Mother Without Child

....

*Contemporary Fiction
and the Crisis of
Motherhood*

Elaine Tuttle Hansen

*University of California Press
Berkeley   Los Angeles   London*

University of California Press
Berkeley and Los Angeles, California

University of California Press, Ltd.
London, England

©1997 by
The Regents of the University of California

Library of Congress Cataloging-in-Publication Data

Hansen, Elaine Tuttle, 1947–
    Mother without child : contemporary fiction and the
crisis of motherhood / Elaine Tuttle Hansen.
        p.   cm.
    Includes bibliographic references and index.
    ISBN 0–520–20577–4 (alk. paper).—ISBN
0–520–20578–2 (pbk. : alk. paper)
        1. American fiction—20th century—History and
criticism.   2. Motherhood in literature.   3. English
fiction—20th century—History and criticism.   4. Fiction—
Women authors—History and criticism.   5. Femininity
(Psychology) in literature.   6. Mother and child in literature.
7. Love, Maternal, in literature.   8. Feminism in literature.
9. Mothers in literature.   10. Women in literature.
I. Title.
PS374.M547H36   1997
    813'.54093520431—dc 20   96–13716

Printed in the United States of America
9   8   7   6   5   4   3   2   1

For Emma and Isla

）

Contents

Preface

Thinking about this project over the past five years or so has been a little like the experience of hearing a new word one morning and then finding it on everyone's lips for the rest of the day. It's hard to say exactly when I first perceived that the story of the mother without child was a pervasive, coherent, and meaningful narrative being reiterated in a variety of ways and places. My desire to attend to this narrative more carefully is certainly attached to the spring of 1991, when my older daughter, now a teenager, was in third grade at Merion Elementary School. One afternoon while I was teaching a course on contemporary women writers, my Haverford colleagues Julia Epstein and Randy Milden came to break the news that there had been an accident at the school, and I needed to go there at once. The details mercifully missing at that point soon emerged: Senator John Heinz's plane had collided with a helicopter over the playground, killing all the adults in the air and two children playing below. As I listened to the first radio coverage in the fifteen minutes that it took me to drive from Haverford to Merion, I heard only that at least two little girls were dead, their bodies as yet unidentified. Along with confusion and disbelief, I remember the clear, quite bodily sensation that I was aging as I drove, that I would never be the same again even if my husband and I were among the lucky parents, as we were, who found their children unharmed.

Before this incident, I had thought about mothers whose children were taken away from them in a few of the novels and stories I regularly taught. In response to an invitation from Maureen Reddy to contribute an essay on Marge Piercy and Margaret Atwood to a volume on mothers and fiction that she was coediting with Brenda Daly, I found my way to an early version of what appears here as chapter 5, "Mothers Yesterday and Mothers Tomorrow, but Never Mothers Today" (reprinted with the permission of the University of Tennessee Press). But after my own mild brush with loss, the issue took on a new weight and urgency, and I began to discover a proliferation of stories that were different versions of the same fundamental narrative.

I am grateful to have had a sabbatical year to devote exclusively to reading and writing about these stories. My leave was supported in part by a fellowship from the American Council of Learned Societies and in part by Haverford College. I am also grateful to the many Haverford students who have enrolled in my courses in contemporary fiction over the years, and I want to acknowledge here their contributions. I appreciate the support of my friends in the Department of English; after hiring me as a medievalist in 1980, the department has generously tolerated and even encouraged my interest in teaching outside my original field of specialization. Other generous colleagues have read or discussed parts of this work with me, and I owe particular thanks to Abbe Blum and Ellen Cronan Rose, who have been characteristically helpful at many stages, and to Sara Ruddick, who took the time to respond cheerfully to an early version of the first chapter. Most recently, I have benefited from the thoughtful suggestions and questions of the anonymous outside readers for the University of California Press and of Gloria Warnke, the editorial board member who considered the manuscript. For editorial assistance, I thank Elsa Efran, Erika E. Büky, and Carolyn Hill, and for last-minute help in getting the final manuscript onto paper and disk, I am grateful to the ever-willing Sue Waddington, Carol Wilkinson, Sharon Nangle, and Chris Steinbrecher.

One

A Sketch in Progress

Introducing the Mother without Child

MOTHER?

Once upon a time, maternity seemed to be a biological fact fixed both literally and symbolically within the private, affective sphere. Now we debate the meaning and practice of motherhood and mothering in many public spaces. A survey of newspapers, bookstores, and academic conference programs yields catchy titles, all ending in question marks: "Whose Child is This?" *Mothers without Custody: How Could a Mother Do Such a Thing?* "Will the Real Mother Please Stand Up?" What is said by and about mothers—full-time mothers, surrogate mothers, teenage mothers, adoptive mothers, mothers who live in poverty, mothers with briefcases—is increasingly complicated and divisive. Language is stretched to describe the bewildering fragmentation of a time in which one child may have a genetic mother, a gestational mother, and a custodial mother, each of whom is a different person.[1]

Although it seems clear that new, unprecedented pressures have recently called into question the meaning of *mother,* this assumption nonetheless simplifies the history of the term. Motherhood has meant many different things in the past, just as it means (and will no doubt continue to mean) different things in different cultures and subcultures today. Looking no further back than the late nineteenth century and no farther afield than England, we see that *mother* was already a slippery word with a complicated history. Like characters in *Desert of the Heart,* Jane Rule's novel about language and motherhood, I often find myself reaching for the dictionary and arguing about the implications that lie just beneath the surface of the lexicographer's formal efforts to capture meaning. As always, that monument of late-nineteenth-century industry and scholarship, the *Oxford English Dictionary* (*OED*), affords a complex and fascinating perspective on the historical semantics of *mother* in which the present crisis—both discursive and practical—is embedded.

The *OED* defined *mother* around 1908, under the editorship of Henry Bradley.[2] The first sense of *mother sb.1* grounds the concept in what until recently could hardly be seen as anything but its natural meaning, denoting a gendered, bodily, and relational identity: "a female parent, a woman who has given birth to a child." The second sense expands the referential field to "things more or less personified": "with reference either to a metaphorical giving birth, to the protecting care exercised by a mother, or to the affectionate reverence due to a mother." This second definition reminds us that long before surrogacy as we know it, the word *mother* was frequently extended from its essential link with childbearing women. But this metaphorical usage is still grounded either in the process of giving birth, at least symbolically, or in mothers' presumed function ("protecting") and status ("reverence due") in English-speaking culture. The third sense reconnects *mother* to a gendered identity: "a woman who exercises control like that of a mother, or who is looked up to as a mother." Like the second sense, this one disengages the word from any necessary connection to actual childbirth but firmly reattaches it to femaleness and again confirms that motherhood is a matter of a particular, clearly understood function—"control" over whatever is mothered—and high status ("looked up to"). In contrast to the insistence on the defining obviousness of the elevated position of the mother in senses two and three, a fourth and last sense indicates that *mother* can be "a term of address for an elderly woman of the lower class." The citations that support this sense reveal that from at least the fourteenth to the nineteenth centuries in England, *mother* sometimes connoted the opposite of what it was normally supposed to mean: not high status, but a devaluation in two critical measures of a woman's worth—age and class.

Bradley and his staff also found an even more devalued sense of the word *mother*, one so fundamentally at odds with their educated, middle-class, late-Victorian understanding that they classified it as another lexical item altogether: *mother sb.2*, meaning "dregs, scum." According to the *OED*, this *mother* was associated with alchemy and used especially in the sixteenth century to refer to the scum of oils and subsequently to the dregs of fermenting liquids. An extensive note preceding the definition explains that etymologists have long puzzled over this usage. Some have argued that the term is actually derived from Dutch *modder,* meaning mud or mire; the *OED* editor insists that there is no evidence for this view, however, and that *mother sb.2* is really an application of *sb.1.* Throwing up lexicographic hands at a debasement of the word *mother* that an English gentleman and scholar would be hard-pressed to comprehend, the editor concludes his lengthy discussion by noting that "the transition of sense is difficult to explain."[3]

Today we might be less surprised by this semantic phenomenon. In the wake of extensive late-twentieth-century feminist debates about the nature, function, and status of motherhood, it is no longer hard to offer reasons why the concept of *mother,* so idealized by the dominant middle-class rhetoric of the recent past, can also carry this barely concealed trace of derogation, disgust, and dirtiness. If there is consensus to be found in these debates, it is that conventional sentiments about motherhood inadequately describe and serve to mystify the actual circumstances of most women who mother, even as they may also sublimate the fear and resentment of men who cannot be mothers, or of the always unsatisfied inner child. It is commonly recognized, in some circles at least, that the position of the mother in our culture and our language is riddled with its history of psychic and social contradictions. Motherhood offers women a site of both power and oppression, self-esteem and self-sacrifice, reverence and debasement.

At the same time, it is striking that other problematic and charged aspects of the concept of *mother* reflected in the *OED*'s definition are at best made visible rather than explained or resolved by the diversity of recent feminist thought. For instance, the slippery and imprecisely overlapping equation of mothering and childbirth, or mothering and women, has been taxed but not exhausted by feminist debates about essentialism and exclusion. Many influential theorists still either root their arguments in a maternal (gestating, delivering, or lactating) body or insist that childbirth cannot simply be ignored as a gender-specific and probably gender-constructing experience. Others wish to see mothering as a more metaphorical act, a social position, available to any and all who choose to do maternal work, but this argument has been no less troublesome. Not only does it leave open to dispute the question of whether men can mother, but it continues to link feminine powers and capacities to child care and family roles, no matter how socially fashioned the position of mother is understood to be. So, too, the divides between women over their relationship to metaphorical mothering as well as biological mothering remain real and vexed, such as those between women who choose to mother and women who do not (or cannot), or between women who adopt and women who give birth.

What is taken for granted, both in the *OED*'s definition and in many recent feminist struggles to interrogate and revise nineteenth-century notions of motherhood, is the *relational* aspect of the concept *mother.* Implicitly, in the *OED* and all subsequent formal definitions I have found, *mother* in the primary sense of the word is someone, maybe a woman or maybe not, who gives birth *to* a child or seeks protection and control *of* a child or is affectionately reverenced and looked up to *by* a child. The force of those prepositions is felt in feminist arguments as well. According to Sara Ruddick, an innovative and influential feminist philosopher who has sought to redefine and revalue mothering, "to be a 'mother' is to take upon oneself the responsibility of child care, making its work a regular and substantial part of one's working life"; "the concept of 'mother' depends on that of 'child.'"[4] By throwing *mother* into quotation marks, feminist thinking challenges us to reconstrue our assumptions about maternity in many ways, but Ruddick's formulation, like most others, reiterates the fundamental relationship to the "child" (a position that may be interrogated as well, but seldom is).

Certainly, we cannot and should not ignore the relational component of motherhood. Yet this component merits and rewards closer scrutiny. Both *mother* and *child* are problematic terms to conceptualize, not least of all because they are relational words, marking partial, quasi-temporary identities. This semantic feature reflects precisely the experiential and political problems that beset us as mothers, as children, and as citizens.

I begin here with questions of lexicography and semantics because definitions often usefully describe and focus attention on complicated problems. As I go on to discuss the importance of listening carefully to the stories we tell about mothers, this premise underlies my arguments: language is a conventional system and what we say always bears the burden of where we have been, what we have done, and what we believe. At the same time, language can function in a prescriptive as well as descriptive way; as others have argued, women have been harmed by cultural, legal, medical, and psychological discourses about motherhood. My purpose in this study, then, is not be to replace the old definitions of motherhood with a new one, but to turn attention to what I take to be the most inadequately explored aspect of *mother* as concept and identity: its relational features. This project needs to be situated, first, in the context that perhaps most deeply informs my thinking, the prolific and still growing feminist critique of motherhood that has evolved over the past three decades.

THE FEMINIST CRITIQUE OF MOTHERHOOD

Often, although not always, the story of feminists thinking about motherhood since the early 1960s is told as a drama in three acts: repudiation, recuperation, and, in the latest and most difficult stage to conceptualize, an emerging critique of recuperation that coexists with ongoing efforts to deploy recuperative strategies.[5] This story usually begins with key first-act figures like Simone de Beauvoir, Shulamith Firestone, Kate Millett, and Betty Friedan, early second-wave feminists who point out a strong link between women's oppression and women's naturalized position as mothers. In retrospect, as others have noted, the arguments of these early feminists may seem more subtle and ambivalent than they have often been taken to be. However, the assumption that feminists reject motherhood is so ingrained as early as 1971 that in an anthology of writing from the women's liberation movement published in that year, essays on "family" are prefaced with this disclaimer: "We are not against love, against men and women living together, against having children. What we are against is the role women play once they become wives and mothers."[6]

In the second act, many feminists seek to reclaim and reinterpret motherhood and revalue difference, although their efforts are almost always coupled with indictments of the negative aspects of "the role women play" as mother. (Some have suggested that this renewed feminist interest in motherhood can be understood as a return of the repressed, a consequence of the fact that many women were encouraged to "deny" or "defer" their maternal desires by the strength of the early critique.)[7] This work begins in the midseventies and takes a wide variety of forms, in the hands of feminists as different as Adrienne Rich, Nancy Chodorow, Dorothy Dinnerstein, and Sara Ruddick in America; Mary O'Brien and Juliet Mitchell in England; and Luce Irigaray,

Hélène Cixous, and Julia Kristeva in France. In the third and as yet incomplete act, critiques and negotiations as well as applications, extensions, and defenses of this work begin to appear in the mideighties and continue into the present.[8] Although some of these critiques tend to reinforce the notion of a historical shift from early feminist attack to subsequent feminist celebration, others point out that the story is, as I have already indicated, less straightforward. Several of these more recent critiques attempt to revive and integrate as well as complicate earlier insights into the oppressive aspects of motherhood. There is also a growing sense of impasse. Feminists have demanded and gained new attention for the previously ignored problems of motherhood, but they have not arrived at consensus about how to redefine the concept or adjust the system. Many (but by no means all) women wish to refuse motherhood on the old terms without abandoning either the heavy responsibilities or the intense pleasures of bearing and raising children. The fear that no one will take care of our children if we don't makes it difficult to go forward, even as it seems impossible to go willingly back.[9]

Ann Snitow's recent efforts to overview and historicize the second-wave feminist debate about motherhood strongly emphasize this frustrating sense of impasse.[10] Snitow divides the last thirty years or so into periods a little different from the ones I have suggested above. Her first period, 1963–1974, includes the publication of what she calls the "demon texts" of writers like Friedan and Firestone, which are (often falsely, she says) associated with the repudiation of motherhood and, as we have seen, have been apologized for by subsequent feminists. The second period, 1976–1979, is for Snitow the great age of groundbreaking feminist work on motherhood, including works by Rich, Dinnerstein, Kristeva, and Chodorow. The third and still current period, starting about 1980 with the "threshold" work of Ruddick, is one of "reaction" and failure to advance the original critique of pronatalism. In this last, comparatively long period, Snitow finds chiefly disarray and division, and she decries the "flaccidity" of the feminist critique. Feminism started out hoping to demolish both pronatalism and its dark underside, maternal devaluation. However, divided and conquered by the eighties backlash, the movement has been less able to achieve the former goal. "Indeed," Snitow speculates, "it may well be that earlier reaction to the pressure to mother was so historically specific that it can have no direct descendants."[11]

Although I can easily understand her sense that thinking about motherhood has reached a kind of impasse, my initial response to

Snitow's argument was that it overstated the case against the current critique. But as chance would have it, a few days after rereading a version of her work published in 1992 in *Feminist Review,* I picked up a copy of the first 1994 issue of *Feminist Studies.* Much to the prospective delight of someone with my interests, the table of contents on the back cover groups seven of the essays, stories, poems, and reviews in a box entitled "Scenarios of the Maternal." Inside, the preface further entices, promising the postmodern thinking about mothers that I am eager to find and engage in: "This recent intellectual and creative strand—skeptical, sophisticated, deconstructing, often playful and impious about maternal verities—is visible in a variety of forms in articles included in this issue."[12] But disappointment quickly set in as I began to read through the volume. Each of the first three essays I mention is a worthwhile contribution to scholarship in its own right, but mothers and the maternal are oddly invisible, and these essays pay little attention to standing and difficult questions about motherhood or the feminist critique thereof.[13]

Iris Marion Young's characteristically thoughtful discussion of pregnant drug addicts, "Punishment, Treatment, Empowerment: Three Approaches to Policy for Pregnant Addicts," focuses on the failures of present treatment policies rather than explicitly suggesting how an addicted mother-to-be in theory or practice might challenge our "maternal verities." Young observes that the rage she thinks is revealed in punitive approaches to pregnant addicts reflects identification with the infant's perspective and the scapegoating of mothers, and implicitly her call for treatment that "empowers" the addict to participate more actively in her own recovery is suggestive. But Young does not elaborate on how this treatment would work or consider questions that her other writings about pregnancy and motherhood might give rise to. Can pregnant women be either "treated" or "empowered" in the same way that nonpregnant women can be? What might or should consciousness-raising (part of the recommended treatment) among pregnant addicts or mothers who are drug users reveal about maternal consciousness? Is there such a thing? Does it differ from and contribute to feminist consciousness? And—a key question for my own project here—if, as Young posits, most drug treatment programs teach women to "earn" their children by being "good," thereby reproducing "structures of privilege," does that mean that better, more effective programs would teach women to be "bad" mothers? What would this mean, for the women and for their children? What are the models of mothering that dissolve or open up "structures of privilege"?

In contrast to Young's piece, Judith Kegan Gardiner's equally interesting essay, "Empathic Ways of Reading: Narcissism, Cultural Politics, and Russ's *Female Man,*" has virtually nothing to say about actual mothers, mothers-to-be, or cultural biases about motherhood. The words *mother* and *maternal* or variants and synonyms thereof are not used in the essay, and the only reason I can imagine that it might be included under the rubric "Scenarios of the Maternal" is that empathy is so frequently associated with "maternal" ways of knowing and thinking. But Gardiner herself does not make such an association. In fact, she might be indirectly pressing a counterclaim when she says in passing, without further elaboration or evidence, that empathy is "a capacity developed through early relations between *parent* and child" (emphasis added) and when she later notes that empathy cannot be claimed by women as "natural."[14]

The third scholarly article, Stacy Alaimo's "Cyborg and Ecofeminist Interventions: Challenges for an Environmental Feminism," criticizes both ecofeminism (presumably associated with motherhood, although this point is not directly made, by its use of the metaphor "Mother Earth") and aspects of Donna Haraway's "cyborg" metaphor, particularly as the latter tends to "bolster a destructive technophilia."[15] Alaimo calls instead for an alliance of "women" and "nature" as agents rather than passive victims. In asking whether this is possible—"Can we construct female alliances with nature that don't mystify nature or pose women as essentially victims or mothers?"—Alaimo may be implying that she wishes to detach women from motherhood. Depending on the stress we put on the word "essentially," she may also be equating mothers with victimization and passivity.[16] But, as in Gardiner's essay, we can only speculate about where the author stands on issues such as the particular problems that actual mothers encounter when they seek to be agents or readers, or the extent to which women might have to change the nature of maternal (or is it "parental"?) work if they became agents in alliance with "nature."

Unlike these three theoretical critiques, Molly Hite's piece, entitled "Mother Underground (Fiction)," turns the focus sharply back onto an actual mother (or at least a fictional version of one; the story reads like autobiography, but the parentheses in the title indicate otherwise). It is described by the preface as "another illustration of the new wave of feminist probing of motherhood—and daughterhood," showing how the daughter is turning in middle age from hate and self-blame to analysis. But it is not clear to me whether this story probes "old verities" or repeats them; it remains rooted in the daughter's point of view and ends on a note of retreat from the problems of mother-daughter relations. The memoir is sparked by the middle-aged daughter's new problem, now that she herself has a child: how to deal with her mother's childrearing advice. This concern leads quickly back to a familiar tale of the bright adolescent girl's struggles with her bright, frustrated, and eventually mad mother. The speaker says, in closing, "I want to be forgotten"; she hopes that she can become "a generic daughter," able to talk to her mother and "able to receive advice as if it came from nobody's mother in particular."[17] The desire to pull back from the relationship in its particulars, to view herself and her mother generically, to forget and be forgotten, could be read as an effort to move beyond the mother-blaming that this story to my mind closely resembles. It also suggests, however, something very like the kind of distancing from—if not avoiding of—the outstanding concerns of the feminist critique of motherhood that we see in the scholarly essays, and such forgetting is a time-honored and dangerous strategy.

Undoubtedly, I thought after finishing the volume, it is unfair to measure these articles against a standard that they never intended to meet. My wish that the authors speak more directly to the way they enter into the feminist critique of motherhood and (re)define the terms *mother* and *maternal* might require retracing old arguments and repeating truisms. The authors may hesitate to say much for fear of saying nothing new—a fear that surely haunts anyone who thinks of speaking about motherhood in the late nineties. As it stands, however, the volume seems to confirm Snitow's sense that the feminist critique of motherhood is becoming more "flaccid" and frustrating rather than more rigorous and effective. But on second thought, something more potentially positive and useful also struck me about this sample collection of what is promoted as the cutting edge of feminist thinking. Despite the varying degrees of aloofness from the unresolved material and theoretical problems of mothers and motherhood in several of these pieces, all of them move tacitly toward taking into the feminist account—rather than just blaming or accepting—either "bad" mothers (pregnant addicts; the bizarre patriarchal mother in Molly Hite's story) or what we might call "metaphorical," nontraditional, nonbiological, maybe even nongendered mothers (readers who read empathically; cyborgs and agents as opposed to Mother Earth and victims).

Framed this way, these essays may not only express a self-protective, if not yet transformative, distance from empirical and historical mothers, but also look toward what scholars have just begun to call for: discussion of the borders of motherhood and the women who really live there, neither fully inside nor fully outside some recognizable "family" unit, and often exiles from their children. After overviewing the ways in which the critiques of essentialism and exclusion problematize feminist approaches to motherhood, Patrice DiQuinzio concludes a recent essay with this recommendation: "Further analysis of mothering would benefit from a focus on nontraditional instances of mothering—for example, lesbian mothering or the mothering of women without custody of children."[18] Jane Price Knowles makes a comparable suggestion in the introduction to her anthology, *Motherhood: A Feminist Perspective:* "The challenge of mothering seems to be not how to be 'good enough,' but to dare to believe in our goodness enough to also be 'bad enough.'"[19] Janice Doane and Devon Hodges similarly note that "the role of the bad mother is, in fact, empowering."[20]

In this study, I demonstrate that if we turn to fiction written in the last three decades—an arena Snitow omits from her purview[21]—we discover the kind of rigorous, daring, and potentially empowering focus that scholars like Snitow, DiQuinzio, and Knowles call for. It is to be found, as DiQuinzio and others might not be surprised to learn, in a number of novels and stories that center on the "mother without child," a rubric that includes nontraditional mothers and "bad" mothers, including lesbians and slave mothers; women who have abortions and miscarriages; women who refuse to bear children, or whose children are stolen from them; and mothers who are, as we shall see, sometimes criminals, murderers, prisoners, suicides, time travelers, tricksters, or ghosts.

In bringing this fictional picture of not conventionally good enough mothers to the fore, we will find it helpful to understand that the multifaceted story of feminist thinking about motherhood is still emerging. Although the broad overviews that periodize the last three decades are accurate and useful in some respects, they may also represent what Biddy Martin, writing about lesbian identities, speaks of as "the too common homogenization of a more complicated past."[22] Martin points to the value, instead, of the kind of work Judith Butler attempts: "to redescribe those possibilities that *already* exist, but which exist within cultural domains designated as culturally unintelligible and impossible."[23] One such domain that demands and rewards further description is that of the mother without child in the kind of contemporary stories I call to attention here.

FEMINIST LITERARY CRITICISM AND MOTHERHOOD

Feminist literary critics, especially those who draw on psychoanalytic theories, have been taking part in the more generalized feminist critique of motherhood as institution and experience for many years. One early and enduring question, particularly for American literary scholars, has been the question of whether mothers can write, or whether writers can be mothers. The theoretical obstacles—especially the position of the mother in dominant theories of language, as highlighted by French feminist thought—as well as the practical constraints on a mother's time, energy, and creative powers have repeatedly been considered. Some have seen a movement across the historical terrain of novel writing in particular that anticipates the pattern of second-wave feminism: from repudiation of the mother, in various ways, by both nineteenth- and early-twentieth-century women writers, towards efforts in the most recent fiction to recuperate her voice or write "as" a mother.[24] A related subtheme of feminist criticism has been the position of the feminist critic as daughter, anxiously trying to sort out her relations to her (literary) foremothers and suffering, like most feminist daughters, from deeply unresolved feelings about mothers and motherhood.[25] In both literary critical and metacritical studies, it is thus possible to note the same pervasive, multifaceted ambivalence about motherhood that we see in feminist studies at large.

An important book focusing attention on the literary ramifications of this ambivalence, with particular interest in nineteenth-century women writers, is Margaret Homans's *Bearing the Word*.[26] Homans at once presupposes and reevaluates a Lacanian theory of language, in which both the speaking and writing subject and the signifier are constituted as masculine, and she argues that this theory has been understandably debilitating for women writers. As many theorists agree, entering the symbolic order is especially difficult if not impossible for the feminine subject, who is associated with the literal or nonsymbolic. As Homans sees it, nineteenth-century women novelists were forced at one and the same time to see themselves as mothers, fulfilling or failing to fulfill the true destiny of the proper woman, and yet in writing to betray the mother, circumventing the maternal (as in *Frankenstein*) or representing the mother as a passive transmitter of the Father's seed or word (as in works by George Eliot and Mrs. Gaskell). Women's very power as mother, given the possibilities for egotism and selfishness, had to be denied by norms of Victorian motherhood.

Marianne Hirsch's *Mother/Daughter Plot* presumes, with Homans, both the historical and strategic absence of the mother's perspective and the theoretical difficulty of representing this paradoxical perspective, or writing "as" a mother. Hirsch locates a major source of this problem in the conventional plots of western literature and the discursive myths of psychoanalysis (hence the missing or silent mother in Greek tragedy, upon which psychoanalytic theories often draw). Writing post-Bakhtin, Hirsch defines the novel as a genre open to dialogue between dominant and subversive voices, but she suggests that it has only recently become a genre in which the mother's voice could be heard. Nineteenth-century plots, on the contrary, are controlled by the family romance and depend on the heroine's "disidentification from the fate of other women, especially mothers"[27]; and so mothers are missing, voiceless, or devalued in novels by writers such as Jane Austen, Mary Shelley, George Sand, the Brontës, George Eliot, and Kate Chopin. Hirsch adds, "The conventions of realism, resting on structures of consent and containment, shut out various forms of indeterminacy, instability, and social fragmentation" (14). The situation changes to some extent in modernist plots, which are "supplemented," according to Hirsch, by the heroine's artistic ambitions and desire for affiliation with other women, so that "for women writers contradiction and oscillation, rather than repetition, bind the modernist plot" (15). Finally, in what Hirsch calls "postmodern" plots, "more multiple relational identities emerge," although the mother remains the one "who did succumb to convention," a negative model from which the daughter must detach herself (10). In texts Hirsch considers by Margaret Atwood, Marguerite Duras, and Christa Wolf, although the mothers are prominent, the perspective remains "daughterly." Only in the most recent fiction—especially, in Hirsch's view, in Toni Morrison's *Beloved*—do "mothers begin to appear as subjects" (11).

Other recent critics consider the impact of dominant myths of phallogocentrism on later women writers. In her study of H.D. and Jean Rhys, *The Unspeakable Mother*, Deborah Kelly Kloepfer supports the view that earlier in this century women writers tended to assume the role of daughters, not mothers.[28] Modernist women writers have also engaged the interest of feminist critics concerned with narratology, some of whom find more departure from the dominant psychoanalytic and discursive models than Homans, Hirsch, or Kloepfer may. Rachel DuPlessis sees twentieth-century women writers as revising maternal myths in order to express "the peculiarities of the female quest,"[29] although, still in keeping with views expressed by Homans and others, she finds that women writers like Virginia Woolf, H.D., and Alice Walker look back to the preoedipal. Susan Winnett suggests, however, that the traditional female experience of birth and breast-feeding has forced women "to think forward rather than backward"; we need to stop reading "in drag" in order to see that narratives for women work differently than theories based on male erotic experience have understood.[30] Ellen G. Friedman also argues that the female modernists, like their male counterparts, yearn for the "unrepresentable." But whereas males see it buried in the past (hence the search for the father), women see it as "the not yet presented," so that their narratives look forward.[31]

Another way in which motherhood has recently entered into literary studies from psychoanalysis is through the notion of the play space or potential space, taken primarily from object relations theory. Following key lines of French feminist thought, Claire Kahane has argued that this space is analogous to the discursive space the woman writer might occupy and that since "poetic discourse [is] dominated by the semiotic," it is the ideal vehicle for a maternal voice that questions "fixed structures of gender" in postmodernist discourse.[32] In *Subversive Intent,* Susan Rubin Suleiman shares this view of the importance of the play space and wonders at the absence of figures of the playing or laughing mother in contemporary women's experimental writing. Instead, she finds that many recent women's texts are like those of the male surrealists, who "repudiate the mother" even as they appropriate her place in their battle with the father.[33] As an instance of this, Suleiman cites Jeanette Winterson's *Oranges Are Not the Only Fruit,* where she reads the mother figure as "an instrument of patriarchy" whom the lesbian daughter-writer must abandon and deny.[34] The positive figure of the mother in writers like Cixous and Irigaray could be seen as a reaction to this patriarchal mother, but she remains a myth and tends to lead to writing in the lyric mode, rather than in the humorous and narrative mode that Suleiman believes would be more subversive.

However, in a recent study of Alice Munro's *Mothers and Other Clowns,* Magdalene Redekop finds evidence of subversive "play and parody" in stories about a certain kind of humorous mother figure. The source of comedy in Munro's magic realism, Redekop argues, is what she calls the "mock mother," a type that includes numerous surrogates: "stepmothers, foster mothers, adoptive mothers, child mothers, nurses, old maids mothering their parents, lovers mothering each other, husbands mothering wives, wives mothering husbands, sisters mothering each other, and numerous women and men behaving in ways that could be described as maternal." Finding in Munro's writing a female version of Freud's "fort-da" game, Redekop argues that the toy in this case is a doll, a mother in masquerade, and that the intent of the game is to subvert traditional definitions of motherhood: "Dancing in front of the erasure, the conspicuous mock-maternal figures do not affirm something inexpressible or sacred. . . . The entertainments of her [Munro's] mock mothers enable us to walk 'disrespectfully' around our idealized images of maternity."[35]

The "mock mother" is clearly analogous to the figure of the mother without child; as Redekop notes, in Munro's stories as in the novels I have assembled here, "'*Where are the children?*' is the question that triggers the collapse of the composition," a collapse that must precede revision and reconstitution.[36] However, with rare exceptions (notably the work of Fay Weldon), the novels I consider are not comic, and the mothers in them often cannot play, laugh, or make other people laugh.[37] This may be in part because theories that link "play" with "autonomous subjectivity" and "total freedom" (as Suleiman characterizes the theoretical insights of Freud and Winnicott) are often constructed from the infant's point of view, not that of the person who mothers. If "play" is a "non-purposive state," it might indeed be incompatible with maternal work and maternal thinking, which, as revalued by theories like Ruddick's, have to be understood as highly goal-directed behaviors. Moreover, as we shall see, these serious, often tragic stories may undercut the premise that (maternal) subjectivity itself can be so readily equated with autonomy and freedom. They also represent another way in which to imagine nonpatriarchal motherhood, a mother in a subversive, "culturally unintelligible and impossible" position.

BEYOND THE PATRIARCHAL MOTHER

Feminists and feminist literary critics have in general assumed that if and when mothers could speak and write, in contradistinction to their earlier silence, they would tell us a new and different story. Some would add that only by telling new stories about their lives can women escape the traditional plots that confine them to the roles of wives and mothers. It is not yet obvious, however, that we have heard either a new or more accurate maternal narrative. In an important sense, many recent stories by or about mothers offer a mirror image of old stories: whereas for centuries the myths and literature of western culture assumed and arguably depended on the absence of the mother, many of our contemporary stories—and particularly the ones I am interested in here— assume and arguably depend on the absence of the child. My goal is to explore what this means. As Sara Ruddick has noted, "Some of the most reflective maternal thinkers have been moved to think deeply about motherhood precisely because mothering does not come easily to them."[38] In this study, I consider a number of stories about women to whom motherhood does not come easily, or in easily recognizable ways, if indeed it comes at all. In all of these stories of the mother without child, the relational aspect of motherhood is disrupted or thwarted and thus thrown into relief.

This figure of the mother without child usefully derives from and elucidates a broad spectrum of experience, ranging from the literal circumstances of a woman who loses or relinquishes custody of a biological child to the psychological condition of a woman who miscarries or never becomes pregnant. One difficulty I faced early on in this project was deciding how to limit the field, how to decide which stories to consider. The more I looked, the more instances I found of what I was looking for. In what follows, I explain why I think the widespread appearance of the mother without child in fiction today is overdetermined and how we might begin to account for that overdetermination. But at the outset, it may be helpful to specify more precisely what kind of stories, what kind of female characters the rubric "mother without child" will comprise.

I have borrowed this rubric from Jane Rule's *Desert of the Heart,* a novel that is the principal subject of the next chapter and also the earliest of the works I include here (thereby constituting a *terminus a quo* for the relative notion of "contemporary fiction" in the present instance). In Rule's novel, "Mother without Child" is the title of a sketch in progress. With multiple ironies, it also describes the two main characters, who occupy one extreme of that broad spectrum: they are lesbians who, voluntarily in one case and involuntarily in the other, have no biological children but are perceived to have a fraught relationship to motherhood and to behave in ways that sometimes resist and are at other times conventionally associated with maternal practice. In chapters 3, 4, and 5 of this study, I trace the figure of the mother without child through a series of biological mothers in novels by the better-known American authors Toni Morrison, Alice Walker, Louise Erdrich and Michael Dorris, Marge Piercy, and Margaret Atwood, whose plots entail the loss of a child or children. The fictional circumstances that disrupt or endanger the mother-child relationship are usually traumatic but highly various. The mothers in these narratives murder their own children, send them away temporarily or give them up for adoption, abandon them, or lose them to an oppressive state. The lines between voluntary and involuntary loss are often, but not always, blurred, as are perceptions about motives. In several of these stories, women arguably act out of fierce maternal love, although in some cases their intentions are misunderstood, and in others those intentions remain unknown, unclear, or unspoken. Finally, in the last chapter of this study, I turn to several novels by the British writer Fay Weldon in which the recurring figure of the mother without child includes not only women traumatically separated from the children they have borne but also instances elsewhere on the spectrum: a woman whose child is stillborn, a woman who murders another woman's infant with severe birth defects, a mother-to-be, a mother whose child is threatened by American presidential politics, and a childless woman who discovers, in her sixties, that she has four clones, thirty years younger but otherwise identical to herself.

These instances of the mother without child by no means exhaust the supply of contemporary stories that could qualify for inclusion under this rubric and that might confirm, extend, or possibly contradict the conclusions I draw. I suspect that most readers, like most colleagues and friends to whom I have described my work over the past few years, will immediately think of characters and stories that I could or should have added or chosen instead. This reaction testifies not only to the limits of any one study and the misjudgments I may have made in deciding what to use but also to the fact that the scope of my concern here is large and still growing and that much remains to be charted. The issues raised in these novels are prominent and pervasive, and the contemporary story of the mother without child, called to attention, demands future considerations.

Primary among my principles of selection was the importance of considering texts that come from more than one of the subcultures comprising that loose collective we think of as first-world contemporary fiction in English. (Quite apparently, the inclusion of some of the "subcultures" I treat also calls into question any notion of a static, monolithic first world.) Although motherhood is often spoken of in terms of culturally homogenizing and universalizing ideals and standards, stories of the mother without child individually and collectively refuse to let us forget that experiences of motherhood depart from the theories that would inform them, and they also insist on embedding mothers in specific historical communities and groups. Looking at somewhat different communities and groups throws into relief the ways in which explicit norms and tacit assumptions about motherhood are compromised by varieties of material circumstances, especially in periods of rapid social and technological change and cultural clashes.[39]

I should say at the outset what will soon be apparent and possibly frustrating to readers of this study: I propose no single meaning to these narratives of thwarted motherhood. These novels and stories raise a variety of questions and represent a variety of takes on that most complicated, confounding aspect of motherhood, its relational nature. Wherever we find examples of the mother without child, meaning has to be constructed locally, specifically, in particular contexts. At the same time, I aim to posit some vital common ground. The number and range of instances that can be aptly described by this rubric, despite their differences, argue for treating them as speaking together, although not always in one voice, to concerns that cut across divisions and differences.

Given both material circumstances and the rise of the feminist critique of motherhood, the appearance of so many fictional stories about women distanced in one way or another from their actual or potential children might appear overdetermined and predictable, and it might seem that we don't need to look very hard to understand the phenomenon: women are writing about loss because they are losing their children, literally and figuratively. I by no means wish to gloss over this concern. To paraphrase one of the characters in Rule's *Desert of the Heart,* the relational aspect of motherhood, so long taken *for* granted, may no longer *be* granted. Even the biological connection, once a solid starting place for thinking about motherhood, has recently been attenuated by the most scientifically advanced conceptive technologies. As

many feminist critiques of medicine and technology have argued, this
is in fact not an entirely new development; mothers and midwives have
been increasingly disconnected from childbirth over the course of the
last hundred years (or more).[40] Some of the latest, more dramatic medical advances have seemed to put new measures of control over procreation into many western women's hands. But what can be viewed
as an unprecedented opportunity for women can also be perceived as
a threat to born and unborn children. Anxiety over how best to use (or
limit) the control women have or want manifests itself most visibly, perhaps, in the abortion wars. Others, meanwhile, have pointed out how
uncertain and ephemeral the benefits of reproductive technology may
be.[41] For some women, anxiety verges on panic when the relentless
progress of technology used for conceptive purposes threatens to reap-
propriate power for the medical profession and at the same time further fragments and controls the experience of motherhood. The ambiguities of medical and technological developments are reflected in the
tension between the simultaneously emerging discourses of fetal rights
and women's rights. Despite their opposing political stances, both
movements tend to call into question the ideal of mother *with* child.

For increasingly greater numbers of women worries about either fetal rights or women's rights are a luxury; the urgent issues are how a
mother can survive and take care of her living children's most basic
needs. Poverty puts pressure on the middle-class norms of maternal-
child relations, and unthinkable numbers of children and their increasingly isolated, unsupported mothers are visibly at risk in ways that
are heartbreaking and resistant to solution. Apologists for "family values" often ignore the actualities of maternal work, and hence they too
may stand between the (biological) mother and any means of meeting
the needs of an actual child. As the editors of a special issue of *Signs*
on "Mothering and Patriarchy" have observed, "Sentimentalized tropes
of idealized mothering—endlessly loving, serenely healing, emotionally
rewarding—have no counterpart in a political and social reality where
the labor of caring is devalued, unsupported, and unseen, and where
mothers are more likely to be endlessly burdened, anxious, and blamed.
Biological motherhood, as a discrete and exemplary feminine event, is
elevated, providing of course it occurs within the prescribed cultural
scenario."[42] Novels by and about lesbians, African Americans, and Native Americans show with particular clarity that the mother without
child has historically been the brutal norm rather than the tragic ex-

ception. As previously underrepresented voices struggle to speak, and as we look more carefully for places in which they have already spoken, it should come as no surprise that we repeatedly hear sad stories about rupture and loss.

It might alternatively be argued that second-wave feminism itself is chiefly responsible, in one way or another, for the rise of stories about mothers who give up or lose their children.[43] Most obviously, in its critique of motherhood as a site of female oppression, feminism, like birth control, seems to threaten to take women away from the children they bear, or ought to bear. More subtly, perhaps, these stories might be read as the work of the feminist-as-daughter, unable to forgive her own patriarchal mother—either for abandoning the daughter, or for failing to let her go—and barely able to imagine herself as a feminist mother or to represent anything but the anguish of motherhood that threatens from all sides. It has been suggested that feminists may devise distancing strategies to avoid confronting their ambivalence about mothering.[44] In Ruddick's view, something like this may be going on, and the resultant distance between feminist mother and child explains the limits of feminist critique: "Partly because they wrote as daughters, feminist writing about mothers wrote very little about the children mothers think and speak about."[45]

Given such ominous circumstances, it might seem inevitable and tragic that we find so many stories about the mother without child, all serving to reflect or critique the ways in which the mother-child bond is (and perhaps for some should be) currently loosened and endangered, if not severed. Why do the novels I consider need further analysis, then? Though I would not wish to deny that these stories express anxieties about a multifaceted, sometimes tragic reality, they offer more than reflection and critique. These narratives can be read in ways that do not forget or transcend but rather remember and look within the sense of loss and impasse. In doing so they insist that we reconsider our assumptions about what motherhood is "really" like, that we resist fundamental theories and practices that would oppress mothers and divide women, and even that we pause before assuming that "the" maternal voice or an autonomous maternal subject can or should be sought.

These stories address several general, often overlapping issues. Both conservative and radical definitions of *mother* oversimplify in assuming that the "mother's" position or identity depends on the presence of the child to whom the maternal figure gives birth, nurturance, protection, and so on. Common experiences alone tell us that there is something left out if we fail to take account of the many moments at which a person might act as, feel like, or be considered a mother in the absence of a child. Before a baby is born, a woman is often thought of or thinks of herself as a mother; whether or not she ever gives birth, both traditional pronatalist and some feminist assumptions define every woman as a potential mother. When a child grows up and stops requiring maternal protection, takes responsibility for caring for himself or herself, or fails to offer affectionate reverence, that child still has a mother, and that mother may still identify herself (or himself) as such. When a mother loses or gives up custody of a child, or gives up hope that a child will live and so stops doing the work required to keep that child alive, or even acts to take back the life she has given in order to protect the child from suffering or to defend some other principle, that person may still be or wish to be considered a mother. In any of these instances where the child is absent, where the relation is, for good or for bad, temporarily or permanently, voluntarily or involuntarily broken off, what does motherhood consist of, what does a "mother" feel like? Does a woman without a child simply become (at last or again) a subject, an autonomous self, free from the claims and contradictions of motherhood? Or does she suffer a tragic, irreparable trauma? The story of the mother without child addresses these questions and thereby brings us closer to that frequently stated goal of feminist study: seeing maternal points of view more fully, hearing maternal voices more clearly and variously, understanding maternal subjectivity more deeply and complexly.

At another level of abstraction, the figure of the mother without child expresses the complexity of maternal consciousness by literalizing aspects of the unconscious. American feminism of the 1970s and early 1980s has been critiqued for ignoring the unconscious and positing a "one dimensional," unitary female self.[46] Stories of the mother without child confront without flinching the often-ignored hate, the fantasies of aggression, the desire even to kill her child that is allegedly repressed by conventional accounts of maternity (including feminist accounts). This dimension of maternal experience is brought out in Elsa First's recent discussion of Winnicott's belief that "hate," for both mothers and psychoanalysts, is a necessary element of "self-respect." As First says, Winnicott argues that the mother must acknowledge her hatred if the child is to come to terms with its own aggression and that "maternal resilience" depends on the mother's ability to "play" with her aggression, to recognize the "constructive energy" of anger.[47] The fiction of the mother without child functions in some circumstances as a way of exorcising fear and guilt and even "playing" with aggression, although the stories may not look "playful" in any recognizably light-hearted sense.

Alternatively, if we are trying to take into account the "unconscious" of mothering, the motif of the mother without child speaks to the perception of recent psychoanalytic approaches that stress the constitutive division of maternity, the mother as "site of an originary, constitutive splitting."[48] Along similar lines, we might consider that the intersubjectivity of mother and child is, from the moment of birth, always and properly tentative and temporary as much as it is fiercely connected and interdependent. In her revisionary reading of Freud, Madelon Sprengnether has argued that the separation of mother and child, again considered at the level of the unconscious, should be seen as fundamental in human development in a positive way: "Mother's 'desire' leads her away from her infant, and her absence in turn elicits the child's creativity."[49] This can be put in less abstract terms: an important part of being a good mother by today's popular standards, as experts and mothers will attest, is knowing when and how to let go. If the mother's work entails preparing the child, from the moment of birth, for independence from caretakers, and thus paradoxically engaging in a relationship whose ultimate goal is greater disengagement, distance, or even dissolution, the story of the mother without child may figure instead of repressing this paradox.

Yet another tightly connected concern involves the perception that the child has come first and overshadowed the mother in the most influential theories. As many have noted, Freud's is an infantile theory of human development; since Freud, it has been difficult if not impossible to express anything but the child's point of view of the maternal object, which later becomes the adult's. As Knowles puts it, it is hard to see the "reality" of mothers' feelings, including their ambivalence, their desire, or even their dislike of bearing and caring for children, in "a world full of adults whose inner children feel impoverished, who still yearn for the good mothering of their fantasies."[50] Children really do need to come first, at many points, and it is hard in practice as in theory not to identify emotionally and rhetorically with their needs. If we do so, however, we may continue to ignore the other half of the relationship. The story of the mother without child frees us, experimentally and provisionally, to focus on the mother, and in doing so to see her as a multifaceted and changeful subject. If narrative theories move away from the preoedipal mother-child bond as the source and site of literary activity, this move may find its narrative form in these stories.

Finally, in order to understand and attend to the emergence at this point in time of a new significance to the fictional figure of the mother without child, we need to set these narratives in relief against the old stories, the available plots and standing myths about mothers who lose their children or are threatened with such loss. My primary interest is *stories* about mothers without children, and stories need to be accounted for not only at the level of how they may represent, reflect, and resist current psychic and social realities or theories, but also in terms of how they engage available narrative patterns, in this case entering into and arguably revising a diachronic tradition of fictionally represented motherhood.

In western culture, stories about the mother without child are not new. Abandonment and separation are common themes, although the point of view from which these stories have been told has been the point of view of the child, broadly speaking, rather than the mother. Most of these stories, perhaps concomitantly, have not sought or served to scrutinize the implications of the relational status of maternal identity, to dislodge conventional, naturalizing assumptions, or to help us see or see with the mother. In fact, quite the opposite is true: the loss or threatened loss of the other member of the dyad, the child, has often been used to define and stabilize a particularly disabling meaning of *mother* rather than to open motherhood up to analysis, to acknowledge let alone express the perspective of a woman who mothers, or to tell the particulars of her experience.

A foundational example of this old story is the biblical tale of King Solomon and two women who both claim to be the mother of the same child. The women are identified as harlots or prostitutes who live alone together with their babies; the story begins when one of them brings the other to Solomon's court to claim that in the middle of the night the other woman accidentally smothered her own child and then switched the babies, taking the living child for her own. Relatively early in his kingship, Solomon uses this case to prove his sagacity, determining who the true mother is by putting (or pretending to put) in imminent danger the life of a child that they both claim. His strategy, indeed, anticipates what I suggest is going on in today's fictional explorations of motherhood: to find out "the truth" about "mother," he creates the fiction that her worst fears for her child are about to be realized. The constitutional paradox or double bind for the "real" mother here is as clear, at least to a feminist reading, as the cleverness of the King's ploy: to claim a child and prove her identity as a lawful mother, to demonstrate the capacity to protect that child as a good mother naturally should, a woman must go so far as to give a child up—that is, to stop being a mother. This is a familiar plot. Women are pitted against each other in a competition for the scarce commodity that proves their fertility and, indirectly, their heterosexual activity and availability. The "good" mother is positioned so that she stands in opposition to a quintessentially "bad" mother, a woman so dangerous that she causes the death of her own child and is willing to see a child murdered rather than give up the irrational struggle for possession. The "good" woman and mother can speak only to erase her authority, to renounce possession, to disown her desire; a mother is someone who sacrifices something she has and wants, or is willing to do so, for the good of another. As we all might have learned from the case of Baby M and Mary Beth Whitehead, to want a child too much—so much that one breaks the law—is still to prove that one isn't really a fit mother, that one can't subordinate one's own needs for the child to the best interests of the child. The good mother understands the limits of her love and power and polices the dangers of maternal excess.

In thinking about Solomon's wisdom in this context and going back to the Old Testament to look again at how, exactly, the story was formulated, I noted something that struck me for the first time as peculiar: from the biblical narrative, it is impossible to tell which of the two nameless women—woman A, the one who brought the case to Solomon in the first place and accused her housemate of child stealing, or B, the one who was so accused—turned out to be the "real" mother, the one whose child was alive (or, in my reading, the one who was willing to sacrifice her own relationship to the child in order to save that child and identify herself). It would seem to be an odd omission of detail, but it is in fact consistent with the understanding that this story, like so many, obscures rather than represents anything about either woman's particular character or practical circumstances. The point is patriarchal wisdom in its starkest, purest form, founded on the construction of self-sacrificial motherhood and control over women whose maternity could otherwise manifest independent sexual and reproductive activity. Tellingly, these are "harlots" living alone, outside the marital bond, on the borders of the law.[51] The point is not to represent maternal subjectivity or maternal experience, and certainly not to explore female desire or agency.

If we focus on these latter-day concerns, we see what we already know about patriarchal wisdom: Solomon, its representative, is not interested in the truth or in the feelings and needs of the women in question. We might also wonder whether he is as wise as he seems, or whether he has been duped. Solomon misses or is unconcerned with the fact that both women are victims. One of them has already lost her infant, and if the mother of the dead child is in fact B, the woman who stands accused of child stealing, then her crime may be understood, if not excused, as a sign of her grief, perhaps even her denial and delusion. Or suppose that woman A is not telling the truth, that she is actually the one whose child died in the night, who then thinks up the clever idea of bringing woman B and B's still living baby to court, falsely claiming that B has stolen that baby. In this case, we might still want to see A as deranged with grief, but her stratagem would suggest that she has become canny, not irrational, in the face of loss. In either event, it seems altogether possible that Solomon (or the teller of the story, who equates the self-sacrificial woman with the mother of the living child) could be outsmarted in another way. How do we know that the mother who gets the child isn't just the better performer, the quicker witted one who understands what words to say in order to prove motherhood? Perhaps the "real" mother of the child is like Lear's truthful daughter, Cordelia, sure that her love is more ponderous than her tongue. Or perhaps she suffers from postpartum depression and, in a moment of great stress, standing before the King, almost welcomes the solution his sword pretends to offer.

We can, it seems, be sure of only one thing: the "patriarchal mother"—a term used by feminist critics to disparage a mother who is complicitous with the system that devalues motherhood and oppresses women—wins the case and gets to keep the child. This, again, is the point of the story.[52] But how might feminist retellings of the Solomon story alter this point? In such revisions, maternal identity as formed in patriarchal contexts might still be tested by the loss or threatened loss of the child, but in that testing new definitions and alternative plots might emerge. In the process, the woman who refuses to perform like a mother might well be the heroine, the one who resists patriarchal law and so ends up losing her child. Indeed, all of the stories of the mother without child that I consider here do just this. They call into question the implications, for women, of Solomon's long-standing wisdom, with its troubling presupposition that, as one Old Testament scholar puts it, "the presence of a love that knows not the demands of ego, of possessiveness, or even of justice reveals motherhood."[53]

Other familiar stories about the voluntary or involuntary loss of a child reiterate the patriarchal definitions of motherhood fundamental to Solomon's wisdom. In Greek myth, mothers often have real power, but typically that power is horrifying and may be turned against a child or children by a vengeful mother such as Medea or Procne or Althea. Somewhat less frequently, a powerful mother is turned into a victim by the loss of a child, as in the story of Demeter. In several eighteenth- and nineteenth-century novels, mothers who abandon their children are invariably portrayed as rogues (like Moll Flanders or Emma Bovary) or victims (perhaps the most pathetic of whom is Isabel Vane in *East Lynne*); in both categories, they often suffer terrible punishments.[54] Recent stories use the loss of a child to represent threatening social change and then reconsolidate a conventional definition of the good mother (as in Miller's *The Good Mother*).[55] Or the story of lost children is used to suggest different definitions of mother, but ones that bring us no closer to a particular woman's point of view. For example, in a recent discussion of maternal identity with an ostensibly far different notion of motherhood in mind, one that aims to de-essentialize the concept of the "mother" and lay claim to "parental" status for fathers, Thomas Laqueur demonstrates his wisdom in a way oddly analogous to Solomon's method. Laqueur suggests that since "facts" (such as whose body bore the child) can no longer prove parenthood, emotions can. To show that "mothering" today is or should be gender-neutral and that fathers do as much emotional work as mothers (or in some cases more), Laqueur cites two instances in which the loss or threatened loss of a child proves parental (or paternal) identity: Gladstone's moving account of sitting for days by the bedside of his dying daughter, and Laqueur's own sadness when his wife miscarried (and was less upset, according to him, than he as the prospective father was).[56]

Such stories about mothers—or in this last instance, fathers—whose relational identity is at once disrupted and confirmed by loss of the child, interesting and affecting as they may be, do not seriously challenge normative, categorical definitions of *mother,* although they may, read from the point of view of feminist critique, expose their faultlines and constructedness. Nor do these familiar stories help us to learn more about the possibilities or implications of a maternal subject somehow distinct from or independent of a relation to a child. They confirm that there is no concept of *mother* unless, as Ruddick says, there is a concept of *child.* The longevity of the Solomon plot also confirms how commanding stories may be, how much they may serve to mold and interpret experience in particular ways.

In the new stories that I consider, the loss or absence of a child may or may not still be presented as tragic or heartrending, and it may or may not literalize a fundamental aspect of human psychology, a "liberatory" political agenda, or a set of deplorable historical circumstances. The important difference, however, is this: these fictional women who are mothers (actual or, in some cases, potential) and their conventional maternal capacities, including their relational, nurturant, and protective abilities, are not utterly devalued or destroyed by the loss of the child, although they may be more or less damaged and are *always changed* in some way. And so the story, insofar as we know it, does not serve to confirm or disprove a fixed and fundamentally conventional *or* unconventional maternal (or parental) identity, be it one that is unified around bonding and self-sacrifice or divided between self and child, presymbolic and symbolic positions, and so on. On the contrary, it leads toward demystification, denaturalization, and reevaluation of the norms and needs of motherhood. It insists that the position of the mother without child is not only a traumatic present reality but also a logical impossibility, a taboo, and therefore a site of instability that facilitates thinking about motherhood and women beyond official logic and conventional possibility. It exemplifies precisely what Butler calls "subversion within the terms of the law,"[57] representing the woman who, unlike the patriarchal mother, is "a mother and outside the father's law at the same time."[58]

The law, in assuming that a mother bears, takes care of, and is revered by a child, at once presupposes and oversimplifies the meaning of the relational aspect of motherhood. Most (but not all) of the female characters in the stories I consider have hoped consciously or unconsciously at some point in their lives to follow this law, but for various reasons they are unable to do so or choose not to do so. In the old stories, a mother is known to the law only by her willingness to sacrifice everything, even her relation to the child; in them, the mother without child can only be either a criminal who breaks the law or a victim of circumstances or evil forces. In the new stories, as we shall see, she can subvert these categories of criminal or victim, bad or good mother, by not fitting comfortably into either or by occupying both at the same time.[59] Emerging in the last three decades in conjunction with both the material crises of contemporary maternal practice and the feminist critique of motherhood, the fictional death, threatened death, or absence of a child thereby serves as the instigation to different ways of hearing, knowing, and being mothers.

Two

Not a Synthetic Maternity

Jane Rule's Fiction

I didn't die, trying to make a new life for myself out of an old
life, trying to be a lover of myself and other women in a place
where we were despised. I didn't die, but by the spring of the
next year, by May, watching the redbud tree drop flowers like
blood on the ground, I felt like I had died. I had learned that
children were still taken from their mothers in that town,
even from someone like me, if by my wildness, by sexual
wildness, I placed myself in the wilderness with those feared
by white Southern men. . . . I had learned that I could be
either a lesbian or a mother of my children, either in the
wilderness or on holy ground, but not both.

Minnie Bruce Pratt, "Identity: Skin Blood Heart"

Richmond, Sept. 7—In an unusual custody battle, a circuit
court here upheld a lower court's decision to take a 2-year-
old boy away from his mother, a lesbian [Sharon Bottoms],
and give him to her mother for rearing.

"The mother's conduct is illegal and immoral and renders
her an unfit parent," Judge Duford M. Parsons Jr. of Henrico
County Circuit Court said.

The New York Times, September 8, 1993

The Sharon Bottoms case, following fast on the heels of the 1993 debates on gays in the military, seemed a superfluous reminder that social change is slow, uneven, and easily erased if not illusory to begin
with.[1] The frank homophobia of a Virginia judge may have struck re-
porters for *The New York Times* as "unusual," delivering "a shock to
the nation's homosexuals,"[2] but it only confirms what many lesbian
mothers say they know. If they want to maintain custody of their children, particularly after a divorce or when there is a biological father

who might sue, they do best to stay at home in the closet, heeding the lesson that women like Minnie Bruce Pratt learned in the sixties and seventies about the distance between the immoral wilderness of lesbian existence and the holy ground of motherhood.[3] A lesbian or a mother, but not both—women who love women and women who are deemed fit to bear or raise children have been construed as mutually exclusive categories, and that presumption is used to coerce and punish women who think of violating the heterosexual norm. Even those who apparently support lesbian rights may draw the line at the right to mother.

The exclusion of lesbians from motherhood has been both contested and appropriated by recent lesbian philosophers and activists. To some extent, motherhood may be less controversial among lesbians than it was a few years ago (hence, in part, the "shock" to homosexuals, if there was one, of Judge Parsons' decision). Although the politics of this trend are disputed and the actual numbers unknown, in the eighties and nineties more and more lesbians appear to be choosing to mother or to support motherhood as a viable option. As Audre Lorde notes, writing in 1986, "These days it seems like everywhere I turn somebody is either having a baby or talking about having a baby."[4] At the same time, in theoretical discussions the issue has been decentered recently by the shift, as Bonnie Zimmerman describes it, from "the lesbian as a unified, essentialist, ontological being" to "the lesbian as metaphor and/or subject position."[5] But there is still no consensus among self-identified lesbians about the best strategic or ethical attitude toward the maternal or about the status of that putative anomaly, lesbian motherhood, as a subversive or complicitous position. Bearing in mind Marilyn Frye's observation that there is disagreement about "practically everything" in the lesbian community, I don't suggest that there ought to be consensus about this one thing.[6] The disagreement itself merits and rewards continued discussion. One place where we can clearly see the value of lesbian thinking about motherhood is in Jane Rule's fiction, particularly in her first novel, *Desert of the Heart,* a remarkably early and interesting effort to imagine ways to move beyond so-called patriarchal motherhood.

LESBIANS AND MOTHERS: LOVE OR WAR?

The debate among lesbian activists and theorists, like the debate among feminists in general, has been dominated by two strong, contrasting positions. At one end of the spectrum are those who focus on the negative demands of mothering as a role and the destructive equation of woman and mother in a culture that simultaneously objectifies and ignores the experiences of both. Declarations of the fundamental opposition between lesbianism and motherhood are most frequently associated with earlier radical separatists, but in fact they can be heard in both extreme and more tempered or distanced arguments throughout the eighties and into the present. Writing in *Signs* in 1994, Jackie Anderson argues that "there are good and sound reasons to consider rejecting motherhood as a value and birthing as a practice." Anderson goes on to reiterate and endorse Jeffner Allen's strong condemnation of mothers, first published over a decade ago.[7] In Allen's words, "A mother is she whose body is used as a resource to reproduce men and the world of men, understood as the biological children of patriarchy and as the ideas and material goods of patriarchal culture." Motherhood is dangerous to all women because in patriarchy "every woman is by definition a mother"; Allen's call to "annihilate" motherhood urges females to be as wild as possible, to refuse to bear children and collectively enact her "philosophy of evacuation," "a removal of ourselves from *all forms* of motherhood" (emphasis added).[8]

Others oppose motherhood more subtly in both personal and analytic terms. Writing at about the same time as Allen but in a very different tone, Minnie Bruce Pratt mourns the loss of her children, whose father was awarded custody. But she implies that it was a necessary sacrifice, radicalizing and freeing her: "To come to a place of greater liberation, I had to risk old safeties."[9] Even the sense of loss may need to be reread: "When we expand our limited being . . . we can experience this change as loss."[10] More recently, in a far less confessional and more theoretical mode, Theresa de Lauretis seems to speak against the valorization and perhaps the practice of motherhood. In an argument reminiscent of the celebration of clitoral orgasm, de Lauretis maintains that it is the possibility of separating female sexual pleasure from procreation that makes lesbian sexuality so subversive and opens up a space for woman as speaking subject. Commenting on Monique Wittig's development of a "cognitive practice" in *The Lesbian Body,* de Lauretis also opts for wildness: "The struggle with language to rewrite the body beyond its precoded, conventional representations is not and cannot be a reappropriation of the female body as it is, domesticated, maternal, oedipally or preoedipally en-gendered."[11]

Two common concerns strike me in these and other articulations of the antimotherhood position. First, the assumption that motherhood entails in whole or at least in part the biological act of childbearing is either endorsed or, more frequently, unexamined. Does Allen include adoption or artificial insemination in "all forms of motherhood"? Is the "maternal" body that de Lauretis speaks of only the body that actually bears a child? Like many pronouncements about motherhood, these are insufficiently attuned to the increasingly difficult problems of who counts as a mother and what we mean by *maternal*. Second, despite efforts to resist "precoded" conventions, many versions of the antimotherhood position ironically confirm even as they invert the value of older, prefeminist views that stressed the nonmaternal nature of lesbians, seeing them as "defeminized" women who resisted their "normal" female roles as mothers.[12] These ambiguities make for odd bedfellows. For example, the patriarchal villain of Sheila Ortiz Taylor's *Faultline,* a father of six children suing for custody because their mother has left him for a colleague's wife, rests his case on the same claim that women as diverse as Anderson, Allen, Pratt, and de Lauretis are making: "Lesbianism and motherhood are at war."[13]

At the other end of the spectrum are arguments by and about lesbians that celebrate the maternal (still generally associated with biological motherhood); such arguments may even base their case for the normality, naturalness, and rightness of female-female love on the alleged ground of a universal human experience: the infant's primary and original love for the mother. Exemplified by Adrienne Rich's influential theory of the "lesbian continuum," such arguments maintain that for women it is the forced disruption of the preoedipal bond, making women heterosexual, that is perverse and unholy. Psychotherapist Meg Turner cites a young female patient who explicitly articulates what we might call the Rich position: "'It's hard when your mother is the first person you love, and then you must also separate from her,' she told me. Marina sounded impassioned: 'In some ways it seems absurd to prescribe heterosexuality after a homoerotic relationship with the mother.'"[14]

Rich herself is careful to say that "I do not, myself, assume that mothering-by-women is a 'sufficient cause' of lesbian existence."[15] But her case for repudiating heterosexuality as a compulsory institution damaging to all women depends on the assumption that women really do have a "primary relationship" with other females from which they are forced to turn away; Rich cites Susan Cavin's work, presupposing that "the original deep adult bonding is that of woman for woman," as "extremely suggestive" (191). Oddly like the antimotherhood arguments in this regard, Rich's position in a sense reaffirms by inverting the claims of prefeminist accounts, in this case the Freudian view that homosexual women represent cases of arrested development, stuck in the preoedipal stage and immaturely fixated on their first love-objects, their mothers. This position tends to totalize and idealize views of motherhood and emphasize thinking about the good or good enough mother while ignoring, as theory or experience, the bad mother.[16]

Set beside each other in the extreme and no doubt oversimplified forms I have presented, these asymmetrically competing views about lesbians and motherhood construct potential impasses for lesbian theorists and activists. If those in the second camp are right, women fundamentally are or should be lesbians because of the primacy of their relations to a same-sex caregiver, a mother (assumed to be a female and birth mother, for the most part). But if those in the opposing group are right, they cannot reproduce this love by passing it on to their own children because it is philosophically and politically vital to resist becoming a mother in discourse or in the material, male-dominated world. This logic strands the lesbian as an adult woman in a place where she cannot become in practice what she still loves in theory. Ironically, to preserve the very identity derived (some say) from her love for her mother, she must (from a certain point of view) remain a daughter: a particular twist to—or negotiation of—the notion that a woman's choice is between fusion and separation.[17] This problem may explain in part why, as Nancy Polikoff notes, lesbians who choose to mother are rarely heard defending their decision with arguments that draw on the power and capacity that might be derived from the maternal role.[18] The polarization of lesbian attitudes toward motherhood thus underscores the problem Martha Gimenez finds in feminist thinking in general: "The hold of the dominant ideology of motherhood over people's minds limits their ability to perceive alternatives. These limits push people into either total acceptance of motherhood or total negation, thus precluding the emergence of a standpoint which, transcending both, could provide an effective challenge to the status quo."[19]

There have of course been various attempts to mediate or embrace the apparent divide between celebrating and critiquing motherhood. Rich herself tries to separate motherlove as symbol or ideal and motherhood as institution, particularly in *Of Woman Born*. As Barbara Love and Elizabeth Shanklin put it, it's inaccurate to say that lesbians aren't or don't want to be mothers: "What is frequently true is that lesbians don't want to pay the price to be mothers in patriarchy . . . but under different conditions, who knows?"[20] One of the most sustained efforts to imagine "different conditions" and thereby reclaim lesbian motherhood as an alternative to motherhood in patriarchy is found in the work of French critic Nicole Brossard. In *These Our Mothers, or: The Disintegrating Chapter,* published in France (*L'Amer ou le Chapitre effrite*) in 1977 and available in English translation since 1983, Brossard proposes two opposing kinds or meanings of *mother:* the "patriarchal mother" and the "symbolic mother." The patriarchal mother is the familiar object of feminist attack, a creation of western, male-dominated reason and myth. Brossard describes meeting "other mothers" of this sort while sitting on a park bench, watching her daughter playing: "Here is the clan of patriarchal mothers. Devoted to men. Raising their young. Who have nothing to say. To exchange a domestic silence. Enclosed."[21] "Patriarchal mothers able only to initiate their daughters to a man. There is no confidence between us. Sold-out, at a loss. . . . Domesticated symbol . . . Ideological dead-end" (18, 23). Also referred to as the "biological mother"(23), this first kind of mother is the one who must be "killed," if women are to become subjects.

For Brossard, it is the lesbian and the lesbian only who commits this matricide: "It is while caressing the body of another woman over its entire living surface that she kills the mother" (23). But the lesbian daughter who destroys the patriarchal, biological mother must also become a "symbolic mother" in a new order. The key distinction between the patriarchal mother and the symbolic mother is that the latter, like the speaker-writer of *These Our Mothers,* has "killed the womb" (13): "Each woman can profit only to the extent that she becomes a symbolic mother. That is when she stopped bearing children" (21). Again: "If she wants to survive, a woman must assert herself in reality and become recognized as a symbolic mother: incestuous in power but inaccessible sexually for reproduction. She then completely fills the space of desire and so can appropriate for herself the work of the other. Strategic inversion: this symbolic woman-mother has lost her womb" (17). No longer procreative, the woman's "difference" is no longer "useful" to men, and so she in turn can "take up ideology. . . . Daughter-mother lesbian, I write down the ultimate contradiction. Undermining from within his-tory in which I can now participate" (36).[22]

Reading, summarizing, and (in my case) translating Brossard is complicated by her dense, nonlinear, highly abstract and experimental writing. Yet I suggest that *These Our Mothers* runs familiar risks. It is not altogether clear whether the "symbolic mother" is a prescription for material mothering of actual children, as it seems at some points, or for voluntary sterility, as it clearly is at others, or how the two practices, normally at odds, might be combined. In either case the prescriptiveness itself invites the critique often made of cultural feminist celebrations of maternal virtues. To what extent is this still a way of reducing womanhood to some kind of motherhood (in this case, lesbian or symbolic motherhood), excluding the nonmother (in this case, the patriarchal mother) from the subject position, the politically valued, or the morally good, and thereby reifying divisions among women: mothers versus nonmothers, (all) straights versus (only some) gays, bad (patriarchal) mothers versus good (symbolic) mothers, women who sell out versus women who go wild?

Moreover, it is necessary to ask whether Brossard's vision is really grounded, as Alice Parker claims, in "the materiality of a lesbian mother's life."[23] It seems hopelessly literal-minded to wonder how the two pregnant women who make love in Brossard's later novel, *Mauve Desert,* manage to conceive; the novel, like the earlier writing in *These Our Mothers,* has little interest in such questions. But if we now turn from the relatively inaccessible "fiction-theory" of a writer like Brossard to the highly accessible, empirical work in Ellen Lewin's more recent *Lesbian Mothers,* it does not seem irrelevant or simpleminded to worry about how women might manage in practice what seems desirable in theory. Lewin's study of the materiality of many American lesbian mothers' lives in the late eighties would seem to offer little current hope that lesbian motherhood can afford the "female self-defense against the violences of patriarchal discourse" promised on the jacket copy of *These Our Mothers.*

Lewin articulates an initial understanding of the structural position of the lesbian mother that sounds strikingly like Brossard's and other earlier theoretical claims: "Insofar as lesbianism and motherhood seem to be culturally (if not biologically) incompatible, they [lesbian mothers] transcend or challenge the ordinary organization of gender in American culture, which conflates 'woman' and 'mother' and defines lesbians as neither. In this sense, claiming the identity of lesbian mother may be construed as an instance of resistance to prevailing sexual politics" (15). But disproving her own hypothesis, Lewin's interviews with seventy-three lesbian mothers and sixty-two heterosexual mothers (including "natural" and adoptive mothers in both groups) reveal the present difficulty, if not the inevitable impossibility, of living as an "ultimate contradiction" or using motherhood as materially experienced to undermine conventional and oppressive definitions of womanhood. Because lesbian mothers *do* mother outside the heterosexual unit, they are often able to avoid one problem that mothers who are also wives face: they may maintain a degree of autonomy and control over their own lives and the decisions that are made about their children. Other common aspects of their situations, however, make it necessary for them to accommodate to conventional expectations. Most notably, they are at great risk of losing custody of their children. To prove that they are fit mothers they may have to hide their sexual orientation. They may also have to give up their friendships with other lesbian and gay people—not only to avoid the appearance of keeping bad company, but because lesbians and gay men are often childless and may either on principle or out of ignorance fail to support lesbians with children (or in some cases lesbians with male children).[24] They frequently have to appease the fathers of their children and the kin from whom they still need and want support.

The problem, as Lewin sees it, goes even deeper. It is not just that women when they become mothers are forced to conform to a law that denies lesbian rights, in which case we might argue about whether their apparent conformity outweighed or sustained their structural defiance. But Lewin also calls into question whether her subjects can be considered defiant at all when she finds a tendency for lesbian mothers to accept motherhood as a "core identity" that dominates other identities and relationships. As I understand her conclusion, she worries that the problem here is not lesbianism and its risks, but motherhood and its all-consuming demands and seductions—not only the institutions that police heterosexuality, but also the complicity of women with them. The lesbian mother, though undermining certain categorizations, does not and presumably cannot effectively counter a general trend—one that is unwittingly supported by feminists and lesbians who "glorify" motherhood—to use motherhood to defuse the threat to traditional gender divisions and the "hegemonic family" that has resulted from a certain (and now apparently illusory) loosening of the rules about who can mother and who can be a family.[25] To defend their rights, lesbian and gay couples may claim to be as good as any heterosexual couple, thereby reinforcing rather than challenging the heterosexual norm. Lewin worries that even as lesbians can and do more frequently and openly choose to mother and thus contest stereotypes about lesbians, stereotypes about women persist. Women are still divided into mothers and nonmothers, and the latter are denigrated, as motherhood and womanhood "continue to be conflated and mutually defined."[26]

One might argue that Lewin's material lesbian mothers are not symbolic enough, by Brossard's definition; they are actually "patriarchal mothers," whatever their sexual orientation. Does this mean that Brossard errs in assuming that "caressing the body of another woman" automatically kills the patriarchal mother? Or did Lewin interview the wrong lesbians? Those who participated in her study were *de facto* the kind of people who cooperate in such projects. The research itself was, as Lewin self-consciously points out, funded by an NIMH grant and designed in part to meet the requirements of U.S. government agencies. The participants were not chosen for racial and ethnic diversity; all but a few were white, and all but five were biological mothers.[27] They were also women who had and wanted legal custody of their children, and who were thus obliged to live within the law. Would the results have been different if she had interviewed lesbian women who had gone underground with their children (like Wanda in Marge Piercy's *Small Changes*), or—more readily available subjects—lesbian women who had in fact lost or relinquished custody of children (like Josie in Jan Clausen's *Sinking Stealing,* or Minnie Bruce Pratt, or Sharon Bottoms)?[28]

Is there indeed a way to move from the place of "patriarchal" mother to that of "symbolic" lesbian mother? Or is the position of the mother who is "inaccessible to reproduction" (and Brossard does not specify how she becomes a mother, how she becomes connected to children after she kills the womb) such a contradiction in terms as to be practically and politically unavailable or unbearable to most women in most places, and so do we only come back by another route to the sense of impasse? Just as "real" lesbian mothers have little to do with "symbolic" lesbian mothers, so Brossard's theory (French, separatist, written in the seventies) seems to have little to do with Lewin's anthropology (American, integrationist, researched in the eighties) when it comes to thinking about motherhood and the politics of lesbian resistance or complicity. The comparison of Brossard and Lewin confirms Bonnie Zimmerman's worried observation that "the discourses of 'common sense' [certainly closer to the discourse anthropologist Lewin offers] and contemporary theory seem to be moving further and further apart."[29]

I have thus far suggested that neither the facts (of common sense and social science) nor the theory resolve (or even in some cases recognize) the problems of lesbianism and motherhood. What about fiction, a discourse traditionally located somewhere between fact and theory, experience and abstraction, and one that has been so deeply linked with and changed by second-wave feminism? At first glance, the answer to that question is that fiction has by and large left the problematic relationship of lesbianism and motherhood untouched, rarely telling stories about lesbians who have mothers or are also mothers. Moreover, as Zimmerman observes, where mothers or the maternal do explicitly enter into the story, romantic and realistic visions of motherhood divide along familiar lines. Although lesbian utopias often imagine new worlds constructed around traditional maternal virtues such as empathy and nurturance, in more realistic fictions lesbianism and motherhood are represented as incompatible.[30] In highly acclaimed works like Winterson's *Oranges Are Not the Only Fruit*, the lesbian heroine's own mother is fully patriarchal, the enemy. In others, the troubled bond between mother and daughter may be something that characters first act out and then grow beyond (such, for instance, is Zimmerman's reading of *Desert of the Heart*). In still others, the character who provides nurturance and empathy in a markedly maternal way to another lesbian may not have her own needs met (this is Zimmerman's reading of *The Cook and the Carpenter*). The only "heroic" lesbian mother figure is, predictably, the one who is fighting a custody suit, which may entail the overt political action of going underground (as in *Sinking Stealing* and the Beth plot of Piercy's *Small Changes*).[31]

Literary critical treatments of motherhood in lesbian fiction are as rare as the fictional treatments themselves, but one of the most interesting to date is Judith Roof's study of the absent mother in lesbian narratives. Roof reads this absence as a telling sign of what distinguishes heterosexual desire from lesbian desire. The silence of most lesbian fiction on the question of mothers and motherhood positively "denies from the start the nostalgic wish and maternal fulfillment" of heterosexual stories, as embodied in the (nonfictional) narratives of Kristeva and Chodorow in particular.[32] Taking Jane Rule's *This Is Not for You*

(1970) and Rita Mae Brown's *Rubyfruit Jungle* (1973) as "prototypical lesbian novels" in this regard, Roof argues that these lesbian *bildungsromans* deny the relevance of genetic origins, defy the notion that history holds the answers, and above all posit "the missing mother as the original model for unfulfilled desire."[33] They thereby define lesbian desire as unfulfillable and "hysterical" ("woman desiring woman") and the lesbian woman as "a completely independent, self-defined, but marginal woman whose fulfillment comes in the understanding that there is no such thing as fulfillment, that desire perpetuates desire."[34]

In the rest of this chapter, I suggest that in the fiction of Jane Rule in particular we find a more salient and pervasive discussion of lesbianism and motherhood than has yet been observed. However, I focus not so much on the telling absence, failure, or complicity of mothers as on another side of the story: the absence of children and, paradoxically, the revaluation and redistribution of conventional maternal functions previously equated with procreative womanhood. Insofar as we construe the division in lesbian thought about motherhood as a debate rather than a constitutive split, I propose that Rule can be seen retrospectively as a moderator—not because she takes a moderate position, but because she refuses, in a sense, to take sides and thereby defies "the dominant ideology" in order to push beyond "total acceptance of motherhood or total negation."

DESERT OF THE HEART AND NONPROCREATIVE MOTHERHOOD

The fundamental outline of what we might term "nonprocreative motherhood" in Rule's fiction is set forth most clearly in her first and in some ways most romantic or optimistic story, *Desert of the Heart*. I speak of nonprocreative motherhood instead of childless or childfree womanhood because, as I hope becomes self-evident in the course of this discussion, the phrase is truer to Rule's vision. One main objective in Rule's fiction is to break up the conflation of womanhood and motherhood. That can certainly be accomplished by women defining themselves in ways that go outside "maternal" roles and capacities and purposively choosing not to have children, to be (more positively) "childfree" or (more negatively) "childless."[35] It can also be accomplished by dispersing and disseminating the practices and "virtues" conventionally associated with mothers who care for children, suggesting that those practices and capacities are not merely compensatory but have value outside the mother-child relationship as models for connection and action. "Nonprocreative motherhood" better describes this kind of extension of the maternal in an affirmative way.

Because *Desert of the Heart* was published in 1964, before any active lesbian separatist movement is usually thought to have been afoot, the timeliness and insightfulness of the novel may surprise readers in the nineties. Without using the word "lesbian" (or any synonyms except the term "homosexual," attributed to a very unattractive male character in the story), the novel considers competing theories about the meaning of motherhood in the formation of lesbian identity. One main character, Ann, is introduced as that familiar type of lesbian described by Simone de Beauvoir in *The Second Sex*, a woman who, lacking maternal affection as a child, feels compensatory adult sexual desire for an older, motherly woman, especially a "detached" woman like the other main character, Evelyn, "who seemed in her eyes to bear a sacred character."[36] Evelyn, in turn, is the classic childless woman also described in de Beauvoir, "the woman who makes a religion of her femininity" and feels a maternal love for other women compounded by "the absence or difficulty of heterosexual contacts."[37] In such stereotypes we see confusion about the role that motherhood plays in shaping female identity and desire. Is it a woman's relationship (or lack thereof) *to* her own mother or her maternal representations, or is it her experiences (or lack thereof) *as* a mother that affect her sexual orientation?[38] By imagining what happens when one lesbian caricature happens to meet the other, *Desert of the Heart* simultaneously entertains this question and suggests the reductiveness of both theories.

The novel compounds the stereoptypicality of the situation by positing a striking physical resemblance between Ann and Evelyn, not only reflecting de Beauvoir's comments on the narcissism and mirroring of lesbian love but also anticipating the more recent theory that lesbianism is the space of "sameness."[39] However, each is represented as a very sophisticated and intelligent woman who is highly self-conscious of the ways in which she is psychologically constructed by her relationship to the maternal and who also in many ways contradicts the very stereotype she initially seems to represent. Ann, the younger woman and daughter figure, is also a mother figure to others in the novel; Evelyn, after she accepts and acts on the "tenderness" she feels for Ann, alleges the discovery that her true "femininity" has little to do with the obsession with motherhood that previously dominated her life.[40] People are constructed by clichés, *Desert* reminds us—but smart people are also often aware of this fact and may therefore stand a chance of discarding the conventions that no longer serve them. Conventions and clichés, as Ann and Evelyn repeatedly and self-consciously insist, are made to be played on, cartooned, taken literally, and otherwise heard afresh and resisted.[41] As Ann and Evelyn come together in the plot, their respective childlessness is revalued. In tandem they represent the possibility of maternal feelings and experiences, detached from procreation, no longer exclusively or essentially defining their womanhood but nevertheless critical to the complex drives and choices that sustain their relationship.

ANN CHILDS: REVISING "HER OWN UNDERSTOOD SELF"

Ann Childs, as her name suggests, functions in important ways as a daughter figure who introduces to the novel one familiar explanation of why women choose to love other women. Ann was abandoned by her mother at the age of six and raised by a dominating, immensely intelligent and attractive father who appears to have urged his daughter to slash her wrists.[42] Expelled at an early age from Mills College for attempting to kiss a special assistant to the dean, Ann, in her twenties when the novel opens, is apparently self-educated in then-current psychoanalytic theories about her own sexuality. She is also aware of the possibly causal as well as explanatory role of such theories and the images they induce in the formation of (sexual) identity: "She was her own understood self" (124). Until her affair with Evelyn, what Ann understands about herself is embedded in the peculiarity and typicality of her childhood and in her resistance to the infantile needs she believes it has left unfilled. She assumes, and other characters agree, that her affairs with older women represent a paradoxical effort to come to terms with her abandonment, to rid herself of "the weight of sentiment she would not carry around with her" (124). In this formulation, love for the mother is figured as a demonic, termless, fruitless pregnancy that the lesbian woman at once acknowledges and tries to abort. Seeking the lost mother in the arms of other adult women, Ann believes she can then go one step further than the syndrome and "smash" the image that tempts her "to a memory of innocence, of virtue, of salvation. Then view the shattered mother with slight distaste or distant curiosity, a little disappointed, vastly relieved" (124). Ann's behavior thus both invokes and defies stereotypes of the fifties and sixties. It also complicates the influential notion popularized in the late seventies and eighties, after the novel's publication, that lesbian sexuality might be a "natural" result of the mother-daughter bond by suggesting ways in which that theory ignores the actual frequency if not inevitability of failed or interrupted motherlove. The novel calls attention to the romantic, nostalgic "weight of sentiment" this belief brings to bear on women and on the mother as symbol.

When Ann succeeds in her antimaternal "campaign" to make love with Evelyn, a woman fifteen years older with an uncanny physical resemblance to her, a further complication arises. Her rational understanding of the ways in which she deals with and thus controls irrational desires falls apart as she falls in love, fails to smash an image, and feels none of the calculated disappointment she sought. "She felt, instead, a ridiculous tenderness that no self-mockery could defeat" (125).[43] After a dream in which she hears her own mother's voice, "hard and clear," Ann begins to reconsider both her explicit assumptions and her embodied memories:

> Odd how clearly she still held her mother's voice in her unconscious, a voice she hadn't heard for nineteen years. "And you're one of the enemies I'm going to have to kill." Somehow linked to that broken and grotesquely mended bone of memory was the lust of Ann's body. . . . If, in making love with Evelyn, her body yearned for obscure intimacies, they must no longer be substitutes for, a defense against, intimacies of person with person. Here was an enemy to be converted. (145)

In this passage, the unconscious roots of lesbian eroticism seem to be realigned with motherlove, maternal representation, and infantile needs, but in ways that neither mother-blaming nor mother-worshipping can adequately account for. The "enemy" is Ann's conventional maternal representation, her projection onto all women of her negative feelings about the woman who abandoned her, but that representation is seen here more clearly for what it is. The acting out of the mother-daughter relationship, on Ann's part, is initially an attempt at exorcism rather than repetition. Ann wishes to unburden herself of a relationship that could never live up to the sentimental ideals that conventionally define it. In this way she is something of an avatar of later radical lesbians who reject motherhood as dangerous to women's selfhood and hopelessly complicit with patriarchy. But her contorted, familiar response to feelings of abandonment, her desire to protect herself against betrayal that gives rise to woman-hating disguised as woman-loving, is in the process of changing. The perceived fact of abandonment has to be self-consciously reinterpreted or "converted" so that it does not stand in the way of the intimacy with Evelyn. Most importantly, the felt correspondence between Ann's "lust" for Evelyn's body and her unconscious infantile desires and habits is neither to be defensively scorned and rejected *nor* accepted at face value. Evelyn is *not* her mother; adult female sexual relationships are not substitutes for a lost, idealized, or demonized mother-daughter bond. Her attempt to exorcise the mother by means of a ritual of contagion fails as such because Ann's relationship with Evelyn, again, is "somehow linked to" but *not the same* as the relationship with her mother.

The novel may also invite readers to wonder about the facticity of this pretextual maternal abandonment. All we are told is that Ann's father blames the mother's behavior on her "nymphomania," but from what little we know of Mr. Childs, it would seem more likely that his wife might have been forced to leave her child in order to escape his possessiveness. However, what really happened—how Ann's mother understood herself and the act of leaving her child—remains untold. The *Childs'* construction of it, named as such to underscore how it combines her father's perspective and her own childish view, is all Ann and her readers have to work with. The fact that the adult woman can move beyond this infantile, paternal, overdetermined construction is what is remarkable about Ann's story.

EVELYN HALL: THE MOTHER FIGURE OF THE MOMENT

The alternative mother's story in *Desert of the Heart* is coded in Evelyn's alternating narrative. Evelyn's story exemplifies the exigency of motherhood for a woman who prefers to love women as it engages the pronatalism of the decades after World War II. Hers is perversely both a story of not being a biological mother and a story in which being biologically mothered seems irrelevant.

Evelyn is never represented as a daughter—at least not the daughter of a heterosexual, procreative mother. In all her self-reflections during the crisis that she undergoes in Reno, waiting for her divorce, she never mentions her family or her relations to her birth parents. But Evelyn does recall in passing a possibly key ancestress—a formidable great-aunt Ida, "maiden and militant," who lived alone in a family house like the one in which Ann and Evelyn meet, and who "had mastered the master bedroom with nothing but her own royal virginity"(9).[44] What brings the aunt to mind, at the opening of the story, is an olfactory memory: Aunt Ida burned incense in her bathroom, as does Frances, the mistress of the house in Reno where Evelyn stays. This sensual, preverbal (perhaps preoedipal?) memory suggests the unconscious presence and importance of an awe-inspiring, powerful, and willfully nonprocreative female precursor. Similarly, Evelyn's surname, *Hall*, symbolic like Ann's patronymic but in the metafictional register, surely suggests another precursor in the nonprocreative female genealogy of lesbian fiction, Radclyffe Hall. In the bathroom, Evelyn cannot "resist the temptation" to light a stick in memory of her aunt, but the odor is too strong for her and she has to put it out. "'Ah, Ida,' she said softly, 'it's true what you used to say: we are a weaker generation'" (9). Although she is a descendant of strong virgins, Evelyn's "weakness" most particularly entails her conservative, conditioned response to childlessness, which has all but "mastered" her life and is now driving her out of the master's bedroom in her own domestic house.

Despite the fact that she has a successful academic career, Evelyn remembers her life before Reno and Ann as an interminable expanse of passivity and frustrated expectancy: "this terrible waiting . . . a biding of time, her waiting to marry George, then waiting for the war to be over, then waiting for the child that did not come." The divorce that she waits for throughout the present-tense narrative of the novel will be a release from this suspension, but at first this release is figured as terminal, not renewing; Evelyn expects "the death of all this waiting" (55). This waiting ends in death because it marks the end of all hopes that Evelyn will bear a child and become a patriarchal mother. Although she has always felt alienated from generalizations about womanhood, there is one she claims to share: "What it was to want a child. Any woman knew that" (68). Ironically, Evelyn perceives that "she had been willing to sacrifice anything in the world" to have a child, but what she ends up losing is her marriage. Her obsessive domestic behavior—doing all the housework, baking bread, sewing her own clothes—is clearly, self-consciously seen, like Ann's inverse bad-girl behavior, as compensatory gender role-playing: "If she could not bear a child, there were a hundred other conventions through which she could prove she was a woman" (117).

Evelyn recalls one protolesbian experience with her wartime friend Carol that again positions her as a frustrated would-be mother who takes up the mannish role of breadwinner while waiting for George to come home. Evelyn and Carol lived together while their husbands were overseas, in a convenient same-sex version of a conventional marriage. Carol, with a new baby, needed money but could not work outside the house; Evelyn, a childless graduate student, needed time to study, so Evelyn paid for the groceries and Carol cooked. When Carol's husband was killed, Evelyn remembers tending her like a mother, holding and rocking the grief-stricken woman as she wailed, undressing her and putting her to bed, and finally, like a parent with a child who cannot sleep, climbing into bed with her. Then, "Carol turned into Evelyn's arms, her face pressing against Evelyn's breast. As she began to suck, the rocking and wailing stopped." Evelyn views the incident as the cruel end of a woman's waiting, "until at last the desire for comfort and nourishment could be nothing more than a perversion of the flesh, a blind sucking"; she knew then that in the morning, "in decorous forgetfulness they would cancel out this night" (115). She tells herself now that there was "nothing unusual" about her friendship with Carol. Grief explains the aberrant night, although she also reveals her Freudian conviction that it is "natural" and therefore, like other aspects of natural human drives, to be redeemed by "good" behavior. "For the rest, the moments of unacknowledged tenderness and vague desire, the unconsenting will must surely ransom nature" (117).

Ann's calculated, self-conscious, and yet stereotypical understanding of herself and her sexual adventures as a reaction to her abandonment by her birth mother is undermined by her love of Evelyn. Just so, Evelyn's sense of herself as a failed mother who covers her inadequacy by performing as woman in the most conventional ways and her equally self-conscious belief that any erotic feelings toward a woman are an effect of a "nature" to be controlled by virtuous and proper intentions are disrupted when she begins to love Ann. She assents at first to the presumption that she is attracted to Ann as a surrogate daughter, the child she never bore (17). Gradually, however, she comes to believe that this is not all there is to it. When she first acknowledges her physical desire for Ann, she already sees her as daughter and as something more: "the child she had always wanted, the friend she had once had, the lover she had never considered" (108). Then she begins to separate herself from such an easy identification: "What she saw was no longer an imperfect reflection of herself but an alien otherness she was drawn to and could not understand" (117). After their affair has begun, when a store clerk jumps to the conclusion that she is Ann's mother, Evelyn speaks aloud her "final" rejection of a maternal relationship: "'She's not my daughter,' Evelyn said . . . her quiet voice so final that the clerk could not even apologize" (141).

As Ann and Evelyn come together and stop performing the parts of bad girl and good mother, they undercut all the contradictory, clichéd assumptions about why women love other women that presume or enable the fetishizing and blaming of the mother and the conflation of motherhood and womanhood. Ann learns that Evelyn is more than "the mother figure of the moment" (79), and she sets aside her cynical self-defense against being hurt again as she believes she was hurt by her own mother. Evelyn rejects the pronatalism that has driven her life, the enervating conviction that a childless woman is a nonwoman, that femininity is equivalent to maternity, and that women can give each other comfort and "tenderness" only when males are absent and the females' primitive, infantile needs—calls of "nature"—are too strong to resist. At the same time, however, this is not just a story about outgrowing the need to be mothered or shedding the internalized shibboleths against sterile women. Ann hears her mother speak in her dreams and acknowledges the fact that she still holds her mother's voice in her unconscious, that it is part of her desire for Evelyn. Evelyn turns out to be almost as strong as her virgin female progenitor, Aunt Ida, who might be thought of as the beginning of a new matrilineage. As we shall see, *nonprocreative* but distinctly *maternal* feelings and practices remain important and ambivalent parts of Ann's and Evelyn's identities and the relationship between them.

TAKING THE RISK

Ann is not only a daughter figure in all the complexity that that entails but also the spokeswoman for voluntary childlessness. However, she combines her self-conscious refusal to bear children with an apparent instinct for conventional mothering behavior: protecting, consoling, tending, healing, responding, and being responsible. Ann's motives are complex. In large part her decision to do childfree but explicitly maternal work, like her initial response to Evelyn, is self-protective, as we see first in her relationship to the five foreign children to whom she sends monthly checks and holiday gifts. Later another self-defensive reason for preferring a surrogate, distanced motherhood emerges as Ann, mourning the death of her friend Janet's son, describes herself as a "grief rider." "'If you don't play, you can't lose,'" she explains to Evelyn (100). Evelyn views Ann's foster motherhood at first as compensatory, like her own domesticity: "'So these are instead of children of your own?'" Ann has a two-part answer, one part characteristically cynical, self-deprecating, and self-preserving—"'It's the easiest and cheapest way. . . . They're so little nuisance'"—and one part hinting at a larger political and ethical critique—children are being "dumped" all over the world, like surplus grain, so only those "really suited to it" should profess motherhood today (70). Finally, in defending the desert against Evelyn's view that it is "sterile" and thus a metaphor for Evelyn's barrenness—"the word a laceration of her own flesh"—Ann explains why for her "fertility" is "a dirty word." She underscores what is self-consciously subversive and self-constructive about her choice: "'I'm terrified of giving in, of justifying my own existence by means of simple reproduction . . . it's such a temptation. It seems so natural— another dirty word for me'" (107).

Ann's resistance to either the "natural" or conventional allure of institutionalized, procreative motherhood is also a rational response to the actual situation of biological mothers in the world of this novel, where the "happy mother" is as much an impossibility as it is in virtually all of the works in this study. As surrogate and parodic mother, modern icon of "the ironic emancipation of woman," Ann works in the casino as change girl; over her uniform of pants, cowboy boots, and big hat, she wears an apron loaded with sixty pounds of silver "very high" on her waist, "carrying it like a fetus in its seventh month." In the "unnatural" world of Reno, where Ann sees herself studying human nature in its purest "nonanimal" form, (re)producing nothing out of nothing, money thus replaces children as the ultimate value, the "world's only passionate belief" (94); potential motherhood is figured in this weight of which the always expectant woman is never delivered. Those women who try to care for children to whom they have given birth seem doomed to fail and suffer. Janet works in the casino to pay the medical expenses of a seriously ill infant who dies in the course of the novel. Joyce, a new change girl, almost faints the first night on the job, only later acknowledging that she has a six-week-old baby at home and is looking for a husband. Virginia, separated from her children while she waits in Reno for a divorce, tries to kill herself. It is no accident that the place where lesbianism renegotiates its relationship to mothers and motherhood is Reno, Nevada. If procreative motherhood is essentially anything, it is a gamble, one in which the odds are by "nature" *and* convention stacked against women who play the game.

Ann's experiences and observations thus anticipate the kind of full-blown feminist critique of motherhood articulated by Lucia Valeska: "Since failure is built into childraising in our society, there is no such thing as a good mother and no such thing as a good self-concept emerging from this work."[45] At the same time, however, the novel insists that the painful work associated with mothering *is* needed and that it is often done by nonbiological mothers like Ann. Ann not only supports her foreign foster children but also demonstrates conventionally maternal competence when she stands with or for the mothers on several occasions: she grieves with Janet, plays with the abandoned children at the casino, protects Silver, covers for Joyce, tends Virginia's self-inflicted wounds, and counsels Virginia's guilt-stricken husband.

Meanwhile, as if trading places with the daughter Ann only appeared to be, Evelyn moves away from her sense of herself as a failed mother and hence a false, merely performative woman. In a key, difficult passage told from Evelyn's point of view, she thinks that by accepting her love for Ann she has discovered an irony:

> It was curious that, at the very time she was giving up all external images of womanhood [her marriage, her conventional goodness and fear], Evelyn should become increasingly aware of her own femininity, and it was not a *synthetic maternity* as she had expected it to be. Oh, at moments Ann sleeping was a child, her child. And sometimes, when she saw the thin, vicious scars on Ann's wrists, she had to fight down an animal rage which was protective. But these emotions were occasional. Now . . . Evelyn wanted to be charming, provocative, desirable, attributes she had never aspired to before out of pride, perhaps, or fear of failure. Now they seemed almost instinctive. She was finding, in the miracle of her particular fall, that she was, by nature, a woman. And what a lovely thing it was to be, a woman. (160, emphasis added)

This may seem a troubling statement to feminists schooled in postmodern and deconstructionist principles, for it raises among other concerns the question of whether Evelyn's reiterated and inconsistent recourse to "nature," along with her seemingly essentialist claims about being "a woman," can be seen as a morally and intellectually dubious evasion of responsibility.[46] But another reading of Evelyn's self-understanding is possible if we attend to the way *Desert of the Heart* seeks to render the *process* through which the characters change their minds and reinterpret their identities. There is a complex and never entirely clear relation between what a character consciously and unconsciously means at a given point in this novel, what the narrator thinks of this already complicated and in no way final meaning, and what readers may wish to conclude.

For Evelyn, at this point in the plot, it is important to detach motherhood and womanhood, maternity and subjectivity, as firmly as possible, since she is learning how the conflation of the two has dominated her life and, coupled with her involuntary childlessness and disastrous marriage, turned her into the monster she wishes to reject. This moment of self-understanding and reconstruction parallels Ann's revised understanding that "the enemy" is not Evelyn, nor Ann's missing biological mother, but her own maternal representation of the bad mother and her belief that she has been indelibly marked by her mother's abandonment. Evelyn's new enthusiasm for instinctive, natural, and decidedly nonmaternal "femininity" is not the novel's last word on the subject. It is instead a necessary, transitional stage in thinking—hers and ours—about the maternal subject. We are set up to be suspicious of anything in this novel that is said to be "by nature," but it is also the case that Ann and Evelyn are trying both to contest pronatalism and express a desire outside heterosexuality and the traditional family. Doing so may appear a falsely essentializing, reifying move, laying claim to the female identity—that "lovely thing . . . a woman"—that the childless are denied. That identity may not, in the long run, express that subject's full desire or represent her best interests.

In this novel, where words are so constantly under the pressure of the characters' intelligence and the narrator's craft, it is particularly important to consider the carefully chosen phrase "*synthetic* maternity." The surprising adjective qualifies the abstract noun in ways that illuminate the meaning of this new, unthinkable, postpatriarchal concept—nonprocreative motherhood. First, it is not an artificial or "manmade" maternity (as in synthetic compounds or synthetic furs); that is, it is not the maternity, expressed in procreative acts and relations, that western culture has traditionally assumed to be normal, right, and natural for women. (Brossard's "patriarchal mother" comes to mind as an analog of what Evelyn is rejecting here.) Second, it is not a maternity that proceeds, as in synthesis, in a straight line from cause to effect or from general to particular. Because females bear children, it is not logically or materially necessary that women are or can be defined by this single function. All procreative mothers may, as things stand, be women, but not all women are procreative mothers. Third, it is not a maternity that involves synthesis as construction, unifying parts into a whole. No whole woman's identity or subjectivity (should such things exist) can be constructed out of her maternal parts, nor are her maternal feelings necessarily unifying, unitary, or constructive. Nor can all women be unified into a category based on traditional motherhood. In the same vein, it is not a maternity that suggests synthesis in the grammatical sense of the term, which would obviously be important in this novel. Grammatically, according to the *OED, synthetic* means "characterized by a combination of simple words or elements into compound or complex words; expressing a complex notion by a single compounded or complex word instead of by a number of distinct words." *Maternity* and *motherhood*, like *womanhood*, are semantically complex words, in our lexicon, that we substitute for any number of "distinct words"; what Evelyn recognizes here is that, perceived as unifying rubrics, these terms may dangerously suppress distinctions and reduce a variety of stories to a single prescribed narrative.

The denouement of the novel belies Evelyn's wholesale rejection of maternity. When she almost succumbs to her traditionally maternal urge to protect Ann by giving her up, she brings to mind Ellen Lewin's "complicitous" lesbian mothers, driven to appease, conform, and sacrifice. At the same time, other qualities associated with maternal practice are valorized in the surprise last-minute reversal in divorce court, when Evelyn takes the stand to testify against her husband, George: "'He's bitter and despairing and frightened,' she said. 'He's afraid to care about anyone. He's afraid of the responsibility, not just the financial responsibility, but the emotional responsibility. Afraid of being destroyed, or afraid of destroying. He can't care about anyone. It's too much of a risk'" (220). Ironically, Evelyn indicts her husband for his failure to behave in the way that mothers are supposed to behave, taking responsibility for free-floating charges of emotional power loosed by love, need, and caretaking. What she accuses him of, moreover, actually describes her own unwillingness to "risk" loving Ann. It seems to be this odd recognition—seeing herself not in the mirror of Ann's face, but in the despairing shell that is George—that makes it possible for Evelyn to change her mind at the last minute and to stay with Ann. The happy ending is at once qualified and firmly distinguished from the traditional closure of marriage, as we learn in the penultimate sentence of the novel, by the experimental, possibly temporary nature of the illicit arrangement the lovers enter into: "'For the while then. . . . For an indefinite period of time'" (222).

Far from simply rejecting the relevance of motherhood to the characters' lives as childfree lesbians, *Desert of the Heart* brings together two women who eventually reject the sway of confused and contradictory mainstream clichés about motherhood and femininity. Instead, they embrace contradiction and resist being lesbian *or* mother. Individually and together they retain conventionally maternal feelings, do conventionally maternal work, and in the end take the conventionally maternal risks of emotional attachment. Their maternal capacities, however, are exercised in the service of a relationship that is explicitly nonprocreative and outside the heterosexual norm. The possibility that "maternal thinking" could and should inform adult relationships in this way is reiterated in Rule's essay "The Question of Children," in *A Hot-Eyed Moderate:*

> The only love in which possessiveness is generally frowned on is that of adults for children. We [speaking especially of gay people, who are often teachers and others in the so-called helping professions] learn to take responsibility for their safety, well-being, and education whether they are ours or not, even without knowing them. Far from being an experience to avoid, it is the model for the concern we might feel for adults as well. (95)[47]

"MOTHER WITHOUT CHILD": THE CARTOON

At the center of *Desert of the Heart,* framing the moment when Evelyn and Ann first act on their sexual desire, the narrative introduces a striking figure for a nonprocreative motherhood that can practically serve a subversive vision. Ann and Evelyn have spent Ann's day off together, shopping for Christmas presents for her five foster children. As they wrap the gifts, Ann, repeating her half-serious, half-joking enthusiasm for this form of surrogate motherhood, is struck with an idea for a cartoon:

"But the lovely thing about these children is that you can have fa-
vorites. You can even like girls better than boys (my preference in the
adult world only), and no one will grow up with bad bathroom habits
or unattractive aggressions. If anyone does, it isn't your fault. Childbirth without pain, Motherhood without guilt, Mother without child."
Ann paused. "I wonder if I could get that: 'Mother without Child.' If I
got it, I couldn't sell it."(121)

Ann doesn't attempt the sketch at this point. Instead, after the gift wrap-
ping is finished, she and Evelyn make love for the first time; she starts
her drawing of "Mother without Child" the next morning. At the end
of the novel, Evelyn may be alluding to this scene when she tells Ann,
"'We're a cryptic cartoon, my darling. It should be one of your best.'"
Ann replies, "'I'll only draw it if I can live it'" (222).

We never know whether "Mother without Child" is finished, but
the novel as a whole clarifies its centrality. It is meant to be one of
Ann's private cartoons, the ones she does not or cannot sell because
they tell hard truths that the world doesn't want to buy. As an idea,
it notably precipitates Evelyn's capitulation to the women's mutual
desire and thus designates the way lesbian sexuality is here connected to the challenging, perverse, and—by standard logic—
impossible sign of the mother without child. The cartoon suggests a
new "maternal subject" seen not from the point of view of the moth-
erless child (Ann's sometime perspective) or the equally child-
obsessed presumption of the childless mother (Evelyn's self-
understanding), but from the perspective of women who together
resist either conscription into reproduction or exile out of womanhood. Such women, like Ann and Evelyn, reject procreation or live
without it, but they do not reject maternal feelings and maternal
work—caregiving, protectiveness, and acceptance of risk and responsibility. Maternal practice can in this way, in some circumstances, become at once transgressively sexualized and actively
politicized, both in acts of "tenderness" outside the law and in words
of witness, like Evelyn's, before the law.

The status of "Mother without Child" as a cartoon is also critical in
several aspects. As Ann's drawing, it marks her role in the composite
or plural figure of the lesbian as artist in *Desert of the Heart*. Evelyn
clearly represents the more conventional part of that artistry: she is a
professional literary critic who teaches Ann about canonical poetry, including the works of her favorite poet, Yeats.[48] Evelyn's learning and

verbal acuity are reflected in the dense intertextuality of the novel, as high literary texts (for example, Dante's *Inferno*) are fragmented, revised, and appropriated in ways that are familiar and exciting to literary critical minds.[49] But it is Ann who studies and critiques real people in the material world ruled by guns, one-way mirrors, and gambling; her eccentric political and philosophical acumen at the very least complements Evelyn's logocentric vision.

The novel itself also prizes by imitation the skills of the cartoonist in particular—seeing and caricaturing, reveling in the gaps between word and image or euphemism and actuality, and visualizing new contexts in which conventions may be demystified. Conveyed by strategies of uncertain irony, broad skepticism, and general alertness to the instability and power of language, the content of the cartoonist's vision, in its most common sense, is political. Cartoons today are frequently comic statements on current events, usually yoking two faculties, the visual and the verbal; double or subversive meanings of familiar names, titles, idioms, and clichés, which often appear in the caption or other verbal part of the cartoon, are brought out by visualizing the literal or perverse meaning. The political cartoon (which may be captionless, or may use words only within the drawing) may also employ caricature, "grotesque or ludicrous representation of persons or things by exaggeration of their most characteristic and striking features" (*OED*). "Mother without Child" particularly suggests this kind of cartoon, for it grotesquely exaggerates the most striking and contradictory features attributed to the lesbian: on the one hand, her affiliation with aspects of maternal experience, and on the other, her childlessness and hence unnatural resistance to the equation of womanhood and motherhood under the system of compulsory heterosexuality. At the same time it evokes a bitter image of one true aspect of motherhood, devalued by the world at large and dangerous to women (and their children) who try to play by the world's rules. Despite the weight of sentiment to the contrary, the mother's loss of the child is the frequent if not universal experience of women. It is the missing child, not the missing mother, that seems to structure female desire; what unites women may be, as Evelyn says, the (often frustrated) wanting of a child, not the having of one, the relationship in potential, not actuality. Finally, "Mother without Child" may also suggest, in another spirit, the impossible figure of the woman who defies patriarchal motherhood but celebrates another kind of mothering.

WHAT YOU LOSE IS WHAT YOU SURVIVE WITH:
MOTHERHOOD IN RULE'S LATER FICTION

"What have you done with Arthur?" Ruth shouted. "What
have you done? They're *my* children, *all* of them, *mine.* You
kill everything. Bastards! Bastards!"

Jane Rule, *The Young in
One Another's Arms*

In thinking about the mother without child as figure, we may also consider the fact that Ann's work on this drawing is incomplete and that the
word *cartoon* meant, in an earlier sense (*OED* 2), a preliminary sketch,
an idea for a later, more finished work. In this way, Ann's cartoon may
suggest that we are at an early stage in the literary (not to mention cultural) ability to understand and represent the relationship between
motherhood and lesbian desire or lesbian identity. It thereby introduces
what I see throughout Rule's later fiction as an ongoing delineation of
this unfinished project. My central focus has been on *Desert of the Heart,*
in part at least because it is relatively widely read, but I conclude now
by suggesting that Rule's first novel can also be seen as a preliminary
work, preparing the ground for her later, possibly even more complicated fictional explorations of the idea of nonprocreative motherhood.

The fiction of Jane Rule has perhaps not been taken up by either
those who celebrate motherhood or those who decry its dangers for
women because her novels call the split between loving and hating maternity into question—just as they call many generalizations about
womanhood, motherhood, and lesbianism into question. Rule's fictional women are not all lesbians, and in fact defining people by their
sexuality or assuming that there are two and only two groups, gay and
straight, is generally seen as dangerous and misguided, part of the mistaken treatment of homosexuality, which Rule herself has said she
hopes will someday be thought of with the "healthy neglect" and moral
neutrality with which we now think of left-handedness (see *Lesbian
Images*). Although many of her fictional women are involved in erotic
relationships with other women that range from brief encounters to
lifelong partnerships, many are not. Within the first group, some are
still more or less closeted but sexually active; some are openly gay but
currently involved in no erotic relationships; some are sexually active
yet homophobic; many are explicitly bisexual. Within the second
group, consisting of women who are primarily attracted to men as

sexual partners, some are homophobic; some are nonjudgmental; and several are involved in primary nonerotic bonds of friendship and love with other women.

The neglect that Rule hopes might overtake our consideration of homosexuality does not extend, however, to her fictional treatment of motherhood, which in the later novels is often a far more important and difficult problem than is sexual preference. But just as all women are not lesbians in Rule's novels, not all women have the same relation to motherhood, procreative or otherwise. Although Ann and Evelyn are both childfree, we have seen that they have arrived at that common position by routes that often set women bitterly against each other—one is a desperate, infertile married woman who has spent years trying to make a traditional marriage work; the other, at the beginning of her adult life, desperately and willfully resists marriage and procreation. Collectively, Rule's later female characters further defy both the categorization and opposition of women as mothers or nonmothers, women with children or the childfree. Some practice the kind of nonprocreative motherhood I have identified in *Desert of the Heart,* and I close this chapter by calling attention to the frequent reappearance of the mother without child in the later novels. But first it is important to notice that other of Rule's female characters, including both gay and straight women, are indeed procreative mothers and that the childfree often have close and supportive relationships with those who bear or raise children.

Pregnant women in particular play a role in many of Rule's works. Most of them—Kathy and Agate in *Against the Season,* Gladys in *The Young in One Another's Arms,* Alma in *Contract with the World,* and Red in *After the Fire*—are unmarried at the time of conception. In this way, pregnant people in Rule's stories are most often positioned, both voluntarily and involuntarily, outside the traditional family structure, and procreation is detached from marriage, so that the maternal work of childbirth itself can continue to subvert rather than reinforce "patriarchal" motherhood. Almost always the character's pregnancy spans the narrative time frame or she gives birth at or near the end of the novel, and so procreative work, analogous to the tentative union of Ann and Evelyn, specifically functions within the domain of traditional narrative realism to provide an alternative plot and anticlosure.[50]

Seen in light of this particular pattern, a subplot in *Desert of the Heart* that is not apparently germane to my earlier discussion of nonprocreative mothers takes on a significance that merits briefly revisiting that novel. This is the story of Silver, a loud, large female friend—and another, very different mother figure for Ann—who works in the casino and makes love to Ann on several occasions. Silver is bisexual, as she explains to Ann; men have been her "profession," women her objects of affection. Two surprising events in Silver's life frame the main plot of *Desert*. Near the beginning of the novel, we learn that Silver is planning to marry Joe, a younger, shorter, Jewish man with a stammer, whose ambition is to write successful pornography. At the end of the novel, on the eve of their formal wedding where ironically Ann will play maid of honor, Silver announces that she is pregnant. With mixed feelings of loneliness and relief, Ann is obliged to join in an "earnest toast to procreation"(191).[51] Ann's friendship with Silver is part of the novel's attention to the difficult but necessary connections between women who want to have children and women who don't, to the need for tolerance and mutual respect. It also suggests the possibility that conventions can be subverted not only by those who refuse to play the game, but also by those who threaten the system from within. Silver cultivates what is often labeled as sin, impropriety, ignorance, and vulgarity, claiming the right to participate in and benefit from conventional practices while parodying, disregarding, and possibly changing the rules. It is crucial, however, that Silver's pregnancy enters into the narrative only near the end. The story of the nonprocreative mother must come first, radically clearing away old notions of what a mother is and thus preparing us to see the possibility for subversion within procreativity.

In the works that follow *Desert of the Heart,* Rule's complex and thorough consideration of motherhood is worked out in the repeated depiction, from as many angles as possible, of two nonexclusive and sometimes overlaid variants of the mother without child: the biological mother who has lost one or more of the children she gave birth to, or who fears that she will do so; and the character whom we might view as a kind of surrogate mother, who does not in the present time of the narrative have biological children, but who serves as both a material and emotional or spiritual mother to others in her community in both traditionally and nontraditionally maternal ways.

"We plant time bombs in our flesh," says Ruth Wheeler in Rule's *The Young in One Another's Arms* (1977).[52] Perhaps the most common characteristic of procreative motherhood, glimpsed first in the sad story of Janet in *Desert of the Heart* and then reappearing throughout

Rule's fiction, is the way in which it makes women vulnerable to pain, loss, and suffering. This seemingly universal vulnerability, however, does not have a seamless meaning, but rather generates a divergence of responses and consequences, depending on the circumstances and the choices that women make. Most of the consequences are highly negative. Stories of women driven by the loss or threatened loss of their children to perverse acts that damage themselves and others occur at every narrative level—in the lives of the main characters, in subplots or pretexts involving minor characters whose acts may have major consequences, and in passing mentions of haunting maternal figures. (The effect, if we consider Rule's novels as a group, resembles the diffusion of stories and the representation of reproductive consciousness that we shall see in *Meridian.*)

One of the six main characters of *Contract with the World* (1980)— and the only one who is given that rare quality in Rule's fiction, a first-person voice—is Alma Trasco, the protected adult daughter of wealthy, indulgent parents. Mother of two sons, Alma breaks up her eleven-year-old marriage when she falls in love with Roxanne, a brilliant underclass musician. Alma insists that she would give up even her children to keep Roxanne, for whose body she feels ineffable passion. But when their mutual gay male friend Alan is arrested and publicly exposed and his younger lover commits suicide, Alma repudiates Alan with just one word—"pervert"—and Roxanne moves out. Ironically, this apparently good mother, Alma, is often irritated by her children and views them chiefly as extensions of herself (a healthy selfishness in that it obliges Alma to train them carefully), whereas the lesbian Roxanne loves them, plays with them, and teaches them. Seen through the eyes of other characters later in the novel, Alma continues to betray her gay friends, choosing not so much her children, but ignorance, selfishness, and the safety and legitimacy of "motherhood" over the risks of uncloseted lesbianism or even support for other lesbians and gay men.

A different version of this phenomenon, wherein homophobia is directly linked to the heightened vulnerability of mothers to conservative moral and social norms, motivates the plot of *Memory Board* (1987). The main characters are estranged twins David and Diana Crown, separated for thirty years by the homophobia of David's now dead wife, Patricia. According to David, Patricia's violent repudiation of Diana and her lover, Constance, was a direct result of the crib death of Patricia and David's son, "her natural young confidence transformed by the death of their first child into protective self-righteousness."[53] In an even more peripheral figure in *The Young in One Another's Arms,* we see a more extreme and tragic response to maternal loss than the self-protective instincts of mothers like the bisexual Alma or the heterosexual Patricia. Boy Wonder, a young black homosexual man on the run, is terrified when one of the women in his new family is about to give birth. He dismisses the reassurance that everything is quite likely to be fine as "white odds," and remembers his five dead siblings: "Last one my mama, she cut off his ear, so God wouldn't want him. God ain't that fussy, turns out" (166).

Yet the consequences of losing or fearing the loss of one or more children are not necessarily homophobia or crazed violence. Like Patricia and like Boy's mother, the central figure in *The Young in One Another's Arms,* Ruth Wheeler, suffers not just the threat but the actuality of loss. But her vulnerability ultimately makes possible a real moral strength, in large part because she is able, unlike Patricia, Alma, and others, to understand the politics and practice of motherhood differently. At the beginning of the novel, Ruth views herself as a maimed, static version of the mother without child; she thinks that the "plot of her life" ended two years before, with the death of her only daughter in an accident at the age of twenty-two. In fact, she has yet more losses to sustain, including the temporary loss of her beloved mother-in-law, Clara; the destruction of a boarding house she has run for fifteen years and the dissolution of the surrogate family who live in it; and most especially the destruction of childlike Willard, a possibly retarded and certainly frightened man whom Ruth accepts, in the face of so much loss, as her remaining responsibility. When Willard tries to stop the demolition of the boarding house by occupying it with a shotgun, he accidentally wounds another of Ruth's young friends, Tom, and is then killed by the police. This combination of loss and near-loss simultaneously repoliticizes and rematernalizes Ruth. She has already begun recovering her dead daughter, Claire, to memory. Then, out of the maternal rage she feels when "her children," Willard and Tom, are endangered, she finds the will to fight back by resuming the responsibilities of nonprocreative mother to her chosen adult children, as the remaining group moves out of the city and into their alternative home and family on Galliano Island. This is not, then, a mother like Evelyn or Alma who is tempted or driven to complicity by the need to protect her surrogate or biological children. Instead, Ruth represents both the inevitability of loss and the capacity to persist with what is left that marks so many valorized characters. When asked why she doesn't resist the demolition of the house herself, she explains the fundamental equation of loss and survival in Rule's fictional worlds: "'What you lose is what you survive with,' Ruth answered, her right arm for a house, her husband for her mother-in-law, two rooms in the basement from the insurance paid for a dead child, and now whatever she could get with this new compensation" (3).

Instead of contracting into fear and hatred, like Patricia Crown, or going mad, like Boy Wonder's mother, Ruth indeed survives with what she loses: her extended, nonprocreative maternal function. She persists because she is already a mother without child in the second, more affirmative sense of the trope as Rule explores it—that is, she is a woman who values and embodies the maternal not as a mark of her proper womanhood or social status but as a life-affirming alternative to dominant norms, choosing connection and responsibility. She is informed, like so much lesbian thinking, by love of her own maternal figure; Ruth married her sad, limited, estranged husband Hal because she wanted to be with the woman she loved, his mother, Clara (who is also a figure of maternal wisdom, although she has difficulty loving her own son). Uneducated, handicapped by the accidental loss of one arm, Ruth has built a life for herself running a boarding house for a variety of young "misfits," including American draft dodgers, a lesbian Ph.D. student, a bisexual teacher of handicapped children, and the limited Willard. When she responds to the loss of her carefully constructed domestic space, the deportation of a young American, and the death of Willard by moving away from the city with most of her remaining boarders, she simply acts out the identity she has already formed for herself, choosing an even more marginal life that values caring, collectivity, and tolerance of various sexual relationships, a life that remains distanced, though not immune, from the control of the law.

In *Desert of the Heart*, motherhood as an institution is strongly critiqued while maternal qualities are celebrated and made available to the heroines; in *The Young in One Another's Arms*, the critique is directed even more at the material reality and social policy that harms all children. Ruth is politicized by the state-authorized loss of her chosen children in a way she is not by the accidental loss of her biological daughter in an automobile accident in part because she can direct her anger at a social cause—the behavior of the police. Insofar as the nonbiological family structure on Galliano Island is more suggestive of an alternative communal and social order than Ann and Evelyn's private choice, and insofar as the novel is essentially hopeful despite all the losses it entails, we might want to see Ruth as a symbolic, utopian mother. But we can't forget she is a real one, too, and a simultaneously domestic and political person who has made her living and her self by traditional maternal activities, feeding and housing young people and taking in homosexuals and draft-dodgers—children abandoned by their own families and exiled from their homes of origin.

The other most important example in Rule's fiction of a mother without child who nurtures both adults and children and supports motherhood as an aspect of rather than synonym for womanhood is Amelia Larson in *Against the Season* (1971), "the lame, old spinster who knew more about motherhood than anyone else in town,"[54] even though she has never borne a child. The aging and crippled Amelia functions as a mother who nurtures, protects, and trains a series of young unwed biological mothers-to-be, to whom she has for thirty years given a room in her large family home and a job during their socially stigmatized pregnancies. The narrative use of pregnancy is foregrounded in *Against the Season*. Here the ambivalence and open-endedness of childbearing, the physical and emotional vulnerability of the mother-to-be, and the contrasting potential for the heroic lawlessness of the unmarried mother is even more dramatically at the center, interdependent with rather than contradictory to the aging, nonprocreative maternal practice of Amelia. Ironically, the true child-centeredness of Amelia's vision is what unifies Amelia in the work of childbirth, her "thirty years of vicarious labor" (66), with these pregnant young women who are soon to be procreative mothers without children. She seems to see the child, not *with* the child nor *as* a child. Whereas her now dead sister Beatrice always worried about the "pointlessness" and "emptiness" that the unwed mother would feel after the birth and adoption, Amelia "couldn't accept or wouldn't understand that. The child was born into the world and for it, whatever the circumstances" (66).

The potent, highly variable image of the mother without child found in characters as different as Ann, Evelyn, Ruth, and Amelia is sketched out in another way in *After the Fire* (1989), in the character of Milly Forbes. Like Ruth—and indeed like most women who, if we are lucky, outlive our fertility by decades—Milly pointedly occupies the positions of the procreative mother and the nonprocreative mother *sequentially* and thus breaks down in a very different way the traditional distinction between the two. Her story centers on the transition between one era in the female life cycle and the next, made more marked and abrupt in her case by a hysterectomy—a killing of the womb, to recur to Brossard's formulation. Milly is an unpleasant, racist, homophobic divorcée whose husband has abandoned her for a younger woman; she is also the mother of three adult children, one of whom has disappeared from her life. After her hysterectomy, however, she finds that the plot of her life as a woman that she thought had ended may begin again. She decides to ask her alienated husband's help in finding their estranged older daughter, Nora, and the novel closes as she takes up a postponed maternal quest that suggests the beginning rather than the end of a narrative. Milly's story deconstructs the false, divisive separation of women into mothers and nonmothers by reminding us that this is actually a division within the adult procreative woman, across her reproductive experience. Liberated by her hysterectomy from seeing herself as object to be used and discarded by her husband, Milly can begin to construct her self in different ways—in her love for the beauty of nature on the island to which she has been banished, in a possibly more tolerant attitude toward social deviance, in a new relationship to her younger daughter, and in the action she may take to find the child she has thought of as lost.

. . . .

The mother without child is a constant yet fluid and complex figure throughout Jane Rule's novels, always pointing towards both utopian and practical revaluations of certain traditional and historically experienced maternal qualities and behaviors, but at the same time always in the context of realistic representations of the problems of mothering in patriarchal worlds. Rule's fictions register the imbrication of complicity and resistance in mothers' stories, but they do not leave us either with the sense that we can never tell complicity from resistance, as Ellen Lewin has suggested, or with the sense of absolute, unbridgeable divisions between the two states that we find in Nicole Brossard. Instead, as I read the novels, a key aspect of Brossard's theoretical position may be brought into closer play with Lewin's empirical findings. Like Lewin, Rule's characters and narrators worry about the conflation of motherhood and womanhood even as they resist the division of women into mothers and nonmothers, fertile and sterile females. Above all, as in Lewin's reports, they are most vulnerable to oppression, complicity, and despair when they face the actual or threatened loss of children. But in some of these cases, as in the autobiographical narrative of Pratt with which I began this chapter, loss or lack of children politicizes Rule's fictional women or represents a willful political stance. Moreover, as in Brossard's theory of symbolic motherhood, it is the multiply realized possibility of what I term nonprocreative motherhood—in Rule, an embodied practice and a way of thinking that has no essential ties to sexuality or gender and may be arrived at through a variety of material circumstances—that most powerfully enables women to resist stereotypes, to experience and gratify sexual desire, and to occupy subject positions at varying distances from the legal system.

Yet the variety of material circumstances through which one arrives at the position of nonprocreative mother makes a difference that merits further exploration. It is one thing for Ann Childs to defy the cultural prescription to marry and become a mother and for Evelyn Hall to shed her conventional belief that because she is divorced and childless, she has failed as a woman. As talented, educated white women with earned or inherited means and the possibility or actuality of a successful career, they can afford to refuse economic dependence on men. Neither has had much of a relationship with her own mother; Ann believes she was abandoned, and the only female ancestor Evelyn recalls in the course of the novel is a masterful virgin aunt. In Reno, Nevada, symbolic capitol of a culture in which money is "the only passionate belief" and divorce is the second biggest business in town, their subversively sterile relationship is as natural as anything else and can be at least temporarily condoned. To say this is not to diminish either the force of Evelyn's guilt and Ann's pain or what I take to be the political and theoretical import of their transgression. But in *Desert of the Heart,* the two women's mutual assumption of the normally inconceivable or tragic role of mother without child—appropriating tenderness, sexuality, and the risks of material and emotional responsibility into a nonprocreative relationship outside the heterosexual family romance—can almost too easily seem viable, probably more intelligent than other choices, and even morally superior to them.

It would be another thing for a southern black woman growing up in the late fifties and early sixties to give away the child she conceives out of wedlock and bears as a high-school drop-out and teenage wife.[55] This is what happens to the figure of the mother without child in Alice Walker's second novel, *Meridian*. When Meridian Hill gives up her son for adoption, her act can be seen as one of defiance and subversion, like Ann's, with an admixture of guilt to be overcome, like Evelyn's. The position of community Othermother that Meridian subsequently comes to occupy, wherein she serves as a kind of impersonal surrogate mother to many women and children, is in important ways continuous with the kind of nonprocreative motherhood that is the central value in *Desert of the Heart*. But neither the story nor the stakes are the same. Ann and Evelyn, most obviously, most critically, are "mothers" in a symbolic or extended sense; their meaning as such depends on the fact that neither bears a child and neither gives one away. Meridian, by contrast, is a procreative mother first, a woman who has given birth to a son and cares for him for an indefinite period of his infancy before giving him up for adoption. Meridian also lives in a radically different American culture, with a different history, both personal and communal, and a different set of values and needs. She believes it is death not to love her mother, and she has a deep sense of a tragic maternal heritage that starts with slavery in America and threatens to end with Meridian herself, a "monster" in her own mother's eyes. I begin to explore in the next chapter, then, what it means to live as a mother without child in different ways and different contexts.

Three
·········

Claiming the Monstrosity in
Alice Walker's *Meridian*

"BAD" BLACK MOTHERS FROM *BELOVED* TO *MERIDIAN*

Feminist analysis of mothering has been faulted for excluding, among
other things, the work of black writers and scholars. African American
literary texts in particular have richly explored the historical importance of black mothers, their indispensable if often unappreciated or
misunderstood power, and the need to recover, revalue, and complicate
our general understanding of this presence. Many of Alice Walker's
well-known essays and stories celebrate the role of black mothers and
grandmothers in sustaining the creativity of their daughters and grand-
daughters against the odds. As Walker puts it in her influential "In
Search of Our Mothers' Gardens," "And so our mothers and grandmothers have, more often than not anonymously, handed on the creative spark, the seed of the flower they themselves never hoped to see:
or like a sealed letter they could not plainly read."[1] Writing a decade
and a half later, critic Joanne Braxton calls attention to another archetype in black women's fiction that grows out of historical maternal
practice. This is an ancestor figure less peaceful, perhaps, than the
grandmother in the garden but sharing in her resourcefulness and importance: the "outraged mother who embodies the value of sacrifice,
nurturance, and personal courage—values necessary to an endangered
and embattled minority group."[2] Barbara Christian identifies the historical figure of the slave mother represented in contemporary women's
fiction as the key element in recent efforts to reclaim the subjectivity
and memory of black slaves, and she points out that "motherhood is
the context for the slave woman's most deeply felt conflicts."[3] The black
mother in American culture is frequently observed in these and many

63

other studies as powerfully present but poorly understood by means of dominant models. Suzanne Carother, for instance, has noted that the conventional assumption in white culture that mothers remain in the private, domestic sphere is simply inappropriate to the circumstances of black mothers, who are traditionally both workers and mothers and who do not raise their children in isolation from other adults.[4]

Whereas many poets, novelists, and scholars have sought to celebrate the often forgotten black mother for her positive creativity, her power to endure, her willingness to protect and nurture despite psychological and material conflicts, other voices have recently called for more negative images of African American people. Mae Henderson urges that we must not avert the gaze of criticism from "non felicitous" images of women in particular. Worried by the "male scopophilia" made possible by Houston Baker's idealization of women and women writers (and I think by the prescriptiveness of this same idealization), Henderson points out that Walker's "mother in the garden," a symbol of birth and renewal, has to be set beside Sula's grandmother Eva, a symbol of death and destruction when she sets her son Plum on fire.[5] Reacting to the criticism of black women writers for their treatment of black men in particular, Deborah McDowell argues in an essay on *Sula* that "the overarching preoccupation with 'positive' racial representation has worked in tandem with a static view of the nature of identification in the act of reading."[6] Hortense Spillers, responding to McDowell's essay, agrees that "the novel and figure [of *Sula*] also offer figures of ambiguity, of 'bad' passions that the heart, the recognition, can no longer afford to deny."[7] And in her own theoretical emphasis elsewhere on the *absence* rather than the presence of black mothers, Spillers similarly implies that it is necessary to confront "monstrous" things when we seek to theorize or historicize black mothers. Moreover, with due respect for critical differences, we might deduce from Spillers' subtle argument that the position of "black mother" is as much a terrifying oxymoron, in its own way, as that of "lesbian mother":

> The dominant culture, in a fatal misunderstanding, assigns a matriarchalist value where it does not belong; actually *misnames* the power of the female regarding the enslaved community. Such naming is false because the female could not, in fact, claim her child, and false, once again, because "motherhood" is not perceived in the prevailing social climate as a legitimate procedure of cultural inheritance . . . motherhood as female blood-rite is outraged, is denied, at the *very same time* that it becomes the founding term of a human and social enactment. . . .

In this play of paradox, only the female stands *in the flesh,* both mother and mother-dispossessed. This problematizing of gender places her, in my view, *out* of the traditional symbolics of female gender, and it is our task to make a place for this different social subject. In doing so, we are less interested in joining the ranks of gendered femaleness than gaining the *insurgent* ground as female social subject. Actually *claiming* the monstrosity (of a female with the potential to "name"), which her culture imposes in blindness, "Sapphire" might rewrite after all a radically different text for a female empowerment.[8]

The distance between those who stress the ignored and devalued presence of heroic African American mothers and those who emphasize the "bad" or absent mother may be more apparent than real, but it reflects a common problem, at the center of so much thinking about motherhood: how best to give voice to the previously silenced, on what terms to bring the marginalized and dominated into historical recognition without downplaying historical reality. One novel, however, has recently seemed to accommodate the desire both to celebrate and to mourn the black mother: Toni Morrison's *Beloved.*

Sethe Suggs, like all slave mothers, cannot claim her children. During a brief period of heroic escape, illicit freedom, and fleshly maternal bliss, Sethe's maternal desire is narrativized in terms perfectly inside the dominant conventions of motherhood, establishing readers' confidence in her as mother and sympathy with her as female subject and victim. But the impossibility of her desire is quickly reaffirmed when the legal owner of both Sethe and her children comes to claim his property. The mother attempts to usurp the slave master's rights, stealing his property (as her historical prototype, Margaret Garner, was convicted of doing) by trying to murder her own children rather than surrender them back to slavery. For many readers and characters this act puts her, for good or bad, where she is historically determined to be, "*out* of the traditional symbolics of female gender."[9] She succeeds in killing only one child, the baby girl who is at least part of what returns to the story as the ghost, Beloved. The novel spirals around this series of monstrous events: a moment of murder, and then years later the ghostly reappearance "in the flesh" of the young girl who is the spirit of multiply deprived, dispossessed, and inadequately individuated identities, including Sethe's dead baby, Sethe herself, Sethe's mother, and the nameless sixty million who died in the Middle Passage. It closes with the exorcism of Beloved and a gesture toward the empowerment of Sethe as female social subject rather than misnamed matriarch. Her final words at once instate and call into question this "radically different" and tentative subject: "'Me? Me?'"

The popular and critical success of *Beloved* verifies the need and effect of telling a story of black motherhood as one of infanticide, outrage, and conflict.[10] The novel is remarkable for its ability to bring the previously repressed or erased preoedipal mother and enslaved subject to the brink of consciousness and language. The publication of *Beloved* coincided with the very earliest stages of my interest in childless mothers in contemporary literature, and in fact the enormous acclaim of the novel in popular as well as more academic circles substantiated my growing sense that the mother without child is one of the key sites of moral and political debate today. However, as I continued to think about the particularities of black mothers in America and the insights and impasses of current scholarship, the questions *Beloved* raises prompted me to greater interest in an earlier novel: Alice Walker's *Meridian*. Given the recent calls for more "bad" African American fictional characters and more nontraditional women and mothers, it may be a good moment to reconsider its powerful and difficult heroine, Meridian Hill, who cheerfully gives her baby up for adoption. At one point, the novel makes it clear that she does so in order to avoid the very same route Sethe planned to take, infanticide followed by suicide: "She might not have given him away to the people who wanted him. She might have murdered him instead. Then killed herself. She might have done it that way except for one thing: One day she really looked at her child and loved him with as much love as she loved the moon or a tree, which was a considerable amount of impersonal love. . . . When she gave him away she did so with a light heart."[11]

What might we learn, after *Beloved* and in the context of a search for the postmodern, maybe postmaternal female subject, by comparing Meridian's and Sethe's "bad" behavior as mothers? By some criteria, Meridian might be judged more guilty and unnatural than Sethe. The twentieth-century black woman's circumstances are far less dire; no one is threatening to take her baby back into slavery. Indeed, Meridian explicitly says that she understands for the first time what slavery is like *after* her child is born, as against her conscious will her body serves his needs. Whereas Sethe is forced to kill what she loves, Meridian freely chooses to give up her son. In the present of the novel, this is a highly atypical act for a black teenaged mother; according to a recent study by Rickie Solinger, it is contrary to both public policy and community opinion about the responsibility for black babies.[12] Although the novel speaks of her "impersonal love" for the child, the perverseness of this choice stands out if we compare it to nonfictional accounts of parents who give up children for adoption. In a study of members of a support group called Concerned United Birthparents, Judith Modell observes that the birth parents she interviewed in fact rejected the rationale that *Meridian* offers, the notion that a mother sometimes gives her child up because she loves it. Instead, in the central "relinquishment" scenes of their stories, they stressed the involuntariness of their act, which they preferred to speak of as "surrender."[13] (Note that there is no noun in our lexicon for what Meridian does: besides loaded terms like "relinquishment" and "surrender" we have only the awkward gerundive phrases, "giving away" or "giving up for adoption," both of which imply at least some degree of ownership and self-sacrifice that does not seem appropriate.) Meridian's dreams are at first haunted by the child, but when she tries to remember him a few years later, she cannot do so. In contrast, the birth parents that Modell studied resist the mandate to forget their children in the very act of telling and retelling their stories. This comparison could suggest, among other things, that Meridian is more selfish, unloving, and unmaternal than Sethe and that Walker fails to see or articulate the outrage of maternal "surrender" fundamental to the historical experience of black subjectivity. Meridian chooses, arguably, what a real mother could only be forced to accept, and she does not even love her child the way most birth parents do.

This is not the way she is usually judged, however. In the second half of the twentieth century, although infanticide is still a crime, giving up a child for adoption is not, and to most readers Meridian's antimaternal behavior is excusable, if not likable, and not "bad" enough to raise the moral, psychological, or political questions that Sethe's does. A few critics have recapitulated the "core plot" of the story without even mentioning this episode.[14] Among the critics who focus at least some attention on Meridian's giving up of her child, the consensus is that Meridian must give up her son in order to pursue her life as a civil rights activist or to realize "self-affirmation."[15] Some readers have even seen the guilt that she feels for doing so as a central problem, the main cause of the illness from which she must gradually recover in the course of the novel's telling. No readers that I know of have suggested that Meridian ought to have kept Rundi with her while she struggled to come of age and join the civil rights movement or waited until he was grown up to become a heroine, and no critics to my knowledge fault Walker for implicitly failing to understand that women's power is deeply rooted in the biological or social capacity to mother that Meridian so blithely seems to put behind her.

I by no means wish to argue that Meridian or Walker should be thus critiqued, but it is important to note that the apparent acceptance, bordering for some readers on approval, of the black civil rights heroine as mother without child rests on common assumptions about female selfhood, (black) motherhood, (white) feminism, and the so-called feminist novel. One assumption is that *Meridian* clearly belongs to and reflects its era, the early days of second-wave feminism, with its allegedly radical repudiation of women's role as mothers.[16] Hence the novel is often categorized as a feminist bildungsroman, the story of the heroine's quest for selfhood set against the forces, including motherhood, that threaten her. Notably selfhood and motherhood are locked in opposition in this typically white formulation, as they are in most thinking about either term (and in many readings of *Beloved* as well). It is further assumed that mothering necessarily entails a sacrifice or at least compromise of an autonomous, cohesive self that some if not all women, often for good reasons, are not prepared to make. The conflict is constructed as a simple one: the interests of the individual woman versus the interests of her child, female self-affirmation versus the institution of motherhood. Women have a right to "surrender" their maternal responsibilities to others (as long as they surrender them completely). Meridian is the case par excellence of the woman who chooses to repudiate motherhood, and having said that, the case is closed.

However, *Meridian* in fact complicates all these rarely challenged assumptions and may open up difficult, usually unasked questions about how and why a black mother would give up her children, what happens to her when she does, and what her story may signify. The claim that Meridian renounces motherhood for the civil rights movement suggests a slightly inaccurate reading of the plot. Meridian gives up Eddie Jr., whom she has already renamed Rundi, not when she volunteers with the voter registration project in her home town (during which time her mother-in-law seems happy to care for the baby all day), but when she receives a scholarship to Saxon College. It is true enough that Meridian has already failed to bond with her child well before the scholarship offer arrives, and the style of activism she has begun to practice, soon to be followed by nights spent in jail, would interfere with primary caretaking of a young child. But Meridian herself never cites her desire to join the civil rights movement as a factor in her decision, and it is important to be precise about the fact that it is her admission to Saxon College, an elite institution of higher education for black women modeled after the elite white women's schools, that precipitates the act of giving Rundi away. Saxon observes the dominant tradition in female education that rigidly enforces the divide between women who are mothers and women who are not, and it dictates that only the latter are permitted to have a life of the mind. However, *Meridian* suggests that this influential white model of independent, educated female identity, which again puts self-development so starkly in opposition to motherhood, misrepresents and erases the experience of black women in America. Saxon turns southern African American daughters into ladies who will not be able to tell their mothers' stories; as Barbara Christian has noted, *Meridian* suggests in other ways too that some African American women themselves ignore their maternal heritage.[17]

It is also important not to put Meridian's choice in terms of activism versus mothering because this way of seeing the problem perpetuates a conception that Walker's novel—and this study as a whole—contravenes: that mothering and political action, like mothering and thinking or writing, are mutually exclusive practices. This is the kind of presupposition that has been used against women of many nationalities and races who do take political action, and it may serve to disarm those who might. It flies in the face of events such as the Latin American motherist movements or, closer to home, the role of women in the peace movement of the sixties.[18] In the context of *Meridian,* it falls into the trap of denying or policing the role of mothers and older African American women in enabling the civil rights movement—a forgetting explicitly deplored in stories like Toni Cade Bambara's "My Man Bovanne" or Walker's own "Everyday Use." And finally it fails to account for what is arguably the novel's most important point: Meridian's highly "maternalized" brand of activism, as we shall see, challenges those dominant notions of the opposition between self-affirmation (or group affirmation) and the work of caring for and about children.[19] I do not suggest that we should entirely set aside the assumption that Meridian gives her child away in order to "find herself" or experience what Lindsey Tucker describes as "mobility," for there is an undeniable validity to such claims.[20] But we need to make them very carefully, because the selfhood Meridian seeks and finds in the course of this novel is not the western autonomous personhood, privileged and upwardly mobile, that we often think of when we speak of the self, and motherhood for black women is not merely the passive, domestic, private, and dependent experience that it is often said to be in dominant white models.

The distinction becomes clearer if we carefully reconsider the notion that *Meridian* is a feminist "novel of self-discovery." According to Rita Felski's persuasive description of this narrative structure, which she claims has emerged in the last twenty years of writing by women, such novels identify "autonomy" and "coherent selfhood" as "women's most pressing need"; gender is seen as "the primary marker" of subjectivity, and other determinants are ignored. Female community is vital in these novels, and concomitantly, "there is no sustained exploration of the interrelations . . . between feminism and the rest of society" and little interest in metafictional questions. Felski subdivides the "novel of self-discovery" into two subtypes: the "feminist bildungsroman," with a historical and linear plot marking progress outward, and the "novel of awakening," in which the discovery entails movement inward to "a given mythic identity" or authentic "innerself." Both presume "a process of separation as the essential precondition for any path to self-knowledge."[21]

Felski mentions *Meridian* twice, both times parenthetically: at the beginning of her discussion she lists it as one of the novels she has in mind, and later she cites Truman as an example of the kind of sexist male radical often found in the "self-discovery" novel. Yet *Meridian* seems to evoke the category of "self-discovery" novel only to subvert it, at least as it is defined by Felski's criteria. Gender is by no means the only determinant of Meridian's subjectivity; her racial, familial, and regional identities are influential too, although often in contradictory ways. Though the "female community" is beyond question important in *Meridian* in ways that I explore in this chapter, it is at best an ambiguous source of support. Meridian remains isolated from many women from whom help and encouragement might be expected, and her foregrounded personal relationships in the novel are to a black man and a white woman. This heroine's journey reverses the normal quest pattern, as it takes her neither outward nor inward but back toward an incomplete but resilient connection between inside and outside, self and community, and past and present. Meridian's quest begins rather than ends in the separation that white feminist novels are often said to require. There is something special and unique about Meridian even as a child, and she detaches herself from the roles of wife, lover, and biological mother early on. But then she returns to the various communities she has always revered, despite her distance from them, to heal herself: the rural South, the Black Church, the principles and practices of the civil rights movement. Her gradual downward social mobility and poverty arrest the apparent progress outward she began when she joined the voter registration drive and entered Saxon College, and near the end of the novel she imagines herself walking behind the "real revolutionaries" (201).[22] Both parts of the old term "self-knowledge" are scrutinized in this heroine's story. Meridian's self is represented as neither cohesive nor autonomous in traditional ways. This character, the soul of integrity, lacks formal, psychological, and epistemic wholeness; the ways we know her and the ways she knows herself and the world around her are not conventional, coherent, or rational.

Reopening and centering the question of why this black mother gives up her son, I suggest that *Meridian* explores the roots of both (black feminist) politics and (black women's) selfhood in a revised understanding of motherhood as a historical and psychological experience of nothing less than trauma, much as *Beloved* does. *Meridian* is not a feminist bildungsroman but a formally innovative and metafictionally self-conscious novel best described by the spatial metaphor Walker herself has used: the crazy quilt. "You know, there's a lot of difference between a crazy quilt and a patchwork quilt," Walker has said. "A crazy quilt . . . only *looks* crazy. It is not patched; it is planned."[23] As Melissa Walker points out, "The impact of a crazy quilt depends on shapes, colors, and textures, but what usually gives such quilts significance and emotional validity is that each individual piece has a history."[24] Patterned in this way, the novel gives far less prominence than *Beloved* does to the individual psyche or subjectivity of a main protagonist. In the first section below, I consider how the history of "each individual piece" in the crazy quilt works to situate Meridian's giving up of her child in what we might call the "reproductive consciousness" of rural southern black females in the second half of the twentieth century. In the second and final part of the chapter, I argue that Meridian's selfhood is not only less separate but also less cohesive than certain conventional models imply, suggesting a psychological model of personality split along vertical rather than horizontal lines—a model often associated only with a "crazy" personality, one who is dissociated and disconnected.[25]

REMAPPING MOTHERHOOD: FEMALE REPRODUCTIVE
CONSCIOUSNESS IN AN AGE OF CHOICE

Questions of women's autonomy and individual female selfhood are in some sense secondary to and completely embedded in *Meridian*'s concern with the way diverse, sometimes conflicting, and sometimes overlapping ideas about motherhood, variously encountered and experienced in everyday life, construct a woman's expectations and understanding of her biological and social being. This concern might well be described by borrowing the term "reproductive consciousness" from Mary O'Brien, who uses it to express her understanding that social, mental, and emotional attitudes toward childbirth and child care have a material base in the biological reproductive process.[26] O'Brien bases the historical difference between male and female reproductive consciousness on the alienation of the male in the act of conception as opposed to the "creative and mediative powers" of female reproductive labor, and her argument has often been criticized for its essentialist and universalizing tendencies. I do not wish to endorse or critique her larger claim here.[27] Instead, I suggest that the concept of reproductive consciousness can be used to describe more culturally specific and locally variable ways in which common social and biological experiences and discourses of reproduction influence a woman's decision to enter into or reject mothering. Pointing to shared, conventional, and constructed aspects of material experience, the term helps to articulate the understanding that individual consciousness will normally be made up of alternative, sometimes contradictory possibilities, which will change over time. It usefully extends problematic notions of authenticity, identity, and intentionality out of the sphere of private, individual experience and into the sphere of ideology, signifying the belief that individual and embodied agents both shape and are shaped by commonly held beliefs about the meaning of experiences. To speak of reproductive consciousness in this way makes it possible to understand motherhood as neither essential nor irrelevant to women's lives, neither universal and invariable nor private, to be freely accepted or rejected. It suggests instead a theory of how women are socially and psychologically designated to do the reproductive work that is necessary to the future of the species, and how that designation can and will be saturated with their varying histories.

Meridian comprises numerous fragments of stories about women, often mothers, other than Meridian herself; these are the pieces of the crazy quilt that I examine here. Each story may seem to function most obviously and conventionally to construct our understanding of the main character by suggesting both analogies and influences, and there is nothing unique about using minor characters in this way. But here the sheer quantity of other women's stories, together with the remarkably clear and signifying pattern of their deployment, urges us to consider that the way these women have collectively experienced the complicated material and cultural facts of motherhood is in and of itself the subject of representation. The diffusion of narrative attention and the accompanying play with point of view decenter the protagonist as conventional self and speaker, and this decentering serves two key purposes. First, it contextualizes Meridian's decision to give up her child in a reproductive consciousness inflected by nearly unspeakable historical atrocities, while at the same time suggesting that African American women's experience is not a seamless web of oppression and that maternal functions performed historically by black women can be extended out of the more limited sphere of biological procreation into the public sphere of political activism. Second, the representation of reproductive consciousness in fragments of women's stories demarcates a space and a language in which the historical traumas of (black) motherhood, at once forgotten or never recorded before yet always serving to control women, can begin to be voiced, heard, and reconsidered; and here Meridian is positioned as a certain kind of receptor and listener rather than as a speaker.

The complexity of the southern black woman's reproductive consciousness is reflected by the intricate arrangement of the fragmentary tales and images of mothers in the nonlinear structure of *Meridian*. Among other intricacies, this structure involves two different but interactive time sequences: what we might think of as "Meridian's time," the chronological order of the events as they happened in the character's life, which we can only partially reconstruct from flashbacks and fragments; and what we might call "readers' time," the order of the events as narrated. For the purposes of analysis, it is useful to divide the mothers' stories into clusters or subpatterns. The first cluster centers on the violent suffering and oppression of black women in America where, as biological mothers, surrogate mothers, and potential mothers, they have been victims and hence victimizers, the latter chiefly in the sense that they cannot protect their children from suffering and death. All of these stories and images are of women who are dead, in the present time of both Meridian and readers. This first cluster is complemented by a second cluster of equally horrifying stories of living characters whom Meridian actually meets at various points in her time. The legendary figures are concentrated in the early chapters of the novel, whereas the living women are encountered mainly in the later chapters, so that in reader's time we move from formative cultural myths—Meridian's reproductive inheritance, as it were—to corroborating instances of ongoing reproductive reality in which Meridian personally participates and to some extent intervenes. Third and fourth clusters of women, one set mostly dead and the other mostly living, are interlaced in the middle of the book. The third group comprises Meridian's troublesome maternal genealogy. The fourth is a set of both near and far relations and friends whose lives, though seen only in fragments and from a distance, offer models of resistance to the weighty paradigm of Black Motherhood elsewhere available in legend and experience alike. I discuss each of these four clusters in some detail, for the most part in the order of their appearance in readers' time, because the details in each case as well as their sequence are important to the complexities of the reproductive consciousness that the novel represents.

MUMMIES AND MAMMIES

The first legendary woman in the novel is Marilene O'Shay, whose story is given privileged status by its appearance in the opening chapter, before readers have encountered Meridian herself. For my reading, the chapter as a whole serves three key functions: it foregrounds widely accepted myths with which white as well as black female reproductive consciousness is imbued; it simultaneously suggests perspectives that debunk these myths; and it introduces readers to Meridian as "a woman in the process of changing her mind" who "volunteers to suffer" (25) for others and is, as on subsequent occasions, associated with the protection and education of children not her own against new and old forms of discrimination and deception.

Marilene O'Shay is the name given to a skeleton, a "mummy woman" (pun no doubt intended) on display in a circus wagon brought to rural Georgia by her husband, who murdered her "'Cause this bitch was doing him wrong, and that ain't right!'" (22). According to the publicity the husband uses to attract a paying audience for his wife's alleged remains, eight words painted on the wagon sum up Marilene's emblematic fate, and retrospectively readers can see that each one of them ironically captions Meridian's story as well: "Obedient Daughter," "Devoted Wife," "Adoring Mother," "Gone Wrong." The relevance of this commodified white paradigm to the central black characters is underscored by the fact that Marilene's husband must reassure his public that his wife *is* white, since her corpse has supposedly been darkened by the salt of Great Salt Lake, where he threw her body after he murdered her. Leached of flesh, this female skeleton is offered as a cultural symbol of the universal woman, an essence underlying racial difference. At the same time, her darkness, the husband suggests, represents her sinfulness, so racial difference can still be confirmed in this display of transracial feminine nature. Marilene notably serves the interests of continuing segregation post–civil rights: a group of mostly black children, now excluded because they are "po" and smell of the guano plant where their parents work, has been told that they can only see the exhibit on Thursdays. This is the restriction that Meridian protests in the opening scene.[28]

The formulaic, marketable, ur-feminine essence imagined by the husband's presentation is undercut, however, from other points of view introduced in the first chapter. Truman, the black male friend of Meridian's through whose eyes we first meet the heroine, immediately observes, "'That's got to be a rip-off,'" and later he assesses Meridian's defiant march in front of an old army tank on the town square as "meaningless action" (26). But Meridian argues that the children, who were bored anyhow, needed to learn the truth for themselves: these least powerful voices in town know now that Marilene is a fake, made of plastic. The poor children represent a disenfranchised, disinterested, and largely uneducated view of the female skeleton and her meaning, and their discovery exposes the most common patriarchal assumptions about women and authenticity as caricature and fraud. Marilene's double status as dominant archetype and marginal joke introduces us to the major concern of this novel with challenging powerful, deadly, yet basically ludicrous assumptions about femininity, race, identity, and power. Furthermore, Meridian's position as a solitary figure volunteering to suffer on behalf of the rights of children to equality and knowledge anticipates her fuller development as an Othermother, standing in for biological mothers, acting on behalf of them and their children, confronting the history of loss and death, and allowing women's stories to be heard from alternative perspectives.[29]

The next legendary figure readers meet, in the second chapter of the novel but several years earlier in Meridian's time, is the Wild Child, who bridges and hence links the two categories—legend and living mother—into which other female figures may be divided. An undomesticated black adolescent girl, she contrasts strikingly with the entombed white mummy who opens the novel, but both figures are punished for wildness: at the end of her chapter, the girl is dead too. The Wild Child is a nameless, homeless orphan roaming the poor neighborhood around Saxon College. She has lived off garbage for several years and on the evidence of advanced pregnancy is recently presumed to have been raped. She is well on her way to becoming a legend in the local community when Meridian, characteristically, tries to rescue and mother her. The girl escapes, however, and is killed by a car in her flight. This pregnant thirteen-year-old female conflates the figures of mother and daughter. The world's indifference to the plight of both is exposed in the refusal of Saxon College, or any other institution Meridian can locate, first to house and then to bury the Wild Child. As the housemother in Meridian's dorm says, on behalf of the repressive force of mothers bent on training their own daughters to survive, "'Think of the influence. This is a school for young ladies'" (37). Meridian, we may assume, comes as close to making a connection with this girl as any other human being, but it is a fragile, barely human one: she leads the girl back to the dorm by tying a catgut string around her arm. The story of Wild Child becomes even more outrageous after the riot that ensues when students are prevented from burying her on the grounds of Saxon, but we know virtually nothing about her as an individual subject with her own point of view. Sister of Caliban rather than Shakespeare, she is heard "cursing, the only language she knew" (36). Marking the impact of this lesson in inhumanity and isolation on Meridian, Meridian's first paralysis, lasting only two days, follows this episode. Retrospectively, this earlier paralysis resembles the catatonic state into which Meridian fell in chapter one, after leading the children to view Marilene O'Shay's remains.

In both contrast to and continuity with Marilene, the archetype of dead white womanhood, and Wild Child, whose speech is limited and whose life is as inaccessible as it is easily destroyed, the third legendary figure in the opening trilogy of chapters is the famous Louvinie, the slave woman and storyteller, a "Black Mammy" whose well-known tale is foundational to Saxon College. A bearer of African verbal powers and a victim of American suffering, Louvinie accidentally murdered the white master's son whom she tended by telling him a story so horrible that it stopped his weak heart. To punish her, the slave owner cut out her tongue. A manifest trope of the African American female verbal artist and monster whose native storytelling power is distorted and then erased under slavery, explaining why black women cannot use the powers they innately have, Louvinie buried her tongue under a magnolia tree on the plantation that later became Saxon. Subsequently named the Sojourner, this tree grew to enormous proportions and acquired numerous legends.[30] As in the telling of Marilene O'Shay's story, multiplicity of meanings—none of which may necessarily give us an authentic record of any woman's actual experience—is privileged over single truth; the stories about the Sojourner are so various that "the students of every persuasion had a choice of which to accept" (45). Louvinie, then, is no more an essential or authentic ancestress of all black women in America than Marilene is the symbol of all white women or the Wild Child of all homeless teenage mothers; in each case obvious symbolic meaning is at once present and complicated both by the multiplicity of others' perspectives and the inaccessibility of one— the woman's "own" point of view, whatever it might be that she would say if she could speak.[31]

However, there is one tale, uniting all "persuasions" of black woman at Saxon in a ritual dance around the Sojourner tree, that clearly figures a key aspect of their common reproductive consciousness. This ritual is based on the less fully known or elaborated story of a fourth legendary figure associated with the Sojourner tree: Fast Mary of the Tower. Whereas Louvinie's status as a biological mother is unknown, Fast Mary represents a subsequent, assimilated generation of African American woman; she is a college girl whose story entails illicit sex followed by pregnancy and then infanticide and suicide. As the story goes, Fast Mary concealed her pregnancy and the birth of a child, "Then . . . carefully chopped the infant into bits and fed it into the commode" (45). Caught when "the bits stuck," she was flogged and imprisoned and subsequently hanged herself. This is the dire consequence of the biological process that is held up as threat to every Saxon woman of every persuasion; it is the plot that Meridian might have replicated, but didn't.

Three even less prominently represented women—one just an image in a photograph, the others bit players in a local story—complete this first, overwhelmingly horrifying set of dead mothers. One day, one of the photos on the wall of the shed that her father built to contain his collection of Native Americana catches the young Meridian's eye. It depicts "a frozen Indian child (whose mother lay beside her in a bloody heap)" (53). Meridian reaches out to touch the picture, as if seeking or even sensing connection across time and distance with someone whose fate she might share. But when her father, who was napping in the room, suddenly wakes up with tears on his face, she runs away in shock and fear. The next, only slightly more fully glimpsed figure is the mother of Daxter the mortician, the man who began sexually experimenting with Meridian in the back of his funeral parlor when she was twelve. His mother was reputedly a white version of Fast Mary, "so the story went," who was impregnated by a black man. When they discovered her condition, her parents locked her in a cellar, fed her pig bran, and when the baby was born, threw it out with the trash. And at the end of the tale of this throw-away baby lurks yet another story within the story of an abused surrogate mother, relegated to two sentences: rescued from the trash, Daxter "was raised by an old woman who later died of ptomaine poisoning. She had eaten some sour, rotten tomatoes Daxter gave her" (65).

It is important to underscore that the reproductive consciousness represented by this first cluster of tragic images and stories is conspicuously not the single true story of an inescapable female destiny. These seven figures of dead women, concentrated in the first fifty pages of the novel, all offer incomplete, incohesive, and possibly false or fictitious images of women whose own voices do not or cannot enter the discourse. The stories also vary greatly in prominence for readers and characters alike. Some have the status of widely known folk tales, some are offered as town gossip, some are not yet stories at all. Unless we are looking for mothers, the frozen Native American woman mentioned in parentheses will hardly seem noticeable or meaningful. Though certain stories, like Louvinie's and Fast Mary's, seem to have a deliberate policing effect on Meridian, it is not clear that she herself knows or remembers others. Moreover, near the end of Meridian's time, she has had her reproductive consciousness raised, as it were, to the point where she is no longer susceptible to the fatal prescriptions inherent in these stories. Whereas readers are likely to make much of Marilene O'Shay, a conspicuous symbol at the opening of the book, Meridian can dismiss her importance: as she says to Truman, the white man is selling something "irrelevant to me, useless" (26).

But hers is a remarkable and unusual realization, and the plot of the rest of the novel follows Meridian's struggle to earn it so that we see exactly what Meridian has escaped, abandoned, subversively inverted, or transcended, depending on one's reading of her status as mother without child. She is embedded in an overdetermined cultural position of helplessness, subjection, silence, and death. At every level of implication, across time, in words and in images, in tales that acquire multiple sets of interpretations and in those that are barely if at all consciously meaningful to those who hear them, in fully developed stories and in the merest, possibly subliminal glimpses, the message that crosses lines of difference among females is insistent: motherhood is cruel, violent, abusive to women; mothers are unable to help themselves, and the only power they have is the power to kill their own children or themselves. The tales and images that deliver this message are stretched through the story in Meridian's time, marking the development of her reproductive consciousness from childhood into womanhood. In reader's time, their placement in the first part of the novel also builds toward the ironically titled eighth chapter, "The Happy Mother," wherein Meridian's early personal experience of motherhood seems to fit inevitably into the negative pattern created by the preceding tales. In this complexly structured way, the legends of mothers out of which the crazy quilt of *Meridian* is pieced collectively attest to the myths of mothering Meridian grows up on and indoctrinate readers into the pervasive horror that marks her female reproductive consciousness.

·······

"No daughter of mine is a monster, surely."
—Mrs. Hill

All the stories I have recapitulated thus far are stories of strangers, more or less, to Meridian; she comes into quasi-maternal or quasi-sororal contact with only one of them, the Wild Child. Her personal female genealogy supplies a far less remote image or myth of motherhood that is at once vital and almost equally fatal to Meridian's development. The stories of her foremothers, which are revealed for the most part after the first cluster of opening legends and after we know that Meridian has given up her own child, are possibly even more terrifying and far more conflicted and conflicting for Meridian. At the same time, even in their uniform report of atrocities endured, her foremothers' stories contain seeds of agency and defiance of the sort already figured in Louvinie's dangerous, fertile tongue.

The horror on her mother's side of the family seems extraordinary, although by the time we come to their stories, we have been prepared for just such unspeakable suffering by the tales of Louvinie, Fast Mary, and the Wild Child. Mrs. Hill's great-great-grandmother was a slave who was finally allowed to keep her two children, who had been sold away from her three times and pursued by her three times at the cost of brutal floggings, "on the condition that they would eat no food she did not provide herself" (122). This is a story of unwitting pelican children indeed: when they reached their teens, the mother finally died of slow starvation, and the children were sold again on her burial day. Meridian's mother's great-grandmother seems to have had a somewhat happier lot. She exerted agency and creativity, buying her freedom and her family's with money earned by painting barn decorations. But her art betrays her otherwise unreadable pain. As a trademark, in each of her patterns there appears somewhere "a small contorted face, whether of a man or woman or child, no one could tell" (123). Mrs. Hill's own mother's story is a more ordinarily painful tale of the "free" black woman's suffering. Mother of at least twelve, she is beaten by her husband and makes many sacrifices so that Mrs. Hill can go to school and become a teacher. With her early earnings, the daughter buys her mother's pink coffin.

The ancestresses' stories are all told briefly, in the matter-of-fact tone that such immersion in horror may come to produce, at a point in Meridian's time when she has been paralyzed for almost a month and is about to be "rescued" from near death by words of forgiveness spoken at her bedside by a surrogate mother, Miss Winter. The narrator introduces the series as "*her mother's* history as Meridian knew it," and then describes the women as "*Her mother's* great-great-grandmother . . . *Mrs. Hill's* great-grandmother . . . *Mrs. Hill's* mother" (emphasis added). This formulation underscores that this is a maternal inheritance and that Meridian has in fact not fully accepted it as *her* history—it is *her mother's* history. Though these historical maternal characters are comparable to the legends and minor characters of the first cluster in terms of the violence and suffering they endure as mothers, a key difference (and an ambiguous glimmer of hope) is that Mrs. Hill's foremothers do not accidentally or purposefully murder or abandon children, as do all the biological mothers in the first group. Instead, they sacrifice themselves to keep their children (barely) alive, nurture as best they can, eventually free, and finally even begin to educate them. Mrs. Hill thinks that she is reproducing this kind of mothering when she submits and endures, even after she discovers that she does not want her children, and in fact is spiritually destroyed, the narrative suggests, by having them. It is for this reason that when Meridian resists the maternal inheritance of self-sacrifice, Mrs. Hill can only think that she is a monster and that there is a paradox here: "no daughter of mine is a monster, surely" (89).

The logical contradiction Mrs. Hill voices reveals the central problems of Meridian's maternal genealogy. The endurance and self-sacrifice of enslaved foremothers colors the reproductive consciousness of their daughters with a heritage of courage, determination, and voluntary suffering for the good of the next generation. This history gives black women a certain subjectivity and power; in doing so, it also defines them paradoxically as quintessential mothers and hence proper, natural female subjects, in dominant constructions of womanhood, in spite of all efforts to deny them the opportunity to nurture, protect, and rear their children. But *Meridian* demonstrates, beginning with the story of Mrs. Hill, how self-defeating this erstwhile model of maternal agency can be, especially if unadapted to different historical possibilities. There is an obvious problem of self-cancellation in the concept of maternal self-sacrifice: if a mother must be willing to give up everything to do her job well, at some point there may be nothing left—not even herself—with which to take care of the children. Moreover, the greater the freedom that each mother makes available to her daughter through self-sacrifice, the more the daughter may in fact be obliged and empowered to pursue alternatives that carry her away from the reigning maternal tradition, even as she still feels bound to the older norms.

Although Mrs. Hill thinks she is imitating her mothers' behavior and demanding that Meridian live up to the family standard, the system has already begun to break down. If we compare the ancestresses' unstinting self-sacrifice with Mrs. Hill's insistence not that Meridian do better, but that she sacrifice herself, we see that Mrs. Hill actually seeks to arrest progress. She keeps Meridian and other black girls, like Meridian's friend Nelda, whom she might have "saved," in ignorance of the reproductive process until it is too late; she then works to block rather than advance the opportunity for education that comes Meridian's way. Legendary aspects of the mothering behavior that was historically crucial to the survival of African Americans and foundational to black women's power and identity are no longer unquestionably appropriate or adaptive. For Meridian to admit this, to give up her child before she murders him or herself, seems, on the one hand, a positive development in light of the versions of infanticide, maternal powerlessness, and neglect she meets in the world around her. On the other hand, to someone who cherishes the past and the collective memories of her people as Meridian does, her behavior seems impossibly selfish and a denial of not only respect for her mother but even her familial identity: "No daughter of mine." Meridian's paralyses embody in this way the impasse confronted by the woman supposedly living in a new age of "choice," when the alternatives offered—selfhood or motherhood—are still seen as mutually exclusive and (therefore) equally impossible.

·······

"The last time God had a baby he skipped, too."
—Delores

A third cluster of female characters, consisting of nameless strangers as well as personal friends and relations, is interspersed and contrasts with the first two clusters to clarify further that reproductive consciousness is not a monotonous story of passive victimization or active but futile sacrifice. Alternatives already exist, consciousness has changed and will continue to do so, and the culture of black women in itself assists Meridian in breaking away from disabling aspects of black motherhood even as she takes with her the best part of her heritage, that drive to protect and lead new subjects into the future by recognizing them and defending their rights. Meridian feels unique at times, and her name suggests in part her status as "the highest point." But she models herself, as she consciously acknowledges at other times, on stories of black women available to her both in legend and life, and she is supported in her decision by at least a small community of other women. These models and friends, barely sketched in, suggest that the agency attributed to the individual protagonist is a more collective force than it might seem by conventional readings of *Meridian* as a novel of self-discovery, and another sense of "meridian" cited in the novel's epigraph suggests this other side of the character: "any of the lines of longitude running north and south." Meridian signifies a particular locus of which there may be an infinite number of other representations, not yet drawn in on most of the available cultural or literary maps of motherhood. Without discounting the enormous power of culture at large (legends, stories, pictures) and family in particular to prescribe and constrain the individual, this cluster of alternatives, fleetingly glimpsed, not yet allowed to speak very often of their resistance, shows us where a space for change has been and can be located.

There are considerably fewer of these figures; change is rare and difficult. The reproductive status of these women is various—we know that some are mothers and some are not, and we don't know about others—which suggests a far more flexible association between the feminine and the maternal than we see in the first two clusters. The first figure mentioned is in fact one of Meridian's ancestresses now on her father's side. This great-grandmother, Feather Mae, was obviously a mother, but we know little about her maternal behavior, for she has two more story-worthy qualities. First, she is a rare instance in this novel of a woman with sexual desire, something Meridian herself rarely expresses. It is "whispered" at least that Feather Mae is "hot" and that she uses her sexuality to prevent her husband from flattening his part of the ancient burial mound in which she, then Meridian's father, and finally Meridian herself experience ecosomatic ecstasy (57). Her bodily desire is compatible with her second important quality, her ability to have an out-of-the-body experience, and in this way suggests yet-to-be explored alternatives to the asceticism and self-denial that we normally see in Meridian.

Another minor character who intervenes directly in Meridian's life and suggests a variant and extension of the biological maternal mode is Miss Winter. A "misfit" at Saxon, like Meridian, she is an unmarried music teacher who came originally from Meridian's home town. Conquering her jealousy of Meridian as a rival (a jealousy that may be a factor in Mrs. Hill's feelings as well), she "instinctively" offers Meridian the maternal forgiveness that she needs but cannot get from her own mother. In doing so, Miss Winter not only releases Meridian from her paralysis but also models the role of nonprocreative Othermother, that culturally common phenomenon in African and African American communities, that Meridian adopts in her relation to so many children and families in the novel.

Meridian's home town also produces two more named minor characters who embody the possibility of resistance when they go with her to break the news to Mrs. Hill that Meridian will attend Saxon and give Rundi up for adoption. Nelda is a version of Meridian's young, passive, accommodating self, kept home from school to care for younger siblings and ignorant of her own body, so that her first teenaged pregnancy comes as a complete surprise. Looked at from another angle, at another point in her story, Nelda might well belong to the first cluster. But when Mrs. Hill tries to offer Nelda as a traditional model to Meridian, Nelda interrupts to speak—not for herself, but on Meridian's behalf. Only the look of hatred she directs at Mrs. Hill, the neighbor who could have given her information she needed, expresses her feelings. Delores, Meridian's second friend, is more openly defiant. She argues Mrs. Hill down, laughs at her, and appropriates her condemnation of her daughter; "'Let's all be monsters,'" she suggests cheerfully to Meridian and Nelda (90). As is true of all the characters, we know nothing of Nelda and Delores before or after this one scene in which they play only supporting (but highly supportive) roles. Whereas the legends, ranging from Louvinie to Feather Mae, have stories that tend to symbolize particular meanings, usually associated with powerful and established assumptions, the living characters in this case and others suggest an open stock of women with ongoing experiences; though these experiences are rarely as yet turned into full-blown narrative accounts, they inhabit a space where, against the odds, we may find the seeds of social change within the reproductive consciousness of black women.

Meridian also lists, at one point after Miss Winter "forgives" her, several individual but unnamed black women whose stories contradict the maternal legacy: a sergeant in the army, a doctor, a schoolteacher, two lesbians, and "the good-time-girls." All seem to Meridian to have achieved success, and she contrasts these surprisingly numerous black women of her experience with white women in a telling way: "Only the rejects—not of men, but of experience, adventure—fell into the domestic morass that even the most intelligent white girls appeared to be destined for" (108). Meridian here draws on another potentially self-affirming side of the history of black women, who have always worked "outside the home" and developed from this experience a power and status beyond the domestic that exceeds white models. She thinks of herself as belonging to the people who produced Harriet Tubman, and the narrator comments explicitly on how this process of finding a new legacy works: "Meridian appropriated all the good qualities of black women to herself. . . . from somewhere had come the *will* that had got her to Saxon College" (109–10).

....

> "I want to be buried on Mother's Day."
> —A dying mother

Readers are not allowed to forget, however, that Meridian's "will," her deliberate choice of those "good qualities" that enable her to resist what is oppressive about motherhood, is both costly and exceptional. For a time, Meridian is divided between the conscious lightheartedness she feels when she gives her son up for adoption and the terrible nightmares that follow, unconsciously expressing what cannot be so easily forgotten. In narrative terms, the unconscious, unintegrated pain of maternal loss and suffering similarly haunts the last part of the story. Here Meridian appears to be well on the road to recovery from her personal traumas, but she proceeds to encounter a set of living mothers who not only reproduce the earlier legendary pattern of misery but also extend the ordeal of motherhood out of past and story into the present actuality of women and children "at risk" in black communities.[32] Closing the novel thus, these figures, like the Wild Child, suggest a reciprocal and even causal relationship between mythic background, historical truth, and individual experience. There is a trajectory of immediacy at work here, as readers' time and Meridian's time merge near the end of the novel. In each of these encounters, however, Meridian acts both *as* (nonprocreative, activist) mother and *for* the (biological) mother, and there is a trajectory of emerging self-representation, as the voices of these living women gradually begin to speak for themselves, with Meridian's help, about the trials of reproduction and motherhood.

The first group of women in this closing set is the still silent, unindividualized, and nameless mothers of a black community bordering on a drainage ditch, where "disobedient" black children wading in the only water available to them are drowned whenever the nearby reservoir is allowed to overflow without warning. The mothers of this community are represented only collectively, as all having lost children this way; their husbands as a group curse the white city fathers and the women as a group take food and "share grief" with the most recently bereaved family. Meridian's role is strikingly emblematic here: she confronts and publicizes the communal distress of maternal loss by carrying "the bloated figure of a five-year-old boy who had been stuck in the sewer for two days before he was raked out with a grappling hook" to the town meeting, where she gives the body to the mayor. Perverse surrogate for the biological mother who cannot bear to touch the "grotesque" corpse of her dead child, Meridian serves once more as she did in the opening chapter, as community Othermother transforming the atrocities of maternal experience into political action, taking risks, and doing the maternal work of impersonal love that is so hard and critical.[33]

In three sequential chapters following this episode, at some unspecified point near the end of both Meridian and readers' increasingly common time, Meridian's ongoing political activism leads her to three black women who speak about mothering in response to Meridian's respectful questions and patient listening. "Travels," the first of these chapters, opens with the word *Mama*, spoken by a half-naked child. Here their voter registration work takes Meridian and Truman to the bedside of a woman dying without medical care who dreams of being buried on Mother's Day: "'I don't know why I want that, but I do,'" she says (204). Her voice is fading and confused, and it bespeaks a desire as perversely apt as Meridian's tender embrace of the drowned boy's corpse. Her dream of a funeral on Mother's Day marks the inherent deadliness of the commercialized national sentiment about mothers and perhaps the gap between the celebration, so important in black communities,[34] and the black reality of mothering as it is represented in this novel: a day for mothers would be a day of a woman's death, indeed. We learn that this woman's wish has been granted when her husband comes to Meridian to register to vote on the Monday after Mother's Day. His act, inspired by Meridian's quiet, local activism, tacitly suggests that it will in some cases take the death of mothers (as in other cases, the death of children) to generate political change.

The next and penultimate woman Meridian tries to help is Miss Treasure, a grotesque figure potentially offering a comic relief or Faulkneresque aestheticization that is explicitly blocked. Fat and of indeterminate old age, Miss Treasure tells Truman and Meridian her story of lifelong isolation on a plantation with her sister. Using both indirect and direct quotations, the novel records the tale. We learn that elderly Miss Treasure has recently fallen in love with a forty-five-year-old housepainter and thinks she is pregnant; she is frightened that if she marries the painter he will outlive her, own her house, and raise her child badly. Truman is ready to laugh at this absurd woman, but Meridian takes her seriously and helps her to a doctor, where Miss Treasure finds that she is not pregnant and is rejuvenated in a "vacancy of grief"(210). This bizarre story suggests among other things that Meridian now does work that her own mother failed to do, relieving Miss Treasure of the ignorance of her reproductive functions that Meridian suffered from before her first pregnancy. It also testifies to the continuity of female fears of pregnancy across the life cycle, fears associated with endangered ownership of one's own domestic space and frustrated responsibility for a child's nurturance and protection.

"And so they must go to the prison. And so they must. And so they must see the child who murdered her child, nothing new" (211). The last, most important, and probably most deeply disturbing of the three chapters in this final cluster is "Pilgrimage," which opens with these three stuttering sentences, as if at once in the middle and at the extreme edge of the ongoing pain of motherhood that the novel has so meticulously documented. There is "nothing new" in this obligatory journey in the sense that the girl in prison for murdering her child is a composite of Wild Child, Fast Mary, Daxter's mother, Meridian herself, and others inside and outside the novel. What *is* altogether new, however, is the narrative perspective that readers are allowed. Whereas in the early chapters, dead women's stories were generally reported from an omniscient third-person point of view with no representation of the women's own voices, in these later chapters we hear at least a few words directly attributed by the narrator to the subjects of the stories, the dying mother and Miss Treasure, some of whose language is reported in direct quotations. Now, taking this move further, a startling meditation by the girl who murdered her baby comes in response to a question that Meridian has apparently asked and a picture of an apple that she has brought to the girl:

Yes. She had bitten her baby's cheek, bitten out a plug, before she strangled it with a piece of curtain ruffle. So round and clean it had

been, too. But not red, alas, before she bit. And wasn't it right to seek
to devour a perishable? That, though sweet to the nose, soft to the
touch, yummy, is yet impossible to keep? It was as if (she said, dream-
ily) I had taken out my heart (red and round, fine, a glistening valen-
tine!) and held it in my hands . . . and it was my heart I bit, I strangled
till it died. I hid beside the river. My heart the roaming dog dug up,
barking for the owner of that field. My heart. Where I am (she continues) no one is. And why am I alive, without my heart? And how is
this? And who, in the hell, are you? (211–2)

The girl's fusion of self and child, her confusion of infanticide and
suicide, her moral logic that responds so clearly to her situation ("wasn't
it right to seek to devour a perishable . . . impossible to keep?"), her
disconnection and loneliness, her challenge to Meridian—and to
readers—as intrusive stranger, all represent in an extraordinary way,
and for the first time in the novel, what and how the mother who murders her own child might think and feel. As in the more extended passages of *Beloved,* the language mimics theorized aspects of the preoedipal or semiotic in agrammatical, disconnected lyricism. As the
culminating figure in the series of women whose stories I have been
pulling out of the quilt of this novel, the girl in prison breaks the silence of the mothers, to speak of her own reality. The fact that the
words are not in quotation marks but in free indirect discourse suggests a merging of the narrative perspective here with the girl's, a strategy that gives her a voice, an "I" in the discourse that Meridian never
has. Notably when Meridian, in tears after this encounter, tries to remember and feel compassion for her own son, she too experiences
from this perspective and so can only feel for and with the girl-mother.
To the girl's final question "who . . . are you?" Meridian may answer
that she is, in a sense, this girl, or she would have been had she not
given her child away.

Like the figure of Fast Mary who closes and unifies the opening tales
of Marilene, Wild Child, and Louvinie, the girl in prison bespeaks the
common (not to be confused with the essential) experience that brings
together women of many persuasions. The novel registers the actual
variety and representational fictionality that constitutes female reproductive consciousness, as well as a common denominator of traumatic
suffering, fear, and loss. After this previously unspeakable story is partially told from a point of view that merges narrator and character, the
novel has little left to do or say. In three brief final chapters, we glimpse

Lynne and Truman, perhaps reestablishing a relationship of some sort; the photo of the stump of the Sojourner, with a little shoot growing out of one side; and Meridian's quiet departure for a place unknown to us, while the newly maternalized male, Truman, falls dizzily into her sleeping bag. Meridian, destination hereafter unknown, has completed a narrative quest that takes her inevitably to the space of the prison in which the maternal has often been confined. There she calls forth the voice that speaks, as in *Beloved,* of infanticide, in a language that expresses confusion, lyricism, and challenge.

In that space Meridian serves still as Othermother, complementing and continuing the role we witnessed in the novel's first chapter. There, she led children (and at another level readers) to see that established and dominant ideas about femininity were inauthentic and worthless. Here, having confronted these ideas extensively in the course of the plot, she revises them by actively seeking out a space in which previously silenced or ignored voices can speak. In this space, Meridian is positioned chiefly as a listener, hearing a story not to be forgotten, resolved, or integrated. She is able to listen empathically because, in giving up her own child, Meridian at once repeats and arrests or alters the transmission of that central element in the African American female reproductive consciousness, the trauma of motherhood. At the close of this chapter, I say more about Meridian's role as witness to trauma, but first I consider her own story from another angle.

REMAPPING SELFHOOD: DISSOCIATION, DISCONNECTION, TRANSFORMATION

> I felt myself entering, to some extent, the underground city of female adolescence, the place where powerful learning experiences were happening. The gateway to this underworld was marked by the statement, "I don't know". . . . Girls, gaining voice and knowledge, are in danger of knowing the unseen and speaking the unspoken and thus losing connection with what is commonly taken to be "reality."
> —Carol Gilligan, *Making Connections*

> "I don't *know* if I could kill anyone. . . . If I had to do it, perhaps I could . . . I would defend myself . . . Maybe I could sort of grow into the idea of killing other human beings. . . . But I'm not sure. . . . I don't know."
> —Alice Walker, *Meridian*

I have argued thus far that Meridian's giving away of her son, like the widespread appearance of the figure of the mother without child itself, is overdetermined, in this case by sometimes overlapping and sometimes conflicting aspects of the southern black woman's reproductive consciousness. I have emphasized that Meridian cannot be fully understood apart from this context, as if she were acting as conventional main character playing her part in the familiar western plot, in quest of separate selfhood. Renegotiating her relationship to her historical maternal heritage, Meridian might also be compared to the female adolescents coming of age in America today that Carol Gilligan and her colleagues are studying, figures of an emergent female subject who, in the process of "gaining voice and knowledge," is "in danger of . . . losing connection." Giving up her own child marks not only Meridian's positive intervention in and subversion of a collective, traumatic past, but also her pervasive personal difficulty in developing and sustaining a coherent self in stable relationship to others. In fact it seems accurate and illuminating to say that Meridian is dissociated, in a clinical sense of the term.[35]

Newly defined and seriously studied in recent decades, dissociation is now considered by psychologists not merely in its major pathological forms, such as multiple personality disorder and various amnesiac states, but as a "continuum" of experiences and behaviors that includes daydreaming, tuning out of a conversation, safely driving a vehicle on a familiar route and subsequently realizing that one has not been attending to the road, and many everyday feelings of adolescence. (My own most frequent experience of this phenomenon is associated with motherhood: reading a story aloud to a small child without comprehending the words I am uttering, while my inner awareness is busily composing a memo, worrying about the next day's scheduling problems, or otherwise dealing with adult business.) Dissociation refers to any "psychophysiological process whereby information—incoming, stored, or outgoing—is actively deflected from integration with its usual or expected associations."[36] And it entails, theoretically, a view of how consciousness is divided that differs somewhat from that of Freudian psychoanalysis. The latter has generally held that the mind or psyche splits along horizontal lines and that repression is the mechanism by which memories are buried, though we proceed as if consciousness were unified. The dissociative psyche is split instead along vertical lines, and the barriers are set up—as in amnesiac states—between experiences and memories usually available to everyday awareness.

At least in its more extreme and pathological forms, dissociation is frequently considered an effect of trauma, and psychology's renewed interest in dissociative problems and theories over the last few decades has often been linked to the rise of patients suffering from what is now identified as "post-traumatic stress disorder." I return to this connection at the end of the chapter, but for my present purposes, I note merely that three categories of trauma are often thought to precipitate dissociation: loss or threatened loss of an important object, situations where an individual can neither fight nor flee, and experiences of "overwhelming impulse" such as suicidal or homicidal urges. Dissociation is also thought to have several adaptive functions including resolution of irreconcilable conflicts, escape from the constraints of reality, and isolation of catastrophic experiences.

The clearest indication that Meridian is dissociated in a more than everyday sense, although not as a result of any known personal trauma, is found in an early description of her moments of ecstasy in the Serpent Mound.[37] The experience begins with "a sense of vast isolation. . . . She was a dot, a speck in creation, alone and hidden. She had contact with no other living thing: instead she was surrounded by the dead." Meridian is frightened at first, but remembers her great-grandmother, from whom she presumably inherits her dissociative powers, and moves beyond fear to something that begins with light-headedness. Then, "it was as if the walls of earth that enclosed her rushed outward, leveling themselves at a dizzying rate, and then spinning wildly, lifting her out of her body and giving her the feeling of flying" (58). Though the out-of-body experience is joyful, it also suggests a dangerous tendency toward a degree of dissociation and disconnection that is at other points profoundly debilitating and painful for Meridian. She is detached from her own body not just in her out-of-body moments but in her deathlike paralyses and her joyless asexuality. To her own bewilderment, she frequently feels cut off from the people around her, friends and family, from the institutions they accept, from the political movement that first "awakens" her, and from conventional ways of making meaning and constructing reality.

In the following discussion, I explore four points about dissociation, a term I reserve for speaking about an internal sense of split consciousness, and disconnection, a term describing the often concomitant

divide between self and an external, usually social reality. First, dissociation can obviously be pathological; in *Meridian,* we see this most
clearly in the person of Mrs. Hill, who serves also to link dissociation
as a pathology with pregnancy and motherhood. Second, dissociation
and disconnection can be responses to a reality that fails to afford the
individual any recognition, any viable means of expressing or connecting her self and her own experience to the world around her. In this
way, dissociative behaviors can be seen as both adaptive, protecting the
sense of self from what threatens it, and potentially resistant to and
subversive of an oppressive reality. Third, dissociation, detachment,
and withdrawal can be means of escaping from one reality in order to
see and make connections with other realities, often with what is normally taken to be outside, beyond, or alien to one's everyday experience. Fourth, dissociation and disconnection may be symptoms of
"powerful learning experiences" and necessary strategies for attaining
personal agency and social change, for rejecting what is self-destructive
in reality—racism, misogyny—and reaching out for new, difficult, and
at best partial connections between a self and others who will tolerate
division and difference and recognize a common traumatic history of
unspeakable inhumanity and loss.

·······

> But in her first pregnancy she [Mrs. Hill] became distracted
> from who she was. As divided in her mind as her body was
> divided, between what was part of herself and what was not.
> —*Meridian*

Some of the pathological aspects of dissociation are outlined most
starkly in the story of Meridian's mother, Mrs. Hill. In the second part
of the opening chapter of the novel, Mrs. Hill appears in Meridian's
introspective reverie as a classic, static figure of maternal absence and
loss. In the first narrative flashback to her early days in the civil rights
movement, Meridian contemplates her inability to commit herself
wholeheartedly to violent revolution and attributes this hesitation to
a lack: "Something's missing in me. Something's *missing.* . . . What is
it? What? What?" (31), she asks herself. In answer to her silent question, Meridian recalls an experience another decade or so earlier that
would seem to locate the "missing contents" in a familiar, unspeak-

able place: "Saying nothing, she remembered her mother and the day she lost her" (32).

At first glance, the following flashback within a flashback (to a scene in church, when Meridian is unable to say "Yes" to Christ, as her mother wishes) seems to confirm a conventional psychoanalytic approach to understanding (female) development, not dissimilar from the underlying assumptions in many readings of a novel like *Beloved*. We seek what is missing, what divides the subject and arrests development, by reconstructing a critical past event that has been repressed. We find that the lack is, as always, the mother's (unavailable) love; we struggle to accept the loss, to integrate the recognition that the mother's love is not unconditional. We finally separate from this cold and rejecting mother, so that the unified consciousness can enter into the father's sphere, represented for Meridian by the "intelligence" and autonomy that she identifies with in Mr. Hill.[38] But looking exclusively to the early relationship with the psychic mother for a full explanation of subjectivity (and often for the cause of pathology) is quickly shown to be inadequate. Mrs. Hill is not just "the mother," an abstract, universal representation of the child's point of view; she has a particular story too.

In what we glimpse of Mrs. Hill's story, it seems clear to begin with that Meridian didn't lose her mother's love at any identifiable moment, because she never had it. Mrs. Hill appears a clarion figure of the damage that can be done to a barely emerging sense of female subjectivity and agency by the experience of maternity. She was "not a woman who should have had children," the narrator observes, because her own southern black female selfhood was particularly tentative and delicate, much in need of freedom: "she was capable of thought and growth and action only if unfettered by the needs of dependents, or the demands, requirements, of a husband. Her spirit was of such fragility that the slightest impact on it caused a shattering beyond restoration" (49).

Mrs. Hill is tricked into marriage and family by the mystification and idealization of motherhood she meets all around her. Maternity seems to promise enriched selfhood, a "mysterious inner life"(51) reflected in the faces of women who have children. But in actuality, becoming a mother obstructs her quest for a more stable, integrated self and renders Mrs. Hill "distracted from who she was," "divided" in both mind and body. Awakened to the reality of mothering in her own experience, she perceives that other mothers too are "dead, living just

enough for their children"; motherhood for her is fundamentally an experience of fatal self-division and isolation, like "being buried alive,
walled away from her own life, brick by brick" (51). In what seems
both resignation and protest against the division and loss of her frail
self, Mrs. Hill cultivates "abstraction," deliberately refusing her own
creativity and actively disavowing any connection with past and present reality outside her narrow sphere of family and institutionalized
religion. Meridian remembers a "perennial" conversation between her
parents concerning the Native American genocide that haunts Mr. Hill;
Mrs. Hill tells him, "'I never worry myself. . . . As far as I'm concerned,
these people and how they kept off mosquitoes hasn't got a thing to do
with me" (29).

Mrs. Hill's sense of distraction, willful self-suppression, and disconnection not only foreshadows aspects of Meridian's own psychic response to maternity, but also suggests that Meridian's upbringing could
only contribute to her characteristically dissociative behavior. According to the narrator, Mrs. Hill displaces the connection she might have
felt with her children (or anyone else) into her ironing, sending the family out into the world "enclosed in the starch of her anger," and obliged
therefore "to keep their distance to avoid providing the soggy wrinkles
of contact that would cause her distress" (79). Though the daughter is
obviously shaped by this maternal anger and withdrawal, they are by
no means the only influences that the novel represents, nor are dissociation and disconnection elsewhere shown to be entirely or necessarily negative, self-destructive responses to circumstances. Meridian has
another parent, a father whose "withdrawal from the world" is of an
equally influential but different nature, and his disconnection also
points to the possibility of a positive separation and distance from
"what is taken to be 'reality,'" one that does not isolate the individual
completely or deny the existence of others but refuses to participate in
the conventional reality of oppression and social injustice.

Mr. Hill, a schoolteacher, is obsessed with the historical injustice
done to Native Americans. Mrs. Hill sees Mr. Hill's behavior as irre-
sponsible and escapist, just like Meridian's response to motherhood:
"'You would just fly away, if you could,'" she tells him (55). But however he fails in her view, he also paradoxically expresses a deep sense
of connection across time and race: "'They've been a part of it, we've
been a part of it, everybody's been a part of it for a long time'"(55). He
tries to give back his sixty acres of rocky land, inherited from his grand-

father, to a Cherokee from Oklahoma named Walter Longknife. Appropriately enough, it is when Meridian meets this stranger that she finds a new way of understanding the man she has known all her life: "He [Longknife] was a wanderer, a mourner, like her father; she could begin to recognize what her father was by looking at him" (54). Seeing from a distance and understanding the known by looking at the unknown has a certain value; it may promote a recognition that is unavailable in more intimate relationships. The night before Meridian hears the news of the firebombing that causes her to join the civil rights movement, she has a dream that reveals the link between her recognition of her father and her own political activism: she dreams of Native Americans, although "she had thought she had forgotten about them" (73). From her father, Meridian may inherit or learn a disconnection that entails the ability to transcend everyday ways of thinking that promote self-protective ignorance of injustice, to make contact with other human beings across difference and distance, and to take responsibility in larger historical and spiritual ways. As we shall see, Meridian both uses and revises this inheritance in ways that are more responsive than Mr. Hill's to the particularities of female reproductive consciousness and maternal experience.

Though the stories of Meridian's parents help us to account for salient features of her character and behavior, the novel does not merely explain Meridian's dissociation and disconnection, for bad or for good, as family traits. It documents instead, in great detail, the circumstances in which Meridian struggles to know and act in a world where she consistently fails to find the recognition necessary for a coherent sense of self in relationship with others. An early key to understanding this struggle is found in the briefest chapter in the novel, "Gold," a scrap of narrative only half a page long and tellingly situated between the stories of Mrs. Hill's loss of fragile selfhood in motherhood and Mr. Hill's escape from a guilty selfhood into history. In "Gold," seven-year-old Meridian digs up a dirty, rusty piece of metal; she cleans it up, and "to her amazement, what she had found was a bar of gold." She runs to her mother, who is shelling peas, and places the heavy object in Mrs. Hill's lap; her mother, like any mother who finds her child's enthusiasms interrupt the mundane tasks she wishes to finish and forget, speaks "sharply" and tells her to "move that thing." This is not just another moment of maternal failure and rejection: Meridian's father and her brothers also fail to be "impressed" by Meridian's finding. She nevertheless polishes it, buries it under a tree, and for a while digs it up regularly to look at it. "Then she dug it up less and less . . . until finally she forgot to dig it up. Her mind turned to other things" (52).

Although it fits easily enough into what we learn about the family dynamics in the Hill household and about Meridian's personality, "Gold" seems to be one piece of the crazy quilt that is not as tightly stitched into a pattern as most of the others are. The main narrative, like Meridian, forgets about the gold; the story is presented not as a distressing or painful experience that was repressed but as one of the many little disappointments that happen and are simply forgotten. But it can at the same time be read as a parable about the model of consciousness and identity that the novel as a whole presupposes and represents most clearly in Meridian. The child is not merely the sum of her two parents; in "Gold" we meet Meridian as a young, developing individual, framed but not exclusively defined by familial genealogy, already at seven an agent of discovery and imagination. This chapter, opening a small space between the parents' stories in the chapters that surround it, represents the embryonic self as a place of mystery, excitement, potentially great worth, and lack of recognition. Worthless in the eyes of the world, soon forgotten by Meridian herself who once knew or imagined its worth, and now buried forever, the gold bar is a projection of a core value that is at once a childish illusion and a lost treasure. It also brings to mind the "mysterious inner life" that Mrs. Hill naively hoped to find in motherhood and her bitter disappointment when that hidden treasure turned out to be the phantom of dead women. In the course of the novel, we never go back to the yard and dig this treasure up; there is no map that shows the way to finding it; it is not in our mother's lap or breast. If we did go back, it is not clear exactly what we might find. Thus if "Gold" signifies what is lacking in Meridian, it suggests that those missing contents always escape full narration, are not a knowable whole; "the past" is made of bits and pieces, some of which might be useful to us now, some of which might not; some of which might be authentic, some of which might be fake.

By such a reading, "Gold" figures the postmodern fragmentation and inaccessibility of the past as originary ground of being and critiques theories of unified consciousness and full interpretation, calling instead for something closer to a dissociative model of the mind. At the same time, "Gold" does not dismiss the intrinsic *worth* of the self, even as it understands the fragility and ambiguity of identity. The chapter speaks a truth about Meridian that no one except the novel as a whole hears or believes: note that the narrator's statement, "what she had found was a bar of gold," either assumes Meridian's childish perspective or avows faith in what everyone but Meridian discredits. The failure of others, particularly parents, to accept Meridian's finding at least partially accounts for her own characteristic, sometimes crippling self-doubt. When she herself listens to and finds value in "Miss Treasure" near the end of the novel, she recuperates something of her self that was buried and forgotten.

"Gold" also introduces us to an early instance of how Meridian deals with the refusal of recognition by linking forgetting and self-protection. At seven, she accidentally finds a fragment of the impersonal past, sees it as beautiful and valuable, and resourcefully buries what she believes is a precious find in order to preserve it, to hold onto it, and to save it from the blatant failure of others to acknowledge and appreciate either the treasure or her own role in finding it. As a consequence, however, she too loses sight of what she once knew or believed to be true. This strategy for protecting her own belief is characteristic of Meridian in adolescence and adulthood, and thinking about "Gold" helps us to see Meridian's habit of dissociation as a risky act of resistance and protest against a reality that neither recognizes nor values her worth.[39]

Recent psychological studies suggest that adolescence is "a watershed in female development, a time when girls are in danger of drowning or disappearing" (10). Though "Gold" implies that this crisis has roots in childhood and in fact refracts an endemic psychic condition, subsequent chapters confirm that adolescence is a time of increasing self-doubt and disconnection, particularly as the female child enters into heterosexual relationships. The keynotes of Meridian's feelings about sex are ignorance, incomprehension, and distance from anything that might be called her own desire; the effect of her sexual experience is disconnection from those to whom she is apparently closest.

Mrs. Hill is presented as initially responsible for Meridian's lack of knowledge of even the simplest facts of reproductive processes and for failing to understand the relation between knowing and doing: "Having told her absolutely nothing, she [Mrs. Hill] had expected her to *do* nothing." Ignorant of the code her mother uses—"be sweet," "Keep your panties up and your dress down" (60)—Meridian has sex as often as her boyfriends want it. Her motive is not pleasure but protection from frightening reality and dangerous knowledge: "It saved her from the strain of responding to other boys or even noting the whole category of men. This was worth a great deal, because she was afraid of men" (61–2). One particularized source of Meridian's fear is her experience, starting at the age of twelve, in the back office of George Daxter's funeral parlor, where the half-white mortician exchanges candy for "a swift, exploratory feel" (66). Here she also meets his assistant, who displays himself to Meridian using only his voice, describing the act of intercourse, to seduce another schoolgirl. Whereas Mrs. Hill's clichés fail to have the intended effect because they lack reference to any meaning that Meridian understands, the assistant's words do what he intends them to; in both cases, however, Meridian's own desires and intentions go unrecognized by those who try to use words to control her behavior, and she becomes increasingly silenced and unsure about what she feels.

Even as she willingly meets her boyfriend Eddie's constant demands for sex, Meridian fails to comprehend her complicity, and we repeatedly hear variants on those key words, "I don't know." "*She could not understand* why she was doing something with such frequency that she did not enjoy"; she didn't even like Eddie's name "and *didn't know* why" (62, emphasis added). When she laughs with Eddie, it is "as if she did it underwater, and the echo of it whirled sluggishly through her head" (63). Pregnant and then married to him, she wonders "who really, he was. What he was doing there in bed with her"; though he seems to work hard for their future, "she could not even recognize it" (63). Her even more patent lack of interest in sex, once she is pregnant, marks "frigidity" as both a self-denying form of resistance and an accurate reading of how little her desire would be recognized by others: "she— her body, that is—never had any intention of *giving in*. She was suspicious of pleasure . . . Besides, Eddie did not seriously expect more than 'interest' from her . . . they never discussed anything beyond her attitude" (68–9).

As was the case for Mrs. Hill, pregnancy, dividing the female subject in a particularly manifest way, is a critical experience for Meridian, promising and potentially embodying the most intimate connection imaginable with another human being, but also entailing confusion of boundaries and inevitable separation. The problem of knowing who she is and what she thinks is compounded when even her bodily integrity is invaded. As mother-to-be, Meridian is utterly confused. She "never thought about the baby at all . . . She knew she did not want it.

But even this was blurred. How could she not want something she was not even sure she was having?" After the baby is born, exhaustion contributes to her befuddlement, making it "futile to attempt to think straight, or even to think at all" (69). Like the mother of object relations theory, Meridian feels her caretaking capacities brought into being by the baby's needs. But this only heightens feelings of internal dissociation—"her body prompted not by her own desires, but by her son's cries"—and disconnection from the infant who thus both divides and dominates her. Given what she knows about reality, this experience seems analogous to the historical domination of her ancestors: "So this . . . is what slavery is like," she tells herself. She begins to dream of ways to murder her child, "because he did not feel like anything to her but a ball and chain." Frightened by these dreams, she substitutes conscious daydreams of her own suicide, finding it "pleasantly distracting to imagine herself stiff and oblivious, her head stuck in an oven. Or coolly out of it, a hole through the roof of her mouth" (70). Ironically able to function only with the help of these dysfunctional fantasies, she takes delight in her ability to fool those who see her as "an exemplary young mother," and living this schizophrenic nightmare, she verges on disintegration: "She felt as though something perched inside her brain was about to fly away" (70). Suicide is averted only by disconnection, a great lethargy that keeps her in a "fog of unconcern" (71) so impenetrable that she is hardly even aware that the baby's father, Eddie, leaves her and the baby.

But motherhood, like unwanted and unsatisfying sex, is only part of the problem, and giving her baby away does not lead to wholeness or freedom. Disconnection is reinforced at the institutional level when Meridian goes to Saxon College. Here, female sexuality is simply ignored, even as the rules that police female students contradict that ignorance, and so too the college simply closes its eyes to the forbidden activism of women who join the civil rights movement. Meridian's experience with hometown boys is cruelly replicated in her affair with the worldly college student, Truman, for whom she does for a time feel desire. Conversation is often difficult with him for an odd reason: he likes to speak French, which Meridian understands but cannot quickly speak. Meridian finds herself pregnant again, after only one sexual experience with Truman—during which he thinks he has deflowered a virgin—and then he abandons her to date the white civil rights worker, Lynne. Meridian has an abortion and sterilization. Then, when the white exchange students have gone north, Truman comes back and tries to seduce Meridian again, whispering "worshipfully" and "urgently," in English this time: "*Have* my beautiful black babies"(116). Expressing the kind of resentment that her mother felt duty-bound to contain, Meridian strikes out before she rationally comprehends her response: "She hit him three times *before she even knew* what was happening" (116, emphasis added).

It is hardly surprising that Meridian withdraws from the everyday worlds of heterosexuality, motherhood, and college, all spheres of "not knowing," where persons and institutions claiming to protect or train or give her pleasure lack any intention or means to recognize her desire. Any effort to discover her self *must* lead Meridian to lose connection with such reality. Just after the abortion and break with Truman occurs (in reader's time), the narrative embeds yet another incident that dramatizes how a girl who begins to think about what she actually knows and believes is distracted and silenced, because comprehension of the lies that pass for reality, as opposed to safe not knowing, stuns her. The story is filtered through Miss Winter's reverie as she sits by Meridian's bed and remembers the first time she saw the younger woman at an oratorical competition at their hometown high school. In the middle of the same memorized speech about the Constitution and the American Way of Life that Miss Winter once performed, Meridian suddenly falls silent and leaves the stage. Trying to explain herself to a shamed, angry, and willfully uncomprehending Mrs. Hill, Meridian says that "for the first time she really listened to what she was saying, knew she didn't believe it, and was so distracted by this revelation that she could not make the rest of her speech" (121).

While attending college and participating actively in the civil rights movement, Meridian finds hope only when she is beaten into unconsciousness by police at demonstrations. So too the paralyses she experiences from her college days into the beginning of the novel's present time mark not only the impasse in her reproductive consciousness, but also the familiar, dangerous effort to escape an unbearable situation. Actually hearing the disparities between self and society, experience and myth, black and white, personal belief and public opinion, means shutting out the rote words, forgetting the available language. It may also mean losing the capacity to speak, burying what might be gold, and seeking unconsciousness to evade the traumas of consciousness and history. To avoid this pathological potential in dissociation as a strategy for dealing with conflicts, escaping the constraints of reality, and isolating unbearable experiences, it may be necessary to focus on the unvarnished truth of loss, to listen to the terrible stories, so that the self is not walled up but newly connected. Meridian's quest, I suggest, follows precisely this course of action.

• • • • • • •

The absence of the child herself was what had finally brought them together.
                                                                —*Meridian*

Lines of latitude running north and south.
                                                                —*Meridian*

In their ecstatic dissociative states, their out-of-body experiences, Meridian and her father are sometimes able to escape a present reality that does not recognize them or many others, and they both find joy in this shared secret power to achieve a "tangible connection to the past" (59). But they disagree about the meaning and purpose of their paranormal ecstasies. Mr. Hill believes that the Native Americans built the sacred coil where the body can be left behind "in order to give the living a sensation similar to that of dying . . . only the spirit lived, set free in the world" (58). Meridian disagrees: "It seemed to her that it was a way the living sought to expand the consciousness of being alive" (59). In contemplating suicide, welcoming police beatings, and seeking more and more ways to dissociate mind from body as a coping strategy, Meridian comes dangerously close to the death that Mr. Hill views as freedom. But she eventually chooses "consciousness of being alive" instead by finding ways of reconnecting with a reality that at once challenges old lies and looks less hopelessly oppressive and unchanging than it once did, and with others who confirm and respond to her own experience rather than ignore and seek to control it. This experience entails "really listening" to stories about a shared history of loss and dispossession, particularly the traumatic loss of children, one of the most horrifying events that can happen to an individual and to a community. To know and live with the truth of her own experience, Meridian must recognize it elsewhere; to take advantage of the possibilities for future change, she and others must reconstruct and mourn the unspeakable inhumanity of their collective history.

There is not just one turning point or moment of connection for Meridian but a more diffuse representation of a series of partial points of contact, all of which turn on this paradoxical presence of connection on the ground of absence. I have discussed some of these relationships, ranging from Meridian's tentative hold on the Wild Child to her empathy for the girl in prison who has murdered her infant. But these are one-way connections, often with a younger or narrowly averted version of the self, who is among the dying. Here I consider in detail two episodes in which Meridian is able to move from the subversive to the reconstructive powers of her disconnectedness by making tentative contact with maimed but living people who are very different and distanced from Meridian, and to whose stories she must struggle to listen.

The first and less frequently noted connection built across difference and disconnection is Meridian's friendship with Lynne Rabinowitz, the white exchange student whom Truman eventually marries and then abandons. This friendship opens the question of connection across racial lines, the dominant image of which is displayed in a button Meridian particularly admires "that showed a black hand and a white hand shaking, although since the colors were flat the hands did not seem, on closer inspection to be shaking at all; they seemed to be merely touching palms, or in the act of sliding away from each other" (81). Lynne and Meridian, white and black woman, have been separated from the beginning of their relationship as much by their competition over Truman as by their race, although the two concerns are tightly interwoven in a way that foregrounds the multiplicity of subject positions a woman actually occupies. But Meridian's first response to Lynne, before Truman has met her, signals the possibility of connection: "I like her," Meridian says, even as she proceeds to tell a story that firmly mocks Lynne for her ignorance of black folks' ways. And Lynne sees Meridian more accurately than any one else in the novel, as Truman recalls when he finally corrects his own view of Meridian and recognizes what "Lynne—who had known her only briefly—had insisted anyone could see": "Meridian, no matter what she was saying to you, and no matter what you were saying to her, seemed to be thinking of something else, another conversation perhaps, an earlier one, that continued on a parallel track. Or of a future one that was running an identical course. This was always true" (141).

Given this rare insight into Meridian's oddly connected form of disconnection, Lynne later comes closer to Meridian than any other character. The tragic precipitant of their eventual bond is the violent death of Lynne and Truman's interracial daughter, Camara. As Meridian helps Lynne grieve for Camara in the chapter entitled "Two Women," they have the kind of ordinary contact that is rarely glimpsed in this novel: watching television, reading poems, combing hair, and sharing political insights. The novel neither romanticizes nor dismisses this connection. Its fragility, and the novel's ambivalence, is seen in the disruption of narrative chronology, so that in reader's time, the chapter in which we see Lynne and Meridian together, at least "touching palms" after the death of Camara, is framed by their meeting a year or so after that period, when Lynne has come south to Meridian's current house to find Truman and the two women seem to be "sliding away from each other."

This substantial episode, which spans seven chapters, focuses on the divisions between white and black women and on the question of how they might avoid competing for men and better listen to each other's horror stories. At the beginning of "Visits," set a year before the opening of the novel, Lynne seems to think that Truman is still having an affair with Meridian, and Meridian explicitly refuses to hear Lynne's story of being raped by one of Truman's black friends, Tommy Odds. This is a key refusal of connection on Meridian's part, suggesting the limits of interracial female friendship, and in her response to Lynne's plea that she listen Meridian sounds just like her mother: "'Can't you understand that there are some things I don't want to know?'" (153). The narrative, however, disclaims or qualifies Meridian's denial. First, it proceeds to tell Lynne's story for the next twenty-eight pages on the presumption that Lynne is talking to herself—"*Perhaps* Meridian wouldn't listen to her, but she could sit there herself and try to remember" (153, emphasis added). The perspective not only moves from the third-person voice of the black author into the first-person voice of the white character, but obliges readers, whatever their color, to serve as surrogate listeners for the black heroine, who apparently falls asleep. In retrospect, the weight of that "Perhaps" increases when we come to the end of the long, multichaptered flashback to discover that Meridian is still in the room with Lynne. When Lynne speaks out loud at this point—"Black folks aren't so special"—Meridian suddenly answers, "'Maybe . . . the time for being special has passed,'" and the narrator adds, "said Meridian, *as if* she had been listening all along" (181, emphasis added). The chapter ends by reporting a gesture that embodies what the novel does to readers here: Meridian winks at Lynne. The entire sequence of events raises the critical question for any discussion of the ongoing, tangled traumas of black people and white people in racist America: just who is supposed to be listening to whom, and who can or will serve as audience to this story that is so hard to tell and hear?

We are left with this uncertain representation of Meridian's ability to make a rare and difficult contact across racial difference, despite or perhaps because of her constitutional and habitual disconnection—tuning into another conversation, falling asleep, passing into catatonic fits. It is useful to contrast this late episode with the opening flashback in chapter 1, where Meridian seems to her revolutionary friends to have fallen asleep but in fact is simply remembering her own past. The attempt to understand the self through intrasubjective reverie, in the first instance, is supplanted in the later chapters by the effort to make intersubjective contact. "Perhaps" this exchange of stories between black women and white women can only be heard conditionally for now, "as if" listening were taking place—just as Evelyn Hall may occupy the position of "the mother figure of the moment." Whether Lynne and Meridian are "touching palms" or "sliding away" from each other when the story leaves them is unclear. But characteristically, Meridian is better at establishing unusual and difficult connections—ones that border on disconnection and demand a higher tolerance for partial, fleeting, ambivalent touching and a conversational engagement that situates the participants on parallel tracks—than the easy everyday ones that may in fact disguise the lack of connection and communication under the illusory notion that it is a simple matter of "telling one's own story" to an empathic listener. And this point of contact, however temporary and hesitant, is forged on the basis of an experience of living with abrupt, painful, and permanent disconnection that Meridian and Lynne share with many women: the voluntary or involuntary loss of a child. Giving away her son severs Meridian's bonds with both the problematic cultural image of the good mother and those persons to whom she would normally be tied in bonds of natural affection, "blood" relatives and heterosexual partners like Rundi himself or Mrs. Hill and Eddie Jr. or Truman. Her unnatural act makes possible, however, not so much her own selfhood but a deployment of the self into connection with many black women and, more surprisingly, Lynne. It also facilitates her move into the position of a listener to whom Lynne, like the girl in prison, can speak.[40]

. . . .

"My son died."
—*Meridian*

A more commonly recognized moment of connection for Meridian, often mentioned as the point at which she "discovers herself," begins to heal, and move forward, comes just two chapters later, immediately before the trio of chapters in which an awakened Meridian exercises her listening skills and we hear three women's voices that speak painfully of reproductive violence.[41] This second moment of connection is tightly and implicitly linked to the relationship with Lynne and the common bond of lost child by the chapter title, "Camara," the name of Lynne's murdered child, which seems at first to have nothing to do with the narrated events. The title's apparent disconnection from events complements the effect that Deborah McDowell has pointed out: *Camara*, as a written word, differs by just one vowel from *camera*, a machine suggesting Meridian's characteristically distanced perspective.[42] In the opening of the chapter, Meridian stands outside the strange church she has come to visit and watches the congregation gather "as if into an ageless photograph," and her initial stance as objectifying photographer rather than participant is reiterated: "And she . . . was not part of it . . . she sensed herself an outsider, as a single eye behind a camera that was aimed from a corner of her youth, attached now only because she watched. If she were not there watching the scene would be exactly the same" (193–4). The feeling of disconnection Meridian expresses here is that of the outside observer detached from a scene; it goes on without her and she cannot change it in any way. This is clearly not a position that acknowledges agency or fosters activism. It disavows the power to alter the world outside the self even as it posits a fragmented, easily dissolved self. In fact, however, Meridian is misreading the scene, as she soon learns, and she also mistakes the relationship between her self and the observed world. In the transformation she is about to experience, as she comprehends a change that has already taken place, it is not a question of whether the scene is the same—it is not—but of how and why she can begin to hear what is different.

It is important to trace in detail the nature and mode of the change that is recorded here, as Meridian moves toward a surprising reconnection with an institution she thought she had left behind long ago (just as she thought she had forgotten about the Native Americans). As so often in her adolescence, she enters the scene moving and acting out of motives unclear to herself. Her feelings of not knowing should by now tell us that something important is being concealed, and so potentially may be disclosed. She has come to a strange church, "perhaps" because of its particularly bright stained glass windows but really "for no reason she was sure of." Inside, she finds herself unable to remember the words to the hymn she hears. Suspicious of words, which have failed to recognize her feelings so often in the past, drawn instead by color and sound, she must consciously resist or defer finding what she was seeking in the very first chapter, the "something missing" in herself that she tried initially to locate in the memory of losing her mother's love. But now, "she did not want to find right then whatever it was she was looking for. She had no idea, really, what it was." This refusal of a particular kind of knowing—like falling asleep when Lynne tells her story—makes possible another kind of hearing and understanding. As the tune of the music changes to "a martial melody," Meridian begins to connect, not at first through words but through the aural, nonverbal experience of joining: "her consciousness was no longer led off after a vain search for words she could not recall, but began instead to slowly merge itself with the triumphant forcefulness of the oddly death-defying music" (195).

Displacing or putting on hold the quest for self and voice in order to feel connection and listen to others is the first step and privileged epistemological and linguistic mode here, as in the scene with Lynne. But this is not a story that celebrates remaining silent, outside language, dissociated, and powerless. Rather, it points to the possibility of collectively appropriating and reinventing discourse. Meridian quickly finds herself adding other words to the hymn, quoting Margaret Walker's "Let the martial songs be written," and it is through these new words authored by the black poet rather than simply through her own sensory intake that she is able to comprehend something that shocks her: the people and their music *have* changed. Listening to the sermon, she first thinks it is a mocking parody of Martin Luther King's style, another instance of tragic misappropriation and disconnection. But then she perceives it as a different mode of connecting with the history and meaning of King, a deliberate, death-defying performance, "keeping that voice alive" so that it can be heard over and over. The understanding of what has changed comes into focus, however, only when the "red-eyed" father of a young man martyred in the civil rights movement, a man who has passed through madness into resigned grief, stands up to speak. His words come through despite an almost paralyzing dissociation that helps him to survive, "from a throat that seemed stopped with anxiety, memory, grief and dope"; "in confusion, in loss," and "inarticulate grief," he utters three words that complete the process of changing Meridian's mind: "'My son died'"(198).

Meridian has hitherto seen the Black Church, like her mother, as a "reactionary power," but now she perceives that the son's death has finally evoked a new anger in the people, who vow to fight. As she "comprehends" this feeling, which touches on her reproductive consciousness of victimization and survival, Meridian's voice is liberated—"as if a tight string binding her lungs had given away"—from the lure of self-sacrifice and the desire to escape her body. As opposed to the pages of not knowing, not understanding, hesitating and wondering why, she "understood finally" that she will fight to live; and at that point she is able to join the congregation of strangers in making the promise to the red-eyed father that she couldn't make to her friends years before: "that yes, indeed she *would* kill, before she allowed anyone to murder his son again" (200).

This affirmation and resolution to preserve someone else's child is immediately qualified and cannot be assimilated into the standard moment of "self-discovery" or philosophical certainty that it has sometimes been taken to be. It is not a pledge to act as an individual self. Meridian adds that any murder she contemplates could only be undertaken in the context of a community aware of its history, "a church surrounded by the righteous guardians of the people's memories"; "only among the pious could this idea [of murder] both comfort and uplift" (200). Moreover, her dedication subsequently wavers; it is not a fixed point that she has reached. She sometimes thinks that she will never "belong to the future" and must "walk behind the real revolutionaries." At other times, however—notably those that situate her as an Othermother and connect to political activism—her commitment returns: "she needed only to see a starving child or attempt to register to vote a grown person who could neither read nor write" (201).

This moment of (partial) revolution, (sometime) change, and (ambivalent) transformation for Meridian is grounded in the story of losing a child, the disconnection between mother (and now father) and child that the novel relentlessly depicts and that Meridian, already disconnected from an unbearable reality, in some sense chooses for herself. In "Two Women," the loss of the known child brings the white and black mothers together. Then the even broader force of the politicized absent body of the child, now also the body of a grown son, is confirmed by the naming of the "Camara" chapter, where the utterly impersonal love of a stranger's dead child—the same kind of love that helped Meridian give away her child rather than murder him—has collective transformative power for Meridian and the Black Church as an institution. Through Meridian's resistance to the conventional prescriptions of motherhood and through her actions in the culturally traditional role of Othermother, the maternal position or subject has come to be understood in this novel as one that demands not only protection of the child but also recognition of the parent, who must survive to fight in a world where protection and recognition are not readily provided. It may be a position that a mother *with* child ironically cannot yet take, at least not unilaterally, because of the historical circumstances that make her solely responsible for her children (and hence so often doomed to maternal failure). Alone, Meridian cannot occupy this position until it is extended to and occupied by not only the father but also the larger community, who resolve to turn grief into anger, anger into action. The metaphor of detachment and one-way relations implicit in Meridian's initial sense of herself as the camera's eye is discarded, and the process of self-discovery and social change as we often see it is at once reversed and made reciprocal. The individual is changed by listening and hearing change in the impersonal, collective action of the community, as opposed to the hero leading the way to change. Meridian may remain outside and behind the community; where she goes after the novel remains unseen.

NOT A STORY TO PASS ON

Disremembered and unaccounted for, she cannot be lost because no one is looking for her, and even if they were, how can they call her if they don't know her name? Although she has claim, she is not claimed. . . .

> It was not a story to pass on. . . .
>
> So, in the end, they forgot her too. Remembering seemed unwise. . . .
>
> It was not a story to pass on. . . .
>
> So they forgot her. . . . They can touch it if they like, but don't, because they know things will never be the same if they do. . . .
>
> This is not a story to pass on.
>
> —*Beloved*

Perhaps the most provocative sentence in *Beloved* is repeated, in one of two variants, three times on the last two pages of the novel: "It was/This is not a story to pass on." Almost everyone who writes and speaks about this novel speculates about the meaning of such a puzzling and ambiguous refrain. Does "pass on" mean transmit, as would seem likely if we are speaking about stories, or "die"? Or, if the stress is on the first word rather than the second, might it also mean "pass on" in the sense of passing judgment? Or could it mean to pull back from engagement, or forget (as in "I'll pass on this one" said while playing poker or refusing a proffered edible)? Many readers have spoken to the first sense of "pass on," even if they acknowledge the other possibilities, and have wondered about the apparent paradox. If the purpose of the story we have read is to remember Beloved (in multiple senses of the word "remember"), why does the novel end with an emphasis on the wisdom of forgetting her? In the third and final iteration, "This is not a story to pass on," the shift from past to present tense and the deictic "this" as opposed to the impersonal "it" anchors us in the narrator's present time and perspective, suggesting that a kind of community and closure has been attained, but doesn't the sentence also enjoin us as members of that community not to do what the novel as a whole and many characters within it have just done? Does the narrator feel guilty for her "complicity" in the act of writing itself, which is arguably a crime of violence against "the mother tongue," and does she "metaphorically slit her own throat" with this statement, as Lorraine Liscio has suggested?[43] Or is it the preoedipal daughter who has been done violence, who "remains outside language and therefore outside narrative memory," even as she "continues to haunt the borders," as Jean Wyatt observes?[44] Let me add yet another possibility to the accumulating commentary on this crux, one that is informed by and hence requires further elaboration of my proposal that both *Beloved* and *Meridian* belong to the literature of trauma and recovery.

According to only recently codified medical definitions, trauma is "an event that is outside the range of usual human experience and that would be markedly distressing to almost anyone"; it entails "a sudden extreme discontinuity in a person's experience."[45] As Judith Herman points out in her study *Trauma and Recovery,* the psychological and public awareness of trauma has an "episodic" history in the last one hundred years. Herman identifies three "waves" of concern with three varieties or manifestations of trauma: hysteria, combat neuroses, and, only recently, sexual and domestic violence. All three syndromes are "one thing," Herman argues, but in each case the systematic study of a particular kind of traumatic experience "depends on the support of a political movement."[46] Her particular concern with rape and domestic violence is made possible by the second wave of feminism. Herman notes that, though psychological aspects of this kind of trauma are consistent with others, the high incidence of sexual abuse challenges the standing definition of trauma as "outside the range of usual human experience."[47] She is also interested in treatment of post-traumatic stress disorder and posits four main components to psychological recovery: a healing relationship (by which she means a relationship with a well-trained therapist); safety; remembrance and mourning, wherein the goal is to reconstruct the trauma, not forget or "exorcise" it; and reconnection with persons or groups, where the goal is to restore the victim's belief that human relationships can be trusted.

In her introduction to a recent journal issue on trauma (brought to my attention by a footnote in Wyatt's essay), Cathy Caruth focuses on a paradox that further problematizes the task of reconstructing trauma. As experienced by survivors, traumatic events belong to what Caruth describes as "a past that was never fully experienced as it occurred"; dissociation, as I have noted, is the main defense against fear, pain, and loss of control during trauma, and hence perception and memory are often distorted. After the traumatic experience is over, it usually remains "inaccessible to conscious recall and control" and comes back in flashbacks and nightmares.[48] Amnesia may coexist with these constant intrusions of traumatic past events, and it has been suggested that the very strength and precision of the involuntary, often disabling recollection derives from the fact that the event has not been "encoded" in normal ways. Herman makes this point too, noting that trauma memories "lack verbal narrative and context," are fragmentary, and are often remembered "in the form of vivid sensations and images."[49] Psychologists stress the difficulty that this causes for recovery, delaying "the necessary working through and putting into perspective" of trauma.[50] Caruth, however, foregrounds an epistemological and historiographical dimension to the problem: the traumatic "event" is in effect a paradox, both true and incomprehensible; trauma "both urgently demands historical awareness and yet denies our usual modes of access to it." Caruth asks, "How is it possible . . . to gain access to a traumatic history?"[51] To be healed, the "patient" suffering from posttraumatic stress disorder needs to verbalize, integrate, and communicate the past in narrative and memory, but in the very act of doing so there is further loss, in at least two senses: the details are often forgotten, rearranged, or blurred (an effect of "putting into perspective"), and the power of the trauma as "affront to understanding" may be, perhaps must be, weakened.[52]

This paradox is expressed at the end of *Beloved* in the refrain: "This is not a story to pass on." The trauma the novel seeks to reconstruct cannot be conveyed, handed down, or judged in conventional ways, but it must not die or be forgotten. To verbalize and transmit it as story, as cohesive and coherent narrative, is to change things as they were, perhaps to make them knowable and bearable but thereby to falsify what was, and should be remembered as, irrational and intolerable about the experience. A case study from the founding theorist of dissociation, Pierre Janet, exemplifies this problem in a way that tellingly links it to the particular trauma that *Beloved* and *Meridian* confront. Janet cites the instance of a patient named Irene, a thirty-one-year-old woman who lost two infants and was subsequently haunted by images of death. Janet treated her with a hypnotic suggestion that enabled her to replace the images of death with images of flowers, and cured, she became a midwife. As B. A. van der Kolk and Onno van der Hart observe, this therapy is effective, but isn't it also a "sacrilege"?[53] It may be better for individuals to forget, but is there a way to register the truth and to survive with what you lose (as Jane Rule's character understands), to avoid losing again what was lost before? As Herman points out and as recent discussions of the Holocaust confirm, the history of trauma study would suggest that it is all too easy to forget or deny that atrocities "really happened."

Caruth cites another possibility for transmitting "the historical truth" of trauma, one that honors "the refusal of a certain framework of understanding" that trauma entails and is resistant to "the platitudes of knowledge" that would diminish the horror and forget the loss. Instead of requiring knowledge in a conventional sense of the term, this strategy calls for "a creative act of listening" to speech that exceeds understanding, listening that "opens up the space for a testimony that can speak beyond what is already understood." This "difficult task . . . of historical listening," this "attempt to gain access to a traumatic history," is also, Caruth says, "the project of hearing beyond individual suffering, to the reality of a history that in its crisis can only be perceived in unassimilable forms."[54] This is not, again, a story to pass on.[55]

Most psychological research on trauma has treated victims of either natural calamity or acts of human violence such as war, torture, rape, and domestic abuse. Morrison's and Walker's novels add black motherhood to the list of atrocities that demand and challenge remembrance, mourning, and reconnection, and as novels they represent the possibility of a safe space and healing relationship within which the work of recovery in two senses of the word—retrieval of the story and healing of the victims—can take place. It is perhaps hardly newsworthy and certainly not difficult to justify this claim for *Beloved*. Morrison's novel obviously presents infanticide as a traumatic experience, a rare event of sudden discontinuity that is unusually distressing. It also confounds our knowledge of who is victim and who is victimizer in the particular trauma of Beloved's death and resurrection (Sethe and Beloved occupy both positions with regard to each other) in order to indict the true perpetrator of the larger, collective trauma that is responsible for the discontinuity of black motherhood: the white slave owner and the system that legitimates his violence (with regard to which Sethe and Beloved are both victims). The trauma of Sethe in captivity reenters the narrative present in a way that registers both necessary forgetting and "abnormal" modes of remembering, here in the form of the ghost story. Beloved herself represents precisely the kind of "reenactment" of trauma, including particularly its nonverbal encoding in sensations and images, that as Herman points out can be both adaptive and dangerous.[56]

I suggest that it is equally if not more important to locate *Meridian* in the literature of trauma and recovery and thus to resist assimilating Meridian's giving up of her child into the familiar narrative of the feminist bildungsroman. It might be argued that I stretch the word *trauma* too far in applying it to Meridian's maternal experience: her unhappiness as a mother, though it contradicts myths of maternal instinct, is hardly a rare phenomenon "outside the range of usual human experience"; few people would agree that giving a child up to responsible, loving adoptive parents is always a "markedly distressing" thing; and the "discontinuity" Meridian feels is more extreme before rather than after she gives her son away. But this is just the kind of stretching that the novel urges us to do. Meridian as mother without child can in fact be seen as a composite figure of the trauma victim, the post-traumatic survivor, and the creative listener and witness who forms an alliance with other victims.

Trauma is reconstructed in *Meridian,* as in *Beloved,* in a way that honors its abnormal encoding in fragments that resist linear narration and mark instead dissociation and disconnection: the form of the crazy quilt, which at once serves to mimic and integrate or reconstruct the psychological effects of trauma. In this form, *Meridian* initially contextualizes the heroine's act in a representation of the southern black woman's reproductive consciousness as collective trauma, not a single event but a communal and ongoing set of historical circumstances that begin with captivity, comprise innumerable stories as "bad" as Sethe's, and do not end with emancipation. Taking us beyond the pathology of "individual suffering," this mother without child is embedded in the history of all black mothers who could not "claim" their children. Meridian's personal experience as an adolescent girl in an age of choice also bears these characteristic marks of trauma, dissociation, and disconnection. Her recovery draws on the more positive or adaptive aspects of dissociation—defense and resistance—and reconnects her to other women and to the community. In this process of reconnection, however, Meridian participates not as victim—a position she rejects—but as a model of alternative, nonprocreative maternal force and "creative listening." Drawing on the "good qualities" of her maternal heritage, she serves as Othermother to children who are not her own, educating and defending the living while witnessing and politicizing the dead. She serves as addressee so that Miss Treasure and the girl in prison can be speakers, and she responds to their crises of motherhood with action where possible, with empathy where there is no hope. In what I have called a kind of conditional listening, "as if" in an altered state of consciousness, she is able to hear (or let us hear) what she consciously doesn't want to know: the story of Lynne's rape, which acknowledges the common vulnerability of women to male violence and complicates questions of racial identity and responsibility. This is a model of what it might mean to be a "creative" listener to speech that is difficult to hear, perceived in ways that in some sense preserve its "unassimilable" form. Her position as reverberant listener reaches its acme in the Black Church, where she is able to hear and then join with a community of victims and witnesses connected by trauma: "the years in America had created them One life." The change in this community from resignation and forgetting to potential recovery through remembrance, mourning, and anger is made possible by a political movement and energized by the "survivor mission," to borrow Herman's phrase, that Meridian accepts: "to continue, against whatever obstacles, to live" and to make that inconstant, collective promise that "she *would* kill, before she allowed anyone to murder his son again" (200).

The history of black motherhood told in *Meridian* and *Beloved* is and should remain an "affront" to our normal ways of thinking and knowing, revising many of our conventional "platitudes," especially about maternal subjects, maternal instincts, and maternal rights and duties. Taken in tandem, the content of these narratives ranges from and thereby links the slave mother's infanticide, an unquestionably complex traumatic event, and the relatively common occurrence of giving up a child for adoption in an age of "freedom" and "choice." Neither story can or should be fully absorbed into our ordinary ways of seeing. There is little risk that *Beloved,* told the way it is, will be. But so too Meridian needs to be claimed in our readings as a type of the impossible figure of the mother without child, not assimilated, as her story so easily can be, into a framework that either cuts her off from her traumatic maternal heritage or assumes the separation and incompatibility of selfhood and motherhood.

Four

What If Your Mother Never Meant to?
The Novels of Louise Erdrich and Michael Dorris

> No matter how we strain to decipher the sound it never quite
> makes sense, never relieves our certainty or our suspicion that
> there is more to be told, more than we know, more than can
> be caught in the sieve of our thinking.
> —Louise Erdrich, *The Bingo Palace*

Following in the footsteps of her father and her paternal grandmother, Meridian Hill taps into the power of Native American traditions when she has her first ecstatic out-of-body experience in the Serpent Mound, an ancient Cherokee burial ground. Mr. Hill is obsessed not with the collective trauma of his own enslaved ancestors but with the injustice done by Euroamerican conquest and settlement to the people who already inhabited the New World. As Meridian discovers through a dream, his outrage is a legacy that she carries with her into the civil rights movement. The rarely explored connection between African Americans and Native Americans as both victims and survivors of American history, only alluded to in Walker's novel, becomes more apparent when we consider the crisis of motherhood in both subcultures.

A familiar image of the Native American mother appears in the photograph that young Meridian sees on the wall of her father's shed, "a frozen Indian child (whose mother lay beside her in a bloody heap)" (*Meridian*, 53). Interrupted as she reaches out to touch the photograph, Meridian runs away from both the sight of her father's tears and their cause: the history of murdered Native American mothers and the children they cannot protect and nurture. The Native American mother, in *Meridian* as in most discourses, remains in parentheses. But we can revisit that photograph and remove the parentheses by turning to the recent fiction of Louise Erdrich and Michael Dorris, where women very much like Meridian and her foremothers—women who lose or surrender their children—abound. Many of these Native American mothers are only a little more clearly and fully seen than the mother in Mr. Hill's photograph, but, read in light of my project as a whole, they confirm and extend what *Meridian* suggests about the function and meaning of the mother without child.

THE POCAHONTAS PERPLEX

That women mother in a variety of societies is not as significant as the *value* attached to mothering in these societies. The distinction between the act of mothering and the status attached to it is a very important one—one that needs to be made and analyzed contextually.
—Chandra Talpade Mohanty,
"Under Western Eyes: Feminist
Scholarship and Colonial Discourses"

Recent scholarship by and about women of Native American heritage suggests that their place in what was once a large number of societies has been misunderstood by European colonists and their descendants. Rayna Green proposes that in commonly accepted accounts of Native American women over the course of the last five hundred years, women have not been forgotten but remembered in selective and damaging ways that add up to what she calls "the Pocahontas perplex: Indian women have to be exotic, wild, collaborationist, crazy, or 'white' to qualify for white attention." In the earliest period of contact, according to Green, "distant princesses were acceptable, but matriarchal, matrifocal, and matrilineal societies were neither acceptable nor comprehensible to members of European patriarchies."[1] More recently, Green observes, studies have tended to be interested less in the romance and more in the pathology of Native American women, seen as emblems of a dying culture.

Paula Gunn Allen has insisted that although the power of women in most gynocratic precontact cultures was rooted in their bodily reproductive function, motherhood was also understood in many Native American tribes as a spiritual and social condition separable from biological identity or sexual behavior—like the "nonprocreative motherhood" we see in Rule's fiction or in Meridian's "Othermothering"—and associated with intellectual and verbal powers, with thinking and creativity. "The status of mother was so high that in some cultures Mother or its analog, Matron, was the highest office to which a man or woman could aspire," Allen claims. Women who did not have children were not excluded from power but "had other ways to experience Spirit instruction and stabilization, to exercise power, and to be mothers."[2] They were also embedded in cultures where, traditionally, care and responsibility for children was dispersed and collective, and so again the link between biological procreation and mothering work was looser. Among the Crow, Brooke Medicine Eagle notes, "There is a beautiful and very functional tradition. When a person has no children, then all the children are their children."[3]

Late-twentieth-century feminism, Allen and others have suggested, needs to recognize its connection with and roots in the gynocratic tribes and principles of precontact cultures. As Kate Shanley puts it, the nuclear family and the "American lifestyle" that white middle-class women are fighting against today has not been adopted by many Native American communities. In fact, she argues, "In many ways, mainstream feminists now are striving to redefine family and community in a way that Indian women have long known."[4] So, too, Beth Brant suggests that while Native American women have been ignored by mainstream feminists, they have "for centuries" been doing what feminists do:

> We are angry at a so-called "women's movement" that always seems to forget we exist. Except in romantic fantasies of earth mother, or equally romantic and dangerous fantasies about Indian-woman-as-victim. Women lament our *lack* of participation in feminist events, yet we are either referred to as *etceteras* in the naming of women of color, or simply not referred to at all. *We are not victims.* We are organizers, we are freedom fighters, we are feminists, we are healers. This is not anything new. For centuries it has been so.[5]

Just as African American women scholars have pointed to the inappropriateness of judging black motherhood by white models, writers like Allen, Shanley, and Brant suggest that Native American women don't need to be liberated because they have not been oppressed in the same way that Euroamerican women have. We will want to be cautious about assuming that Native American mothers feel the need to be relieved of either the burdens of child care or the dominant myths of motherhood in order to develop the kind of autonomous selfhood or freedom from the oppressions of femininity that mainstream Euroamerican culture—along with many of its feminist critics—valorizes.[6]

Arguments emphasizing the ongoing, culturally specific presence and importance of Native American mothers and childrearing traditions may counter the tendency to reify, romanticize, and possibly overstate the case of the vanishing American Indian, male or female. At the same time, they do not mitigate but instead deepen the enormity of an historical reality: despite the spiritual power and communal face of motherhood in indigenous myths and norms, despite the social and political status of women in contemporary tribal affairs, generations of mothers descended from and in some cases still participating in Native American societies have had their children taken from them, along with all the other things they need and value. As lesbians have been denied legal custody of their children, as slave mothers watched theirs sold by their owners, so too Native American mothers have lost children to disease, to boarding school, and to adoption, so that here again the figure of the mother without child is more likely to represent the historical norm rather than the exception. And again the problem goes beyond the pathos of individual losses to systemic injustices that persist into the present time. As Louis Owens points out, "On reservations today, more than 90 percent of Native American children up for adoption are adopted into non-Indian families, an institutionalized 'mainstreaming' of Indian children into Euroamerica that results in widespread loss of cultural identity as well as a feeling by Indian people that their children are being systematically stolen away."[7] Patricia Hill Collins, seeing this as one dimension of the widespread crisis of maternal empowerment for women of color, also argues that "physical or psychological separation of mothers and children designed to disempower racial ethnic individuals forms the basis of a systematic effort to disempower their communities."[8]

Until very recently, an increasingly recognized and growing body of contemporary fiction written by and about various Native American people has focused on the traumatic history of deculturation in which the mother appears as victim of the colonizer's efforts to disempower native cultures. Like most scholarly approaches, these novels exemplify Green's "Pocahontas perplex" in their obsession with the painful pathology of absent mothers and lost or orphaned children in twentieth-century Native American life.[9] In many versions of the same story, the mother stands for a lost past of harmony with nature and tribal wholeness. Native Americans are abandoned by the Mother Earth who once protected them, and their children are seen, as in the final dream vision of James Welch's novel, *Fools Crow,* standing alone, without mothers or fathers, outside a circle of happy white children. In other novels of the so-called Native American Renaissance, the image varies only to admit a more complicated narrative about broken homes, homeless men, lost children, and the dead mother or absent maternal function.

Much of the fiction written as recently as the mid-eighties contains two specific versions of the figure of the Native American mother without child. In the first version, she is a secondary female character who would mother if she could, but either her biological children (usually male) are killed by forces associated with white domination or she has lost most or all of her "native" maternal powers, including her childbearing capacity. In Leslie Marmon Silko's *Ceremony,* Tayo's surrogate mother, Auntie, is one good example of this kind of mother; in Welch's *The Death of Jim Loney,* Jim's successful, childless sister Kate, in very different ways, might be another. A second version of the mother without child overlaps the first in presuming the fundamental absence of maternal function. In several of these latter instances, a birth mother is either dead or as good as dead, missing from the main narrative and the waking lives of its characters yet often appearing as a nameless figure who intrudes, like unassimilated trauma, in dream or flashback. She is consciously remembered only as a crazed victim, who has abandoned her child or children as well as her culture. She may have done so in a desperate attempt to save her victimized self or even her child, but we cannot know this, because her story is as lost to memory and verbal representation as she is lost to her family and her people. Jim Loney's absent, probably institutionalized mother, Eleta, and the dead, unnamed woman who bore and then abandoned Tayo are just two of the many examples that might be cited.

Judith Antell has discussed in detail this absence of "the loving Indian mother as a significant literary character" in novels where all the heroes lack mothers, suffer deeply, and may even die from endemic maternal deprivation.[10] As Antell points out, the figure Jim Loney meets in a central dream vision without knowing who she is might speak for these elusive Native American mothers when she describes herself as "a Mother who is no longer a mother."[11] To account for what she sees as this "truly disturbing figure" of the dead or otherwise absent mother, Antell offers interesting suggestions. As she sees it, Native American men as fictive protagonists may serve as more "tragic" figures than their female counterparts because their traditional function has been more completely destroyed. They represent more clearly the defeat of what "white America" sees as most threatening in Native American culture, and so at the same time their alienation is more comforting to the dominant culture. Often thought to represent continuity rather than tragic disruption of traditional ways, Native American women are more easily "discounted," in Antell's view, by the "colonial scenario," the male-dominated Euroamerican cultural tradition within which to varying degrees these novels are written. But implicitly agreeing with Allen that many traditional Native American cultures centered on the figure of the mother, Antell argues that these novelists in fact also record the importance of "the feminine principle"—entailing survival, continuity, healing, and ritual transmission of the culture—by dramatizing the suffering of a male protagonist in his alienation from the mother; she points out that the plots of these novels often entail reunification with the feminine and maternal after ritual healing.[12] In light of the recent work by Green, Brant, and many others, we might worry, however, that the repeated fictional picture of the absent (Native American) mother serves less to celebrate than to limit or distort woman's traditional power and obscure her active presence.

In the last decade, the publication of Louise Erdrich and Michael Dorris's fiction has foregrounded and complicated the representation of Native American motherhood.[13] Most obviously, their stories challenge both the homogenization and the erasure of these women, so that what we may think of as "Native American literature" can no longer be said to reify either woman-as-absent-mother or "the feminine principle" in quite the same way. Although there are significant numbers of abandoned children and dead or maimed mothers in Erdrich and Dorris's fiction, at last there are also complex, fully present female characters and narrators, some of whom are even nurturant and devoted mothers. In her first novel, as Robert Silberman has noted in an essay subtitled "*Love Medicine* and the Return of the Native American Woman," Erdrich "takes apart and puts back together the traditional narrative" of the alienated Native American male.[14] Reversing the familiar trajectory, the story begins rather than ends with the death of June, whom Silberman and many other readers see as the central figure of the book. June, like earlier fictional mothers, may be dead, but her "sadness" lives on, not unconscious or repressed but a "fundamental subtext." With more particular attention to the question of Native

American mothers, Hertha D. Wong has also pointed out that mothers and mothering relationships are prevalent in *Love Medicine* and the next two novels Erdrich published, *The Beet Queen* and *Tracks*. Wong suggests that these novels represent the realistic plight of the Native American woman, unable to sustain bonds or protect and nurture children, after conquest and defeat of the culture. For the most part, she argues, Erdrich's mothers are what I would call mothers without child, "strained" and "troubled" figures.[15] Wong suggests that this reflects the cultural alienation of the entire Native American community; under the circumstances of white conquest and reservation life, "abandoning one's child is not an act of selfishness; it is an act of despair or an act of desperate mercy."[16] Wong observes that the novels also represent the survival of the long-standing custom of sharing mothering among other members of a clan. On the reservation at least, someone cares for abandoned children, and the hope of the future, in Wong's view, are these "thrown away" children and the mothers who adopt them.

With the recent publication of the much-anticipated fourth novel in the tetralogy, *The Bingo Palace,* the subject of mothers and mothering in Erdrich and Dorris's fiction becomes even more prominent and difficult. This latest novel brings back June Morrisey (from *Love Medicine*) as a ghost and Fleur Pillager (from *Tracks*) as a trickster and wise woman living once more on the margins of the reservation and pushing even harder against the limits of realism. It is strikingly clear that neither June's death nor her abandonment of her son Lipsha has been fully exorcised, as readers may have logically but erroneously assumed, and that the representation of mothers and the value of mothering exceeds, although it by no means ignores, the demands of a realistic picture of either cultural alienation or the resources of collective child care. In retrospect, it is evident that Erdrich and Dorris's novels to date consistently engage the possibility of recovering the role of the mother and revaluing the status and power of Native American women. At the same time, however, haunting figures of the mother without child become *more* rather than less disturbing in successive narratives. In what follows, I trace in detail this increasingly vexed figure of the mother without child, which I understand to be a centripetal force, an insistent goad to storytelling, and a key to reading five collaboratively written novels—the four published under Erdrich's name and Dorris's *Yellow Raft on Blue Water*.

My efforts to track this one motif throughout several novels may at points run counter to what I see as the best work to date on this fiction, which has stressed Erdrich and Dorris's innovative and powerful use of multiple voices, fragmented plots, and inconclusive, ambivalent, and pluralized themes.[17] There are many other ways to approach and make sense of these five books, individually and collectively, and I hope that concern for this one thread (admittedly, in my view, the most vital one) in a complex pattern is not construed as a quest for the single or definitive key to their meaning. Taking a cue from the collective, communal, and metafictionally engaged "we" narrating parts of *The Bingo Palace*, it may be appropriate to claim an urge to interpret that, like an urge to tell, can separate the quest to know from a guarantee of security or certain discovery: "We were curious to know more, even though we'd never grasp the whole of it. The story comes around, pushing at our brains, and soon we are trying to ravel back to the beginning, trying to put families into order and make sense of things. But we start with one person, and soon another and another follows, until we are lost in the connections."[18]

The mother without child is the salient figure in these novels because she stands at the critical point where connections are inevitably sought, and she represents the epistemological possibility of a difficult, limited, entangled knowing that acknowledges loss. Like *Meridian* and *Beloved,* these are novels of trauma and recovery, and "this is not a story to pass on." I try to "make sense of things" by constructing a trajectory leading from the earlier novels up to *The Bingo Palace*. Throughout, the appearance of the mother without child, realized with variation and constant revision as Ida George, June Morrisey, Adelaide Adare, Pauline Puyat, and Fleur Pillager, manifests both the inevitable, imaginative raveling back and the impossibility of grasping the whole of it. Read in a certain sequence, these novels increasingly discover that (Native American) mothers cannot be recovered or remembered in narrative as a fixed origin. Like the figures of maternal trauma in Alice Walker's and Toni Morrison's fiction, they are not so much memorials to lost plenitude as elusive points of a persistent presence and connection. The mother without child motivates the quest to know yet is always perceived in unassimilable forms, disruptive to rational ways of understanding the past and everyday notions of making sense. Focusing on this figure concomitantly suggests and accounts for a generic drift in these postmodern Native American novels from the mystery story to the ghost story.

I AM THE STORY: *YELLOW RAFT ON BLUE WATER* AND *LOVE MEDICINE*

> At Laguna Pueblo in New Mexico, "Who is your mother?" is an
> important question. . . . Of course, your mother is not only that
> woman whose womb formed and released you—the term refers
> in every individual case to an entire generation of women whose
> psychic, and consequently physical, "shape" made the psychic
> existence of the following generation possible. But naming your
> own mother (or her equivalent) enables people to place you
> precisely within the universal web of your life. . . . Failure to
> know your mother, that is, your position and its attendant
> traditions, history, and place in the scheme of things, is failure to
> remember your significance, your reality, your right relationship
> to earth and society. It is the same as being lost—isolated,
> abandoned, self-estranged, and alienated from your own life.
> —Paula Gunn Allen, *The Sacred Hoop*

In both *Yellow Raft on Blue Water* (1987) and *Love Medicine* (1984),
the paradoxically absent center of much previous Native American fiction, the mother, is brought to life and to diffuse, decentered narrative
presence.[19] What was a seemingly inevitable and monotonous story of
maternal abandonment turns out to be the primary subject of variation
and revision. It is misleading to speak of *the* plot in these fragmentary,
nonlinear, multiply told narratives, formally analogous in ways to the
"crazy quilt" of *Meridian*. But it is fair to say that as novels these texts
cohere around the quest to know mothers' true stories—already "we
are trying to ravel back to the beginning," where the beginning is apparently both cultural or historical (the social, the past) and psychological (the personal, the unconscious, the preoedipal). As this difficult,
elusive knowledge is pursued—and to varying degrees attained—in the
course of the storytelling, a child's perspective on the mother is frequently corrected. As the trauma of Native American experience is revisited, the fact or perception of abandonment may not be completely
erased and the mother may still be dead or dying, but the story is never
what the abandoned child originally assumed it to be. Directly or indirectly, the woman known as mother may be understood and forgiven,
if not in all cases fully recovered *as* mother. What links these two novels, then, is their seeming optimism about understanding and coming
to terms with lost connections and their common equation of storytelling that is culturally and personally empowering with rediscovered
and revalued matrilineage.

Although published three years after *Love Medicine* (and one year after *The Beet Queen*), *Yellow Raft* serves to introduce this perspective more directly and single-mindedly. The novel structurally as well as thematically foregrounds both the difficulty and traditional importance of knowing who your mother is and why she acts as she does. It comprises three distinct but overlapping first-person narratives, presented in reverse chronological order—moving from youngest to oldest speaker and hence in part from present to past—by three generations of women: Rayona, a biracial teenager; Christine, her Native American mother; and Ida, Christine's mother. Although fragmented and overlaid, the pieces are clearly connected by their presentation in novel form into something like the clinical tool known as a genogram, one story about matrilineage that situates individual mothers in wider contexts and understands them as having other lives, beyond the maternal function.[20] As genogram, the narrative is full of secrets and surprises for the daughters, Ray and Christine, each of whom misunderstands her mother's history, behavior, and feelings. Even as the story moves backward in time and maternal generations, it also looks forward to newly discovered truth about mothers' love, more complex notions of maternal experience, and the heightened possibility of (re)connection between the persons and positions of daughter and mother. Most notably, for my purposes, what looks like the problem of maternal abandonment in each of the first two sections turns out to be something different, and the daughters, first Ray and then Christine, move in their respective sections as readers move in the novel as a whole: from misreading and mistrust to fuller and more accurate understanding of the complexity of the woman who has apparently abandoned her child. This prepares the way for the final narrative, where one mother without child speaks.

At the outset of the novel, in Rayona's section, the first misreading of the often disguised and disingenuous mother establishes the basic pattern of each segment and the overall narrative. The story opens in an Indian Health Service hospital in Seattle where the teenaged narrator is playing cards with her sick mother, Christine. Although she is losing, bored, and eager to leave, Ray is reluctant to go home to the empty apartment she and her mother share. Loitering around the hospital and then walking slowly to the bus stop, Rayona comes upon what she thinks is a "fat candy striper" trying to steal her mother's aging Volare from the parking lot. Determined to stop the theft, she rushes to the attack, only to discover that the thief is none other than Mom herself, who escaped from the hospital in a stolen uniform and intends to drive her car off a cliff so that Ray can collect the insurance money. This is a variation on a recurring theme of maternal abandonment rewritten as maternal sacrifice, seen first in *Love Medicine* when King Jr. buys a car with the insurance money from his mother June's death, which was perhaps suicide. Completely baffled in this instance by her mother's bizarre behavior but stubbornly clinging to her, Ray refuses to let Christine go alone, and then the plan is foiled when the car runs out of gas. Having failed to commit suicide, Christine decides to take Ray back to the reservation in Montana, where she abruptly deposits her in the care of Christine's mother, "Aunt Ida," and disappears.

What Ray can see only as her mother's sudden and inexplicable act of abandonment turns out to be something else. In the second part of the novel, Christine is the new first-person narrator who reveals what neither readers nor Ray previously knew: the IHS doctor has just told Christine that she has six months to live. In increasing pain, afraid to tell Ray that she is dying, and deeply worried about her daughter's future, Christine brings her to Ida because she is the only person who might care for the girl after Christine dies. In this section of the narrative, we learn how wrong Ray is to doubt the strength of her mother's love for her. Although she has not always provided Ray with the material and emotional stability assumed in dominant models to be the best environment for child development, Christine views her daughter and her own motherhood as the only good things in her life, as sources of identity and compensation for the failure of other female roles and familial connections: "I was nobody's regular daughter, nobody's sister, usually nobody's wife, but I was her mother full time" (222).[21]

We go on to discover that Christine herself, as daughter, misreads *her* mother. She believes that Ida never wanted her and always loved her less than she loved Christine's younger brother, Lee, who is now dead. But in Ida's section, the third and in some ways most important story is told. Christine's reading of her disguised mother, like Ray's, turns out to be another oversimplification of the story, flawed by vital, missing information and a foundational lie about biological maternity. Ida reveals that she is in fact Christine's cousin and half-sister, not her birth mother. Christine's birth parents were Ida's young aunt, Clara, and Ida's father, who impregnated Clara during Ida's mother's illness. To keep the scandal quiet, the family asked Ida to pretend that she was the pregnant one; Ida and Clara were sent to a convent in Denver where

Clara bore the child and wanted to give her up for adoption. Young Ida resisted Clara's plan and took the newborn Christine back to the reservation, where she brought her up as her own child (and again had to outwit Clara when she came back, when Christine was four, and tried to reclaim her daughter).

Christine's feelings of rejection reflect an even more complicated mix than Rayona's of the misunderstandings and realities surrounding the mother's story. The woman Christine thought was a bad birth mother turns out to be a good enough adoptive mother, yet Christine *was* abandoned by the woman who bore her. The novel thus validates the oft-noted collectivity of mothering in Native American groups without sentimentalizing or oversimplifying the social or psychic difficulties of this practice, in postcontact times, for both the child and the Othermother. Ida's insistence that Christine call her "Aunt Ida" rather than "Mother" enunciates deeper, conflicting truths. Christine assumed, like other people, that Ida wanted to be known as "Aunt" because she was ashamed, but in fact what was perceived as a lie and mark of rejection ironically reveals the secret Ida otherwise refuses to tell, except finally in the narrative addressed to readers of the novel. And Ida's reason for insisting on being called "Aunt" turns out to be a form of self-defense against her well-grounded fear of losing Christine to her biological mother. Suggesting what we have seen in earlier chapters and what we shall see again throughout Erdrich's tetralogy as the possibility of resistance inherent in the figure of the mother without child, Ida self-consciously adopts the name of Aunt rather than Mother as a kind of self-inflicted torture to toughen her self, ironically made vulnerable and connected by maternal work, against the constant threat of loss: "And every time she said it, the feelings for her I couldn't help, the feelings that came from being the one she came to when she was hurt and the one who heard her prayers, the feelings I fought against, got flaked away. That was as I intended. Someday Clara would arrive at the door and might steal Christine back" (325).

Both maternal concern and fear of loss are at the center of each mother's tangled story. Motherhood, the novel implies, can be comprehended only as a highly complicated narrative, told from sometimes conflicting, sometimes overlapping perspectives, full of selective recall and secrets that are perceived as necessary and strategic in situations where women are at once highly vulnerable to loss and all too aware of both the value and risks of holding on to a child. Conversely, narrative is driven by the need to know, and repeatedly, the daughter's misunderstanding of who her mother is, what she feels, why she does what she does, is to some extent corrected. Collectively, the stories not only revise what individual daughters think they know about their mothers, but also rewrite several dominant myths about motherhood. For example, *Yellow Raft* debunks the notion that mothers are the only influence that determines the identity of children. Important as the bond between mother and daughter is in each woman's life, these stories also speak repeatedly to the limits of the mother's power and the impact of other psychological, social, and political forces. Relations with peers and siblings, for instance, are especially critical to the development of a gendered identity, as we learn from the role of her brother Lee (Ida's biological son) in Christine's story. In Rayona's case, the absent father of another race is a fact to be reckoned with.

Similarly, these maternal revelations call into question the association of motherhood with women's lack of volition. Until recent technology brought us to the so-called age of choice, women were assumed to have little control over their procreative lives. Both Ida and Christine, however, stress the fact that they *chose* to become mothers, and in a world where they otherwise have little control, motherhood is a clear source and proof of identity and agency. The power to choose is also demonstrated by decisions *not* to mother: Christine refuses to have a second child because she fears that Ray would feel "out in the cold" (232), as she did when her brother Lee was born. Sara Ruddick has recently argued that the first step in reconceiving childbirth in a "respectful" way is "to represent birth as a chosen activity requiring commitment and responsibility." As Ruddick adds, "In current political conditions . . . it is an anticipatory utopian act even to begin to represent birth as a chosen activity."[22]

Yellow Raft is not utopian fiction; Ida remains an isolated, somewhat resentful woman, and Christine will soon die, perhaps without even knowing what readers know about her biological mother. (The only follow-up to the story so far comes in *The Bingo Palace*, where there is an allusion to the lavish memorial dance a woman named Ida sponsors in memory of her dead daughter.) But the novel is nevertheless optimistic: Ray, half Native American and half African American, is conspicuously presented as the hope of the future.[23] Not only is she smart and brave and probably luckier than Christine and Ida, but she is potential heir, at last, to the story never before heard, the story that

Ida as the first woman "carries." As Ida announces at the beginning of her section, third and last in the novel:

> I have to tell this story every day, add to it, revise, invent the parts I forget or never knew. No one but me carries it all and no one will— unless I tell Rayona, who might understand. She's heard her mother's side, and she's got eyes. But she doesn't guess what happened before. She doesn't know my true importance. She doesn't realize that I am the story, and that is my savings, to leave her or not.[24]

Lacking either a vital traditional community or a viable place in mainstream culture, Native American mothers in this story give voice to their worries about finding or constructing an inheritance for their children. Yet there is a growing richness and indigenous, self-reflective, and self-constructive quality to the things Christine and then Ida decide to leave to Ray. At first Christine suggests that two rented video tapes will serve as her legacy to Rayona, but later proposes to leave her a silver ring in the shape of a turtle, valued as a symbol of her self: "'He always reminded me of me,'" Christine tells Ray; "'Slow but gets there in the end'" (292). Ida's even more valorized and essential bequest (which she may or may not choose to make) is her story, at once answering and complicating the question, "Who is your mother?" Her claim that the narrative of her life is the most valuable heritage she can pass on to Ray is in keeping with the fundamental importance of storytelling and the Grandmother or Spiderwoman figure in so many Native American myths and ritual practices. Louis Owens argues for the power of resistance inherent in this figure: "Ida becomes a storyteller, like Nanapush in *Tracks,* the grandmother in *Winter in the Blood,* or Francisco in *House Made of Dawn,* the bearer of the identity and order that are so fragile they may perish in a single generation if unarticulated. With Ida resides the power to abrogate the authority of that 'other' discourse assaulting Indians from the media of Euroamerica."[25]

As Ida's claim suggests, the authoritative western theory that culture and language are founded on the loss or absence of the mother's silent body is reversed in *Yellow Raft,* where the mother speaks. So too the tale of how Rayona got her name, told in two different versions, indicates how the mother, in naming, may use language to exceed the limits of referentiality. Ray has been told repeatedly that her name comes from "rayon," the word printed on the tag in Christine's nightgown. But Christine later explains it another way, saying that "Ray-

ona" was "like nothing," invented in part as a feminine version of Ray-
mond, the name she had chosen for a son, but also a totally new name.
Like Ann and Evelyn in *Desert of the Heart* or like Meridian, Christine thus arrests the pattern of repetition that actually blocks matrilineal development. Similarly, Lee and Christine never know the name of
the father; they come from "nothing" but Ida, and patrilineage, like
referentiality, can thus be set aside. And Ida, we are told, speaks Indian
in preference to English in order to preserve her "soul and grammar"
from salvation by the nuns; throughout all the stories, the native
tongue, which Ray only partly understands, appears as a kind of secret (maternal) language.[26]

An anecdote reported in an interview with Dorris and Erdrich underscores my claim for this novel's central mission. Hertha Wong, the
interviewer, observes that Rayona (whom Wong describes as the "protagonist" of the novel), was initially conceived of as a male character,
and asks why she became a female. Describing the collaborative process
of writing and revision by which all their fiction is said to be gener-
ated, Erdrich answers that the couple occupied themselves during a
drive from Dartmouth College to Minnesota discussing the novel, and
Dorris adds:

> When we left New Hampshire the book was about a young boy who
> was coping with his mother's death, and by the time we reached Min-
> nesota it was about a young girl whose mother lives. Since then it has
> expanded into three parts. One of which is the mother's voice, and the
> next is *her* mother's voice. All of that really evolved out of changing
> the main character from a male to a female. Louise, I think, proposed
> that originally.[27]

Somewhere on the road from New England to the upper Middle West,
Native American literature took a major turn. What was once the classic story—"a young boy who was coping with his mother's death"—
was altered slightly: the boy became a girl. What "evolved" from this
sex change was startlingly different in certain ways. The girl's story
grew into a braid, three intertwined tales told by her mother and her
grandmother too.[28] With the female character brought (back) to narrative life, a univocal tale of absence became a multivocal tale of complicated, ambivalent, intermittent, and powerful presence, nurturance,
flexibility, and continuity. It is tempting to add that obviously it would
be Louise who "originally" urged this change, because this is the same

tale, I argue, that she is telling in the four novels published under her name to date, although doing so in the straightforward way of *Yellow Raft* becomes increasingly more problematic. Maternal absence and the problem of lost children, tragedies in the lives and literatures of Native American people, are not forgotten or triumphed over. Instead, the question of how to represent these problems is at once consistently central, increasingly complex, and unsatisfied by narrative realism.

....

Love Medicine, published three years before *Yellow Raft*, chronologically initiates the effort made throughout the tetralogy published under Erdrich's name to pass on a Native American (maternal) heritage, paradoxically by reconsidering the commonplace cultural and psychic story of the Indian mother who voluntarily or involuntarily abandons her child. The "original event" of this narrative, as Silberman points out and as so many other commentators have observed, is in conventional plot as in actual experience more often thought of as an ending point: the death of the mother without child, June Morrisey, in chapter 1.[29] Much of what follows that death can be read as a mystery story, with a secret about parental identity and intention at the center. The mystery is more fragmented and more difficult for readers to solve than the one told in *Yellow Raft on Blue Water*, as we must try to figure out, from a slim assortment of narrative clues, who June was and why she acted as she did. (There is also a significant hint here of the ghost story, when June's former husband Gordie thinks that the deer he has run over and put in the back seat of his car is June, but this approach is not fully developed until *The Bingo Palace*.) Although the overarching narrative structure of *Love Medicine* in this way might suggest the theory discredited in *Yellow Raft*—that is, the notion that the loss of the mother's body requires and hence instigates symbolic practice—the diffuseness of the plotting and voicing in the novel counters any such simplistic notion of what stories do and where they come from. Moreover, conventional assumptions about the fictional archetype that June so clearly evokes, the missing Indian mother, are undercut in two key ways that correspond to and develop the central revelations of *Yellow Raft*. First, through two female characters in *Love Medicine*, Lulu Nanapush and Marie Kashpaw, the presence of the loving Native American mother who faithfully nurtures the children she bears or adopts is rein-scribed as both social reality and psychic fantasy. Second, from the in-creasingly important perspective of June's son, Lipsha Morrisey, a bio-logical mother's failure to hold and nurture is understood in a new way and, in the climax of the novel, overtly forgiven.

Love Medicine reaffirms the presence of the strong, enduring, and nurturant Native American mother and grandmother, who was con-cealed and protected in the misunderstood figure of Ida in *Yellow Raft*, by delineating her traits in more than one female character. Although, as Wong notes, there are many "strained" maternal relationships in the novel, we also observe mothers in *Love Medicine* who do *not* abandon their own biological children or who take in children whom others have orphaned or left behind. We learn in the later novel, *Tracks,* that the two most important of these good mothers, Marie and Lulu, were aban-doned or sent away by their own biological mothers, so in retrospect the popular notion that one can only parent as one was parented is countered. In the "new and expanded edition" of the novel, it is made even clearer that these two are also figures of the Native American (grand)mother as political activist and traditional leader, a role only prefigured in Ida as the grandmother-storyteller.

Marie is at first the more fully and realistically evoked figure of the loving, hardworking Native American mother. As a girl of fourteen with a "mail-order Catholic soul" (41), she envisions herself as a saint with diamond-tipped nipples. Ironically saved by the loss of her bor-rowed faith, she grows up into a different kind of Saint Marie, at once more down-to-earth and nurturant. To her husband Nector, at the peak of her fertility she seems to have babies tucked everywhere, her own and other people's. When she believes that Nector has left her for Lulu, she responds by peeling all the potatoes in the house and waxing her linoleum floors, finding strength in mundane and fragile acts of inde-pendent maternal work, labor that at once recognizes constant threat and takes action against lurking danger to the child: "It was one of my prides to keep that floor shined up. Under the gray swirls and spots and leaves of the pattern, I knew there was tar paper and bare wood that could splinter a baby's feet. I knew, because I bought and paid for and put down that linoleum myself. It was a good solid covering, but un-der it the boards creaked" (127).

From the perspective of western ideas about good mothers, Lulu is presented as a more ambivalent figure, combining prolific and devoted biological motherhood with a seductive sexual power that threatens erstwhile western-style monogamous families like Nector and Marie's.[30] Her behavior suggests that the creative order of Native American motherhood, as we see in *Yellow Raft* and elsewhere, has little to do with the social order controlled by the Euroamerican institution of marriage and dominant notions of licit female sexuality or chastity. With no permanent husband or father in her home, Lulu raises a large family of children variously sired by undomesticated men and in extradomestic relationships with other women's husbands or lovers. Her numerous sons adore her and obey her completely, although the realistic limits of her control are recognized in the fate of Henry Jr., a Vietnam veteran who commits suicide. But in a key scene in which Lulu feeds her pack from her spotless kitchen, in a half-comic, half-lyrical vision of her powers, the novel invokes the magical capacities of the nurturant mother and parodies the image of the vanishing Indian woman:

> Lulu was bustling about the kitchen in a calm, automatic frenzy. She seemed to fill pots with food by pointing at them and take things from the oven that she'd never put in. The table jumped to set itself. The pop foamed into the glasses, and the milk sighed to the lip. . . . The boys began to stuff themselves with a savage and astonishing efficiency. Before Bev had cleaned his plate once, they'd had thirds, and by the time he looked up from desert, they had melted through the walls. The youngest had levitated from his high chair and was sleeping out of sight. The room was empty except for Lulu and himself. . . . She turned to the sinkful of dishes and disappeared in a cloud of steam. (86–7)

Near the end of the novel, when both Marie and Lulu are old and Nector, the man who came between them, is dead, Marie also becomes an odd, fantasylike surrogate mother to her former rival. After eye surgery, Lulu needs drops put in every day, and Marie volunteers to do the job. As Marie administers the eyedrops, Lulu's thoughts confirm that Marie is a figure for preoedipal perceptions of the plenitude of mother love: "She swayed down like a dim mountain, huge and blurred, the way a mother must look to her just born child" (236).[31]

Marie and Lulu thus bring to life and celebrate maternal powers previously represented in contemporary Native American novels as tragically lost, or as something that even Ida and Christine are able to speak about only in retrospect. At the same time, the novel complements this perspective by replaying the story of the mother without child in the figure of June, who frames the novel. June's son Lipsha

Morrisey's quest for his parents is sometimes read as primarily important for his closing discovery of and reunion with his still living father, Lulu's son Gerry. But the maternal side of the quest seems to me more critical, because it is what links the end of the novel—Lipsha's new understanding about June, his recently discovered birth mother—with its beginning, June's death.

Lipsha is a minor character in the first section of the novel. But when his voice takes over the first-person narration of the last two chapters, he assumes a privileged narrative position in this multiply told story. For Lipsha, the discovery of his biological parentage serves as a traditional epiphany. An "odd" and "troubled" figure, a "lost" youth in earlier episodes, Lipsha indicates a new sense of identity, purpose, and connectedness at the novel's conclusion. At the same time, however, thanks to Erdrich's complex narrative presentation, readers have in fact known since the first chapter who Lipsha's biological mother is, as have many members of the community he grows up in. The conventional force of epiphany is thus diminished by the privileging of a secret that is not really a complete secret, an effect that might be compared to the ironic protection of the secret of maternal (non)identity in *Yellow Raft* that is achieved by spelling it out in the name "Aunt Ida." The important thing about Lipsha's new understanding is not only or not so much the identity of his mother, but the way he changes his mind about why she gave him away in the first place (a question that never arises, it seems, in his thinking about Gerry).

In the first chapter, when the narrator Albertine Johnson begins to hint that the Aunt June they have just buried was his mother, Lipsha refuses to listen. He interrupts Albertine with a melodramatic rendering of the moment of his abandonment:

> "Your mother . . . " I began.
> "I can never forgive what she done to a little child," he said. "They had to rescue me out of her grip." . . .
> "She didn't do that," I said. "She wanted you."
> "No. . . . even if she came back right now, this minute, and said 'Son, I am sorry for what I done to you,' I would not relent on her." (36)

Albertine tries one more time before she gives up; "'What if your mother never meant to? . . . What if it was just kind of a mistake?'" But Lipsha cannot hear. At the end of the novel, however, after his paternal grandmother Lulu forces him to listen to the truth about his parentage and he meets his biological father, Gerry Nanapush, Lipsha implicitly revisits Albertine's question. The novel ends with Lipsha's new, corrected understanding of what June's abandonment meant, which now accords with Albertine's opening hint. "I tell you," says Lipsha in the penultimate paragraph, just before heading home to the reservation with his maternal legacy, the car purchased with his mother's insurance money, "there was good in what she did for me, I know now. The son that she acknowledged suffered more than Lipsha Morrisey did. The thought of June grabbed my heart so, but I was lucky she turned me over to Grandma Kashpaw" (272).

Lipsha's change of heart is retrospectively supported by scraps of information about June embedded elsewhere in the novel and seemingly designed to ensure a sympathetic reading of her character. Marie, known to Lipsha now as "Grandma" Kashpaw, was also June's adoptive mother, and from her we learn that June herself was an abandoned child, left in the woods to survive on pine sap when her own mother died. Marie tried to care for the vulnerable, appealing June, but the girl preferred to be raised by her Uncle Eli, a "traditional" man who lived alone in the woods until June came along. Everyone in the family, even Eli who adores her, agrees that grown-up June wasn't much of a mother, but Albertine testifies that she was a good aunt. When Lulu finally tells Lipsha about June's affair with young Gerry, she insists that "'June was real upset about the whole thing'" and "'Gordie [June's husband, a Kashpaw] couldn't handle another man's son.'" When Lipsha wonders whether June ever mentioned him, Lulu says, "'She watched you from a distance, and hoped you would forgive her'" (245). Lipsha at last fulfills that hope; the framing lesson of the story of the dead mother offers a revised and compassionate understanding, as in *Yellow Raft,* of why she acted as she did and (at least some of) what she really felt.

In this newly heard version of the story of the mother without child, forgiveness is possible in part because the mother herself is construed as a victim who made the best choice she could for her child, and in part because the community has a well-established tradition of providing alternatives when the biological mother cannot or will not care for her child. And just as maternal responsibility is a collective responsibility, shared among male as well as female adults in this Native American community, so too a child himself or herself is shown to have a responsibility for identity formation, where identity is a matter both of knowing kinship and of making choices.[32] Gerry Nanapush passes on these words of wisdom to his son Lipsha: "Belonging was a matter of deciding to" (255). This principle extends the argument of *Yellow Raft* that the fate of the child is not the exclusive and enduring responsibility of the biological mother. Just as others may help to raise the child and many forces shape identity, so the child must take action and accept responsibility.[33]

If the story of the mother without child ended here, with Lipsha's recognition and forgiveness of June, a reading of the novels in the order in which they were published—first *Love Medicine* and then *Yellow Raft*—might emphasize a positive movement toward the articulation of what was silenced, the recovery of what was lost: a maternal voice, a mother's presence. First the mother (June) is more clearly understood by the narrative and forgiven by the child, and then she (Christine, Ida) is allowed to speak for herself, to tell her own story. However, as readers of the subsequent novels know, the mother who abandons her children or who is at least thought to do so reappears in the form of both new characters and, in Erdrich's fourth novel, old ones—the ghost of June and the person of Fleur Pillager, from *Tracks*. In retrospect, we can begin to identify in *Love Medicine* part of the reason why the problem of maternal abandonment refuses to go away and why the mother's story is so hard to discover and represent in a narrative form that attains closure or puts doubts to rest. What I have identified in *Love Medicine* as two complementary ways of revising the fictional story of the absent Native American mother—Marie's and Lulu's stories, on the one hand, and June's, on the other—also have something in common: their quality of fantasy. Lipsha's forgiveness of his mother resembles those other moments of idealized maternity in the novel: Lulu's magical nurturance of her pack and Marie's seemingly inexhaustible store of maternal energy for the protection of her children and later for her former rival, Lulu. These moments are depicted in romantic and tender scenes, contesting in important ways the novel's more realistic emphasis on "strained" maternal relationships, and thus echoing the message of *Yellow Raft* while evoking a kind of sweetness not seen there. But thinking back to Lulu's analogy, when Marie puts the drops in her eyes, suggests one problematic implication of this fantasy: even as we are relieved of our blind misunderstanding of the mother, can we really ever see her as anything but "huge and blurred"?

In *Love Medicine*, it would seem not. Indeed, Lipsha's belief that his mother abandoned him is amended, and Marie and Lulu represent both the reality and the myth of the strong, present, nurturant Native American (grand)mother. However, it is still the absent mother's full story that remains a motivating mystery, resists discovery, and appears only as a lost connection that cannot be fully recovered in language. June has no narrative voice, no speaking part; we never hear her version or understand her choices. The only time we even see events briefly narrated from her point of view by a limited omniscient narrator, we know little about what she is thinking, and we glimpse her feelings of fragility and fragmentation from some distance. What we have of June's story includes two possible attempts at suicide, one as a child, when she lets her cousins try to hang her, and the other, in the opening scene of the novel, when she sets out to walk home to the reservation in a wind that some say she must have known portended a blizzard. But no one ever decides whether she meant to kill herself on either occasion. Representing her voice, identity, and intentions with any kind of certainty remains outside either the interests or, more likely, the self-defined capacities of this novel, even as it desires to know her story. Albertine's initial question to Lipsha—"'What if your mother never meant to?'"—remains only partially answered, and the mystery of June bears witness to the difficulty of escaping the circumstances of both psychic and social loss that simultaneously blur and enlarge the picture of the mother, so that there is always more to try to bring into focus.

THE ONE YOU WILL NOT CALL MOTHER:
THE BEET QUEEN AND *TRACKS*

Erdrich's second novel, *The Beet Queen,* turns to a largely new set of characters but is tightly connected to the other novels in the tetralogy by the way it reengages the plot of the mother without child. Like *Love Medicine* and *Yellow Raft,* it substitutes a closing vision of maternal presence and revision of the child's perspective for an initial scene of abandonment, so that overall narrative movement is toward recuperation of and reconciliation with the mother. *The Beet Queen,* however, balances in a different way the forces of maternal idealization, seen previously in Lulu and Marie or in Ida as she finally reveals herself, with those of maternal absence, seen in June or in Ida as she is thought by Christine to be. Whereas in the earlier novels it is the absent mother herself—Christine as seen by Rayona, Ida as seen by Christine, and June as seen by almost everyone—who is more or less recovered and at least partially understood in the course of the storytelling, this is not the case

in *The Beet Queen.* Instead, the mother with whom a child is recon-
ciled at the end of the novel is not the same character whose abandonment of her children instigates the plot. The problem of maternal abandonment is initially represented in a story that in some sense stands,
like June's death, as an original event, never to be fully explained: Adelaide Adare's flight from her children, Mary, Karl, and Jude. The strong,
loving (Native American) mother, in contrast, is represented in the realistic, nonmysterious, and far more fully developed story of half-
Chippewa Celestine James and her daughter Dot, the eponymous Beet
Queen. The dichotomy between the present mother and the absent
mother contained in Ida, or represented by Marie and Lulu, on the one
hand, and June, on the other, becomes in part at least a difference of
race: the absent mother, Adelaide, is apparently white,[34] whereas the
present mother, Celestine, is half Native American.

Celestine resembles Ida, Marie, and Lulu in that she is a strong, "stat-
uesque" (31), sexually and socially independent woman, the daughter
of a Chippewa woman and a white man.[35] As adults, Celestine and
Mary Adare together run a butcher shop, and eventually Celestine takes
Mary's ne'er-do-well brother Karl as a lover. She becomes pregnant,
and from the moment her baby Dot is born, she adores the child as
much as Christine adores Rayona, with what can only be called "passion," a feeling "even stronger than with Karl. She stole time to be with
Dot as if they were lovers. . . . Her love for the baby hung around her
in clear, blowing sheets" (175).

Although such motherlove is enormously powerful in this novel, it
is not particularly pleasant, peaceful, or in any way sweet. Dot is a difficult child, full of violence and passion herself. Celestine is the kind of
mother who brings jello laced with nuts and bolts to the school pot-
luck supper as a practical joke. She has to compete with two other childless adults—Mary, the baby's aunt, and Wallace, Celestine's neighbor
and Karl's ex-lover—who also want to parent Dot. Her jealousy and
her empathy with them are vividly depicted; we are reminded that parents, both biological and surrogate, need children as much as children
need parents and can feel abandoned when children leave them, as they
usually do. We see this too in the briefly glimpsed figure of Catherine
Miller, whose husband Martin finds (or steals) the abandoned baby
Jude Adare and brings him home three days after their own child has
died. Catherine cherishes the clothes the found child was wearing "on
the night he came to her rescue" (47).

Despite all the historical and psychological problems that realistically strain Celestine and Dot's relationship, the novel ends with an image of patient, enduring maternal love and a reconciliation of sorts between the daughter and half Native American mother. The final scene inverts and rewrites the opening "flight" of the white mother, Adelaide. At a fair in Argus where Dot has been named Beet Queen (and has just discovered that Wallace has rigged the contest so that she will win), Dot flies away with the skywriter who has been hired to spell out her name. This move on the part of the daughter, escaping the overly intense, often embarrassing, and unwieldy passion of her mother (and in this case her surrogate mothers, Mary and Wallace), seems at first to enact the more familiar late-twentieth-century white mother-daughter plot, but such a reading is quickly blocked when airsick Dot returns to the fairgrounds a short time later. Only Celestine is still waiting for her when Dot comes back down to earth, and they go home alone together. After a meal, Dot thinks, "I want to lean into her the way wheat leans into wind," but she resists the urge and each woman goes to her own room. As she waits to fall asleep, Dot welcomes the sound and smell of rain, and the last image is of a fragile, nonverbal, prospective, and imaginative bond between late-adolescent child and mother, in separate but adjacent parts of the same house: "I breathe it in, and I think of her lying in the next room, her covers thrown back, eyes wide open, waiting" (338). Although there is still distance between the mother and daughter and no dramatic scene of reconciliation, closure comes with Dot's implicit recognition of her biological mother's persistent, fertile, patient, and expectant love. Like the forgiveness of the mother at the end of *Love Medicine,* this scene suggests that narrative resolves not only with homecoming but also with a sense of beginning, anticipation, and going forward together rather than ending.

The final chapter of *The Beet Queen* addresses not only Dot and Celestine's strained yet enduring relationship, but also the larger problem with which the story began—Adelaide Adare's flight from her three children, Mary, Karl, and baby Jude, at the Orphans' Picnic in Minneapolis. The position of this flight at the chronological beginning of the plot indicates an originary cause or at least instigating narrative complication. The setting ironically suggests a perverse carnival of lost familial connection and a subworld of mothers (and fathers) who abandon their children, willfully or not. The story begins in 1929 as the Depression sets in. Adelaide and her children have recently been cast into utter desperation by the death of the married man, Mr. Ober, who fathered and supported this illicit family. Homeless and penniless, Adelaide spends what is probably her last dollar for a ride with a stunt pilot, a ride from which she never returns. The baby she leaves behind is taken by Martin Miller, that passing stranger whose own newborn recently died, and the older children, Mary and Karl, run away to North Dakota, where they hope to find their mother's sister, Fritzie.

Adelaide's initial abandonment complexly marks several of the main characters of the novel for life, and none of them ever forgives or fully understands her. Mary, the daughter, is in some sense complicitous in their lifelong separation. She was already jealous of what she perceived as her mother's preference for Karl, although the only independent evidence we have suggests that Adelaide was more worried about Mary's future than her son's. When Adelaide, who seems to know that her children are with Fritzie, sends a postcard that attempts to make contact— "I am living down here. I think about the children every day. How are they?" (56)—Mary uses her aunt's name and handwriting to break any future link: "All three of your children are starved dead" (58). Conversely, in order to cement their budding friendship, Mary tells Celestine that her mother is dead and that she is an orphan, like Celestine. In contrast to Mary, Karl tells himself that his mother couldn't have run away from him; he can only imagine that she was kidnapped by the pilot. Both children, then—the daughter who never relents against the mother and the son who immediately forgives and never recovers from her loss—get the story wrong. Late in the novel, Mary and Karl's cousin Sita, who has also been shaped by Adelaide's flight and Mary's usurpation of her place as only daughter, adds another perspective. Disagreeing with those unspecified persons in the community who saw Adelaide's flight as "cold-hearted," Sita says that she wishes she had flown away too. Since Sita has no children, her comment links the mother's flight to an escape not just from the weight of maternal responsibility but from a feminine role of passivity and dependency.

Any clear-cut judgment that Adelaide was either selfish or desperate—or maybe even subversive—is complicated by the fact that her story is told chiefly from the disparate points of view of the children she left behind or of the other characters who figure in their subsequent searches for love and connection. Only in two brief chapters do we get a closer perspective, still not from Adelaide herself but from Omar, the pilot who flies her away. Twice we see Omar watching Adelaide in pain. The first time, she lies in a hospital bed after their plane has crashed;

Omar is unhurt, but he is worried that Adelaide will die. Her first words when she regains consciousness make him jealous: "'I've got to send Mary a sewing machine. . . . If Mary learns how to sew, she'll always have a skill to fall back on'" (60). At this point, Omar delivers the brutal postcard from Mary, announcing the children's supposed death, which he has previously concealed. Adelaide's response is unnarrated; her embryonic language, as a mother, never develops beyond the telegraphic speech of her own postcard, which her daughter mimics in their only narrated exchange.

We meet Omar a second time, several years later, now settled down in the aviary he and Adelaide run (and hence still associated with flight and air). Listening to Adelaide breaking every glass in the kitchen in what seems just one of many wordless, self-destructive rampages he has witnessed over the years, Omar waits with empathy and frustration for her rage to pass: "He felt her pain like it was inside him, but could do nothing" (231). In our final glimpse of Adelaide, she stands with a broom in the middle of her kitchen, her feet bleeding and her hands shaking. How much of this rage is grief for her children, who never rescued her, we cannot say, just as it seems impossible to determine whether there is justification for a sympathetic reading of this character, or whether the novel takes its own revenge against her. But in either case, the specter of the silent woman bleeding on the floor covered with glass that she herself has shattered manifests the enduring pain, inexplicable rage, self-inflicted punishment, and wordless grief of the mother without child. Associated with the birds whose flight is arrested because they are trapped in the aviary, Adelaide never tells us how she feels, and the interpretations offered by other characters in the novel are limited and inadequate. Adelaide was not simply a powerless victim, forced by circumstances to abandon her children, but neither was she "cold-hearted" or liberated by her flight. What she was remains a mystery.

. . . .

Tracks takes us back to the familial past of several of the characters from *Love Medicine,* mostly full-blood or self-defined Indians, and it too arises out of—and revises—misunderstood or never-before-told stories of maternal abandonment. Two first-person narrators, Grandfather Nanapush and Pauline Puyat, speak alternately; both tell parts of the story of Fleur Pillager, a character mentioned only briefly in the earlier novels, who emerges here as another Native American mother who at the time of the novel's telling is no longer a mother, who has lost one baby and is accused of abandoning her daughter, the same Lulu Lamartine we met in *Love Medicine*. The motive for Nanapush's storytelling, explicitly addressed to Lulu as audience, recalls Albertine's efforts to change Lipsha's mind in the first chapter of *Love Medicine*. Nanapush says he speaks in order to revise Lulu's understanding of why Fleur, "the one you will not call mother" (2), sent her away to the dreaded Indian boarding school, from which he eventually rescues the child: "Maybe once I tell you the reason she had to send you away, you will start acting like a daughter should. She saved you from worse, as you'll see. Perhaps when you finally understand, you'll borrow my boots and go out there, forgive her, though it's you that needs forgiveness" (210–1).[36] The hope that his storytelling itself can heal the breach and reconnect Lulu to her mother corresponds to what we see elsewhere as the positive role of words, both spoken and written, in resisting physical and cultural loss and restoring Native American life. In two earlier moments of rescue Nanapush saves Lulu from freezing to death by talking to her, and he resorts to learning the white man's written discourse in order to manipulate bureaucratic channels and retrieve her from boarding school.[37]

In *Tracks* itself we never learn how Lulu responds—that is, whether she, like Lipsha, is persuaded to revise her understanding and forgive her mother, as Nanapush hopes she will do. However, as Nanapush tells it, the story of Fleur, like the story of June, insists that such forgiveness is justifiable. Neither woman acts arbitrarily or selfishly but because circumstances make it impossible for either of them to hold onto her children. June is prevented from mothering in part by the traumas of her own childhood. Fleur is prevented by the tragic and collective consequences of white conquest. Fleur's case for forgiveness is stronger than June's in two regards. First, she is portrayed not as a broken woman who lacks maternal competence, like June, but as a strong woman and a good, loving, nurturing Native American mother who suffers deeply when she loses her second baby and clings all the more strongly to Lulu, her firstborn, until she loses her too. Second, Fleur is explicitly associated with supernatural powers, and Fleur sends Lulu away only because she must use her powers to protest and subvert conquest.

Mystery surrounds Fleur's inherited, ancient spiritual force, and she is feared by the remnants of the Native American community. She has many characteristics of the traditional trickster figure more often noted in the character of Nanapush.[38] Twice as a girl she comes back to life after drowning, although drowning is "the death a Chippewa cannot survive" (11). Each time she is resurrected, according to Pauline, she is thought to send others to death in her place. One of the last two survivors of a family that is decimated by contact with whites, she is reputed to be a witch who is desired by Misshepeshu, the monster of Lake Matchimanito, a devil attracted to "the strong and daring especially, like Fleur" (11). Again according to Pauline, many want to drive Fleur off the reservation but do not dare to do so, and before they can find a way she leaves for Argus, where again "things happened" once she arrives (12). The paternity of her children, born after she returns from Argus, is questionable: Lulu could have been conceived when Fleur was raped by white men in Argus, or perhaps Eli Kashpaw, who falls under her powerful spell, is the father. When Fleur becomes pregnant a second time, Eli wonders if he or Misshepeshu, the spirit under the water, is responsible.

But in this time of conquest and extinction Fleur's archaic, supernatural powers cannot coexist with an endangered maternal practice; at this point in history, her deep and threatened love for her biological children only weakens her. After a difficult first childbirth, Fleur is brought back to life by Lulu's cries, but she almost loses her powers when her second baby is born prematurely and dies. The novel does not blame the loss of children solely on white conquest but suggests that the old gods have stopped favoring their people: Fleur gambles with the dead for the life of her baby, and whereas she always beats white men at cards, this time she does not win. After that she clings to Lulu obsessively until the white-owned lumber company moves to evict her from her land. In such historical circumstances, the strong Native American mother who bears traditional powers ironically has to relinquish custody of her child to exercise her destructive force without destroying the child too. As in the story of Ida, who tries to toughen herself against the potential and dreaded loss of Christine by denying her bond, the strength and cunning needed for a Chippewa woman to survive on or off the reservation may be at odds with the vulnerability born of postconquest maternal experience. The point seems clear: the victimization of mothers is an effect of white cultural domination. And unlike the mature Ida, the otherwise forceful Fleur at this point in her life lacks the power of storytelling. As Nanapush puts it, "She was too young and had no stories or depth of life to rely upon. All she had was raw power and the names of the dead that filled her" (7). Here, it is the figure of the grandfather, not the (grand)mother, who tells Native American stories and uses the power of words, saving both himself and Lulu by talking and later writing.[39] Nanapush's purpose, with its personal as well as political ramifications, recalls Ida's: he too is passing on his "savings" in the form of the mother's true story to the future generations.

Although Fleur, caught between the roles of native trickster and loving Native American mother, cannot tell her own story, another mother without child, Pauline Puyat, is the second first-person narrator of the novel. Pauline's narrative develops Fleur's story from an alternate, often far less sympathetic point of view than Nanapush's, but at the same time it also relates Pauline's own history. Her story surprises readers of *Love Medicine,* as the book's characters are often surprised, by a sudden revelation of an intimate and mysterious secret about maternal origins: Pauline turns out to be none other than Sister Leopolda, the crazy nun who torments Marie in Erdrich's first novel and is now shockingly discovered, in the later one, to be Marie's birth mother. Ironically, this mother—one of the few in Erdrich's books to have a first-person perspective—speaks chiefly of her desire *not* to be a mother. Long before the baby is born, she utterly repudiates the product of her affair with Napoleon Morrisey. Hoping to induce an abortion, she repeatedly thrusts her stomach against an ax handle but is prevented from further self-mutilation by Bernadette, Napoleon's sister and a mixed-blood widow who has given Pauline a home and a job. Later, in the final stages of labor, Pauline tries to hold the baby in by refusing to push, but Bernadette ties her down and delivers Marie with forceps.

Pauline's most obvious motive for refusing motherhood is her shame, born of her obsession with Catholicism; she rejects her child, "already fallen, a dark thing" (136), as tainted with the sins of her own flesh. Just before the delivery, another aspect of her resistance to giving birth may also be suggested. "If I gave birth," she says, "I would be lonelier"; she tries to hold the baby inside her body, "clenched" around the child "so that she could not escape" (135), and when Bernadette succeeds in pulling the infant out, Pauline says simply, "We were divided" (136). There is a sense in which Pauline seems at this most gruesome, unnatural of moments to belong with other women who are forced to separate from their children. Her resistance to delivery itself marks in a perverse way her impossible desire not only to escape her unloved, unconnected body and the role of mother in the dominant religious discourse, but also to hold on to what no mother of any culture can keep—the perfect and inviolable intimacy with the child inside her body before birth.

Pauline has been read in a variety of ways. She is perhaps most frequently understood as a version of the unreliable narrator, characteristically disrupting any smooth, linear flow of plot or any single narrative of interpretation.[40] Thought to be crazed by the demise of her clan and her jealous desire to be loved both as Fleur is loved by men and by Fleur herself, Pauline has been described as "a mean-spirited woman who is a proven liar," "confused and psychologically damaged," with "a bizarre amalgamation of Chippewa belief and Catholicism."[41] In more mixed readings, Pauline is seen to have certain powers and to wield her own distorted version of the native supernatural force that Nanapush and Fleur possess. According to Nancy J. Peterson, Nanapush's perspective is finally the one that the novel affirms, but it is the contrast between the interpretations offered by Nanapush and Pauline that grounds history here in conflicting visions and thus guarantees an "'indigenous' account of what happens," one that comprehends both oral and textual history.[42] In contrast to most other readers, Daniel Cornell is suspicious of the view, promoted by Nanapush, that Pauline is insane and ludicrous. To accept this, he argues, implicates us in Nanapush's efforts to "objectify" Pauline and deny her demand for the "constituting gaze" of subjectivity that belongs only to men in the Euroamerican order.[43]

Although it is important to recognize the disruptive voice and practice of Pauline, it is equally important to distinguish between what it means to reject the position of woman as mother in Christian tradition from what the refusal to mother might signify in what is left of the Chippewa community. Nanapush may be misread if he is too simply understood as a figure of maleness who wants to dominate and objectify women. Like any good trickster, he occupies many positions, including the role of surrogate parent first to Fleur and then to Fleur's daughter Lulu, and he aims in his storytelling to repair one forced breach in the matrilineal order that has been opened up by white encroachment. Whatever else it does, his narrative follows the yearning of narrative in *Yellow Raft, Love Medicine,* and even *The Beet Queen* toward the forgiveness of the mother who appears to have abandoned her child. Pauline's story represents among other things a counternarrative in which a mother defies on her own behalf this appeal for forgiveness—this mother asks nothing of her child, at least at this point—in a quest for self-definition that can only look unstable and irrational, given the options for survival. Read this way, both Pauline *and* Fleur are not only tragic figures, whose spiritual powers at this historical moment of racial and cultural erasure are not strong enough to permit them to hold onto their children, but also trickster figures, in their own ways, certainly defying among other things "the Anglo bias of identifying Indian women with stability" (18).[44]

Pauline's story further suggests that it is not just having a voice that matters. Language is explicitly politicized as it is in *Yellow Raft*, so that it is not just whether you speak but what tongue you choose or are allowed to speak in that matters, and nonnative languages can constrain more than they can express the (maternal) subjectivity of Native Americans. Whereas we are asked to believe that Ida tells her empowering, self-fashioning story in the old language, Pauline will speak only English. She repudiates her mother tongue along with her Native American heritage—both of which have been almost obliterated. She comes from the Puyats, a mixed-blood family "with little to say," and from a "clan for which the name was lost" (14). Pauline is lighter-skinned than her sisters, and when she leaves the Chippewa to go to the white town, she says: "I wanted to be like my mother, who showed her half-white. I wanted to be like my grandfather, pure Canadian. That was because even as a child I saw that to hang back was to perish. I saw through the eyes of the world outside of us. I would not speak our language. In English, I told my father we should build an outhouse with a door that swung open and shut" (14). But Pauline's dreams of self-improvement and survival, initially tied to speaking English and learning from the nuns how to make lace, are impossible. When she goes to the white town to live with her aunt, she ends up sweeping floors in the butcher shop where Fleur works. Longing to survive, suffering from guilt over her part in the deaths of the men who raped Fleur, extremely jealous of Fleur's sexual allure, and frustrated over her own failure to attract a husband, Pauline begins to have visions and seeks her vocation in the Catholic church. The Church, however, "discounts" Native American women. The order receives word that no Indian girl can join, so Pauline cunningly has a vision from Christ, who sits on the stove beside which she sleeps and tells her that she is not who she thought she was: "I was an orphan and my parents had died in grace, and also, despite my deceptive features, I was not one speck of Indian but wholly white. He

Himself had dark hair although his eyes were blue as bottleglass, so I believed" (137). "'The Indians,'" she begins to say, "'them.' Never *neenawind,* or us" (138). She learns from Christ, however, that she has a mission not to turn her back on her native ways but to convert and save the Native Americans. In return for the powers of salvation that she will wrest from the Satanic force of Fleur, her own powerful will must completely submit: "I must dissolve" (141).

In the Christian symbolic order, woman's highest and oldest road to salvation demands this repudiation of the self, the flesh, the literal, the Eve-like desire that brought sin into the world. One inevitable cost of that repudiation, in Pauline's case as in so many early female saints' lives, is the abandonment of her own child, a mark of sin. The perfect Christian mother is Mary, whose image compensates for the loss of the real mother and represents the fantasy of total and absolute maternal omnipotence together with submission of the female self to the male child. Mary defines woman as mother and only as mother, but paradoxically the mother of no human being, a mother who is no longer a mother, who has lost her child; she is a disembodied figure of self-sacrificial power, alien to the mythic and social figure of the Native American mother. The power of the native mother is erased, silenced, and distorted into Pauline's nightmare visions. The novel raises the question of whether the ability to talk only in this language, to know and be only this story, is perhaps worse than having no voice at all.

From *Love Medicine* through *Tracks,* Erdrich's novels thus register what we have seen in *Desert of the Heart* and *Meridian:* increasing rather than decreasing difficulty in representing—in English—an unproblematic, unified, individual maternal subject, a synthetic maternity, or the mother as nonvictim and not absent. In *Love Medicine,* forgiveness is made possible by epiphany, and alternative models are presented in Marie and Lulu, but the mother also remains "huge and blurred." Problems are displaced onto a white mother, Adelaide, in *The Beet Queen,* while Celestine carries on the maternal lineage of Ida, Marie, and Lulu— women who are not sentimentalized but represented as strong, nurturant, and present mothers. *Tracks,* however, returns to problems inherent in the Native American mother figure who is almost synonymous with problems of recovering the cultural past, the precontact identity and community; two versions of the problem are explored in Fleur and Pauline. Both are tricksters, figures of resistance, inciting narratives, pursuing alternative paths in an effort not to be victimized, but both paths necessitate voluntarily occupying the difficult position of a mother without child, giving up the child who cannot be held.

THERE IS MORE TO BE TOLD: *THE BINGO PALACE*

> The red rope between the mother and her baby is the hope of our nation. It pulls, it sings, it snags, it feeds and holds.
> —*The Bingo Palace*

The Bingo Palace introduces a major new female character, Shawnee Ray Toose, who seems to inherit the maternal powers of creativity, nurturance, and sexuality suggested in Marie and Lulu in *Love Medicine* or Celestine in *The Beet Queen,* while countering even more unambiguously than they do the old images of "strained" mother-child relations and pointing to a new, anticipatory model of cultural revival. Shawnee is a young unmarried mother who is beautiful and talented in both traditional and new ways. She wins dancing prizes wearing her brilliant homemade costumes; she uses her prize money to go to college. She is unswerving in her devotion to her young son, Redford, fathered by Lyman Lamartine, successful tribal leader and owner of the casino. As the collective voice of the novel's opening chapter suggests, it is as a result of her motherhood and the strong pull of that "red rope" binding her and her baby that Shawnee is saved from wildness and pulled back to the world of responsibility and care, "outraged and tender" (6). Notably, the alternative to wildness here is not the holy ground occupied by the white models of nuclear family and heterosexual marriage; it is the resilient, extramarital connection of mother and baby, sometimes supported by the extended family (Shawnee's sisters and a surrogate grandmother, Marie's daughter Zelda) but also capable of moving outside the community. In the interests of herself and her son, Shawnee is resourceful and independent: she refuses to marry either Lyman or the more appealing, unstable Lipsha Morrisey, who returns to the reservation and falls desperately in love with her. Lipsha's passion for Shawnee is the realistic motive for much of the action, and it is made explicit near the end of the novel that he wants her to be his mother as well as his wife.

The optimistic cultural and personal future imaged in Shawnee is at the same time deferred by the complications of the plot; there is old business to be settled with the earlier maternal figures. Picking up threads from both *Love Medicine* and *Tracks,* the plot of *The Bingo Palace* takes Lipsha not forward to fulfillment of his sexual desire for Shawnee but back to sadder and more terrifying, ancestral female figures: his birth mother, June Morrisey, and his paternal great-grandmother Fleur Pillager. The status of the mother without child as a liminal figure reaches its fullest realization here. June returns as an alluring, enigmatic ghost, and Fleur is an ancient, still-powerful, and highly feared "medicine woman" living geographically on the margins of the tribal community but psychologically and spiritually at its center. With the reappearance of these characters, we revert to the problem that is a driving force in Erdrich's novels—the difficulty of knowing or telling the story of maternal abandonment in any single, true, or empowering form, together with the impossibility of forgetting it. But now, after three attempts that in different ways treat the mother's story as fundamentally a mystery story, the narrative turns more completely to the genre glimpsed in *Love Medicine* and then reintroduced in *Tracks,* where events we would normally divide into realistic and supernatural spheres are interwoven in a ghost story.[45]

....

JUNE

Just as the mystery of June's death and the question of her maternal intentions frame *Love Medicine,* so too the haunting tale of her return as an apparition frames *The Bingo Palace.* In the opening chapter, the first-person-plural voice of the community—or some unspecified portion of that community, suggesting what Kathleen Sands calls the force of gossip—is watching and talking about Lulu Lamartine and her son, the famous criminal Gerry Nanapush.[46] This collective persona self-consciously understands itself to be "trying to ravel back to the beginning, trying to put families into order and make sense of things" (5). But starting with Lulu quickly leads to one thing and another, "until we are lost in the connections," and one of the unavoidable tangles is June, suddenly recalled along with the thoughts of a late spring blizzard. June is identified from the outset by this "we" as a ghost, said to be walking still in the snow but also recalled as "a beautiful woman, much loved and very troubled" (5).

In the chapter entitled "Transportation," the ghost of June appears for the first time to Lipsha alone, in the middle of the night, to take back the car that appeared at the beginning and end of *Love Medicine,* a blue Firebird purchased by King Jr. with June's life insurance and then won in the poker game by Lipsha and his father, Gerry Nanapush. After a brief conversation with her son, June gives Lipsha a lucky set of bingo tickets; her appearance thus entails both cultural updating and maternal rebuke, as she takes back the previous maternal legacy, the car from *Love Medicine* that no longer runs, and proffers a dubious new heritage, the winning bingo cards. By way of both explanation and outcome of this provocative nocturnal visitation, June's life is revisited and revised at several points in the novel. In these additional episodes of her story, the supernatural, the fictive, and the actual are complexly and unstably mixed in the memories and visions of the living characters.

Near the beginning of the novel, from Marie Kashpaw's singular and somewhat more intimate point of view, June is remembered differently than she was in *Love Medicine.* There Marie tried to assure Lipsha that his mother loved him. Now June is recalled as a child Marie tried to mother, "but it had been too late to really save her . . . June was damaged goods. . . . Some children, you could not repair" (27–8). Marie's daughter Zelda is the next to offer us a contradictory and less pleasant version of June's story. Her tongue loosened by unaccustomed amounts of gin, Zelda shocks Lipsha by bringing up "the raw specifics" of his mother's abandonment, the story he has heard alluded to before but has dismissed as a joke. "'I hate to talk about it in front of you,'" Zelda claims, and then goes on to insist that she was there when June threw baby Lipsha into a slough, in a gunny sack filled with rocks. "'I should know. It was me who dragged you out,'" she adds. What bothers her still is the mystery of why the baby, who was under water "a long time," didn't drown. Without complete success, Lipsha tries to convince himself at this point that Zelda is wrong, that the story he accepted at the end of *Love Medicine* is the truth: "I was given to her [Grandma Kashpaw] in a sad but understandable way by a mother who was beautiful but too wild to have raised a boy on her own" (52). But then he dreams of "frightening water," and when he goes back to the bar for a drink he encounters June, looking the way she did when he was a child and offering no excuses.

The next brief chapter, following Zelda's revelation and June's first visitation, is entitled "June's Luck." Here, it is as if her ghost has finally brought into narrative reach some fragment of her consciousness, in this instance a classic "recovered memory." In the third-person past tense but clearly from June's point of view, we hear the grim tale of June's childhood before her mother's death. June is treated more and more cruelly by her mother, Lucille, especially when Lucille is drunk. One night, when June fails to heed her brother's warning to run away and sleep in the woods, her mother ties her up, and sometime later her mother's drunken boyfriend rapes her. June survives the ordeal, as victims of abuse are so often said to do, by dissociation, becoming

> just a burning dot, flung star moving, speeding through the
> blackness . . . until she finally escaped into a part of her mind, where
> she made one promise before she went out.
>   *Nobody ever hold me again.* (60)[47]

After June's trauma breaks through forgetfulness and voicelessness into narrative, so does Lipsha's. In the wake of this newly presented information about June, just before her second and last appearance in the novel as a ghost, he has a vision in which he reexperiences his drowning as an infant and connects it to June's own trauma and subsequent inability to hold or be held. As at so many points in this novel, comedy and tragedy as well as phantasmagoric and rational worlds easily intersect in Lipsha's experience. The memory of his infant self has been summoned up by Lipsha's apparently unsuccessful ritual quest, where he has met only a mysterious speaking skunk. Felt as well as understood, this traumatic memory now escapes from Lipsha's consciously forgetful self into his first-person narrative. With the conviction that comes from the irrational knowledge gained by intrusive sensation, Lipsha feels certain that he knows what June did to him and that June meant to do it. At the same time he interprets and rationally encodes her act in a way we can understand, as an inevitable repetition of her own trauma: "I remember the sensation I spent my whole life trying to forget. . . . I hear my mother's voice, feel her touch, and by that I know the truth. I know that she did the same that was done to her—a young girl left out to live on the woods and survive on pine sap and leaves and buried roots" (217).

More uncannily still, Lipsha finds in his own recovered memory the answer to the question that bothered Zelda: How did he survive for so long under water? Appalling but plausible experience, the mother's attempted infanticide, is inextricably accompanied by the implausible and supernatural, as Lipsha remembers being under the water, in the sack, for an indefinite period, and then being saved by something with "fins and horns . . . and long and shining plant arms" that rock him: "Its face is lion-jawed, a thing of beach foam." To Lipsha this "something else" has the face of "unburied goodness, the saving tones" (218), yet it also resembles Pauline's description in *Tracks* of Misshepeshu, the demon of Lake Matchimanito with "horns, fangs, claws, fins" and "the body of a lion . . . made of black moss" (*Tracks*, 11) that saved Fleur from drowning.

From this moment on in Lipsha's story, real and unreal, comic and tragic are not only permeable but completely confused. In a surreal closing escapade in which Lipsha's "luck" seems to take a serious turn for the worse, Gerry is on the run again, and the Nanapush father and son are escaping in a car they have stolen without realizing that there is a baby in the backseat. As they drive through a blizzard that clearly echoes the opening storm in *Love Medicine,* the ghost of June, driving the Firebird, suddenly reappears to both Gerry and Lipsha. Gerry drives off the highway to follow June across a snow-covered field. When the Firebird comes to a halt, Gerry stops too, looks at Lipsha "with an air of sad puzzlement and hard choice," and then joins June, "lost in the surge of his own feelings" (258). Reversing the movement toward reconciliation and reunion at the end of *Love Medicine* and indeed all the earlier novels, Lipsha is once again abandoned by his parents. Yet the last time we see Lipsha, stranded in the field of snow where Gerry and June have left him, he simultaneously relives his psychic conviction that he was abandoned and acts with confidence and clarity to invert his mother's legacy, to save as he was saved. To do so, like Nanapush who mothers Lulu, Lipsha takes the maternal part, as he zips the baby he and Gerry have accidentally kidnapped into his jacket with just one resolve: "At least I can say . . . here is one child who was never left behind" (259).

Among all the puzzles and ambiguities of *The Bingo Palace,* readers may well wonder how much to trust either Lipsha's visions or his explanations of June, given the way the apparent "truth" achieved at the close of *Love Medicine* is exposed as self-deception in *The Bingo Palace.* Even the way Lipsha formulates his newly recovered memories here—"*I know* the truth. *I know* that she did the same that was done to her"—recalls the wording he uses at the end of *Love Medicine*— "there was good in what she did for me, *I know* now" (emphases added)—and thus the finality and reliability of what he knows is rendered problematic. But whatever else we believe, it is difficult not to conclude that here June has been reclaimed as the restless ghost of the mother who really does "mean to" abandon her child. Maybe Lipsha is right now, and she did mean to hurt him as she was hurt; or maybe he is still wrong, and she acted to put the child she could not hold out of its misery. In either event, June's return as an embodied ghost with her own traumatic history prompts (or perhaps is prompted by) an undoing of the resolution and forgiveness of the mother that closed and for many readers unified *Love Medicine*. In the last chapter of that novel, Lipsha says, "I couldn't linger too long on sad facts" (265), but in *The Bingo Palace* he has been forced to do just that, when his hopeful reconstruction of his mother's act of abandonment as a blessing in disguise is explicitly revised again, this time apparently irrevocably.

Although June's behavior is far more difficult to judge than Sethe's in *Beloved*, the story of June and Lipsha may best be understood as analogous to the story of the slave mother and her baby daughter in that it is "not a story to pass on." Like *Beloved*, it is told and understood as a ghost story in which there is no question that the ghost is real. Both narratives seek to record what is an affront to understanding, what is impossible to know in rational, historical modes of knowing, even, perhaps, what must be kept secret lest it, too, be stolen, at the same time that the story must nevertheless be brought to consciousness and memory. This story, as constructed by the sequence from *Love Medicine* to *The Bingo Palace*, does not go fully or only forward to the mother who holds and offers hope, but also goes back to June as a figure of traumatic loss and failure of connection who cannot be repaired or recovered or forgiven, even as she is still "much loved." Attempts fail to assimilate or repress either the real atrocity that "damaged" her to begin with or the disorientation that her own abandoned child in turn undergoes. At the same time, Lipsha, unwitting agent in the separation of another parent and child, tries not to "pass on" the story as he received it.

FLEUR

In *The Bingo Palace* there is a partial, tenuous, and enigmatic reconnection of that other liminal mother without child, Fleur, to her descendants. In *Tracks*, readers never find out what Lulu, a virtually uncharacterized listener in that novel, thinks of Nanapush's attempted vindication of her mother, Fleur. In *The Bingo Palace*, however, when

Lipsha assumes that Lulu still hates Fleur, Lulu quietly corrects him in a way that suggests she was able to hear Nanapush: "'I don't hate the old lady . . . I understand her.'" In the chapters Erdrich has recently added to *Love Medicine,* we learn more about Lulu's longing for her mother, and at times of trouble Lulu still hears her mother's comforting voice saying "'N'dawnis,' my daughter" (69, 83, new and expanded edition). In *The Bingo Palace,* however, what Lulu or anyone else might "understand" about Fleur is rendered, like June's story, in such a way as to exceed what we might normally think of as rational understanding. And although it might have seemed to be the case in *Love Medicine* and *Tracks,* as Scott Sanders has observed, that "the wisdom of healing and intimacy with the ancient gods is dying with the old women" (9), this conclusion too is revised by Fleur's role in *The Bingo Palace.*[48]

Already associated with ghosts, the dead, and fearsome supernatural powers in *Tracks,* Fleur returns in *The Bingo Palace* as a surpassingly old but still extraordinarily powerful woman, a "healing doctor witch" feared by the community, which assumes that she is waiting to pass on her knowledge to Lipsha, her great-grandson, before she dies.[49] When Lipsha timidly introduces himself to Fleur, she leads him back to her home in the woods around Matchimanito Lake. There Fleur has apparently learned what she did not know in *Tracks:* she has tapped into the power of words and writing that only Nanapush wielded in the earlier novel, appropriating writing for her own purposes of resistance and cultural survival, not assimilation.[50] Lipsha finds his great-grandmother's house full of papers stacked to the ceiling, and every available surface, including walls and tablecloth, is covered with a spidery writing that Lipsha cannot decode. When he asks her for love medicine to help him court Shawnee Ray, the already surreal scene fades as Fleur seems to turn into an animal and Lipsha faints. Just what the old woman means or does remains, as ever, terrifying and unclear.

But at least a little more of the story can be told. Just as the story of "June's Luck" follows on Lipsha's first sighting of her apparition in the bar of Lyman's casino, his uncertain and frightening meeting with Fleur brings another piece of her experience into narration in the next chapter, with the parallel title "Fleur's Luck." Here we learn more about one segment of Fleur's mysterious life after the end of *Tracks* (although we still lack many details). This chapter tells of her last return to the reservation, at some unspecified point, with an expensive white car, wearing an elegant white suit and bringing with her a mysterious white boy, who may or may not be her son. Whoever he is, she uses the boy in her successful effort to resist the colonizer, to win back the Pillager land by playing cards with the white agent. Whereas "June's Luck" confirms and accounts for the damage done to June as victim, "Fleur's Luck" extends the story of Fleur as trickster and avenger.[51] In both cases, what happens in the traumatic or supernatural moment or what the ghostly, dissociated June or magical figure Fleur intends is obscure, but the consequences of Lipsha's encounters with them are clear. Somehow they afford at least a window onto understanding, a slightly fuller but by no means fully rational or complete narrative of that which is so difficult and crucial to know and tell, the mother's story.

The novel closes with what we can take to be Fleur's death, following on and seemingly in response to Lipsha's failed attempt to rescue his father. The last chapter in Fleur's story and the novel, however, does not have the status of epiphany or final revelation or even clear, coherent narrative. From the point of view of the first-person-plural voice with which the novel opened, it is represented as a puzzle whose solution resists or escapes certain knowledge: those who come to Fleur's house after she is gone partly "*decipher,*" partly "*imagine*" what happened. According to their recreation of events, Fleur sets out in the blizzard on her last journey, at once imitating and reversing June's journey into the snow at the beginning of *Love Medicine.* Fleur goes to take her place among the dead at last, standing in for "the boy," presumably Lipsha, whom we last saw marooned in the snow: "Annoyed, she took his place" (272). On the basis of imagined "tracks" in the snow, as mysterious and unreadable as the "tracks" on her walls, it is rumored that Fleur turned into a bear as she headed back to the cave on the island where her cousin Moses and all the dead members of her family waited for her. It is also said that "she still walks"—like and unlike June, who still drives at least—and watches the community at their gambling. Read as figures of the mother without child, Fleur and June both remind us of the intricate patterns of loss and desire, of all that we will never fully understand, while promising that there is more than can be known and narrated.

MAKING DO AND DOING SOMETHING

Two recent short stories by Linda Hogan, a member of the Chickasaw tribe, and Georgiana Valoyce Sanchez, from the Pima/Papago and Chumash tribes, may help to clarify the two main threads of a tradition within which the figure of the mother without child works in the juxtaposed stories of June and Fleur.[52] In Hogan's "Making Do," an unidentified third-person speaker briefly recapitulates the story of Roberta James's experience as a young mother. Roberta "became one of the silent people in Seeker County" when she lost her first child, a daughter who died at the age of six. In quick succession, Roberta loses a second child, a son who is strangled by his umbilical cord at birth, and then her third and last child, a daughter who dies of some unspecified fever. Leaving her family of equally bereaved and "broken" people, Roberta goes alone to a small town in Colorado where she works part-time in a convenience store, whittles small birds "as toys for the spirits of her children," and otherwise waits in vain for her soul to leave her body. In the second section of the story, a first-person speaker who appears to be Roberta's sister comments on her reasons for deciding not to go to comfort Roberta when she hears the news of her troubles. "I knew this much," the narrator says:

> Roberta would need to hold on to her grief and her pain.
> Us Chickasaws have lost so much we hold on to everything. Even our muscles hold on to their aches. We love our lovers long after they are gone, better than when they were present. (204)

In what remains of her part of the story, the speaker appears to forget Roberta. But in fact she transforms Roberta's experience into parable, as she elaborates on her theory of how her people "make do," saving and reusing whatever comes to hand—bottlecaps, old jars and cans and shoes—in order to save themselves from the repeated history of losing everything. For many, the price of this kind of saving (in both senses of the word) is denial, the speaker adds; the occasional act of angry protest is just "a tidal wave in the ocean of our history, an anxiety attack in the heart monitor of our race" (205). However, she ends with an anecdote that suggests how quiet, apparently submissive "making do" can be, in its own way, a means of simultaneously remembering and surviving loss:

> Once I saw a railroad engineer's hat in a museum. It was fully beaded. I thought it was a new style like the beaded tennis shoes or the new beaded truckers' hats. But it was made in the late 1800s when the Lakota were forbidden to make traditional items. The mothers took to beading whatever was available, hats of the engineers of death. They covered colony cotton with their art.
> We make art out of our loss. (205)

In this story, the mother who loses three children does not, like Adelaide Adare or June Morrisey, purposely abandon them, but like Adelaide and June she is one of the innumerable "silent" ones, "damaged" and "broken" in some irreparable way, who cannot use words to reconnect to others, to express or relieve their loss by telling their own story. Her sister, the contemporary storyteller writing in English, respects this silence and the grief it contains, recognizing both as ways of holding on to loss when loss itself is paradoxically all that is left. Like the storytellers in Erdrich's novels, she thereby seems to frame and reinforce the impenetrability of the mother without child. In her telling, Roberta's story becomes both a paradigm of the traumatic history of "Us Chickasaw" and a springboard to reflection on how survival and art—as well as survival through art—are possible in the face of the decimation of families, tribes, and cultures. In the last anecdote, "the mothers" are also those who represent this continuity—not immediately or easily recognized as such—despite loss, and who express it in their "saving" art forms.

In Sanchez's "The Heart of the Flower," a more active, immediately recognizable, although not necessarily more effective political response to maternal loss (that is, a woman's loss of a child) is imagined. The story sets a tale of private tragedy inside a historical crisis, an episode of dramatic public protest. The time is March 1973, and the pregnant first-person narrator gives birth to a stillborn baby on the tenth day of the siege at Wounded Knee. Before the loss of the baby, she has been daydreaming about joining American Indian Movement (AIM) activists and finding herself in increasing disagreement with her husband Ed, a veteran who disapproves of AIM's militancy, prefers to ignore his Native American identity, and believes "the old days are gone" (258). Afterwards, the narrator associates her own stillborn fetus with the death and pathology of Native American culture. Despite Ed's disapproval, she decides she must take some small part in the action at Wounded Knee by donating food to the AIM headquarters in Los Angeles. As she sets off with the groceries, she cries because of the growing rift between herself and Ed, but she sees and articulates clearly the way in which loss of the child has politicized her: "There I was going off on some maybe hopeless vision quest only I couldn't pull out because the child had died. Would never be born. And, oh God, I had to do something" (263). Here, as in so many other historical circumstances, the mothers—especially the mothers who are no longer mothers—survive to do something, in this case making trouble as well as art out of loss. The point is the same as Ruth's claim, in Jane Rule's *The Young in One Another's Arms*—"What you lose is what you survive with" (3).

Erdrich and Dorris's insistent recursions to and variations on the theme of the mother's loss or fear of loss evoke these two fundamental patterns (and in many cases, one character can do both). In the first, recording and making "art" out of loss without assimilating it or forgetting it recognizes the mother's silence as a way of holding on to the loss itself, when loss may be all that is left. In the second, finding in her loss the impetus to take action with what is left opens the possibility of "doing something," however hopeless it may seem. June's story, in the context of many others, might be understood primarily as a version of the former, Fleur's a version of the latter. In the trajectory I trace here from *Yellow Raft on Blue Water* to *The Bingo Palace,* there is decreasing certainty that the story of the mother without child can be told once, resolved, recuperated, known, and forgiven. Instead it is divided into these two complementary myths, both of which require a narrative that finally turns into a full-fledged ghost story. Like the sister's narrative intervention in "Making Do," the ghost story in Erdrich's latest novel puts June back into the narrative without violating her silence or taking away her pain and the pain she has given, without absorbing pain and loss into our normal ways of remembering, which can also be ways of forgetting. Like "The Heart of the Flower," *The Bingo Palace* underscores the simultaneous political resistance and commitment to survival through tradition that is at the heart of Fleur's actions, her mysterious existence, and her supernatural force. The story of the mother without child can thus represent both the trauma out of which we can never—and should never—quite make sense and the power that exceeds the sieve of rational thinking.

With this development of the Native American mother without child, we see the obverse of Judith Antell's argument about the figure of the absent mother in much previous fiction. Contradicting their images in Euroamerican representations, women of Native American descent have been able to play their traditional role and sustain the continuity of their tribal culture through times of crisis. To the extent that they do so, female figures—like Fleur or June or Pauline—are even *more* threatening to the "colonial scenario" and certainly cannot be "discounted." Erdrich and Dorris put the mother without child into narrative as a figure of both "tragic," irrecoverable loss and the "threat" of survival and resistance.

Five

Mothers Yesterday and Mothers Tomorrow, but Never Mothers Today

Woman on the Edge of Time and The Handmaid's Tale

> The loss of the daughter to the mother, the mother to the daughter, is the essential female tragedy.
> —Adrienne Rich, *Of Woman Born*

> Though human mothers can, in an ultimate existentialist sense, do other things than give birth, their choices to do so or not are usually highly constrained.
> —Virginia Held, *Feminist Morality*

The stories I have considered thus far explore three disparate subcultures wherein the loss of children is the historic norm, and most of the mothers in question are positioned as deviant and marginalized persons—lesbians, black women, Native Americans, and people of mixed blood. Having begun at these margins, I move now towards what might be thought of as the center or norm. Here too, however, we find that things aren't so different for many mothers. In the remaining chapters, I turn to fiction authored by two well-known white North American writers, Marge Piercy and Margaret Atwood, and the prolific British writer Fay Weldon. Collectively their stories of the mother without child underscore what is in some sense the most urgent message of all the novels I consider: no woman, whatever her class or race or nationality or sexuality, is immune from the crisis of motherhood.

In some ways the two novels I pair in this chapter, *Woman on the Edge of Time* and *The Handmaid's Tale,* presume the most conventional models of motherhood and offer the least ambiguous figures of the mother without child that I have yet examined. The protagonists are both heterosexual. Connie Ramos, in *Woman on the Edge of Time,* is Chicana, but her ethnic identity, although it contributes to her problems as a mother, is not the focus of the story. The Handmaid is a white, well-educated, and still relatively privileged woman. In what precedes the present time of the novels, both women have given birth to healthy daughters whom they love, and neither has given up her child willingly. Apparently they would be quite traditional wives and mothers if only they were allowed to be, but circumstances mark them as victims of oppressive, male-dominated societies. At the same time, by setting all or part of the action in each novel in a future world where women have either voluntarily surrendered their reproductive functions (Piercy's utopia) or involuntarily lost control over them (Atwood's dystopia), both novels articulate serious worries about conventional motherhood, particularly insofar as it enables actual and potential abuses of the fact that females bear children. Together, moreover, these two novels afford a wide range of reinterpretations of the notorious female tragedy, "the loss of the daughter to the mother."

A POWERFUL AND UNUSUAL MIX

In *Woman on the Edge of Time,* the story's problems and solutions and the protagonist's weaknesses and strengths are tightly connected to the heroine's behavior as a biological mother and to ideological or theoretical notions of what it means to mother and be a mother. As a story of time travel, the plot moves back and forth on two time lines, one present and one future. In the present, sometime in the second half of the twentieth century—we might call this "real time," for short—Connie Ramos is an unlikely heroine: an unfit mother, previously committed to a mental hospital for abusing her four-year-old daughter, Angelina, who was subsequently taken from her for adoption. The so-called caring professions into whose hands she falls label Connie "socially disorganized" (377), a rubric that accounts for the contradictory observations the professionals make—she is "cooperative," on the one hand, and "hostile and suspicious toward authority," on the other (379). The final diagnosis at Bellevue is "Schizophrenia, undiff. type 295.90" (378) and at Rockover State Psychiatric Hospital, "Paranoid schizophrenia, type 295.3" (379).[1] Such dehumanizing labels are offered only at the very end of the novel, however, in a brief epilogue of sorts, closing the fictional story immediately after Connie has done what Meridian Hill only thought she might be able to do: she has will-fully murdered in a righteous cause, for the revolution. In ways I ex-plore later in this chapter, the epilogue abruptly puts this violent mother without child with mothers like Adelaide Adare or June Morrisey, be-yond the imaginative reach of novel writing, fictional authority, or read-erly apprehension. It also sets novel writing and fantasy making in re-lief as discursive modes that see the mother unofficially, differently, more compassionately, and more honestly. Contrasting sharply with the clinical judgment, the fictional story that constitutes the bulk of the novel indicts not Connie but rather, among other things, the crude and cruel failures of institutional psychiatry and social work.

As the official, reductive diagnosis ironically indicates, Connie in real time indeed embodies all that is normally perceived as paradoxical in our culture's myths about mothers and mothering. She is vulnerable, passive, submissive to the will of others, empathic, and self-sacrificing; at the same time she is powerful, tough, violent, resistant to the will of others, and self-absorbed. In the novel, however, this paradox or dou-bleness is not represented as an index of an internal, individual bind or an inevitable split, for good or bad, constitutive or otherwise, in the maternal as type of the subject.[2] The point instead is that the negative consequences of the apparent dichotomy in Connie's personality and behavior are a function of the social and political context in which this woman is positioned as a mother. Like the communal destruction of the Sojourner tree in *Meridian* or Fleur's devastation of the woods sur-rounding her home, Connie's anger and consequent violence are viewed both as self-implosive reflexes of her particular oppression and as po-tential tools of collective empowerment.

Taught by her ethnic and class background to be a good woman—a passive, submissive, complicitous victim—Connie is brutalized and aban-doned by a series of men and institutions who are allegedly her protectors: her father, brother, lovers, husbands, professors, doctors, family, the wel-fare state, and the hospitals she is imprisoned in.[3] She is in turn unable to nurture and hold onto her child. Connie sees herself in this daughter, and after losing her, comes to believe that some of her occasional anger towards the child was self-abusive. "She should have loved her better; but to love you must love yourself, she knew that now, especially to love a daughter you see as yourself reborn" (62). The story opens after the loss of the daugh-ter, with an act of violence aimed at the real enemy—Connie smashes an empty wine jug into the handsome, evil face of her niece's pimp, Geraldo.[4]

The instrument of violence Connie chooses—apparently because it is nearest to hand—symbolically identifies her, from the outset, with the biological mother and the female reproductive body. The empty bottle, one of the few decorations in Connie's bleak two-room flat, contained dried flowers and grasses gathered on a rare family outing, a picnic with her estranged brother, her niece Dolly, and Dolly's baby daughter Nita. What Connie remembers most about this picnic is that Nita, just learning to walk, fell asleep in her arms and that she was allowed to hold her: "She had sat on the blanket burning, transfigured with holding that small sweet-breathing flush-faced morsel" (34). It is the almost erotic, sensual, transformative possibility of "holding" a baby that Connie summons up and throws away when she scatters the "nostalgic grasses" (16) and breaks the wine jug over Geraldo's nose. Yet she does so in order to preserve other conventionally maternal functions. She takes the offensive as a surrogate mother, on behalf of other biological mothers who are still trying, against the odds, to hold onto their born and unborn children. She acts to protect not herself, but her niece Dolly, the unloved and illegitimate daughter of the brother who later betrays Connie; Dolly, "her almost child" (20), has come to her aunt bleeding from Geraldo's beating—he wants to abort the baby he has fathered on her. Connie thus tries to defend her niece both as almost daughter and as almost mother. The wine bottle foreshadows a smaller bottle, disguised as a container of shampoo, in which Connie will conceal the poison she uses in the matching act of violence that closes her story. Both wine jug and shampoo bottle—emptied, curvilinear spaces no longer holding what they were designed to contain, and fragile, easily shattered yet dangerous vessels—clearly image the female womb, denied its reproductive burden, as a vengeful weapon.

In part, it may be the greater distance between niece and aunt that enables Connie to fight for Dolly, whereas she could see in Angelina, her birth daughter, only her hated, defeated self. The surrogate mother or Othermother, as we saw so clearly in *Meridian* and in Erdrich's plots, often has a power that the birth mother finds more difficult to exercise.[5] But more importantly, the novel insists, it is because Connie has already lost her own child, together with the capacity and right to mother any other child, that her anger can now be directed outward against her oppressors rather than inward against herself and her daughter. Like members of Latin American motherist movements or characters in Jane Rule's novels, this heroine is explicitly motivated to protest social injustice not because as a mother she has special political insights or powers, but because as a mother whose child has been taken from her, she has so little left to lose. She articulates this herself at the end of the novel: "'If only they had left me something. . . . Only one person to love. . . . For that love I'd have borne it all and I'd never have fought back. . . . But I have nothing. Why shouldn't I strike back?'" (372).

The opening episode of the real-time plot anticipates and encapsulates central arguments of the novel as a whole: women mother under the logic of either-or, whereby characteristics like passive and active or complicitous and subversive are seen as mutually exclusive. Consequently, the only power of the biological mother, in present circumstances, is no more and no less than a reflex of her vulnerability. A woman can exercise one kind of maternal power only if she (willingly or unwillingly) gives up the other. Connie's sacrifice prefigures and implicitly prepares the ground for the future world, in which women have given up biological motherhood in order to bring social justice to all.

Seen from the more enlightened perspective afforded by the novel's interwoven construction of a utopian community, schizophrenic Connie and the mutually exclusive, self-destructive maternal capacities she embodies are relabeled. Connie turns out to be one of a handful of people in our time who can travel to the future *because* they have conventionally feminine or maternal qualities: they are passive, submissive, penetrable. In the terminology of time travel here, Connie is a natural receiver, and Luciente, the woman who fetches her from the future, notes: "'It's odd. . . . Most we've reached are females, and many of those in mental hospitals and prisons'" (196). This statement draws on familiar myths about creativity and madness, but it also begins to erode oppositions between active and passive, mind and body, rational and irrational, suggesting that mental creativity or imagination can be facilitated, not blocked, by what is considered in our time to be part of the self-denying, other-oriented side of mothering. The novel thereby confirms in its own way feminist theories like those of Julia Kristeva and Hélène Cixous that attribute special imaginative and discursive powers to the subversive feminine or maternal. It becomes gradually clearer, moreover, that Connie is not just a receiver; to forget present pain, she learns to thrust herself into the future. Luciente soon realizes that Connie is a potent force in her own right: "'Grasp, you could be a sender too. What a powerful and unusual mix'" (113). To the future, then, what we call schizophrenia is a combination of those qualities usually considered to be in binary, gender-specific, irreconcilable opposition. The novel suggests that both sets of qualities will be necessary to the successful redefinition and revaluing of mothering, on which a better society for all depends.

But in real time, women are punished for striking back; Connie is beaten and incarcerated for her opening act of maternal violence. As she lies strapped to a hospital bed, drugged, her burns and broken ribs untreated, she articulates her own understanding of both the connection and the difference between the self-implosive anger that caused her to lose her daughter and the potentially empowering rage that she has turned on the pimp: "She hated Geraldo and it was right for her to hate him. Attacking him was different from turning her anger, her sorrow, her loss . . . into self-hatred, into speed and downers, into booze, into wine, into seeing herself in Angelina and abusing that self born again into the dirty world. Yes, this time was different. She had struck out not at herself, not at herself in another, but at Geraldo, the enemy" (19–20). Connie thinks, mistakenly, that she can make this protest work—"this time" will be "different" in that she will know how to convince the authorities that she is sane, violent in a just cause, so that she can "get out fast." The story demonstrates instead that she will never get out. In the present time of social injustice and inhumanity, a mother's righteous, deadly anger cannot disguise itself as so-called sanity and will not serve to reunite her with her lost daughter, save her niece, or allow her niece to mother again.[6] In Connie's last reported act, she attacks the enemy once more, successfully and self-destructively poisoning several doctors who conduct mind-control experiments on mental patients like herself. Connie's premeditated murder is depicted as both heroic and self-sacrificial; as political commentary, the novel thereby registers the powers, limits, and costs of maternal violence in a context where the maternal is still exclusively tied to—and so often denied to—the devalued body that reproduces.

In Connie's case, the experience of time travel—a metaphor for and a realization of imaginative power—is consistently linked to aspects or consequences of her thwarted biological maternity, and so it is difficult for her or the novel to get beyond the logic of either-or. The first visit with Luciente comes immediately *after* Connie has passed a playground full of brown-skinned girls that she imagines to be just about her daughter's current age. She weeps with pain at the loss of Angelina, and with characteristic self-reproach thinks herself "sentimental"—"Anybody would think that she had loved her daughter." In the next sentence, Luciente comes through—"A shadow across her" (40). The second time they make contact, Connie is in the hospital, locked in seclusion, physically suffering from burns and beatings and mentally reliving the horrible moment when she hit Angie too hard and the child fell and broke her wrist. As she tries to forget the pain of losing the girl, she consciously lets herself feel Luciente's approach (and on this visit she travels to Mattapoisett herself for the first time; 60–3). Later, when she learns to travel in time easily, she deliberately calls on Luciente—for example, when she wants to stop herself from dwelling on memories of Angelina (113).

Through this strategy of initiating time travel with memories of the lost daughter, the novel connects Connie's mental receptivity with her traumatic maternal experience in the real world and underscores the link between maternal oppression and maternal resistance. But at the same time, the plot does not merely rewrite the victimization of women as a potential source of strength and power; the powerlessness of this mother without child as it is experienced in the here and now blocks further progress on the road to the future. So, Connie's constant recall of Angie may trigger her imaginative insights into the future, but just as often the pain of those memories stays with her in future time and, when it becomes too strong, breaks the connection. When Connie visits the utopian "brooder," a building full of tanks where fetuses gestate, she learns with initial disgust that each test-tube baby will have three comothers of either gender. Provoked, she recalls her own embodied experience of bearing and nursing her child too intensely; the tie to the future is broken, and she suddenly finds herself back in the mental hospital. Again and again, when Connie in the future remembers the reality of her disabled mothering or the injustices of motherhood as an institution in America in the second half of the twentieth century, the link dissolves (114, 125–7, 160, 183). Only in utopian Mattapoisett is this mixture of passivity and activity, of felt maternal empathy and principled maternal violence, understood and experienced as a positive, powerful conjunction rather than a pathological or psychotic split; and Connie and the novel, both committed to present-day political theory and action, cannot remain in the future. As Connie's real-time purposiveness and outwardly directed rage against the conditions that make her an "unfit" mother take stronger shape, she travels to the future less and less frequently, and Luciente comments on the unreachable "hardness" in her mind (370). After Connie has irrevocably committed herself to murder—the insecticide is already in the doctors' coffee maker—her time travel ends, and the novel has only a few pages to go: "She thought of Luciente, but she could no longer reach over. She could no longer catch. She had annealed her mind and she was not a receptive woman. She had hardened" (375).

Does this statement imply that it is impossible in actuality, rather than in fantasy, to escape the logic of either-or that Connie as biological mother is trapped in? Isn't Connie's real-time behavior, celebrated by the novel, in fact inconsistent with the utopian presumption that women would voluntarily give up their reproductive powers, the fiction upon which Mattapoisett is premised? In light of questions such as these, how seriously do we want to take Piercy's apparent prescription for feminist action—is she suggesting that in the quest for an end to domination, women have to or inevitably will give up their special, sometimes celebrated powers of receptivity and creativity, often seen as extensions of their biological capacity to give birth, as Connie does? This is the way many readers have interpreted the frequently quoted passage in which Luciente tries to explain to Connie how and why women, on their way to the future, voluntarily gave up their procreative function:

> "It was part of women's long revolution. When we were breaking up all the old hierarchies. Finally there was that one thing we had to give up too, the only power we ever had, in return for no more power for anyone. The original production: the power to give birth. Cause as long as we were biologically enchained, we'd never be equal. And males never would be humanized to be loving and tender. So we all became mothers." (105)

Critics have argued that Piercy, like other "demon" feminists, is actually guilty of reproducing here a patriarchal move by rejecting the female body and excluding the biological mother from utopia. The grounds of this criticism are obvious and undeniable, but it begs the fraught question of women's relation to biological motherhood and oversimplifies if not mistakes the genre as well as the politics of the novel.

To say, as one critic does, that the novel aligns "motherhood" with "machinery" (in the brooders of Mattapoisett) is to presume only the narrowest construction of motherhood.[7] Universalizing and conflating "*the* female body" with its reproductive function, this reading ignores among other things the fact that Piercy's utopia is welcoming to other somatically female characteristics that Connie is trained to view negatively, like the wide hips that fit comfortably into Luciente's expandable drawstring pants. It also ignores the final aspect of Luciente's explanation: "So we all became mothers." Here, as in all the novels I have considered thus far, there is a dispersal of "the" mother that merits attention. No longer linked in any essential way to the reproductive function, motherhood in the future of this novel is imagined as a powerful position or set of behaviors available to everyone.

We might exercise caution in taking Piercy's fiction too prescriptively, forgetting its speculative function. As Luciente says, late in the novel, "'The vestiges of old ways will fade. . . . We can only know what we can truly imagine. Finally what we see comes from ourselves'" (328). The novel is "didactic," as Piercy is often accused of being, in its critique of real-time motherhood. But we may be reading too literally if we think the novel seriously instructs women to stop either mothering or imagining in order to take up revolutionary, guerrilla warfare. It realistically apprehends the complexities and compromises of trying to take care of children, be politically active, and do creative work, and it resists the notion that the power of imagination it both idealizes and embodies is sufficient unto itself, independent of political purpose and action. Primarily, *Woman on the Edge of Time* urges the necessity of redefining motherhood so that it is a collective as well as a personal project and so that good mothering, like good fiction writing and good political action, unifies and legitimates the "powerful mix" that Connie, a sender and a receiver, can be in a better world.

It is important to emphasize that this is more a prescription for parthenogenesis than one for androgyny because Piercy does not attribute one set of binary traits to women, one to men, and urge that they be combined into a fuller human essence.[8] Instead, the novel locates the "powerful mix" most specifically *within* what is falsely conceived of and punished as the mythic maternal split or paradox. Child abuser and sterile woman, markedly *without* the only child she will ever bear, Connie is paradoxically the constantly evolving figure who takes care of the future, who remains committed to mothering work even as her notion of what that means changes, like her own behavior changes. Only after Connie has glimpsed the possibility that her daughter Angie has been reborn in Luciente's daughter, Dawn (140), is she able to free herself sufficiently from her own complicity and self-loathing to think of fighting back again—this time to do serious harm instead of just lashing out. Giving Angie to the future and assenting to the utopian repudiation of the biological role of women as mothers are turning points for Connie; thereafter she dreams of becoming a co-mother herself (249), and the last thing she sees in Mattapoisett, before she poisons the coffee, is Dawn/Angie. It is made pointedly clear that Connie knows the difference between her real loss and this imaginative substitution—the visionary imagination is not romanticized as an escape or retreat to an alternative reality—but the utopian dream nevertheless fires the real crime. As she tells a fellow inmate, "'I dreamed of my daughter, safe, happy, in another place,'" and this complicates the perception that it is her absolute loss of anyone to love that empowers her vengeance. It is also her dream of a world where the community shares and makes possible her mundane goals as a mother—to see a child "safe, happy"—that inspires her to take subversive action.

In real time, Connie has suffered for trying to embody one side of the falsely dichotomous maternal personality, ironically the one most frequently enjoined upon women in patriarchal prescriptions for motherhood, marked by passivity, vulnerability, empathy, lack of self-control, and irrationality. These are the qualities that empower her fantastic journey in time; and although the novel identifies with and revalues these capacities, it does not sentimentalize or idealize them and thereby merely project the work of good mothering onto the minority female figure. Instead, *Woman on the Edge of Time* suggests that Connie has other valuable strengths that in Mattapoisett would make her a good mother: her aggression, her emotional and physical endurance, and her drive to protect those she loves and to fight for her beliefs. In real time she can only be punished for those qualities, and the novel finally refuses to forget that Connie will never mother her own birth daughter.

GIVE ME CHILDREN, OR ELSE I DIE

In *The Handmaid's Tale,* published almost a decade after *Woman on the Edge of Time,* the problem of women's biological link to mothering is perhaps even more obviously and single-mindedly at the center of the story. The dystopia Margaret Atwood constructs illustrates by counterexample the proposition that we might all get to a better world, one without injustice and inequality, if women gave up their one apparent power, the capacity to give birth. It also confirms another feminist insight that may be implicit in Piercy's portrayal of Connie's obsession with biological motherhood: the work of mothering is often divided along racial and class lines. The most privileged women, in various historical periods including our own, have been tacitly and legitimately able to "slough off" the more onerous parts of mothering onto working class and minority women. This division among women serves the purpose of maintaining patriarchal formations; as Evelyn Nakano Glenn argues, "Because they gain these privileges, white, middle-class women have less impetus to challenge an arrangement that ultimately oppresses them."[9] In Atwood's dystopia, "ultimately" has arrived, all women are oppressed, and any "impetus to challenge" is contained by coercive pronatalism and the tightly controlled division (and repression) of reproductive and nurturant labor.

In the future world of the early Gilead era, biological mothering (and to a lesser extent the institutions that control it, including marriage and domestic life) is indeed women's *only* power. In a fantastic and prophetic caricature of actual surrogacy practices brought to national attention in the Baby M case shortly after the publication of Atwood's novel, the gestational and caregiving aspects of maternal experience are strictly divided. The system is sanctioned by association with the Old Testament version of surrogacy practiced by Rachel, Jacob, and Bilhah. Gilead's women of childbearing years recite the ancient words of Rachel quoted in one of the novel's epigraphs: "Give me children, or else I die" (Genesis 30:1). The survival of the protagonist depends completely on her biological capacity to give birth. The state protects her only because she once bore a child, a daughter earlier confiscated and given to a childless couple of the elite, and because she still has viable ovaries. If she or any other Handmaid fails to conceive and bear a healthy baby after three postings with the aging, probably sterile leaders of the regime, she will at best be deported to "the Colonies," where the powerless clean up toxic wastes until they die hideous deaths.

Concomitantly, as the unevenly intersecting lines of class, race, age, and gender difference are reinforced by the totalitarian, patriarchal regime of Gilead, women are at once categorized as the same (powerless and subject to men) and divided among themselves (so that they will compete). One of the regime's first important steps was to fire all female employees and freeze every woman's financial assets. Now females are strictly divided into women and unwomen, and those in the first category are further sorted according to task and status within the strictly regulated domestic and reproductive sphere: Handmaids, Marthas, Wives, Aunts, Econowives, and so on. Ludicrously and cruelly, women who have argued against feminist reform and in favor of conservative values that privatize and domesticate the female have been taken all too literally. Serena Joy, the wife in the Handmaid's household, is a former television personality who once made speeches, the Handmaid recalls, "about the sanctity of the home, about how women should stay home" (60).[10] "How furious she must be," the Handmaid thinks, "now that she's been taken at her word" (61).

Atwood's novel thus conflates conservative and radical notions of the special difference and power of the female body and the sacred, redeeming experience of maternity to show us what they have in common and how readily they fuse into one horrifying, logical extreme. The pessimistic insistence on the ease with which feminist gains of the very recent past could be swept away even as feminist celebrations of motherhood and childbearing recoil against women seems percipient and urgent in light of political developments in the decade since the novel's publication. Atwood's indictment of patriarchal control over the female body and its procreative powers is at least as biting as Piercy's; both bear witness to the difficulty of conceptualizing a reproductive female body outside the control of a patriarchal state.

As a dystopia, however, *The Handmaid's Tale* offers nothing like the programmatic recipe for change that is available in the utopian fantasy of Piercy's work. In the epilogue, "Historical Notes on *The Handmaid's Tale*," we are offered a brief glimpse of a better or at least more familiar future (the year is 2195), wherein both male and female academics analyze the tale at a conference of the Gileadean Research Association. In this short episode it is clear that although the atrocities of Gilead were finally eradicated, things have changed very little in some ways. The male keynote speaker's references to putatively obsolete sexist language evoke laughter and applause (381), and the speaker takes an apolitical stance when he eschews "passing moral judgment upon the Gileadeans": "Our job is not to censure but to understand. (*Applause.*)" (383). Insofar as the nightmare of the Handmaid's story demonstrates that the job of getting out of Gilead and into any remotely tolerable future would require not just censure but subversion and revolutionary violence, Atwood's satire targets academic complacence and the notion that simply installing new identities in old structures will bring about social justice.[11] More indirectly than *Woman on the Edge of Time*, the novel similarly implies that there are limits to "understanding," that empathy may have to harden itself when revolution is called for.

This implication is conveyed, however, by a heroine who is the opposite of Connie Ramos in most respects and whose lack of heroic qualities is thoroughly consistent with the post-Gileadean return to business as usual, or with only a slight difference. In Connie, we see a woman who embodies and reconciles both sides of the mythic mother, her "clean anger" and her remarkable empathy, and her imaginative fusion of these qualities makes Mattapoisett a possibility. In the Handmaid, we have no such "unusual and powerful mix," but rather a woman who is much more ordinary, the typical protagonist of Atwood's fiction that her readers have come to know since the stolid Marion of *The Edible Woman*.[12] This woman is both less powerless and less powerful than Connie. On the one hand, the Handmaid is not (in the present of the telling) drugged or considered insane. She has an education, is white, and is therefore genetically acceptable for the elite position of Handmaid. In pre-Gileadean society, she had a good job and money of her own. Her memories of motherhood imply that she had no problems, as Connie did, in loving her daughter adequately.

On the other hand, it sometimes seems that the Handmaid's strongest capacity is her tolerance of boredom. She never tries to escape; she contemplates a variety of subversive, criminal acts but never commits them; she is always cautious, or almost always. The most dangerous thing she does is to risk her life for sexual satisfaction by carrying on an affair with Nick, the man who may betray her or may save her, but whom she cannot resist. In the end she waits (as Connie waits, although the Handmaid's punishment is less certain), to be destroyed or rescued. She speaks of herself as a coward, terrified of pain, who wants to survive; to that end she tries hard not to feel, and she certainly succeeds in suppressing any signs of the rage that empowers Connie. In the very beginning, she announces: "I try not to think too much. Like other things, thought must be rationed. There's a lot that doesn't bear thinking about. Thinking can hurt your chances, and I intend to last" (10). Like most of Atwood's earlier heroines, she is aware of and even seems to relish her own ordinariness, her limits and weaknesses, her failures of courage and wit. When the Commander takes her to an illegal nightclub, she calms her nervousness: "All you have to do, I tell myself, is keep your mouth shut and look stupid. It shouldn't be that hard" (306). She admits to admiring what she cannot be, the heroine that she sees in her friend Moira, and worries about the double standard she holds for herself, on the one hand, and Moira, on the other:

> How can I expect her to go on, with my idea of her courage, live it through, act it out, when I myself do not?
>   I don't want her to be like me. Give in, go along, save her skin.
> That is what it comes down to. I want gallantry from her, swashbuckling, heroism, single-handed combat. Something I lack. (324)

What this narrator is guilty of, or capable of, by her own account, is not the overtly criminal, antisocial behavior of a woman like Connie but everyday, "usual" behavior. Commenting on her past life, she says: "We lived, as usual, by ignoring. Ignoring isn't the same as ignorance, you have to work at it" (74). Now, although she tries not to think or feel too much, because she understands how dangerous that would be, she does want to know, or at least this is what she finds herself telling the Commander that she wants. However, any use of her knowledge seems beyond her self-reported, strategically limited capacity.[13] This mother without child is someone knowingly caught in the middle between knowledge and ignorance, action and inaction, anger and numbness, resistance and submission—all too aware of what she lacks but incapable of changing. As she says near the end of her story, "I would like to be ignorant. Then I would not know how ignorant I was" (340).

What do we make of such a heroine, whose self-protective stupidity and complicity (or at least failure to fight back) seem to be, as she says in one of the last of her self-criticisms, "the point"?[14] Is she another one of Atwood's depressing postfeminist types from whom women readers can take no pleasure, no positive inspiration?[15] How do we read her ambivalence about heterosexual relations and about feminism itself, seen particularly in her portrayal of her own lost mother, who chose to be a single parent, as a somewhat pathetic and stereotyped seventies radical? Comparison with *Woman on the Edge of Time* suggests a variety of answers.

Concerning the mother's body and female powers of reproduction, the novels express a shared understanding from opposite directions. The Handmaid is unable to act, at this level of interpretation, precisely because she remains hopeful that she will be saved by biological motherhood. Her complicity with the regime is assured, as her captors probably intend, by the promise that she *might* be one of the lucky few who can conceive. This desperate hope of pregnancy motivates her one subversive act, the affair with Nick, which is perhaps not so subversive at all—Serena Joy suggests it, to begin with, and Nick might be a member of the secret police. The futility and danger of this faith in salvation or even just survival through reproduction ought to be clear to the reader and to the Handmaid when we witness the treatment of the other handmaid who gives birth in the novel, Ofwarren (like our Handmaid, the mother in pre-Gileadean times of a child now lost). A few minutes after birth, the biological mother is ignored, even though she is in pain, while the Wives name the infant; after a few months of nursing, she will be forced to relinquish the child altogether. Every woman, even the procreative mother, is a mother without child in Gilead, where children belong to the male-dominated regime.

This reading explains what at first puzzled me about the plot: Why doesn't such a technologically advanced society fight infertility with conceptive technology instead of ritualized, regulated copulation? It is because the very scarcity of children is calculated to reinforce the systematic oppression of women. The rarity of pregnancy, the fragility of procreation, in the ruthlessly pronatalist and antifeminist world of Gilead, keeps women in place even more than fertility, however controlled, would.[16] It keeps the Handmaid focused inward, centered on her womb; as she says, "I can't think of myself, my body, sometimes, without seeing the skeleton. . . . A cradle of life" (143); or as she observes at an earlier point, "I used to think of my body as an instrument, of pleasure, or a means of transportation, or an implement for the accomplishment of my will. . . . Now the flesh arranges itself differently. I'm a cloud, congealed around a central object, the shape of a pear, which is hard and more real than I am" (95). As Handmaid, valued only for her womb, she is hardly "real" to herself, fragmented and left with just enough confused hope of survival and love that, unlike Connie who has "nothing" left, she is unwilling to "strike back." In this way, despite the differences between them and their situations, the experiences of Connie and the Handmaid tell us the same thing about the volatile, easily controlled, usually constraining equation of women and reproductive power under a forceful pronatalist order.

Both novels critique other aspects of present-day motherhood as well. As we have seen, they disavow the mythic duality, paradox, or split in the mother, her overweening power and her absolute vulnerability, her overshadowing presence and her fundamental absence. Connie as mother is both grandstanding heroine and helpless victim; more realistically, more pessimistically, the Handmaid is neither. (In this way, of course, the Handmaid may also counter the myth of self-sacrifice as a model of female behavior that Connie reaffirms, despite her avowed commitment to the new model of mothering in Mattapoisett.[17]) Similarly, both narratives counter and interrogate the myth of the mother's ultimate and sole responsibility: comothering in Mattapoisett fosters collective accountability and care for children, and the Handmaid, by virtue of her blandness, ordinariness, and willful lack of power, challenges any ideal of maternal omnipotence. Susan Rubin Suleiman has asked recently why women are reluctant to give up this myth of ultimate responsibility,[18] and it is perhaps because giving up such fantasies leaves us with unsettling characters like the Handmaid. As Atwood's protagonist says, "Those who can believe that such stories are only stories have a better chance"; whereas Connie's comparatively conventional heroism offers hope to everyone but herself, it is perhaps harder to believe that the Handmaid's story is only a story. The absence of even the kind of speculative utopian message that *Woman on the Edge of Time* provides—at least imagine a world where everyone who wants to can mother, where child care is valued and collective, and maternal behavior is dispersed and cherished—suggests the risky proposition that we need to be outspoken in our criticism of old ways without knowing yet exactly what to put in their place, where new ways might take us.

By virtue of her status as ironic first-person narrator, the Handmaid speaks to another standing question about mothering that Piercy's work addresses in a different way. The Handmaid is an archly self-conscious narrator who often pauses to discuss her distaste for the story she must tell, or to assess the difficulty of telling the truth, or to offer alternative versions of certain episodes. Sometimes these passages raise that old idea, broadly implicated in the link between Connie Ramos's receptivity and time-traveling capacity, that the (female) artist's storytelling is a type of reproduction, a metaphorical, surrogate mothering, so to speak, in its own right. Again, whereas *Woman on the Edge of Time* is fairly optimistic about female powers of imagination, *The Handmaid's Tale* is more ambivalent. At two particularly interesting moments at either end of the story, the narrator speculates whether the imaginative artist can create her audience by telling her story; the answer differs on each occasion.

In the first of these passages, the narrator remembers how her captors convinced her to become a Handmaid: they showed her a picture of her lost daughter with another woman, presumably her adoptive mother, and they told her, "You are unfit, but you want the best for her. Don't you?" She reports that her reply was, "You've killed her," and adds, "She was wearing a dress I'd never seen, white and down to the ground." Then immediately follows this typical digression:

> I would like to believe this is a story I'm telling. . . .
> But if it's a story, even in my head, I must be telling it to someone.
> You don't tell a story only to yourself. There's always someone else.
> Even when there is no one.
> A story is like a letter. *Dear You*, I'll say. . . .
> I'm not in any immediate danger, I'll say to you.
> I'll pretend you can hear me.
> But it's no good, because I know you can't. (52–3)

The Handmaid attempts to recuperate, through storytelling, the control she has lost over her life. She struggles, at this point futilely, to create an audience, a listener, "someone else," "you"—perhaps, in psychoanalytic terms, the other. This effort can be read as a (failed) metaphor or displacement of biological reproduction, not unlike Connie's travel in time, coming as it does immediately after the memory of her daughter's picture and her own disbelief in the daughter's existence. The Handmaid can no longer care for her lost child, or even, it seems, imagine the possibility of her. At this moment she is more like Connie—she has reached rock bottom, with nothing left to love—except that she isn't quite as free to protest as Connie is, because she is desperately hoping to give birth to another child, which she will also not be allowed to mother. Storytelling in these circumstances is implicitly a necessary self-deception, a defense mechanism, an imaginative but not empowering hope of giving birth to "someone" even as the narrator despairs that she will ever mother again, or that someone, anyone, can hear her words. The speaker's conclusion that "it's no good" suggests another way of saying what Morrison says about trauma that escapes narrative and resists ordinary ways of knowing and telling: "This is not a story to pass on," in this case because it isn't a story, and because no one is there to receive it.

In a second passage, the teller's power to give birth to an audience, to imagine the other, and hence to pass on the story that is not a story is more firmly maintained. Almost three hundred pages later, near the end of the novel, chapter 41 begins with the confounding statement: "*I wish this story were different"* (343). The Handmaid goes on to explain, however, that she cannot refashion the intrusive, traumatic past:

> I'm sorry there is so much pain in this story. I'm sorry it's in fragments, like a body caught in crossfire or pulled apart by force. But there is nothing I can do to change it. . . .
>
> I keep on going with this sad and hungry and sordid, this limping and mutilated story, because after all I want you to hear it, as I will hear yours too if I ever get the chance. . . . By telling you anything at all I'm at least believing in you, I believe you're there, I believe you into being. Because I'm telling you this story I will your existence. I tell, therefore you are. (343–44)

The Handmaid still associates telling her story with not just remembering but also reexperiencing pain and lack of control, and the most painful parts of the story involve the trauma of losing her child; as she says of her recurring nightmare of the failed escape, "Of all the dreams this is the worst" (98). In this passage, moreover, the fragmented story is compared to the female body in Gilead, divided "like a body caught in crossfire or pulled apart by force." But here the cause and effect of her compulsive narrative labor is affirmed as a more solid, subversive "you" and "your existence," critically situated in "some other place." The Handmaid seems to suggest that artistic creativity, doomed in this instance to repeat a painful experience, does not constitute an imaginative escape from the present (as it did not, finally, in *Woman on the Edge of Time*) and does not offer the female artist a fully imagined, positive, liberating alternative to thwarted, traumatic motherhood. It may be instead, in its own right, a torturous giving birth—not to the speaking subject, the "I" (here referring to the fragmented female), but to the lost "you," to someone else, to again unspecified alternatives, and to new conjunctions and relationships in the future. Whether this represents anything more than the narrator's passing mood we cannot be sure. But to the extent that the tale itself survives to be read—as the epilogue insists that it does—the Handmaid as storyteller has mothered, in this sense: tale and epilogue together embody her final optimistic notion, "I tell, therefore you are," and "you" includes her fictional readers, brought to life in the epilogue, and her real readers. To the question of how maternity and creativity are related, *The Handmaid's Tale* offers a provisional answer as affirmative in its own way as Piercy's. The novel does not situate "the mother" in a single position; the Handmaid is a woman who has mothered and may mother but does not mother now. Yet it tentatively proposes that mothering and storytelling are not mutually exclusive activities and that creativity itself entails a maternal relation, in an extended, indeed "nonprocreative" sense of the term maternal, to the future and to the possibility of a "someone else, You."

I WILL NEVER TOTAL IT ALL

In Piercy's real-time America and Atwood's not-so-far-off Gilead, Adrienne Rich's assertion is borne out: "The loss of the daughter to the mother, the mother to the daughter, is the essential female tragedy." Although Rich continues, "There is not presently [in the 1970s] enduring recognition of mother-daughter passion and rapture,"[19] the separation of Connie and Angelina and of the Handmaid and her daughter *are* two potent contemporary expressions of the mother-daughter story, two complementary versions of "the essential female tragedy"—"essential," that is, given an ideology and practice of motherhood rooted in the pronatalist conflation of woman and biological mother that both novels strenuously indict. In Connie's story, we see how loss can, in extreme cases, make political action possible and be recuperated as a chosen renunciation. In the Handmaid's case, this same point is made by counterexample, and the Handmaid's complicity may be attributed to the shred of hope, the calculatedly slim chance of viable pregnancy and birth (or even of reunion with the lost daughter) that the regime holds over women.

With some of the open-endedness that both narratives structurally enjoin upon us, I want to close this discussion by proliferating ways of reading the story of the missing daughter as Piercy and Atwood tell it. In my own thinking about the mother without child, these were the two novels I began with, and I register, in what follows, the stages I went through in trying to understand and connect what I was seeing. In some of these readings, the erasure or loss of the child can be seen as regressive or self-serving, whereas in others (the ones I have tended to privilege throughout this study) it is speculative and exemplary; taken together, both perspectives underscore that the figure of the mother without child is complicated and multiply significant.

It might readily appear that by telling the mother's story as a tale of the inability to mother, these novels actually sustain the ambivalence about mothering that has historically been expressed in many myths and narratives and that late twentieth-century feminists have reiterated in the movement from rejecting to celebrating (and then rejecting again?) the maternal. This, I take it, is the view of those who criticize Piercy in particular for writing the mother's body out of utopia. Although this ambivalence is attributed in both novels to the conditions under which we mother, it is nonetheless real and problematic to feminism in theory and in practice. One of the first readings of these stories that occurred to me, along these lines, was that in both cases the loss of the protagonist's child solved the practical problem of what to do with the kids while having either a utopian or dystopian vision. Flippantly (and admittedly from the position of a mother of two young daughters) I noted that the absence of her child effectively emancipated each protagonist from the cares and constraints of mothering a preschooler on her journey into the future. Were Connie still single-handedly in charge of Angelina, her expeditions to Mattapoisett would be impossible; she would hardly have the free time necessary for a quick nap, let alone an extended daydream or out-of-body experience. Who would baby-sit during her sudden transports? Suppose the Handmaid, in turn, had found herself in the position of an Econowife in Gilead—one of those women she sees on the street, unattractively dressed, lower-class, who have to be wives, bear children, and care for them all at the same time. The escape that makes it possible for her to transmit her story—and hence the very premise on which the tale is founded—would be far less likely to be undertaken. She would hardly have the opportunity or time for an affair with a man like Nick, who rescues her from sexual deprivation and then (maybe) from Gilead; and not only romance but any life underground would be difficult to imagine with a young daughter in tow. The impossibility of escaping *with* a child is literalized in that "worst" of dreams, the most prominent and painful episode the Handmaid relives, when she and her husband tried to escape across the border. If the child could have run faster—or if she hadn't been responsible for the child at all—couldn't she have made it to safety? Did her husband, who apparently left her with the responsibility of carrying the little girl, sprint across the border?

By this same reading, the loss of the child might be viewed as a less than fully satisfactory solution to the problems, both literal and symbolic, of combining motherhood and creativity. On the question of whether female artists can mother, too (or whether mothers can be artists), both novels may hedge by developing figures of the visionary or storyteller who *have* mothered, who love their daughters and long to mother, but who do not *now,* in the time of visioning or speaking, mother. In this way, do these stories really give us the mother's story that feminists have called for, or do they only seem to? Is there still no sign in our fictions of the actual, daily, ordinary aspects of the mother's story?

Another, not necessarily incompatible way of reading the loss of the daughter is as a manifestation—and perhaps then an exorcism—of potent and well-documented fears: fears that if the child doesn't kill or silence the mother-writer, the mother-writer will neglect, abuse, or kill her child; or any mother's seemingly inevitable fears of losing her child.[20] No matter how perfect the world were to become, children would be vulnerable to our self-centered desires, and there is still war even in Mattapoisett. But if we imagine the worst, perhaps it will not happen; things almost never happen quite as we worry and dream that they will. Atwood's novel gives a special place to this side of maternal experience in the very first memory of her daughter that the narrator shares, a typically mundane one that contains, like most ordinary life, a record of real and imaginary terror. As she purchases a chicken wrapped in paper for her Gileadean household, she recalls the plastic shopping bags of former times, which she used to save for no reason until the pile under the sink spilled out onto the floor. Then her husband used to throw them all out: "She [this is the first cryptic reference to the never named daughter] could get one of those over her head, he'd say. You know how kids like to play. She never would, I'd say. She's too old. (Or too smart, or too lucky.) But I would feel a chill of fear, and then guilt for having been so careless. It was true, I took too much for granted; I trusted fate, back then" (37).

In both novels, there is this reminder that mothers, while they live with the all too easily evoked fear of loss, also take too much for granted. This is especially true for Connie, who never fully comprehends what her child means to her, how much she loves her, until she cannot have her. The everyday, confounding experience of mothering seems to be captured here: when we are with our children, they are often irritating, demanding, boring, unreasonable, and unlovable. How much more can we feel our love when they are asleep, at day care, at a distance, when we look at a picture of them, when we read a newspaper story about a missing child, or hear a television report about an abused one?

As this last question suggests, there is a danger of oversentimentalizing the experience of motherhood. This is one of the risks spoken about by Kathi Aguero, a writer with young children who explains why she has written very little about her experiences of motherhood: "I find it a little hard to know how to write about it without being sentimental."[21] By avoiding writing about mothering directly, are both Atwood and Piercy skirting the risks of romanticizing and idealizing the child, the mother, and the always vulnerable relationship between them?

The reasons why both women can't mother, in the narrative time of each novel, may also indict the complicity of mothers in the institutions that make mothering so difficult and conflicted. This is not to say that either novel should be accused of encouraging us to blame the victim. Connie's oppressors are so vividly realized and horrible, Gilead so terrifyingly powerful and plausible, that I find it hard to imagine readers who would feel, on the whole, anything but sympathy for the protagonists and anger at the injustices done to them. At the same time, it is clear to Connie herself that she lost Angie in part at least because she chose to mourn her dead lover at the expense of nurturing her child. The Handmaid is guilty of taking too much for granted, and more seriously perhaps she is guilty of ordinary behavior, of "ignoring." Could she, if she had paid attention, have seen what was coming sooner? Could she have taken her child across the border before it was so risky to do so? Did she, like Connie, put her relationship to her male lover first? Did she fail her daughter by trusting a man to protect her and to make arrangements for their escape that were obviously not adequate?

We can read these mothers' fears, failures, and losses of their daughters in yet another way that brings us back to other familiar issues: the problem of respecting the female reproductive body; the difficulty of theorizing the relations between the maternal and the feminine, given that *only* women give birth but *not all* women are (birth) mothers; the further gap between theorizing the maternal and practicing mothering. Read with an eye to these issues, the characterization of Connie and the Handmaid as women who have mothered in the past, who show us what mothering might look like in the future, but do not mother in the present may at once figure and circumvent (rather than just hedge, as I suggested earlier) such concerns. Connie and the Handmaid speak for and about women who mother as well as women who don't mother. Like other representations of the mother without child, they thereby bridge traditional divisions between women as a group, comprehend a versatile, fluid, unsettled relation of maternity and femaleness or femininity, and resist any fixing of the mother or motherhood as a complete human identity, a transcendent, full, or atemporal, ahistorical essence. Evaluating and critiquing the "maternal metaphor" in French feminism, along with metonymic American feminist alternatives that she also sees as "utopian," Domna C. Stanton has argued that "an initial counter-valorization of the maternal-feminine as a negation/subversion of paternal hierarchies" is an important first step, "an enabling mythology"; "But the moment the maternal emerges as a new dominance, it must be put into question before it congeals as feminine essence, as unchanging in-difference."[22] *Woman on the Edge of Time* and *The Handmaid's Tale* give flesh to this argument, demonstrating initially the positive (Connie's enabling time travel) and then the negative (Gilead's surrogacy practices) effects of "counter-valorization of the maternal-feminine" and putting any congealed notion of the maternal (be it patriarchal or feminist) into question.

In the process of putting maternal dominance into question, *Woman on the Edge of Time* and *The Handmaid's Tale* subvert the mythic notion that the single figure or person of the mother—as biological birthgiver, caretaker, or position in language—has or should have complete individual responsibility for the psychological and physical well-being of the child. So too, by virtue of this interrogation of old myths, the novels question whether any single theory (or any one reading) can be ultimately responsible for meaning, can completely contain or even accurately describe motherhood. This does not mean that critical theories—plural—aren't valuable; I mean rather to say something close to what bell hooks says when she warns that "feminist theorists . . . need to be conscientious about not supporting monolithic notions of theory. We will need to continually assert the need for multiple theories emerging from diverse perspectives in a variety of styles."[23] These novels suggest in particular that the relations between mothering and novel writing, between maternity and creativity, are consequential yet always mobile, precarious, and uneven, rooted in histories of great complexity, as resistant to any monologic theoretical resolution as they often are to practical combination. Thus our maternal figures, Connie and the Handmaid, are also figures for the creative, imaginative faculty, but the analogy between protagonist and visionary artist can be taken only so far in each case. Significantly, neither protagonist has complete responsibility for the story, and neither's voice or narrative corresponds exactly to the novel as a whole. Connie's story is told in a third-person voice that sees almost exclusively from her point of view and records her innermost thoughts but sees other things too—possibly more than Connie does. The Handmaid is a first-person narrator, but her tale is followed by a story of how it was transmitted by others. Piercy, like Atwood, uses an epilogue; in both cases, the main story, a fantasy, is thus closed by the fictive voices of official, nonfictional discourse: the putative institutional files on Connie and the imaginary proceedings of the conference of the Gileadean Research Association. As I noted earlier, in each case this gives weight to the fantasy by demonstrating how much more believably it speaks, how thoroughly the novel escapes and subverts other discourses that try to read and theorize about the protagonists' experiences.

At the same time, the presence of the epilogue also serves to establish a difference and a distance between novelist and character. This distance suggests, among other things, that full understanding of the fictional character exceeds authorial or readerly control and that the novelists thus see not exactly *with* their characters, but *as* their characters see—partially, but in telling detail. The central, supposedly visionary heroine of *Woman on the Edge of Time* is often and increasingly "confused," a condition noted by psychiatric diagnosis and by her own account. One of her final visits to Mattapoisett, during which she fights in an air war with Luciente and sees the doctors who have operated on her brain in the enemy's ships, is ambiguously rendered. It may be a hallucination, or, as Luciente suggests, it may have taken place in another "continuum" (367), or it may retrospectively call into question the status of all the earlier visions. As Connie says, "'Pues . . . never mind'"—it doesn't matter anymore, as it once did to Connie, whether her visions are imaginary or real; the clarity of her moral purpose is inversely correlated to her concern with rationality. Similarly, the Handmaid stresses the precariousness of her hold on rationality. She tells a story that is fragmented and reconstructed, as she repeatedly says, because she does not know any version that is whole and original and also because she wants in her own way to resist the version that is promulgated by the rulers of Gilead *as* whole and original, authorized by the Bible and enforced by state terrorism. From under her heavy white winged headdress, designed to keep her from seeing or being seen, she learns instead "to see the world in gasps" (40), a way of seeing that is compatible with rethinking "the mother" not as an autonomous, unified person but as a fragmented role, a postmodern subject, and a collective project.

Both Connie and the Handmaid see in much the same way as another one of our rare instances in imaginative fiction of a mother who tells her own story: Tillie Olsen's first-person narrator in "As I Stand Here Ironing." Until the very end of the story, this mother speaks in the literal absence of the child, and she tells a story that verges on the tragic about her attenuated connection to a partially lost daughter who was once separated "for her own good" from her mother and whom the mother has not loved as well, she says, as she loved her later children. As the mother sees it, the daughter's potential is therefore stunted: "All that is in her will not bloom" (20).[24] It is "too late," in the present narrative time, for the love the mother would like to give, and the mother accepts this fact and resists the call to intervene in the daughter's life. To the unnamed interlocutor whose request for a conference about the child prompts the story, the narrator expresses only a refusal: "Let her be." The story is thus written as one that the mother, because of her position *as* mother, will never pass on:

> Even if I came, what good would it do? You think because I am her mother I have a key, or that in some way you could use me as a key? She has lived for nineteen years. There is all that life that has happened outside of me, beyond me.
>
> And when is there time to remember, to sift, to weigh, to estimate, to total? I will start and there will be an interruption, and I will have to gather it all together again. Or I will become engulfed with all I did or did not do, with what should have been and what cannot be helped. (9)

Here Olsen suggests that the story of the missing daughter embodies what our culture wants to deny, the most necessary, painful, disempowering, enabling aspect of mothering: the inevitable separation of the mother and child that begins at birth. In Mattapoisett, this ongoing process is embodied and celebrated, not repressed or psychoanalyzed, in a ritual ceremony called "end-of-mothering," when a child reaches adolescence and names herself or himself. This ceremony entails a rite of passage whereby the child is left alone in the wilderness for a week. Connie views this as cruel abandonment, but Luciente explains to Connie, "'We set our children free'" (116). Like Atwood and Piercy, Olsen explicitly challenges the basic assumption of virtually all the child-oriented theories of human development that our culture has depended on. As her mother-narrator says again at the end, "I will never total it all." Such theories (like teachers and counselors, like social workers and doctors in *Woman on the Edge of Time* and ideologues and academics in *The Handmaid's Tale*) are often assigned and expected to choose, divide, set out limits, explain, "to sift, to weigh, to estimate, to total"; that is often how they conceive of their job. It is not the job, not the way, both narratives suggest, of mothers or of novels.

Six

Fay Weldon's Mad Dolls

I want to lead people to consider and explore ideas that aren't
very popular, which many people would rather not think about.
—Fay Weldon, "Me and My Shadows"

Fay Weldon's prolific fiction is frequently praised for its biting wit and
quirky humor, and Weldon is usually read, for better or worse, as an
equally quirky feminist, a woman's novelist with a capacity to capture,
albeit in satirical form, the so-called reality of female experience, including motherhood.[1] On this particular topic, Weldon's novels might
be readily assimilated to the popular view that feminism has gone
through three stages in its difficult encounter with maternal identity:
harsh repudiation; sentimental recuperation; and confusion, conflict,
and a silencing sense of impasse. Her books in the seventies, such as
Female Friends, Words of Advice, and *Praxis,* could be viewed as
mother-blaming stories, exploring the failure of an earlier generation
of women to nurture and the compensatory anxiety of their daughters,
who must struggle to escape exploitative heterosexual relationships and
the pronatalist mandate. That struggle culminates with a heroic antimaternal (that is, for the sake of the mother, not the baby) crime in
Praxis. Her novels in the eighties, starting with *Puffball* and including
The President's Child, The Hearts and Lives of Men, and *The Cloning
of Joanna May,* seem to reinstate motherhood as an authentic female
experience, repudiated only by monsters like Ruth in *The Lives and
Loves of a She Devil,* who parodies the grotesque extremes of the seventies vision. Men are the enemy chiefly insofar as they purposely or
accidentally cause women to lose their children or, as in *Cloning,* try
to steal female reproductive power. Closure in these stories comes with
the birth of a child or reunion with the lost daughter or threatened son.

Weldon's nineties novels, like *Darcy's Utopia, Life Force,* and *Troubles,* might reflect the sense of postfeminist, postmaternal impasse in that their attention to motherhood is uneven and unsettled, revisiting old issues and offering no resolution of the major dilemmas.

But Weldon fits the image of the popular feminist writer, flip-flopping on or finally evading the problems of motherhood, only in vastly reductive readings. Because her work in fact engages and critiques such reductive views of feminism and motherhood, readings in Weldon may serve as both an extension of and a fitting conclusion to this study. The conflict between repudiation and celebration of motherhood is not linear in her novels—nor, for that matter, in "feminism" (mis)understood as a movement. In Weldon's work to date, maternity is repeatedly revisited as a central and difficult space for the cultural and material construction of women. This is not to say that there is no change, growth, and movement in Weldon's fiction, for there is. Hers are "historical" novels, responsive to contemporary shifts and debates, often anticipating the popular trouble spots with the uncanny power of fiction. The history her novels write, however, is a history of necessary ambivalence and confusion, uneven change, sudden leaps forward, and violent backlash. A vital and flexible thread woven through this vexed history is the many-sided story of the mother without child. It marks here as elsewhere an intense engagement with prevailing (and so often contradictory) wisdoms about women and motherhood and a determined quest for revised models of relations between female identity, maternal experience broadly construed, and narrative.

In this chapter, I follow this thread through five of Weldon's novels where it is especially conspicuous: *Female Friends* (1974), *Praxis* (1978), *Puffball* (1980), *The President's Child* (1982), and *The Cloning of Joanna May* (1989). *Female Friends* is a particularly useful starting point for a reprise of many of the issues explored in this study. The novel directly indicts the pronatalism of post–World War II England, a climate of opinion that relentlessly impinges in a variety of ways on American works as well. More specifically, it supports a critique of the influential work of "attachment theorist" John Bowlby and its popularized dissemination, often referred to as "Bowlbyism." The plot of *Female Friends* arises from the same historical circumstances that brought Bowlby to prominence, at a moment that anticipates (and is implicated in) the crisis we seem to face today—a moment when the relational aspect of mothering is endangered, and the separation of mother and child is at once mandated and deplored by official and expert forces. The novel imagines what happens to three girls thrown together in late childhood as a result of a controversial social policy in wartime England, the evacuation of children from London, without their parents, to rural towns and villages. This is precisely the policy that Bowlby, early on in his career, was asked to study.

As Denise Riley points out in *War in the Nursery*, Bowlby had been interested since 1940 in the effects of wartime evacuation of children. From a study of forty-four juvenile thieves begun before the war, Bowlby had concluded that childhood delinquency was caused by separation from the mother.[2] He therefore urged wartime policies that kept mothers and children together. After the war, based on the strength of his previous work on the separation of mother and child, the World Health Organization (WHO) invited Bowlby to prepare a report on the mental health of homeless children. Summarizing several psychological studies in Europe, Scandinavia, and the United States, Bowlby wrote then that the dangers of what he termed "maternal deprivation" had been conclusively established. The WHO report, in a simplified version, was published in 1953 as a popular volume entitled *Child Care and the Growth of Love;* Bowlby's beliefs were later promulgated in the three-volume study, *Attachment and Loss,* published between 1969 and 1980. Meanwhile, as Riley sees it, postwar government policy, sanctioned by such expert opinion, could take the cost-effective step of closing wartime crèches and passing ultimate and often unassisted responsibility for nurturing, protecting, and training future generations of English men and women back to those who did the job (or ought to) for love alone—individual mothers.

Feminist psychologists and theorists have offered divergent assessments of the impact of Bowlbyism. Jessica Benjamin presents it as just one aspect of British object relations theory, which she believes profoundly challenged American ego psychology and paved the way for her own feminist understanding that if the self is fundamentally social, the mother must be recognized as an independent subject.[3] However, Bowlbyism, critiqued by psychologists as early as the fifties, has more frequently been attacked by second-wave feminists. Writing in the seventies, Juliet Mitchell deplores the oversimplifications in Bowlby's conclusions and the way those findings were interpreted to focus sole responsibility, as always, on mothers: "Evacuee children were 'maternally deprived'—bombs and poverty and absent fathers didn't come into it."[4] According to Ann Dally, though Bowlby's work brought new and needed attention to the psychological needs of children, the idealization as well as the blaming of the mother that it encouraged had more lasting and unfortunate consequences for women, and Bowlbyism is in fact "a fundamental reason why . . . women's liberation has never come to terms with motherhood."[5]

Both Riley and Dally take pains to remind us that Bowlby is not single-handedly responsible for the popular belief in the necessity of continuous maternal presence. His work meshed with that of other child psychologists, the needs of government and industry, and a climate of pronatalist opinion in the postwar period, and understanding the effect of this pervasive and multifaceted rhetoric on the experience of women is a difficult task. Weldon's writing often thematizes this problem by offering a particularly complicated sense of how people simultaneously participate in, ignore, and resist the various discourses that are available to them. In keeping with Weldon's characteristically wry, dark humor, the specific instance of child evacuation that brings Chloe, Grace, and Marjorie together in *Female Friends* is marked from the outset by error and incompetence: a train full of children from London is disembarked at the wrong rural station, Ulden instead of Egden, because the conductor misreads his instructions. Here as in all of Weldon's stories, social policy and its attendant rhetoric rarely accomplish exactly what they mean to do; they are instead frequently derailed by human error, intentional misbehavior, fate, magic, and random luck. Efforts to control people always have unpredictable side effects, and in that unpredictable space between public discourse and its effects, the very constraints that pronatalism seems to mandate can sometimes be subverted and appropriated. Many factors other than "maternal deprivation," as we shall see, come into Weldon's representation of human development and her repeated efforts to understand how women's liberation might come to new terms with motherhood. Invariably, however, her novels insist that the mother *with* child remains at risk and that loss or threatened loss of a child is, if anything is, the common and potentially unifying female experience. Motherhood, then, is an experience and an idea about which some unpleasant and unpopular truths must repeatedly be told.

A FEMALE GROUP IDENTITY?

Pronatalism generally implies, and sometimes explicitly claims, that all women share an essential identity based on their reproductive capacity. Although they disagree with many pronatalist conclusions, feminists have sometimes concurred with this assumption. It is reflected, for example, in the notion of "reproductive consciousness" discussed in chapter 3, the formulation used by Mary O'Brien to express her understanding that common social, mental, and emotional attitudes toward childbirth and motherhood have a material base in the biological reproductive process.[6] Although O'Brien has been accused of essentialism, the concept of reproductive consciousness can be used to describe culturally specific and locally variable ways in which both social and biological experiences shape female identity as such and have a collective dimension. Indeed, because reproductive consciousness is by definition conventional and collective, it will inevitably change over time, especially when aspects of not only the social climate but even the biological experience are in flux. In Weldon's fiction, the evolving nature and meaning of "a female group identity," as one character calls it, is frequently explored. We see that women share in the common reproductive consciousness of their time, but we also see that this does not necessarily reduce their agency, as coercive pronatalism might suggest or indeed insist. Instead, collective awareness can be an uneven but real source of energy and change.

As its title indicates, *Female Friends* focuses on the increasingly public influence and celebration of bonds between women, also known as "sisterhood," that has been both formative of and responsive to the reemergence of feminism in the second half of the twentieth-century. In the novel, this increased interest in female friendship and solidarity is set in relief against a background in which we glimpse women of the previous generation. The protagonists' mothers, Helen, Esther, and Gwyneth, seem to have no female friends, at least in what little we see of their lives; they live in isolation from or competition with other women, including their daughters, and are dominated by their relationships to men. The already existing possibility of an alternative female orientation is noted, however, if only in the even more distant periphery of the narrative. When Grace's mother Esther dies in childbirth after a late pregnancy, her baby is sent away to be brought up by his distant aunt Elaine, a widow in "shirt, tweed suit, and brogues" who raises dogs with her friend Olive, "a lady companion with a definite black moustache."[7] Stereotyped as they may seem in this brief description, Elaine and Olive are models of nonprocreative maternity who replace the dead birth mother to rear a child "in happiness and contentment," something that none of the biological mothers in the novel is able to do.

Although the three protagonists of the novel frequently reproduce their heterosexual mothers, both in imitation and in rebellion, they are explicitly concerned with shaking off debilitating aspects of the maternal past. To do so they turn, with complex emotions, to each other. As the novel opens, seemingly in the early seventies, the three friends are entering middle age, and the first-person sometime-narrator Chloe is exhausted, she says, with the effort to practice her mother's self-negating philosophy of compassion and forgiveness. Seeking revitalization, she wonders whether she can get help from the childhood companions with whom she has maintained fraught ties as an adult: "Marjorie, Grace and me," she thinks, invoking the threesome in a refrain that henceforward punctuates the novel.[8]

This refrain, "Marjorie, Grace and me," signals one of the most important formal changes in the novel, and arguably one that is brought about by changes in reproductive consciousness and by women's friendship: a trio of women has replaced the individual female protagonist or speaker who is conventionally isolated from or in competition with other major and minor female characters. Chloe functions as both narrator and individual protagonist only to a certain extent. She tells a large part of the story of Marjorie, Grace, and herself from a first-person point of view, and it is at least possible that she is also the author of the third-person segments. At one point we learn that she has recently completed an autobiographical novel, which her husband forbids her to publish; it does not seem farfetched to imagine that after the ending of the story, when Chloe leaves her husband, she writes again and that *Female Friends* is the product of her next autobiographical venture. But whether Chloe is the narrator of part or all of the novel, the privileged position of central character and subject is still broken up, either because her perspective and her experience comprise only roughly one third of the story and even so are interwoven with the stories of Marjorie and Grace, or because she fragments herself, from the authorial position, into first and third person.[9] This is one of the earliest instances in contemporary fiction of a strategy harking back to Woolf's image of a pair of female characters, Chloe and Olivia, who break with traditional narrative, contest the dominance of *I,* and point to the unwritten future of female fiction. Here and in the work of other contemporary novelists, including Margaret Drabble and Margaret Atwood, the female dyad is further diffused into a trio in order to develop an even more complicated narrative of female friendship as a force in women's lives. *Female Friends* affords one of the most interesting instances of how this strategy represents a more postmodern, less firmly bounded notion of self as an aspect of female identity and weakens the apparent hold of the individual character on both plot and voice in the novel.[10]

In *Female Friends,* the content of this multicentered story of Marjorie, Grace, and Chloe emphasizes their culturally specific and currently evolving female reproductive consciousness. The narrated interactions among the three women cluster around reproductive experiences, broadly construed. In childhood and adolescence, the friends have formative connections to a single maternal figure, Grace's biological mother, who functions as surrogate mother to evacuee Marjorie and to Chloe, only child of a devoted but ineffectual widow. In late adolescence and into adulthood, they all have close affective and sexual ties to one man, Patrick, who fathers illegitimate children with both Grace and Chloe and lives for a time in Marjorie's house. At one point Chloe thinks of herself and her friends in a way that even implies a collective maternal experience, although in fact Marjorie has no successful pregnancies: "How foolishly we loved. . . . We have had six children between us" (18). Despite Grace's efforts to starve herself and upset the common cycle, as girls they menstruate in unison. When many years later in the narrative present Marjorie and Chloe meet for lunch, they discover that they are both having their periods, and Marjorie wonders, "'Do you think it means anything at all? Do you think there's a kind of inner force which drives us all? Perhaps we have a female group identity, as black-beetles do?'" To this possibility, Chloe answers shortly: "'No'" (93).

As Chloe's and Grace's frequent resistance to their often unhappy interconnectedness suggests, and as anyone familiar with Weldon's refusal of both sentimentality and simple solutions would predict, there is no romance of sisterhood here. Marjorie, Grace, and Chloe, like earlier generations of women, often seem bound more by competition—first for mothers and later for men—than by mutual affection and a feminist spirit of collaboration. They frequently tell each other hard truths. Sometimes they trust each other's advice, and sometimes they do not; sometimes the advice is sound, and sometimes it is not. But still, Chloe's late judgment that "our loyalties are to men. . . . We are divided amongst ourselves. We have to be, for survival's sake" (249), is a judgment that is *not* in fact fully supported by the novel as a whole. [11]

Instead, the denouement that follows swiftly on the death of Marjorie's cold, beautiful mother, Helen, closes the novel by at least gesturing toward what have become feminist clichés, although in *Female Friends* they are at once confirmed as such and undercut by comic obviousness: the possibility of mutual support, the fluidity of female identity, and the way in which women's lives as daughters *and* mothers—their reproductive lives—interpenetrate. In the penultimate chapter, the three friends wait together for a bus that will take them home from the hospital where Helen has just died. Marjorie sits with her mother's handbag on her lap and asks "'What shall I do with it? . . . I can't bear to go through it.'" "'Leave it in the waste bin'" (307), Chloe says, thus firmly advising Marjorie to do what she herself hoped to do in the opening of the novel—to dispose of the "baggage" inherited from her mother, which is only painful to contemplate and is not apparently useful in solving the daughter's adult problems. Marjorie follows Chloe's advice and throws her dead mother's handbag into the trash, but it is not so simple as it seems to disavow the maternal legacy. Some honest person finds the bag, and Marjorie is obliged to collect it again from the police. Something about the act of throwing away "holds good," however. If ties to mothers cannot be absolutely broken and the mother's handbag and story demand exhumation and examination, things can nevertheless change to some extent for daughters, thanks to female friends. In the very last chapter, we learn that Chloe is finally able to leave her odious husband and take her children with her because Marjorie also gives away more family baggage—her mother's house in London—to her friend, who appropriates it for her own needs.

. . . .

In Weldon's numerous other novels, similar strategies call traditional notions of individual character and fixed or separate identity into question and represent female reproductive consciousness in complex ways. In several, there are pairs of women who at first seem to stand for conventionally opposing attitudes and experiences. *Words of Advice* (1977) pairs Gemma and Elsa—barren, paralyzed middle-aged woman and fertile younger woman, witch and princess, storyteller and captive audience. Gemma's female lineage similarly consists of two traditionally opposing models of femininity: her dead biological mother, who represents impurity, sexuality, danger, and failure to nurture; and the aunt who raised her, who represents safety, virtue, caretaking, and self-sacrifice. What is a conventional way of dividing women into mothers and nonmothers, good and bad, is thus articulated first as a distinction *between* sisters; then, as the plot develops, the familiar categories and identities first emerge and finally blur *within* women too (Elsa escapes, probably bearing a child conceived with Gemma's husband; Gemma's paralysis is cured). Other pairs of women in Weldon's novels whose reproductive lives intersect include Mabs the witch and Liffey the innocent victim in *Puffball;* in *The Lives and Loves of a She Devil* (1984), Mary Fisher the childless adulteress and Ruth the scorned wife trade places. Three women, again related by hatred and sympathy as well as by their sexual involvement with a single male, appear in *Remember Me* (1976); here, two of them even briefly share the same body after one has been killed in a car crash. The number of female friends connected and divided by their sexual relations with one man expands to four in *Life Force* (1992). In *The President's Child,* the same questions of women's bonds, shared and divergent experiences, and the evolution of reproductive consciousness are displaced into the frame, which I return to in the epilogue.[12]

Perhaps the most explicit and affirmative treatment of the question of "female group identity" after *Female Friends* appears fifteen years later with the publication of *The Cloning of Joanna May,* where an extraordinary figure of the mother without child materializes as a woman past childbearing age, who has never been pregnant but discovers that she has four genetically identical clones thirty years younger than herself. Notably, the original Joanna May belongs to the same generation of women that Chloe, Marjorie, and Grace do. Postwar pronatalism is again the explicit historical setting in which Joanna's reproductive consciousness is formed, and here the mandate to mother is shown to have a persistent but not single, simple, or unbreakable hold on at least two generations of women. Cloning is associated at first with a kind of perverse coercive pronatalism that desperately needs to reduce female identity to a quantitative, biologically based substance—the sum of woman is her reproductive life—in order to assuage male fears of mortality. At the time of the cloning, unwitting Joanna believes she is being forced to have an abortion because her husband Carl wants her to be his mother and no one else's. In fact, she has experienced a hysterical pregnancy—another subversive manifestation of the mother without child, as Carl understands.

In secretly cloning Joanna, the demonic husband intends to punish his wife (for the crimes his own mother committed against him) and affirm his power, as he later admits: "There are many of you and many of you gloated Carl May and that means there are none of you because you amounted to so little in the first place. . . . I am master of mortality."[13] Carl's intentions go unchallenged for the thirty years during which neither Joanna nor the clones know of each other's existence. Then in a fit of anger Carl tells Joanna what he did to her egg, and the plan begins to backfire. Initially she feels ashamed and frightened of his destructive malice. But as Joanna also says in her very first defiant reaction, perhaps he has not in fact diminished but expanded her power: "All the more of us to hate and despise you." In a paean to the triumph of a postmodern female subjectivity that mocks the god-trick,[14] Joanna goes on:

> Multiply me and multiply my soul: divide me, split me; you just make more of me, not less. I will look out from more and different windows . . . and there will be no end to my seeing. I will lift up my heart to the hills, that's all, to glorify a maker who is not you. I should carry on if I were you, cloning and meddling, you might end up doing more good than harm, in spite of yourself, if only by mistake. (110)

The denouement of the novel confirms that female power is multiplied for the good, not reduced, when identity is dispersed and shared. The point is analogous to what we have seen in other novels where the negative effects of pronatalism are undone by the utopian reappropriation and redistribution of female identity. In *Desert of the Heart*, Evelyn rejects "synthetic maternity" and is not thereby reduced, as she had feared, but expanded by her "barren" relationship with Ann. In *Meridian*, redefined maternal identity is socially and politically expansive, and in the history of Mattapoisett, women have allegedly given up their sole and singular power so that everyone has more.

LOCALIZED AMNESIAS

We are, then, beginning to construct new models of self that can encompass both the sense of coherent separateness and meaningful connection as emergent structures throughout the life span. The old lines of movement from fusion to separateness, from domination by drive to secondary process, and from undifferentiation to differentiation are presently being questioned. A major flaw in existing theory has been the lack of elaboration of the developmental lines of connection and relationship; there has been a tendency to resort to either the now questionable model of the fused mother-infant pair or heterosexual genital union to conceptualize intimacy and self-other connectedness. . . . It has been noted, particularly in understanding female development, that this model is sadly lacking and even distorting; I think as we begin carefully to explore empathy and relational development we will see that the model misrepresents self-experiences of both males and females.

—Judith V. Jordan,
"Empathy and Self-Boundaries"

Weldon's *Female Friends* carefully explores the shared, collective aspects of feelings and behavior that constitute what it is useful to conceptualize as female reproductive consciousness, and the novel thereby considers what Judith Jordan calls for, the possibility of enabling connections to same-sex peers rather than to mother, child, or heterosexual mate.[15] *Praxis,* published four years later, seems at first glance to turn back to the individual and to reject "sisterhood" even more firmly than Chloe sometimes does. But as I read the novel, *Praxis* in fact considers the concept of identity from the other side, so to speak. Here female selfhood is difficult to find and preserve not because women have innately fluid ego boundaries, relational capacities, or common reproductive functions, but because in the course of her development the main female character experiences sharp discontinuities across time and within the feminine roles she plays at various stages of her life. The problem of renegotiating a relationship to the maternal heritage entails a change not only in the reproductive consciousness and "meaningful connection" by which the individual is attached, willy-nilly, to other women, but also in women's sense of their "coherent separateness." As we see in *Meridian* and the novels of Erdrich and Dorris, dissociation and disconnection are more common responses to the modern traumas of female development. In both Walker's novel and *Praxis,* self-division and detachment from others are represented in large part as disabling effects of the titular heroines' external circumstances. At the same time, just as the notion of reproductive consciousness can be used to expand as well as reduce female power, so too dissociation and disconnection can be enabling as well as debilitating. Praxis, like Meridian, inhabits her fragmented self in ways that also permit her to resist the culture's efforts to erase or reduce her experience and deny her knowledge.[16]

Formally, *Praxis* exploits the resources of the novel as a mode that can reveal both the division within the putative individual and the possibility that despite the flux of experience and the would-be cultural erasure of what women know, a less rigid, more integrated sense of self-in-relationship can be preserved and articulated. This is fundamentally a picaresque narrative, and as such it breaks narrative sequence by questioning or revising not so much linearity and separate selfhood, as *Meridian* does, but cohesiveness. Instead of the collective protagonist of a book like *Female Friends,* we meet here the complementary figure of a single protagonist fragmented into many stories and multiple voices. Like any picaresque hero, Praxis is a rogue, and the plot of her life story is episodic; her adventures can be neatly divided into discrete, chronologically sequential segments embedded in a present-tense first-person narrative that occasionally interrupts the retrospective narrative. However, one central difference between Weldon's version of the picaresque and standard examples of the genre from *Don Quixote* to *Tom Sawyer* is that whereas the conventional picaresque hero is more or less static in character, Praxis is a postmodern hero who undergoes so many changes that readers may wonder, as she often does, whether she is a single character. The problem of the instability of her identity is both echoed and resolved in the narrative structure, which divides Praxis into present-day first-person narrator of the novel and youthful third-person subject of the episodic narrative contained within the first-person frame. The picaresque genre is also revisited in Weldon's most well-known novel, *The Lives and Loves of a She Devil,* but there the danger of picaresque is more completely realized, and the instability of female identity leads to a dissolution of self that threatens readers' ability to know the character sufficiently to be in control of their sympathy. We might say that in the later novel character is sacrificed or sacrifices herself to the demands of social critique. Praxis is saved by her complicated connection to other women through narrative in a way that Ruth, the she-devil, is not.

The discontinuity of Praxis's self is represented from the beginning of the story as part of her female legacy, specifically as an inheritance from her mother, Lucy Parker. For the first five years of Praxis's life,

Lucy has a guilty secret. She is a Christian woman living in sin with Jewish playboy Ben Duveen, who is the father of Praxis and her sister Hypatia. The mandated repression of female sexuality makes women like Lucy feel divided into incoherent configurations by their bodily desires and unable to reconcile the urgings of "lust" and the demands of motherhood. When Ben threatens to rape her during their last big fight, Lucy is horrified and confused by her own arousal:

> She is far from frigid: she is ashamed of her own response to his violence: frightened of being out of her own control—is she not a mother? And mothers must be on duty day and night.
>
> "Animal." She bares her teeth. She would crawl around on all fours, she would, the better to excite herself, and him. Oh, horrible!
>
> He forces her down upon the ground. Does he force, or does she sink? (13)[17]

To avoid such painful, imponderable questions of agency, responsibility, and maternal identity, Lucy disavows her experience (and later projects her bad side onto Praxis). Wondering whether her mother really slept with the lodger she took in after Ben left, Praxis observes: "Mother would have denied it and believed her denial, whether she had or whether she hadn't. At a time when women's instincts were so much at a variance with the rules of society, such localized amnesias were only to be expected" (37).[18]

For Praxis, the anxiety of lacking a single, knowable identity and failing to belong is initially fueled by the disintegration of the patriarchal family, which normally functions to provide at least some sense of self and connection. After Praxis's father leaves, his daughter is known by many names—Praxis Parker, Patricia Duveen, Pattie (or Pat) Fletcher, to mention a few—and the confusion of names signals divided and disconnected female selfhood. At the same time, it affords the possibility of escape, disguise, and evolution to a more integral, coherent, and connected selfhood located outside the law, the family, domesticity, motherhood, and other conventional containers of female identity. The positive benefits of exile from patriarchal protection emerge only after a great deal of suffering, however.

Both within and among the various lives of Praxis/Patricia/Pattie/Pat, the external discontinuities marked by the instability of her name are matched by pervasive feelings of division both between self and reality and within each of those terms. For Praxis, like her mother and

like the young Meridian, such feelings are a consequence of quite ordinary and common female experience. As Praxis moves from one heterosexual relationship to another, her habits of dissociation mirror the
way she is treated by men. Talking to her first lover Willie at a dance,
she realizes that "he wasn't listening. His eyes were on her breasts"
(84). The separation of mind and body suggested by such experiences
shapes Praxis's sexual life. Passively accepting Willie's obsessive atten-
tions, "sometimes six or seven times a day," Praxis responds "politely,
kindly and affectionately" but remains detached from any sexual feelings of her own (91). In fact Praxis stays with Willie because she thinks
she is in love with the handsome Philip, his roommate, but this romantic
notion further compounds the division of mind and body: "with Willie
around, about and into her body, [she] loved Philip with her head"; she
cherishes her "secret knowledge" of him (93). Years later, when Praxis
leaves her husband Ivor and their children to marry Philip at last, that
sexual fulfillment she only dreamed of comes true, but orgasm is not
the answer to her problems. "Dizzy with desire by day, weak with sa-
tiation by night" (188), she still feels detached from reality and unsure
of her own knowledge or agency: "Blinkered: her focus limited to what
was in front of her: everything else blurred, or black; she was unable
to register the implications of what she had brought about." She feels,
as she felt with Ivor, "as if she too were now some part of Philip's imagination. What she saw lacked solidity" (189).

As this comment and others like it suggest, a part of Praxis always
knows that something is wrong. Like her mother, however, Praxis has
"localized amnesias"; "She had a wonderful, useful gift for forgetting
the events of the past. Useful, at any rate, to everyone except herself"
(216). For many years, the most she can do from her position of vague,
forgetful dis-ease is what many women do: wait. When Ivor asks her if
she is happy, she is puzzled by the question. "How could she know if she
were happy? She felt neither happiness nor unhappiness. She waited, and
for what she had no idea: she endured, why she could not tell" (169).
Like Evelyn Hall, she attempts to fill the gap, the waiting, the emptiness,
with children, and she bears Ivor a son and a daughter. But the birth of
the children only increases Praxis's dissociation and disconnection; she
believes that even as infants her daughter and son, who feel like strangers,
also "recognized her instinctively as the impostor she was" (165).

In the penultimate episode of Praxis's retrospective narrative, she becomes a feminist and begins to glimpse the possibility of both greater
connection—not to men or children but to other women—and a more

continuous and stable sense of herself. It is not in her feminism per se, however, that the blinkers are removed, and epiphany based on an understanding of a single, fixed doctrine or mystical loss of self in communion is explicitly rejected. As the successful editor of a feminist newspaper, Praxis remains functionally dissociated, using her writing skills to compose editorials "which she half believed, and half did not, in the same way as she had half believed, half not" when she wrote advertisements for the Electricity Board during a previous incarnation (233). She feels temporarily "elated" and "safe" through the illusion of merger with other women, "having lost her little loves, her shoddy griefs and pointless troubles—lost them all in the vast communal sea of women's tears" (234). But feminism as a religion, experienced as immersion in the consciousness of victimization, is not the final answer; in "the vast communal sea of women's tears" Praxis is still in danger of drowning. As always in Weldon's novels, conventionally (or unconventionally) pat answers and safe harbors are deceptive.

At the same time, Praxis's dissociation—her inability to know or remember who she is, what she knows, or how she feels—is strategic, like her multiplicity of names. She protects herself by learning to detach herself from pain. With Willie, she preserves some part of an independent self by leading a double life, caring for Willie and the quasi-adopted Mary Leonard most of the day but spending the lunch hour as a prostitute. Like her sexually satisfying relationship with Philip, prostitution is an experience of self-division for Praxis. But while heterosexual union is not a form of connection in these circumstances any more than it is with Willie, Ivor, or Philip, the illicit and hidden nature of her sexuality in this case nevertheless makes it potentially subversive, offering a sphere of material and emotional autonomy from the pervasive Willie.

Symptomatically, it is in her work as a prostitute that Praxis comes into contact with a part of her lost past that she needs to reconceptualize in order to feel and act. An attractive older man whom Praxis services after lunch one day turns out to be her father. When she realizes what has happened, she is at first stunned and defensive, telling herself that this could not be incest, because a man who abandons his family is not really a father. Then, after a second, this time knowing orgasm, she laughs "with bitterness and exultation mixed" because in purposely having sex with Ben she has "demystified" him, "turned him from saint to client, from father to man, from someone who must be pleased to someone who could pleasure her" (131). From this first illicit encounter, simultaneously violating the incest taboo, redefining and inverting and denying it, Praxis finds new resolve and takes a step on her journey out of patriarchal daughterhood toward self-knowledge and connection to past and present reality. She leaves Willie, taking baby Mary with her, that afternoon. Praxis is by no means autonomous yet, and later she is forced to revise her understanding of even this seemingly liberating experience when she discovers that her sister has kept in touch with their father all along. She begins to suspect that he may well have known who she was when she slept with him in Brighton but rejects the need to pursue the matter further: "There was no obligation, after all, to know the truth, let alone face it." The important thing, she believes at this point, is that she liked her father, a feeling that affords Praxis a glimpse of relationship if not the autonomy she thought it afforded: "The realization cheered her up, made some kind of rent in the mist between herself and other people" (232).

To break through the mist completely, however, requires even more difficult and defiant actions in which Praxis both knows and faces "the truth." Praxis must demystify not only her father but also the conventional ideals of motherhood that even more deeply prevent female autonomy, in an act more criminal and subversive than prostitution, certainly, or even incest: the murder of an infant, Mary's third child, born with severe defects. She must also reveal the truth of her story to others, in a double narrative act that gives the cohesiveness and connection of a moral structure to her disconnected, conventionally immoral life. Before discussing these aspects of *Praxis*, I consider how Weldon's next novel, *Puffball*, continues to address the problem of women's dissociation and disconnection, locating and exploring them within another taboo, the pregnant subject.

WHAT ABOUT YOU, BABY? THE MOTHER *BEFORE* CHILD

> For if there's one thing that's been repressed, here's just the
> place to find it: in the taboo of the pregnant woman.
> —Hélène Cixous,
> "The Laugh of the Medusa"

> It is crucial, I believe, that we now shift our [feminist]
> discourse and strategies away from an abstract rhetoric of
> choice to one focused on (1) exposing the contradictions in
> our legal tradition regarding bodily integrity . . . and (2)

> challenging the fetal-container conception, by reclaiming
> (from the right wing, which now holds a monopoly on such
> ideas) the view of pregnancy and abortion as *experientially*
> *profound events*. . . . Feminists may be made queasy, too, by
> the idea of emphasizing the experiential significance of
> pregnancy and birth, out of a fear of the conceptual
> proximity of such notions to constructions of mothering as
> the one true destiny for women. I believe, however, that we
> stand a better chance of successfully contesting such ideology
> if we engage in the construction of a public, feminist
> discourse on pregnancy and birth rather than leaving it in the
> hands of the "pro-lifers."
>
> —Susan Bordo,
> "Are Mothers Persons?"

The plot of *Puffball,* published only two years after *Praxis,* centers on the pregnancy of a female character, Liffey, which ensues from her dream of escape from urban corruption and decay into rural domesticity. At the close of the novel, she gives birth to a healthy infant and is about to be reunited with the baby's father in their conventional marriage. *Puffball* has thus seemed to many readers to reverse what is often taken to be the "out and out feminist" message of *Praxis:* now that they have the right to choose, women may have to repudiate motherhood in order to "find themselves." A brief review of the novel in the *Atlantic* notes that "readers who have been drawn to Weldon's books because of her feminist concerns might have trouble with it," although for this reviewer (who by implication lacks feminist concerns), "the assertion of the primacy of physical destiny that lies at the center of *Puffball* gives the book a surprising seriousness and an impressive optimism."[19] Though hinting that there is more to the book than meets the average eye, Anita Brookner also suggests in her review that this reading is a likely one: "*Puffball* seems to establish pregnancy as the only experience a woman can rely on for authenticity or indeed for validation." Brookner adds, "Superficially, it is a great leap backwards for the stereotype feminist . . . a fantasy for the tired businesswoman."[20] Paulina Palmer strongly disapproves of it for just these reasons: its "cultural feminism," "romanticizing" and valorizing the pleasures of motherhood, is disturbingly "regressive."[21]

All three of these readings share the common assumption that feminists are rightly or wrongly hostile to motherhood and pregnancy, although Brookner at least hints that this is a "stereotype," and Palmer, writing from the perspective of the late eighties, understands that another well-established kind of feminism, which was in fact emerging into popular perception at just about the time *Puffball* was published, seeks to reclaim motherhood as a source of power rather than oppression. Both the general stereotypes and the specific reading of *Puffball* that they give rise to are, I think, mistaken. Pregnancy is hardly romanticized or valorized by this novel; it may be, to use Susan Bordo's term, "reclaimed." As Bordo argues in the quotation cited epigraphically, we need "a public, feminist discourse on pregnancy and birth."[22] If women really have the right to choose, as opponents on the left insist, they must have the right to choose to mother as well as not to mother. *Puffball* explores the profound causes and effects of doing so, thereby challenging ideology on the right and deepening the discussion of what a feminist discourse about pregnancy might entail. Together with *Praxis, Puffball* bespeaks an ambitious project theoretically called for, rarely attempted, and at stake in all the stories of the mother without child considered in this study: what Gayatri Spivak speaks of as the need "to denormalize uterine social organization" without writing it off.[23] *Praxis* challenges previous models of selfhood by exploring the notion that dissociation and disconnection are more or less predictable effects of the experiences women have and prevailing attitudes toward them; these mental states may in fact have self-protective as well as self-destructive uses. *Puffball,* continuing and further specifying this insight, suggests the intensity with which a pregnant person challenges in other ways those concepts of separateness, singleness, and integrity that we normally take to be basic to selfhood and agency. As Iris Marion Young for one has put it, the pregnant "subject . . . is decentered, split, or doubled in several ways."[24] *Puffball* anticipates this theoretical claim and changes the conjunction. The pregnant subject in this novel is both "split" or divided, like Praxis, *and* "doubled."[25]

Concomitantly, though it may not be immediately apparent why I include this novel in a study of the mother without child, *Puffball* belongs here as much as *Praxis* does for two reasons. First, in its careful discussion of pregnancy as both an embodied and social experience, the novel serves to remind us that a pregnant woman is also on the border of motherhood, a mother *before* child, not a mother *with* child. Maternal capacities we may either ignore or take for granted as innate or automatic are set in relief—and thereby potentially open to revision and revaluation—as they are shown emerging, developing, and being formed by the biological and social experience of pregnancy. Even those who would argue for the social construction of motherhood rarely consider that it begins with, and must be understood in the context of, pregnancy.[26] Parturition is more frequently identified as the onset of motherhood, but *Puffball* insists that mothers do not spring forth full-blown at the moment of delivery. Second, the anxieties felt by most women during pregnancy not only resemble but may actually exaggerate those same characteristics that come to the fore when a living child is endangered. This possibility is underscored by the plot of *Puffball,* as the unborn child is threatened by both the biological accident of placenta previa and the social misfortune of a malevolent female friend and an inconstant father.

Liffey's reproductive experience before pregnancy is marked by discontinuity; she feels as confused and disconnected at many points as Praxis does. In her story, however, the emphasis is not only on the specific circumstances that make women in particular feel dissociated, but also on the constitutional dividedness of human nature, the split between mind and body. This division is reflected in the use of two different narrative registers, one voicing a more or less conventional third-person narration, the other speaking a language about reproduction borrowed from medical textbooks.[27] The medicalized or scientific discourse is featured in chapters ironically entitled "Inside Liffey (1)," "Inside Liffey (2)," and so on, although it is not confined to these segments.[28] The repeated *inside* is ironic here insofar as getting inside a character or person would normally be thought of as a technique for seeing more about that character's or person's genuine self. We tend to privilege the inside as a site of truer, private, more authentic experience—just as many believe that the biological is a ground, origin, or just plain hard reality that cannot be escaped no matter how much social or cultural effort we exert. What is "inside" Liffey, however, is none of these things, exactly. The language readily available to describe the body makes physiological processes at least somewhat intelligible, but it can only describe them partially.[29] It cannot integrate bodily processes completely with conscious experiences, and it does not provide access to an authentic, knowable bedrock of self or invariant measure of value.

As the dominant narrative voice tells us, disconnections between inside and outside, unconscious and conscious experience are accepted, even welcomed by most people, who like Liffey would rather not think about what they cannot control: "Liffey, unlike her mother, but like most women, had never cared to think too much about what was going on inside her body. She regarded the inner, pounding, pulsating Liffey with distaste, seeing it as something formless and messy and uncontrollable, and being uncontrollable, better unacknowledged" (22). Although the narrator's superior technical understanding of the body may seem at first to imply criticism of "most women" for their willful ignorance, several authoritative pronouncements about Nature (always capitalized) mitigate any such view. The narrator notes that even if we try to pay attention to the formless and uncontrollable body, we will find that this body—especially if it is female—is not a stable ground of experience:

> It was not even possible to accept, as it were, a bodily status quo, for
> her body kept changing. Processes quite unknown to her, and indeed for
> the most part unnoticeable, had gone on inside Liffey since the age of
> seven when her ovaries had begun to release the first secretions of
> oestrogen, and as the contours of her body had begun their change
> from child to woman, so had vulva, clitoris, vagina, uterus, fallopian
> tubes and ovaries, unseen and unconsidered, begun their own path to
> maturity. (22)[30]

The narrator asserts that the body's reproductive processes and potentials, not routinely susceptible to verbal or conscious control, serve or at least express the blind force we call "Nature." Just as Praxis sententiously alleged, Nature is interested only in procreation and what is good for the species, not the individual. In efforts to understand and thereby exert control over what is happening to their individual bodies, people may assign rational purpose to the force of Nature. Because she is unaware, for example, of all the "statistical probabilities of conception" that make pregnancy a quite rare consequence of intercourse, Liffey fears "some cosmic punishment had been visited upon her" (29) when she does not conceive in the first two months after she stops taking birth-control pills. But it is nothing so consequential or personal; blind Nature "works by waste . . . Auntie Evolution; Mother Nature; bitches both!" (108–9). If we were able to be "in touch" with our bodies, *Puffball* suggests, we might not be healed or liberated, but only the more appalled, terrified, silenced, and divided by their workings.[31]

The narrator further reminds us that Nature, for all its relentless drive, is not the only force that makes things happen. Beside the emphasis on biological matters in *Puffball* stands the equally insistent representation of other contending and inextricably entwined powers, including both human will and emotion and superhuman magic and witchcraft. The narrative voice speaks authoritatively about the complex interactions of these powers but often resists taking a final stand on questions of agency and causality. Events are usually given and left with alternative explanations. Sometimes, the narrator points out, human emotion can change human biology: "Sexual desire itself can on occasion prompt ovulation, overriding the pituitary's clock-work timing" (28). So too, sometimes, human will can override the emotion (or chemical reactions) of desire: "Mammals have the gift of consciousness: decision can over-ride instinct, and often, but perhaps not as often as we assume, does" (136).

If "Nature" or "the body" in particular cannot be fully understood, articulated, or controlled in its blind drive to procreation of the species, it is no greater friend to women in *Puffball* than in *Praxis*. Like *The Handmaid's Tale*, *Puffball* suggests that celebrations of biological motherhood can make odd bedfellows. This novel pokes fun both at conservative sociobiological arguments that would seek to explain femininity as an effect of anatomy and at feminist-inspired arguments that find an alternative to male-dominated culture in a reading of "Nature" as feminine or in an *écriture féminine* that writes the body, an articulation of feminine knowledge based on an "embodied" experience. The pregnant body is more clearly than ever a body in flux, no longer even appearing to offer a fixed ground of individual identity. Pregnancy, like other biological processes, is an experience of self-division, "a thrilling era of the body," as Cixous proclaims it, only insofar as the heightened perception that one is not in control, that one is not one, in fact, might indeed be thrilling.[32] The danger of basing women's social and discursive powers on procreation is caricatured in Mabs, the local witch who is trying to get pregnant throughout the novel, and also in Helen, a one-time friend of Liffey's who moves into her London apartment with her pregnant sister, Lally, and becomes a spokeswoman for the urban, upper-middle class rhetoric of "natural" childbirth. Helen and Lally see themselves as feminists and repudiate doctors as "an essential part of the male conspiracy against women" (92). When Lally has severe pains, Helen denies that she is in labor by making a semantic distinction familiar to the discourse of the natural childbirth movement: "'You don't have pains when you're having a baby, you have contractions. All that stuff about pain is part of the myth. Having a baby is just a simple, natural thing'" (92). Later, six weeks overdue, the baby is stillborn.

Helen and Lally oversimplify and ignore the risks of female bodily processes, but there is truth to part of their claim.[33] Liffey's experience with a country doctor partially confirms their assessment and supports a feminist critique of reproductive technologies that isolate and erase women's experience. This doctor helps to save Liffey and her baby's life when both her husband and her female neighbor Mabs abandon her. Yet this caring, competent man admittedly has trouble keeping his "respect" for pregnant women; "They seemed to him to belong so completely to the animal kingdom that it was almost strange to hear them talk" (169). The doctor scorns Liffey's pleasure when she hears the baby's heartbeat: "'Anyone would think it was your doing. All you have to do is just exist. The baby uses you to grow. You don't grow it'" (180). His approach, like the technical discourse of the "Inside Liffey" chapters, does not ignore women's bodies but in fact serves them as well as it can, within the limits of its purview, and in this case provides new access to what is inside but would otherwise remain unnoticed and unrepresented—the fetal heartbeat—through the use of scientific instrumentation. However, technology cannot so easily tell us what or how the inside signifies; it cannot cross or heal the perceived divide between body and mind, nature and culture.

When her doctor reminds her that she is, in his professional view, merely a passive container for the fetus to grow in, Liffey disregards the obstetrical interpretation and affirms her own knowledge of the fetus and her relationship to it: "Liffey knew better. She hugged her baby in her heart. Ah, we: we have done it. We are doing it" (180). To Liffey, the heartbeat that medical technology makes audible signifies not her passivity but her collaborative action. Because of this active, resistant construction, in pregnancy she experiences for the first time in her life a meaningful connection with what is "inside" her bodily bounds and can no longer be ignored, the fetus. Indeed, this fetus speaks to Liffey at an early stage of its development. When she first recognizes the new material vulnerability she will suffer as a mother, Liffey contemplates abortion, but she changes her mind after a mystical encounter with her baby's spirit speaking clearly to her: "'It's me . . . I'm here. I have arrived. You are perfectly all right, and so am I. Don't worry'" (139).

By representing the unborn child as an articulate speaker with a fully formed and confident personality, *Puffball* raised the problem of fetal rights a decade before it became the hot issue that it is today. In doing so, the novel runs the greatest risk of being read as a reactionary enterprise, contributing to the new construction of what some have called the "public fetus," so often used to control and silence women's experience of pregnancy.[34] Yet exactly the opposite reading is more accurate. Rather than affirming a fetal right that is brought into public perception by medical technology and stands in opposition to maternal need or desire, *Puffball* gives priority to the mother-to-be's perception of the fetus and suggests that she and the child-to-be have a far more difficult relationship to conceptualize and verbalize than we have yet understood. They are neither fused nor entirely divisible into "self" and "other," and their relationship is at least as subject to highly variable cultural construction as any other human interaction. In *Puffball*, the pregnant subject can be understood as doubled as well as divided, in ways that may both serve and disserve, expand and constrain a woman's subjectivity and agency, even as they consistently challenge common misconceptions and oversimplifications. Given the importance of this perception, we need to look closely at the reasons for reading the fetal voice in *Puffball* as part of the construction of a feminist challenge to "rightwing" arguments.

First, as represented here, the voice of the fetus underscores the moral and epistemological authority of the pregnant woman. This point does not depend on whether we believe that the fetus "really" speaks. Thought of as fact or fantasy, the sound of fetal speech is something to which *only* Liffey has access, so among the fictional actors in the narrative—doctor, husband, interfering or neglectful friends and neighbors, the state—she can make the most informed decisions about their mutual needs and best negotiate any differences between them. She has superior information about the fetus's perspective and may therefore act on knowledge that goes far beyond what scientific instrumentation can register or legal advocates or enemies of the fetus can consider. Although this does not necessarily guarantee that Liffey will always interpret what she hears (or believes she hears) correctly, the novel suggests that during gestation mothers-to-be may develop resources needed not only to make decisions that respect the rights of an other but also to take actions that implement those decisions. Before her pregnancy, Liffey feels, like Praxis, increasingly ineffectual, insubstantial, and disconnected as a self, isolated by her move to the country (which was intended to relieve the alienation she felt in the city) and her growing sense that everything is unreal. Gradually, however, because she comes to feel united with the baby in a mutual endeavor, Liffey gains a stronger sense of her own reality and power. She also discovers moral capacities and virtues she may not have recognized in herself before. For example, she violates the lifelong understanding between them to ask her mother who her father was because "lying, which had once seemed an essential part of Liffey's life; the very base, indeed, on which it was founded—though a changing, shifting base, the consistency of an underfilled bean bag—now seemed inappropriate. The baby gave her courage: compounded the reality of her existence. She could not be wished away, or willed away" (179).

A second and related point is that the mother-to-be's particular knowledge of the baby's existence and perspective comes from aural, not visual, perception. The power and acuity of maternal hearing as opposed to the cultivated inadequacy of our everyday ways of listening is further underscored when Liffey's unique perception of the baby's spirit-voice, her ability to perceive what is not said aloud or available to ordinary hearing, extends to other voices as well. When her mother-in-law responds to the news of her pregnancy, Liffey clearly hears the "shock and despair" belied by the words of congratulation. Feminist scholars have repeatedly pointed out how visual images and visual technology are used to create a public sense of a fetus taken out of the context in which it actually exists, the mother's body, and the relation between seeing and domination in western culture is a topic of great concern in many academic disciplines today.[35] Liffey's experience and capacity counters public visualization with a private maternal auditory perception that gives the fetus its voice. Whereas visual images tend to silence and speak for the represented subject—a topic Weldon also explores in *Praxis* and *The Cloning of Joanna May*—hearing as opposed to seeing suggests taking a position that is respectful of newly emerging speakers. Liffey's auditory facility also recalls the way in which Meridian functions as a listener more than a speaker, suggesting that if it is redefined in a way that takes into account the experience of the mother without child, maternal perception is as much about creating a better space for connection and exchange as it is about articulating a maternal voice.[36]

Yet a third, related consideration emerges from Liffey's experience as a listener who hears her baby's reassuring voice and infers their mutual collaboration. As others have recently pointed out, both the

fetal rights movement and the reproductive technology it often uti-
lizes may entail a troubling expansion and intensification of maternal
responsibility.[37] We see this most clearly in many recent and controversial cases of mothers-to-be who are held responsible for alleged
crimes against the fetus or for merely disagreeing with medical opinion. *Puffball* by no means suggests that women are not responsible
for the well-being of their children-to-be, but the novel puts a different spin on the question. Here, the fetus inside Liffey is not totally
helpless and dependent but is far more confident and self-assured than
Liffey herself. In such a version of the relationship between mother-
to-be and fetus, the former is in a sense liberated from the demands
of total responsibility for the latter's well-being even as she is given
strength and may find support and guidance in this new, uniquely intimate connection.

The final and perhaps most important political point to note about
Liffey's experience is that the confident fetus ironically reassures and
strengthens the dependent, embryonic selfhood of its mother-to-be at
a point when her independence is threatened *not* by the baby or by the
idea of the baby per se, but by her sudden recognition that as a woman
who has carelessly spent a private fortune and lacks a job or skills valued in the real world, henceforward she will be dependent on her husband (or someone else) for both her own and the child's support. Here,
then, "fetal rights" suggests a very different and quite straightforward
political argument. The well-being of the baby is threatened in this story
not by the mother-to-be's behavior, but first by the kind of biological
accident that medical technology is as yet powerless to control and then
by the socioeconomic system in which the rights and needs of both
mothers and children come last.

Because in all these ways *Puffball* suggests what we might call a
counter–fetal rights discourse that underlines the mother-to-be's privileged, even empowering access to the baby's "spirit," it is easy to understand why readers have feared the romantic celebration of motherhood in this novel. To prevent just such slippage, however, the benefits
and privileges of the mother-to-be's position are carefully and clearly
qualified in key ways. Making decisions based on the assumption that
the baby already occupies the linguistic position of speaker and addressee leads Liffey to stay in the world and act, and to that extent *Puffball* constructs a reverberant maternal subjectivity that is neither victimized by nor hostile to the fetus. But this maternal subjectivity is not

autonomous, in any ordinary sense of the term. Even as Liffey emerges into the position of a mother with attendant power and takes active responsibility, the novel undermines any notion that maternal agency always or consistently works either to clarify or serve the interests of the pregnant subject. The narrator repeatedly calls into question whether the actions Liffey takes are "hers," properly or conventionally speaking, or whether she acts for the baby, channeling his needs and interests, rather than her own, through her body.[38] When she goes into labor and manages to walk a long distance, bleeding, to the hospital, her extraordinary courage and strength are described in terms that could make them sound instinctive rather than purposive: "She did not suffer, particularly. She travelled because she had to, as a bird might travel to a warmer climate, or a salmon cross the sea to the river it had to find" (252). What we would probably want to call Liffey's own free choice gets her started on the journey—"No use lying down. . . . If I do nothing, I will simply bleed to death," she thinks. But even that sense of initiative is qualified as she goes on to privilege the baby's needs: "If it was only me, I wouldn't mind. I really wouldn't. I am not sure, on my own account, that I wish to stay in the world, considering its nature. What about you, baby?" (251).

Consulting the baby in this case helps to save both lives, but as narrated it also underscores the obvious: the two points of view, so interdependent, are not the same or necessarily in harmony. In fact, the interests of mother and child are increasingly competitive and divergent, especially from the baby's point of view. Whereas Liffey thinks of herself and the fetus as *we,* the baby's spirit uses the first-person singular, and his first words in the womb assure his mother that as a separate self he exists quite apart from her: "It's me . . . I'm here." Later, closer to parturition, the baby's spirit expresses his growing sense of Liffey's relative unimportance: "It's not what you want, it seemed to say, it's what I want" (217). Immediately after his birth, Liffey "sensed its triumph." Events in Liffey's life, the newborn says, "were peripheral events, leading towards the main end of your life, which was to produce me. You were always the bit-part player: that you played the lead was your delusion, your folly" (264). In Weldon's fiction, women who are or want to be mothers play the lead far more frequently than in most fiction, where they have traditionally been consigned to the bit parts. But as *Puffball* insists, motherhood as both psychic and social reality offers women at best temporary and equivocal stardom.

The ending of the novel reminds us that motherhood often obliges a woman, once her baby is born, to make more self-defeating compromises in order to protect the child and their relationship, even as she loses some of the seeming powers of pregnancy. In the last chapter, Liffey's newborn quickly becomes a more ordinary infant: "It gave up all appearance of being in charge, of knowing best. It left all that to Liffey, now" (271). Liffey as mother *with* child rather than mother *before* child finds herself in a position that demands that she act for the good of another who is even more clearly not herself. She no longer has special access to the baby's comforting "spirit," but is single-handedly responsible for the care of a passive, speechless, helpless being. There is nothing romantic about the course she chooses to follow in order to meet her new responsibility. The self she has become takes pleasure in the maternal work of caring for the baby, but in what is expressed as a defeat she also feels that she cedes to conventional wifedom a degree of control over her developing selfhood: "She thought that she too had become what Richard wanted. He had triumphed in his absence" (271). The trap that she entered into when she saw Honeycomb Cottage in the first paragraph of the novel springs on the last page when a contrite and forgiving Richard returns and she opens the door to him, "not without reluctance," but for the baby's sake.

MATERNAL DEPRIVATION REVISITED

> Oh my friends, my female friends, how wise you are to have
> no children or to throw them off. Better abort them, sterilise
> yourselves, or have your wombs cut out. Give birth, and you
> give others the power to destroy you, to multiply your hurts a
> thousand times, to make you suffer with them.
> —*Female Friends*

At the close of *Puffball,* Liffey's diminished powers, as a mother *with* child, link her to the women who appear and reappear in many of Weldon's other novels: women who are vulnerable to loss and suffering from the moment they give birth. To focus more directly on this problem, it is useful to look again at *Female Friends.* The novel rethinks Bowlby's concern with "maternal deprivation" by viewing it from another angle: what if we talk about mothers, not children, who are deprived? A minor character, Mad Doll, stands both as a marker of this previously ignored point of view and a symbol of the pervasive significance of losing children in the consciousness of Marjorie, Grace, and Chloe. Mad Doll emerges in and through the narrative like an archetype swimming in language and consciousness, occasionally bobbing to the surface and only gradually brought into partial representation. She is mentioned first in a passing allusion (95) as if she were a shared reference for narrator and readers. Later, when Chloe refuses to believe Grace's claim that her father raped her, Grace again alludes to the as-yet untold legend of a woman who apparently refuses to face tragic reality: "'Sometimes you act like Mad Doll, Chloe. You won't believe what you know to be true'" (119). The whole of the next brief chapter, midway through the novel, finally tells Mad Doll's story (120–1). She was the working-class mother of sons who were evacuated from their London school to Ulden; she and the boys' father were neither told ahead of time nor given information later as to their children's whereabouts, and Doll had to sleep with the schoolkeeper to find out that they were somewhere in Essex. She came to Ulden seeking them the day after both boys, while trying to run away home to their parents in London, drowned in a chalk-pit. When the vicar told her they were dead, she refused to believe him and continued to haunt the village every weekend, begging for news of the missing children whose loss she still mourned and denied.

Behind the particular figure of Mad Doll stands another group of mothers who refuse to accept state-mandated separation from their children. The comedy of adult errors that brings Marjorie, Grace, and Chloe together culminates when the staid village of Ulden happily accepts the wrong trainload of children, relieved because this lot is from the West End, not, as they expected, the East End. East End evacuees, it is said, are less desirable not only because they are stupid, but because their working-class mothers interfere with government policy and middle-class complicity. These women are too wildly if unavailingly protective. Evacuee children from such families "are followed everywhere by cunning, foul-mouthed, ferocious mothers, whom neither manners, lack of a bed, nor Government decree can keep away" (36).

Mad Doll and all those ferocious East End mothers have something deeply in common with Marjorie, Grace, and Chloe. For all three of the main female characters, living in a pronatalist peacetime does not solve the problems of real or felt loss of children to forces of law and the middle-class sentiment it subtends. As adults, all three friends are at least as troubled by their failures *as* mothers as they are by the failures of their own mothers. Each, however, escapes madness and suggests in her own way hope for change that recognizes the truth about maternal deprivation.

Marjorie represents one of the least dramatic yet most common and most debilitating forms of this phenomenon. Only a mother insofar as all women are equated with the maternal function, particularly in the rhetoric of pronatalism, she is an involuntarily childless woman whose first and only pregnancy ends in a stillbirth in the sixth month. Suffering through most of the narrative from her failure to remarry and bear a healthy child in a culture where doing so is woman's highest calling and first duty, she escapes only at the end of the novel to a new life that is not narrated, where key psychological, biological, and social circumstances liberate her from her procreative obsession and sense of failure. After her mother's death, Marjorie has a medically necessary hysterectomy and breaks away from England to a world in which women have other things to worry about. She goes to Israel as a producer of BBC films and in the war-torn culture ironically finds a certain peace: "Without her womb and without her mother, she seems cheerful enough. She is brown, weather-beaten, and handsome at last, in a country where to be devoid of juices is not remarkable, and to be alive, male or female, is commendable" (311).

Chloe, in contrast, represents the problems of felt childlessness and maternal failure that affect even women who have many living children, in part because motherhood is at once such an idealized and compromised function that no one could or perhaps should feel adequate to its demands. She introduces herself to readers as the mother of five, two of whom she bore, three of whom are more or less adopted. We later learn, however, that even this woman who behaves and understands herself as a deeply maternal person has a long history of miscarriages.[39] Remembering the anxiety she felt when her son at nine suffered a nearly fatal fall occasions the apostrophe to the vulnerability of mothers quoted at the beginning of this section. Despite the ironic tone—"how wise you are to have no children or to throw them off"—Chloe's advice suggests another truth about maternal behavior: what counts as maternal indifference is a social convention and may be a strategy for self-defense, survival, and endurance in the face of hard realities.[40] (This is an idea that is also seen in a rather different way in Dorris's Ida, that will be elaborated in Grace's story, and that suggests some broad connections to the analysis of mothers who "neglect" their children in other cultures.) Chloe, however, does not act on her own bitter wisdom, and her anxiety about losing her children causes not only personal suffering but what might be construed as immoral behavior, leading her to stay with and condone the cruelty of her insufferable husband Oliver for almost twenty years. What another of Weldon's characters calls "motherlust" also lays Chloe open to Grace's charge that she steals other women's children, a crime to which Chloe later admits her guilt.[41]

Grace's story suggests yet a third hazardous path for women coming of age in a pronatalist climate, and she stands as a prototype for Weldon's later mothers without children. Unlike Chloe and Marjorie, Grace is all too fertile, and at first, in Chloe's telling, she seems to be an ironic foil to her friends as she willingly throws away the children she too easily conceives: "Everyone says how heartless Grace is, what a selfish, unmaternal, unnatural woman" (249). When we meet her in present time, she has apparently had several affairs and several abortions, and she claims to enjoy the latter (124, 194–5). At Chloe's insistence she has carried one illegitimate son to term but is neglectful and lets Chloe take over his care when the boy is three. However, the narrative inexorably and with increasing detail undercuts easy assumptions about Grace's unnaturalness. Gradually it reveals the circumstances of her early marriage to a ruthless architect who designs buildings that are structurally flawed—potentially and in one prominent case actually deadly for the people who live and work inside them. Grace "intemperately" (155) loves the two children she bears with this man, but the marriage falls apart because Grace fails to be as completely blind to her husband's fatal architectural mistakes as he wishes her to be. In retaliation he charges Grace with madness and promiscuity, and the court awards him custody of the children. Like Mad Doll, Grace at this point in her life suggests the fate of women who actually embody the culture's precepts all too "intemperately," who care more about their children than their own sanity and survival. When her husband locks her out of their house, with the children inside, she scratches at the walls until blood and stucco mix. The very strength of this anger and grief at the loss of the children seems even to her friends to confirm her husband's accusations that she is insane (234).

But Grace stops her futile, self-mutilating struggle and does not become Mad Doll. Instead, she resists this escape, this victimization, and takes the alternate route to survival that Chloe ironically praised but never practiced, cutting herself off from her thwarted love for the children. She pulls herself together, makes herself "unmaternal," with rationalization. The children are better off with their rich father than with her in the cheap two-room flat she can afford, and she can have more fun without them. She is perceived as damaged by this strategy: Chloe says Grace's husband "battered the maternal instinct out of her" (195), and later the third-person narrator observes that "it's as if part of her brain has been burnt out" (234). Yet Grace's "selfishness" keeps her alive, and at the very least she persists in reminding her victimizers of what they have done. Even after she has given up the struggle to get her children back, she harasses her husband's second wife until prevented by a court order. As she tells Chloe, that epitome of passivity, "bad behaviour is very animating" (210).[42]

In a surprise twist at the end of the novel, middle-aged Grace announces that she is pregnant. Whereas Marjorie flees pronatalist England altogether and Chloe at last breaks free of her husband, Grace reverses the seemingly liberating trajectories of her friends' lives and settles down in middle age with her younger lover to raise the baby. The desire and capacity to mother has not in fact been battered or burnt out of Grace, it seems, but it can only be realized in circumstances that are both lucky and illicit. Given the dominant conception of the "good mother," *some* badness is needed to stay alive. What happens to Grace at the end of the novel is inconsistent only if we misunderstand why she acts so selfishly and unmaternally for most of her life.

As *Female Friends* thus gradually complicates and revalues any simple or conventional reading of the unnatural mother, it suggests that the neat division of women into those who surrender their children voluntarily and those who involuntarily lose them is not merely too facile but almost impossible to make. Cumulatively reinforcing this point, mothers in several of Weldon's later novels reflect isolated, recombined, told and retold aspects of Grace's story. Superficially, one can divide female characters of subsequent novels into two groups: those who choose to leave their children behind, give their children away, or murder an infant, as in *The Lives and Loves of a She Devil, Praxis,* and *Life Force*; and those who involuntarily almost lose their unborn babies or have their children (or clones) stolen from them by bad men, as in *The President's Child, The Hearts and Lives of Men,* and *The Cloning of Joanna May.* But *Female Friends* should warn us at the outset not to assume that it is so easy to judge and categorize these women. It is not simple to determine the psychological and social effects of "maternal deprivation," as Bowlby defined the notion, nor is it right to slide from partial and probably partisan observation into a universally enforced policy and morality, from the one-sided and highly limited study of "child development" as it emerges in the twentieth century into pronouncements about how all women must feel and behave.

·······

Following up on some of the possible implications of this understanding, I want to revisit and explore more fully the climactic episode in Praxis's career as the mother without child, the murder of her surrogate daughter's three-day-old baby. Long before she commits her sensational crime, Praxis gives up her own children to the care of their father, Ivor, for multiple reasons. Some of these reasons she recognizes at the time; some are understood only later. In part, her status as mother without child reflects her extreme dissociation. She is so deeply disavowed by Ivor and divided from herself at the time that she cannot feel like a mother; as she says later, "I did not really feel good enough or whole enough to have children" (178). She also needs to save herself from a progressively degrading relationship with her husband and from the numbing routine that threatens her children's identity as well as her own: "When she collected them, she found it hard to distinguish them from the other children; or herself, for that matter, from the other mothers" (167). She believes that her children will grow without her and that Ivor is better at caring for them and happier without her. At the time she leaves, however, she knows too that her motives are selfish, that if she ruins Ivor's life or the children's "it was just too bad" (176).

In the present-tense narrative, Praxis affirms another important truth that can be acted on only from the position of the mother without child. Although alone and injured in her basement room, Praxis cannot be pitied as a sad, neglected old woman, she says, because she has one important blessing that most women lack: she is "not anxious; not plagued by the Worm Anxiety, which gnaws away at the foundations of female experience, so that the patterns of magnificence fail, time and time again, to emerge." This Worm Anxiety is most frequently fed by fear on behalf of children; it "plagues the maternal life, animal or human. It starts before the child is born. . . . There is no end to it. . . . the Worm Anxiety snips some nerve in the minds of women, and keeps their heads bowed" (120–1). Praxis expresses pride that she set her own children free; they are "ungrateful," and that is good, because they are "free to grow away" from her in a way that she was not free to grow from her mother.

Prepared by the unnatural crime of abandoning the children she bore to the custody of their father and eventually free from anxiety about them, Praxis is the one who can act in a way that the woman who fully and successfully occupies the legitimate position of mother cannot. What she does can be seen as a complexly empathic gesture. She takes on the responsibility that mothers whose ultimate goal is to protect their children may be constitutionally unable to take, in circumstances when the "truth" may be that a child should not live. Her rational motives for murdering Mary Leonard's baby defend the morality of her act and the obligation of mothers to make hard decisions. They include the principle that "logically there was no difference between contraception and abortion: that the termination of pregnancy at any stage, whether the foetus was minus nine months, six months, three months or plus one day, must be the mother's decision" (244). She questions, moreover, any glib definition of "life." The baby would have either destroyed Mary's life or would have been looked after "as the helpless were looked after—cruelty alternating with kindness" (245). The truth, in this case and others, is excruciating—but Praxis now knows that it is important to feel pain when it is really there.

At the time, however, Praxis can only "half believe" these rational arguments. Although she acts on principles, they do not spare her from weeping for Mary's deformed baby, and she is ambivalent about how her act might more widely represent mothers and motherhood. Praxis acts in large part out of "irrational" motives, prompted not by the desire to sacrifice self for others, but to find self and connection; she knows that she is right, through other modes of knowing, and senses that in murdering the baby she is also seeking to destroy the passive, helpless part of herself that has been dependent on the cruelty and kindness of others. More positively, her crime is inspired by a mystical conviction that she is in touch with a power outside and beyond herself that has spoken to her through the star, Betelgeuse, once identified as the soul of Mary's mother, Miss Leonard, the teacher who took young Praxis in. Representing the self glimpsed in adolescence in her relationship with Miss Leonard, the self that has known what it could not say, that has waited throughout Praxis's years of disguise and self-deception, Praxis's act is one of self-knowledge and self-affirmation because it tells truth to the world. As she forces the unwilling doctor to tear up the death certificate and press criminal charges, she insists that the baby would have lived "for another forty years of semi-vegetable living, but because of something I did, deliberately, it is now dead. That is the truth." It is finally for Praxis an instance in which fact can be firmly divided from fantasy, and the division matters both to the integrity of her self and her connection to others: "What she remembered and what had happened were identical. She had passed into the real world, where feelings were sharp and clear, however painful" (243).[43] When "women's instincts were so much at variance with the rules of society," women could rarely talk about or add up the sum of their experiences, even to themselves, and so dissociation and disconnection, however crippling, were sometimes the only available strategies for survival. Praxis herself used such strategies repeatedly as she moved numbly through the roles of abandoned and then seduced daughter, exploited and ignored mistress or wife, whore, mother, even feminist. It is now crucial to start telling the painful truth, particularly about the price of self-sacrifice that mothers have historically been asked, been told, been willing to pay.

·······

Puffball resists the notion that mothers are powerless, speechless victims, but it too ends on a note of truth about the price Liffey must pay to maintain her connection with her baby in a conventional marriage. In Weldon's next novel, *The President's Child*, the tale of Isabel Rust takes us behind the scenes of a different kind of marriage, one that seems at first glance to be a feminist dream come true. As one neighbor puts it, Isabel and her husband Homer have "the perfect companionate marriage. The true, the new, the sharing!" (6). Things are seldom what they seem, however; this marriage turns out to be another trap for a woman threatened with the loss of her child or herself.

Isabel is not, like Liffey, financially dependent on her husband, a sensitive American named Homer. She has a successful career as a television journalist and a healthy six-year-old son, Jason, and Homer does half of all the child care and domestic work. But this domicile of shared parental responsibility is soon revealed to be a house of cards built on the lie that Isabel has told about Jason's paternity and the lie that Homer has told about his identity and his political allegiances. In fact, Jason's biological father is not Homer, but an American presidential candidate named Dandy Ivel, whom Isabel met while covering the first flight of the Concorde from London to Washington. A stereotype of the handsome, florid candidate-as-womanizer, Dandy swept young Isabel off her feet and into a hotel room for several weeks, where she lived in dazed orgasmic bliss until she began to feel imprisoned. Escaping, or so she thought, from the dangers of self-submersion is this affair, she met Homer on the plane back to London and fell just as quickly, if not as blissfully, into bed and then marriage with him.

All goes well, it seems, until six years later, when the American presidential campaign heats up. People begin to notice the physical resemblance between the little English boy and the face on the television news, and the dangerous agents of Dandy Ivel's backers, who have kept careful track of Isabel and Jason, decide that it is time to do something about this visible reflection of and hence threat to the candidate's image. Eventually Homer's lie is disclosed, too. The perfect new husband is actually a secret agent, working for Dandy's interests and sent from the moment Isabel "escaped" to keep her under surveillance. Anticipating a debate that is probably more intense today than it was when the novel was published, *The President's Child* uses this blatantly melodramatic plot and a characteristically wry humor to assault postfeminism, to challenge the presumption that feminist arguments about oppression and domination either were simply paranoid overstatements to begin with or have been outmoded by rapid changes in the relations between men and women.

Like so many of Weldon's protagonists, postfeminist Isabel is vulnerable, despite her financial and sexual independence, for one reason: she is a mother. In other novels, mothers' anxieties about losing their children are often complex projections of the difficult and inevitable divisions between mother and child, divisions caused by both the "natural" process of child development and the needs of women to develop and sustain their own lives apart from their work as mothers. In many cases, the actual loss of children is also glimpsed, but often it is cushioned. Chloe's son falls off the roof, but survives; more miraculously still, in *The Hearts and Lives of Men*, parents are reunited with their lost daughter after fifteen years and a series of near misses; and in *Life*

Force, the son that a woman sells in her youth to a childless couple comes back, as a young man, to find and forgive his outwardly successful but inwardly lonely and unloved biological mother. In other cases, giving children away or even letting them be taken is necessary for a mother like Praxis, better for the children in question, or compensated for by later experiences of motherhood, as in Grace's story. The Worm Anxiety is more imagined than real for many of these fictive mothers—though possibly all the stronger for that. In *The President's Child,* however, imaginary fears that a child is in danger turn out to be all too real,[44] and Isabel, lulled by apparent well-being, is caught off guard: "She had grown careless and sleepy, as a sentry might who has occupied an uneventful post too long; who has heard too many twigs snapping to believe them footsteps any more" (137).

Motherhood is by no means a completely powerless experience for Isabel. Awakened by the necessity of protecting her son from her mistaken reliance on Homer and the surrender of both sexual and moral self that this entails, Isabel finds resources in her role as mother and some of the strength and conviction of self that Liffey finds when her unborn child is in danger. It is not only frightening but liberating to recognize that Homer, the perfect husband and father, has been wearing a disguise for six years and is actually the enemy (199). One by one, the scales fall from Isabel's eyes. Eventually she comes to recognize that even the orgasmic relationship with Dandy Ivel was an illusion of love. Everything she thought she was doing as an agent of her own destiny—escaping Dandy, finding and marrying Homer, betraying Homer with a colleague—turns out to have been set up by her enemies; she has been manipulated from the beginning, except in her decision to bear Jason in the first place. It is thus clearer here even than in *Puffball* that maternal practice itself is not what primarily threatens a woman's well-being. Although Isabel's motives in having Jason may have been mixed, the work of raising the child is said to be an unmitigated good. "The sheer boring repetitive, purposeful nature of the task," notes the didactic narrator, "is a great purifying agent" (130). The evil that threatens mother and son is not inherent in the work of mothering, but reveals the banal, clichéd, outdated reality of a male conspiracy, in this instance one aimed at controlling arguably the most powerful position in the world, the presidency of the United States.

The suspenseful climax of this story poses a question similar to the one that novels like *Praxis* and *Meridian* raise: at what point do the demands of maternal work, in itself necessary, valuable, and "purifying," become so great that there is nothing of the mother herself left, in this case not even the possibility of life? Initially, in her efforts to protect Jason, Isabel is willing to take the first, easy step of acquiescing in a lie that she hopes will save her son—agreeing that he is Homer's son, not Dandy's—and thus putting the child's welfare before the mother's ability to tell the truth. As in *Praxis,* maternal truth telling is particularly difficult if not impossible when the truth might mean that the child cannot or should not live. When this compromising strategy fails, Isabel considers going to Dandy himself and promising to keep silent, "to render herself passive, agreeable, invisible" (186). But it is too late for this traditionally feminine mode of willing self-denial; Isabel's previous displays of independence and courage are in this case liabilities, and the danger that a woman like her might at some point speak or become visible is too risky. Homer arranges, then, for the only viable solution; Isabel must die, so that Jason can live (as Homer's son). In the last suspenseful moments of the story, Isabel accepts the inevitable and heads down a long flight of stairs to the street, consenting to a plan that seems to caricature women's worst fears about what happens when they become mothers: she will step cheerfully into the road and be run over by a truck while she deliberately looks in the other direction.

As Isabel descends to her death, she grasps at conflicting feelings and motives in an attempt to control the meaning of the situation and find some scrap of self-affirmation. She feels real, as Liffey did, under attack, but she also feels that if Jason died, she would be too wounded to go on without him. She thinks of herself as moving "down to the origins of her being" as she climbs down the stairs, but when she reaches the bottom she is only "confused," because there seems to be no original self to return to. The self-sacrificial maternal subject implodes, in a sense, at the bottom of those stairs, and the plot refracts this discovery in a lucky coincidence that spares Isabel: Dandy has a heart attack, and the news is broadcast just before she is to step out into the traffic.

As we have seen elsewhere in Weldon's fiction, forces that women fear—men, social policy, their own reproductive nature or socialization into motherhood—are not always as powerful as people think they are, although this is a near miss. Isabel subsequently makes good her escape from what she has learned about the real dangers of the western political world, taking Jason back to her native Australia where we are also led to imagine that she will have a reunion with her own previously distant mother. One way to read this ending that makes *The President's*

Child a key part of the sequence of novels I group together here is to reiterate that all these stories of mothers who suffer from the felt, threatened, or real loss of children lead to the same conclusion. The work of being a mother is good, if you can afford to do it, but in the world as it is now organized, motherhood is rarely a position in which subjectivity, autonomy, and integrity, as we normally understand these concepts, can be easily attained; material circumstances, moreover, make the job difficult if not untenable for many women today. Lucky women may escape, like Marjorie in *Female Friends,* from pronatalist coercion, or like Isabel from the greed and envy of powerful men—but only, it seems, by passing beyond the borders of England.

·······

Or beyond the borders of realism: in *The Cloning of Joanna May* (1989), Weldon brings my study of the figure of the mother without child to one possible closure by transforming the protagonist, in the course of a plot bordering on science fiction, from a familiar old version into a revolutionary new and improved variety, speculatively discarding and reinventing motherhood on the most radically innovative terms that Weldon has yet proposed. The outrageous "cloning" of Joanna's ripe egg, without her knowledge or consent, would seem to parody the violation that feminist critiques of medical technology have deplored.[45] Like other such critiques, this novel suggests that reproductive technologies, as presently controlled by men, are designed to extend male domination, assuage male envy of female reproductive power, and treat women as passive vessels rather than rational agents. They also support and exploit the coercive pronatalism of culture at large. But in this case female power is multiplied, not divided as Carl intended when he cloned his wife. With the help of other responsible people, the coalition of cutting-edge science and husband-patriarchy is thwarted; the doctor who did the cloning and the husband who funded it are at once defeated and co-opted.[46] Even more important, this victory is accompanied by an empowering revision of women's role as mothers that is made possible by the very technology that was previously used to control female reproduction. *Cloning* thus suggests that to some extent men are less frightening and less powerful than women thought and that some aspects of the role of mother as we have known it are less vital to female identity than women have understood and may be refashioned in ways that better serve women's interests.

Ironically, in this feminist fantasy, the end result of reproductive technology liberates women from the burdens of conventional motherhood while enabling them to control and enjoy the benefits of female friendship and the virtues of maternal work. At first Joanna—our most bizarre example of the mother without child—can only think of her unnatural and hitherto uncharted relationship to her clones as a variety of maternal connection. An older clone would have to be "a kind of extra mother, dreadfully like oneself" (128). So too her motives in seeking out her clones initially seem stereotypically maternal: she refers to the clones as "my babies" (195), and she wants to protect them from Carl and possess them for herself—"I want them. I need them. They're *mine*" (188). But a little later Joanna acknowledges that she wants to meet her clones in order to understand something about the construction of her own identity, to see "what I would be, born into a newer, more understanding world: one which allowed women choice, freedom, and success" (202). This is in fact what she does see; more surprisingly, perhaps, she also finds that she is not too old to experience change, "choice," and "freedom" of her own. In the scene where Joanna and her clones finally meet, the older woman's status as mother is critiqued and transformed. When they first see her, the clones cry, "'Mother! . . . It must be Mother!'" (249), and childless Joanna quickly assumes the role she has often longed for. As mother, acting the part that her own mother acted, she is immediately required to give the clones her opinion of them, as they seek "what every daughter wants, a mother to wholly appreciate them" (250). Her "maternal view," however, turns out to be quite critical of their looks and behavior—"for their own good"—and within seconds the newfound "daughters" start resenting "mother." She and one of the clones agree that this is how mothers behave; they can't help it, particularly as they need to make the daughters as like them as possible and "unthread, unknit, the father in her" (250).

But Joanna has no actual need to "unknit" the father in Alice, Julie, Jane, and Gina. Products of female parthenogenesis, they have no genetic material from anyone but Joanna herself. Joanna is therefore able to renounce this now unnecessary aspect of motherhood, which can only divide mother and daughter: "'If this is motherhood, save me from it. I always wanted it, but this is all it is! Nag, nag, nag!'" (251). Casting about for another role in the limited and tired repertoire of family relations, the clones reject Joanna as sister because she is too old and will be jealous of their youth. They finally decide to go outside the nuclear family altogether for a paradigm of association and collaboration that qualifies the power of the leader. Joanna is named "chairperson" of the group—"someone who controlled an agenda but couldn't vote" (251–2).

In the denouement, we see that although they have given up the name and a large part of the baggage of patriarchal motherhood, Joanna and three of her clones have retained and dispersed certain necessary, good, and pleasurable aspects of mothering work among themselves. That division of women's labor, so oppressive when orchestrated to serve the interests of male rulers in *The Handmaid's Tale,* is appropriated here by women who control the means of reproduction. Joanna promises the dying Carl that she will clone him; with the help of a co-opted Dr. Holly, she does. To everyone's surprise it is the most beautiful and selfish clone, Alice, who volunteers to bear the baby, but she relinquishes him happily to Joanna when he is six weeks old, and Joanna takes over the job of giving Little Carl what Big Carl wanted from her, the loving care that his own abusive biological mother failed to provide. Meanwhile Gina, the only clone who has already borne children, willingly gives her two sons and a daughter away to childless clones Jane and Julie; the former takes in the girl, Sue, and lets her longtime boyfriend move in to do much of the child care, while Julie, whose husband is sterile, adopts the two boys and contentedly stays home to care for them. Happily childfree at last, Gina goes to medical school and back to her husband, Cliff, who still beats her up at times. Just as the clones do not blame Gina for giving away her children, they resist any inclination to criticize her for putting up with Cliff's abuse (and perhaps finding pleasure in it): "We've had so many oughts and shoulds, all of us, we've all but given up being critical of one another. Good for her, we say" (265). The vision of a frankly better but not fully utopian future for female identity and motherhood that closes *Cloning* thus affirms that traditional aspects of maternal work can be dispersed and shared among women who freely choose the part they want or are suited to have and are not divided by their different choices.

Epilogue
Feminism Is [Not] a Luxury

Many people, both in academic and nonacademic circles,
have come to regard feminist arguments concerning the
biases and exclusions of western culture either as outmoded
by progressive changes in gender relations, or as paranoid
delusions, fueled by a mania for "political correctness" rather
than truth. These notions persist despite increasingly strong
cultural evidence to the contrary.
> —Susan Bordo, "Are Mothers Persons?"

If there is, as some feminists want to suggest, a universal
sisterhood of women, and I doubt it, but if there is, it would
have its origins in this collective comforting of those weeping
women, like the biblical Rachel, whose children are no more.
> —Nancy Scheper-Hughes,
> *Death without Weeping*

"Loss suffered by any woman is every woman's loss."
> —*The President's Child*

I MUST OFFER YOU WHAT I CAN: STORYTELLING AS
NONPROCREATIVE MATERNAL PRACTICE

My primary interest is in the *story* of the mother without child; the
works I have considered are novels, not arguments or conduct manu-
als, and what conclusions I can offer must grow out of that understanding. As a literary scholar I have been particularly interested in the
ways these stories variously work within and against the conventions
of classic realism, playing with traditional notions of character, plot,
and genre and often urging upon us a model of listening rather than a
model of speaking as a way of engaging the so-called maternal subject
or voice. Let me begin to end, then, by returning briefly to Weldon's

Praxis and *The President's Child,* both of which offer framing narratives that underscore metafictional concerns even as they point toward the most immediate and urgent implications of this study as whole.

Praxis implicitly shares Ida's understanding, in *Yellow Raft on Blue Water,* that "I am the story." However, whereas Ida can purportedly tell her story in a tongue other than English, Praxis seems doomed to recapitulate the progress of the woman writer who can speak only in the language of western culture. In the third-person past-tense episodes of the novel, Praxis moves swiftly through the written genres that have historically been opened up to increasingly more women. First she keeps a diary, then she composes academic essays, then ad copy, and finally feminist propaganda. Her experience at each stage forces us to question just how progressive this apparent evolution actually is and how much language really serves women and gives them access to useful agency and knowledge. Unlike many heroines of contemporary fiction, Praxis writes easily and effectively. She does not lack a vocabulary or fluency with words; she has to try hard not to earn top marks at university, and later she effortlessly earns a good living as a writer and editor. At each stage, however, she is forced to suppress what she feels and knows as she repeatedly discovers how dangerous it can be for a woman to tell the truth. Her most highly paid writing—advertisements for the Electricity Board that appeal to the ideal of the thoroughly domesticated woman—directly contradicts the life she is living at the time.

Praxis's first attempt to put what she knows into words, in the "part fact, part fantasy" of her adolescent diary, is exemplary in this regard. She tries to record events and feelings in what she later calls "simplified" form—that is, in a form that expresses what they mean to her, what they say about her own fears and desires. The vicar's exposure becomes rape; her unspoken crush on an older schoolgirl, Louise, becomes a secret kiss. When her mother finds and reads the diary, however, disaster strikes. Lucy, we recall, survived by ignoring, compartmentalizing, and forgetting; when she faces Praxis's efforts to acknowledge, connect, and remember, she believes (or pretends to believe) it all really happened, goes berserk, and is finally hospitalized. At the same time, the female imagination has the frightening power to make wishes come true: when Louise, the distant schoolmate who has never before spoken to Praxis, hears about Praxis's diary, she kisses "Patricia" for real, saying "'Now it's not a lie'" (46). The effect of this first narrative act on the reality around her thus dramatically seems to foreclose the possibility of writing to escape the consequences of desire—men's unsolicited desire for women or women's illicit desire for each other. At university, where she learns to suppress her own ideas or pass them off as Willie's in order to keep his love, and again in her successful careers as ad writer and feminist editor, Praxis further demonstrates that women's writing pays off, in one sense or another, only when it expresses popular, normative myths and thus ignores the true facts and puzzling contradictions of experience.

Yet the novel as a whole finally defies this lifelong, necessary habit of self-defensive self-editing—and serves, just like the crime it records and justifies, as a blatant act of resistance, self-recognition, and connection to the world outside the self. A first-person present-tense frame situates Praxis, while narrating the third-person past-tense chapters sometime after her release from Holloway Prison, in the painful isolation of her basement flat. She has recently been immobilized by an accident. An independent young woman in high heels has carelessly trod on her foot, and Praxis feels ignored by the world, "alone in the reality I have created for myself" (77).[1] The novel thus begins as notes from the underground woman, but the position of the lone, alienated, and subversive female hero recollecting experience in the tranquillity and superior consciousness of self-imposed isolation is not celebrated. Instead, the narrative moves to heal and reconnect the maimed female subject, in this case a first-generation feminist wounded by the consequences of the political change she has helped to create. Praxis's professed intention in telling the truth this time is not to serve others on whom she is dependent or, indeed, to fashion or defend herself: instead, thinking that she is soon to die, she repeatedly insists that she want to leave her legacy to other women, so that they can learn from it. Marked as mother without child, she substitutes this new didactic narrative for old maternal anxiety, literary production for reproduction. At the same time, she figures her writing now as a motherly gesture in its own right, addressed like the Handmaid's tale to an anonymous community of prospective readers:

> I must offer you what I can.
> Watch Praxis. Watch her carefully. Look, listen, learn.
> Then safely, as they say to children, cross over. (101)

In keeping with this new view of storytelling as a nonprocreative maternal practice, Praxis constantly interrupts herself with a first-person counterdiscourse of sententious generalizations that directly attack the old myths of motherhood and female identity.[2] The first-person speaker

is a voice of unconventional, postmaternal feminine wisdom who reverses the role of the feminist writer as daughter and at the same time
revalues the connection with "female friends."

In the course of articulating and passing on subversive and newly
empathic insights into the reasons why so many women suffer in the
affective and reproductive sphere, the first-person speaker in the present tense begins to feel better. As she accepts responsibility for her isolated position—"If I am alone now, I deserve it"—her cat comes back
(178). After she has narrated the last retrospective episode, in which
she commits her crime and thus most fully inhabits her original name—
praxis means practice, conduct—by acting as agent of the mother and
the truth, she manages to get to the hospital. There a young female
doctor identifies her as the heroine, Praxis Duveen. "Everyone" knows
her, the doctor says, from the documentary her ex-husband Philip made
for the Women's Movement, entitled "The Right to Choose," but because she came out of prison as Pattie Fletcher, her supporters thought
she was dead. In the hospital, where she is recognized, valued, and nur-
tured, Praxis discovers that she is not as old as she pretended to be and
suffering not from senility but from malnutrition. Although she claims
not to want all the attention she receives—flowers, visitors, "a babel of
people, mostly women"—her last words affirm the pleasure she takes
in feeling connected, perhaps for the first time: "The wall which surrounded me is quite broken down. I can touch, feel, see my fellow human beings. That is quite enough" (251).

Like all the stories in this study, *Praxis* suggests that crimes against
the Euroamerican domestic order are inevitable when women tell the
truth about experience and act on that truth. The paradigmatic female
speaker-teacher here is once more the quintessential female criminal,
the mother without child, who occupies this position first out of necessity, in order to survive, and then out of empathic choice, in order
to protect another woman who would otherwise attempt to sacrifice
herself to motherhood. The cure for a life of fragmentation and lies is
not the outlaw's autobiography per se, but this record of experience
and analysis offered as a sententious, maternal legacy to other women.

YOU MUST LEARN TO SHARE ME:
A COMMUNITY OF LISTENERS

First-person narration is not the perspective of choice in most stories
of the mother without child. Where it does appear—as in *Female*

Friends, Praxis, The Handmaid's Tale, and *Yellow Raft on Blue Water*—it tends to be interrupted, intermittent, shared among more than one "I," or framed in some way. More often, a flexible third-person point of view is used to tell the mother's story. Weldon's narrative strategy in *The President's Child* helps to clarify why this is so.

Here we find what is in some ways the most complicated and interesting metafictional frame of any of Weldon's novels. As in *Praxis,* a third-person past-tense story—now the saga of Isabel Rust and the transatlantic plot to kidnap her child and kill her—is bracketed and interrupted by a first-person present-tense narrative. But the narrator of Isabel's story is explicitly not Isabel herself, from whom we remain relatively distanced and who perhaps never becomes a fully trustworthy voice. Instead, the story of this mother without child is told by a blind woman named Maia. She and her audience are only briefly glimpsed; in the first chapter we meet Maia and a small group of female neighbors, all living on the same street, Wincaster Row, where Isabel and Homer used to live before their sudden disappearance. Jennifer, Hilary, and Hope have come on a rainy Sunday afternoon to visit Maia out of kindness. She says that she offers them the true story about Isabel for two reasons. The first reason suggests that she begins in part where *Praxis* left off, establishing connections: she wants to "reciprocate" her neighbors' kindness and caring since the accident that blinded her. Her second reason reflects didactic purposes that also recall Praxis's or Ida's motives but position the narrator inside the group as well as in the role of teacher: she hopes that together "we" will "know more than we did before" (5).

What we learn about Maia and her audience suggests that this is a story about storytelling itself in a specifically postfeminist political climate. The characters in the frame story are postfeminists in that they enjoy many of the gains that feminism and other progressive movements have made for a fortunate few. As a group of neighbors, caring for each other, Maia believes that she and her friends are "good" people, more or less. They are chiefly "communicators," representing the worldwide "culture of kindness" maintained in such "enclaves" around the world, marked by "self-doubt" as well as "aspiration" (8–9). They particularly hope for change in gender relations and resolution of the conflict within and between motherhood and wifehood, but they can express this hope only in the interrogative voice: "Surely men and women can be friends and lovers too? Be both parents and partners?" (10). And to preserve this possibility, they must turn on the central heating and draw the curtains against the weather; they live in smug, isolated places where privileged people choose not to look outside. The women of Wincaster Row need to hear about Isabel, Maia says, because they have not only benefited from feminist change but also forgotten or ignored one of the first and most fundamental principles of the feminist movement: they still suffer under the illusion "that people and politics are entirely separate" (5). Isabel was a neighbor, someone they once knew and lived with, and the story of how her personal gains as a new woman were so easily erased by men's old political interests is meant to reassert among other things that no one is immune. "The river flows at the end of the garden; what's more, it's deep, wide, muddy, and tricky: not the tranquil flowing stream you might hope for. Isabel almost drowned!" (5).

Maia is a participant observer in this culture of kindness, and as blind storyteller she stands partially inside and partially outside the community in these postfeminist times. As insider, she sympathizes with the illusions that her neighbors, like Isabel, prefer to accept. Maia is herself, in fact, the most dramatic exemplar of the wish not to see. Her doctors think her blindness may be psychosomatic, and as the story unfolds we learn why she might not want to face the crisis of her reality. The immediate cause of the accident that blinded her was betrayal: her husband was having an affair, and in the midst of a quarrel she ran weeping, carelessly not looking, into the street where she was hit by a car. Before that, she too had occupied the position of the mother without child; she had a baby, born without reproductive organs, that died within five minutes of birth. "Cling to a sense of self through that, if you can" (46), she says. At points Maia explicitly warns against seeing too much and directs her larger audience—we, the readers—to be grateful for the protection we can find in not seeing, not fearing, not connecting too far outside the cozy circle. Recalling the Handmaid's strategy and the sardonic advice Chloe offers in *Female Friends*, Maia says "Draw the curtain" against the rain, and "try not to see too much, but just enough for survival's sake. Preserve your peace of mind. There is not much time; all things end in death. Do not lament the past too much, or fear the future too acutely, or waste too much energy on other people's woes, in case the present dissolves altogether" (17). Although there is undoubtedly irony in her tone, Maia's advice reflects realistically on the function and limits of storytelling, fiction writing, and reading (just as Praxis's experience highlights the constraints imposed on the woman writer). Narrator and audience form a safe, temporarily assembled community where horrible things happening just outside the carefully maintained boundaries of their present reality can be talked about, imagined—even, in Weldon's novels, laughed at—and hence endured. Narrative can in this way reinforce rather than transcend the willful ignorance that supports privilege, a danger recognized by Atwood and others. Near the end of the novel, Maia again invites the reader outside the frame to join her where it is peaceful in the dark, where we too will be spared the sights of personal and public betrayal, decay, suffering, deformity, and death. We can live instead in the middle class, with the kindness that only the middle class can afford. "Of course I cannot see. I do not want to see. Do you?" (193).

At the same time, a more resistant model of narrative emerges in the course of Maia's story, not necessarily negating her more cynical moments but suggesting an alternative possibility. Maia's blindness, like her storytelling, has a double valence. It may be a form of self-protection from pain, like Lucy's madness, the Handmaid's ignoring, and Praxis's or Meridian's or June's dissociation, but for this late-twentieth-century female version of the sightless Miltonic bard, it also serves as a complex source of wisdom and deeper insight. As a disability, a misfortune, it connects her to others less privileged than her seeing self and her healthy middle-class English friends, to people less lucky, less liberated than Isabel and others on Wincaster Row think they are. From this perspective, the point of view of the maimed and unlucky as well as the enslaved and colonized, she avers that "feminism is a luxury," unaffordable by women who simply cannot be materially independent, for whatever reasons. Since her accident, she too has found herself willing to do mundane household chores that she formerly scorned, just to be useful, and she comments on this apparently "regressive" behavior: "I stick by a division of labour that never in the past suited me, but now does" (115). In this way she forms a tenuous connection with other women who are "unfit" for the independence demanded by western feminism.[3]

However, like Chloe's perception that women are divided, Maia's claim that feminism is a luxury is by no means fully endorsed by her own experience or subsequent reflection in the narrative. Although her situation of dependence teaches her that mainstream western feminism may serve the privileged few, Maia's experience and insights as a blind person confirm that some foundational feminist principles still hold and are needed by all. For example, with the stereotypically heightened auditory powers of the blind—which are comparable to Liffey's powers in the early days of gestation or even to Meridian's capacities as listener—Maia hears the *cris de joie* of orgasm all through the night in her neighborhood. Meditating on their significance, she understands why Isabel was so deluded by her passion for Dandy: those cries of sexual pleasure "almost, but not quite, blot out the tears of misery and fear which follow them" (82). Maia tells the unknown story of Isabel and her sudden reversal of fortunes because she wants her neighbors too to listen better, to attend to the misery and fear, to be aware, again, that people like themselves are not as protected as they think, not immune to real danger.

Maia's storytelling has the same effect on the teller as Praxis's autobiographical act. At the very end of the novel, when she has reached the depths of despair and given up all hope—like Isabel as she descends the stairs, or Connie as she hits rock bottom—Maia's sight is miraculously restored, just as Isabel is suddenly reprieved and Connie "catches" the future. As in *Praxis* and possibly *The Handmaid's Tale,* it seems that storytelling and truth telling—equated and set in contrast to women's lives that are built on localized amnesias or deliberate lies, often told for the sake of the children—have healed the narrator. Yet because Maia tells this story not about herself, but about another threatened mother, its implications are different. First, there seems to be a kind of healing by analogy or contagion here, as Maia has told the true story of a betrayal that is in some ways parallel to her own story. She cannot speak directly of her own trauma, but after she has managed to record it in a bearable form because it is displaced, she can look with seeing eyes at the loss of her own illusions about both heterosexual connections and motherhood. Second, she has also caught "a glimmer here and there" of a hope that may make her willing to see again, after she tells her story. In her closing overview she brings us up to date on some of the main characters in a way that contradicts the bleakness of her earlier perspective. Isabel and her son are safe in Australia, and Jason, although physically still "his father's image," represents a possibly better future for men too: "Perhaps he will belong to a new generation of man, who can find power enough inside themselves, and not go seeking for it in the exploitation and pillaging of women and the world; who can find their kingdom in inner and not outer space" (218). Even Homer, Maia reveals, has changed a little since he left Isabel, with the help of his new wife, for "the habits of culture and kindness are catching—it is one of the few hopes we have" (218). Like the botched evacuation in *Female Friends*, the cloning that was ironically fatal (and eventually transforming) for Carl rather than Joanna May, or the presumed downfall of Gilead and the possibility of Mattapoisett, the denouement of Isabel's story suggests that male conspiracies may fail, and in their wake things may actually be better for (some) women and men.

Third and most important, Maia's cure may come because she herself has found in and through telling the story a way of connecting with others—not just with replicas, retrospective versions, or metaphors of herself, but with women who are in ways quite different. More strongly even than in *Female Friends*, *Praxis*, or *Meridian*, a tentative and argumentative solidarity among a small group of women replaces the two paradigmatic models of connection that have failed in Maia's own life as in so many of the lives around her: romantic heterosexual connection and maternal connection, insofar as the latter entails the notion that bearing a child is in itself a sufficient proof or lasting guarantee of female selfhood and relationship. If heterosexual relationships frequently fail and becoming a mother is a highly risky, ambivalent and instable experience, perhaps we can go back to female friendship, another early feminist ideal. This is an issue never full-blown here, as it is in a novel like *Desert of the Heart,* into a coherent story that represents itself as a viable alternative, and it is not directly stated, like other messages, in Maia's sententious glosses on her tale. Nevertheless, the frame narrative presents us with a representative community temporarily joined in the act of listening and interpretation.

In these present-tense chapters, we learn only a little about the chiefly but not exclusively female neighbors who form this fictive audience, each of whom seems to have a story that might be as interesting as Isabel's. As different as the characters brought together in this study, the women of Wincaster Row have found various ways of dealing with gender and sexual relations, whether in defying them or retreating to the protection of conventional models of good female behavior. "Cross Hilary" is a lesbian; "pretty, clever little Hope" is a single thirty-year-old who enjoys sex with men but rejects marriage and reveals, near the end, that as a teenager she was in prison for six months. "Earth-mother Jennifer," in contrast to both these more subversive types, was an anthropologist, but she "ran back home" (69), married a man with four children, and had four more of her own. Unlike the clones of Joanna

May, "the women of Wincaster Row don't agree, of course," and they do not yet refrain from criticizing each other's choices. To Hope, for example, Jennifer represents "excessive and dangerous motherhood" (70). From their different positions, they take different attitudes toward the female condition and the peculiarly doubled and divided potential of motherhood, that position of vulnerability and power. For the duration of the novel, however, they come together as a community of listeners to hear the same story and to offer their attention as a gift of "kindness" to the storyteller. The framing narrative thus brings to mind the chapters in which Meridian seems to sleep while Lynne tells the story that Meridian ostensibly refused to hear. Across racial divides in *Meridian,* and across differences in sexual and political orientation in *The President's Child,* women are connected in the scene of qualified, generous listening that replaces seeing and certain knowing. As in *Puffball,* the privileged mode of (maternal) perception and communication is aural as opposed to visual or verbal.

At one point near the end of this collective narrative experience, Maia and her three female friends (joined on this occasion by Oliver, another neighbor) speculate about the feelings of cave women, sleeping around a dying fire with their children, hearing the approach of a saber-toothed tiger. This parable points both to the central questions that the novel addresses and to the primal parental fears that underlie every story of the mother without child that we have considered. What do mothers, living not in caves but in postfeminist, urban middle-class London, do in a time of crisis, when they discover that their children are still in danger of savage, deadly attack, and what do their actions tell us about reproductive consciousness, female identity, and maternal subjectivity, viewed for the sake of argument as having transhistorical elements? Is motherhood a position of weakness or strength? Are women helpless victims, unable to protect themselves or cope with the additional burden they bear as mothers? Or can they resist, have they in fact always had more power than history reveals, and is that power in fact connected in some positive way to their obligations as mothers to protect others who depend on them, for a while at least?

It is at once ironic and appropriate that Hope, who was apparently so dangerous as an adolescent that she had to be imprisoned and who now resists traditional roles for women, holds the more negative view of women's maternal powers. Thinking about the cave women, she assumes that they lie there "gibbering with fear" while their children sleep in the ashes, "maimed, dirty, and wild." Jennifer, who "retreated" to motherhood, has the greater sense of women as agents. She argues that the cave women would build up the fire and sharpen their stakes, while their children lay in rows on "proper clean beds of moss and straw" (176–8). Jennifer's version seems most particularly to contradict what we see in Isabel's story, where little agency is left to the mother and she is spared only by luck. The disagreement between Hope and Jennifer is not resolved; the two perspectives don't cancel each other out but can coexist, at least at the level of interpretation. In any particular case, one version may be truer to the facts than another, but both are possibilities for reading.

Maia's response to the hypothetical case of the cave women suggests another possibility. She does not resolve the debate; she reframes the lesson. The point is not to determine whether women were or were not agents in history (or prehistory), but to recognize that the danger is still real and that it is in attending to this reality that women's solidarity, to use a cliché, resides. Maia, at the close of the scene, has the last word:

> Patter-patter. If there's nothing else to fear for the children, fear a cold in the nose.
> I have no children, but I too suffer from fear; I wake in the night with a start, sure there's someone, something in the room. And I can't even turn on the light. So I invite the fear in, I speak to it: I say, tell me why you are so much greater than any individual fate could merit— and it replies, because I am all your fears; you are all one, you are not as many as you think you are: you must learn to share me. Loss suffered by any woman is every woman's loss. . . .
> Nor do I believe that the sound of pattering every stops: the soft insistences of fear outside the fire's light—just that from time to time I sleep, and can no longer hear it. (178)

"I WILL NEVER TOTAL IT ALL": ONE THING AND ANOTHER

The issue Maia and her friends can never decide—whether mothers are empowered or disabled by the soft insistences of fear, the transhistoric, crosscultural threat of loss that seems endemic to their relational identity vis à vis children—is akin to the questions that readers may ask—indeed, have asked—of this study. Does the story of the mother without child, as read here, in fact confirm the notion that women have to give up mothering? Are abandonment, infanticide, Othermothering, or nonprocreative motherhood necessary forms of empowerment, or are they metaphors? What does all this add up to, in other words; how can readers integrate into their own practice the lessons learned from listening to these stories? What message should they take away from this book?

These are legitimate questions, but the story of the mother without child stubbornly resists short, straightforward answers to either-or inquiries, to hopes of full explanation, final reconciliation, or total understanding. What is most interesting about the figure of the mother without child—and herein, no doubt, lies any message this book might offer—is the way it can hold and foreground the real contradictions of motherhood as a relational identity, without rushing to impose inadequate resolutions or to make sweeping claims for reform. In this sense the narratives considered here reinforce what I take to be the most fundamental insight and difficulty of the feminist critique of motherhood to date: the position of the western mother is one of profound social and psychic division.

As studies by Ann Ferguson and Miriam Johnson, among others, suggest, *woman* is a category not only oppressed by the historical roles of wife and mother, but often divided between them by the contrasting status and function accorded to each of these relational identities.[4] As a result of competing ties between self and mate, on the one hand, and between self and children, on the other, there are constitutive contradictions both within motherhood and between motherhood and other positions a woman might occupy at a given point. In response, the feminist critique of motherhood necessarily set out to do something that also appeared to be—and often was, practically speaking—contradictory. Its bipartite goal was to attack pronatalism and to revalue the function and status of mothers. Using the language of deconstruction and postmodernism, feminists today seek to dislodge motherhood from old, essentializing definitions and, in some theories at least, to lay claim to a place for women as mothers outside patriarchy and phallogocentrism. At the same time, they wish to address the real atrocities of matrilineal histories, the empirical concerns and conflicts of women who are mothers, the actual silencing of mothers who would speak. Although these goals of feminism are not mutually exclusive but in fact constitutionally connected, they have nevertheless been difficult to reconcile. Perhaps recuperation of motherhood, as Snitow argues, has turned out to be an easier achievement in theory, but this is hardly so in material practice. As Terri Apter says, "It is one thing to occupy the place of the mother as a successful discursive strategy and another to be voicelessly immersed within it."[5]

In the fictions I have considered here, all of which respond to the feminist agenda, the figure of the mother without child is *both* one thing—a mother—and another—a not-mother. It serves as a kind of "double strategy," to use the term with which Paul Smith describes the strength born of tensions within the feminist critique of the meaning and status of *woman*. As Smith says, feminists are often torn between seeing *woman* as a unified category or centered subject and understanding *woman* as a false construction and a heterogeneous category or subject. But this seemingly contradictory position can be seen as strategic and appropriate, "the tactic of doing two or more things at once, or of putting ostensibly contradictory but overlapping items on the agenda."[6] It is tempting to add that this tactic is just what motherhood, even more than feminism, is really about. Most mothers do "two or more things at once" both in practical, mundane senses—working the double shift; juggling the competing needs of mate, children, and colleagues; cooking dinner and supervising homework; marching for peace and adjudicating sibling rivalry—and in a variety of psychic and figurative ways as well.

The story of the mother without child, construed as double strategy—"one thing . . . and another"—embraces the loss of children as both tragic and liberating, and it translates poorly into clear prescriptions for individual action. At the same time, it does suggest that certain strong, collective remedies are in order, and perhaps if we reformulate the questions it *can* answer, this will be clearer. These are some of the questions that have motivated this project: is it possible to look at the mother more fully and clearly, as a subject? Like Maia's friends, can we listen to her story communally, with empathy and kindness, even when we disagree about meaning or act otherwise in our own lives? If we were thus able to see and hear differently, provisionally, collectively, creatively, could we learn to resist, revise, and reclaim the role of "mother" for women in a way that serves everyone better, as Joanna May and her clones seem to do?

To the first two questions, the widespread and various appearance of the mother without child in contemporary fiction serves as a double strategy, answering "yes and no." In the particular works I have considered and in others like them, undoubtedly we see more than has ever before been visible or legible about mothers; what we see, however, may not be mother as subject, and it is very difficult to listen to a voice that barely speaks, and whose story is painful to hear. Motherhood is not a core identity for women, not a "synthetic," unifying role. Dissociation serves more aptly as a model of maternal subjectivity and more frequently than not as an inevitable response to trauma and a strategy for dealing with loss. There is no individual or original maternal subject, voice, or perspective to be captured in the conventional narrating "I." Concomitantly, motherhood is not locked in opposition to some alternative, autonomous, or cohesive female selfhood that may or should be chosen instead, because no such coherent female subject necessarily exists. When women act on truths of experience such as these, they are likely to commit crimes, especially the crime of refusing to be the patriarchal mother, and violence may be a response to oppression. Insofar as there is a story to be told, a maternal legacy, it is a legacy of trauma and fear. For this reason, because we would rather not see and because we cannot easily assimilate the truth, the mother without child haunts narrative; hers is the story that can neither be fully told and clearly heard nor put to rest.

We strain to hear, then, what is only beginning to be audible, in stories that *precede* any longed-for revision and reconstitution. Or to put it once more in the words of Toni Morrison, "this is not a story to pass on," in both senses of that ambiguous statement. The story of the mother without child is not a story to hand down, to replicate; none of these novels urges women to give up their children. But neither is it a story to forget or let go; none of these novels makes it easy to accept pronatalist prescriptions or remain content with old definitions of *mother*. The story must instead be heard and reheard, precisely because the meaning of *mother* can't be "totaled." Both telling and listening to this story can be positively construed, at best, as a nonprocreative maternal practice, and the resources of fictional discourse can be deployed to work within and stretch the limits of language, making both art and politics out of loss. Dissociation and disconnection can be represented, not assimilated and forgotten, by the division of single characters into first- and third-person narrators in the space of a single novel; by the juxtaposition of different types of language, also within a single novel; or by the breaking up of linearity, cohesiveness, and unity in the variety of ways we have witnessed. From *Desert of the Heart* to *The Cloning of Joanna May,* both the complexity of female reproductive consciousness and the possibility of alternative plots for women can be expressed as a multiplication of characters and speakers, a proliferation of points of view.

To my third question—could we learn to define *mother* differently if we could listen to these and similar stories?—I hope this study as a whole points to an affirmative answer, even if the question itself must remain in the conditional mode. It is possible if not inevitable that we can read the new narratives of the mother without child as representing motherhood in ways that are truer to the problems and challenges of the relational aspect of mothers' experiences and maternal work, that resist pronatalism in its reductive and coercive forms, and that do not erase or divide women. "Look, listen, learn," Praxis advises her fictive readers, and to the questions with which this study begins and ends, this is perhaps the best answer I can offer. Situated in the literature of trauma and recovery, the story of the mother without child provides us with images of victims, survivors, and witnesses who model the possibility of alternative stories and call in turn for an alliance of creative, generous listeners.

Notes

1. This fragmentation is noted by Donna Bassin, Margaret Honey, and Meryle Mahler Kaplan, eds., *Representations of Motherhood* (New Haven: Yale University Press, 1994): "The quest for the symbolic control of the term *mother* powerfully illustrates how language defines and constructs reality. Is she the egg that holds the genetic code, the womb that sustains and nurtures, or the person who practices maternal work?" (19).

2. I cite from *The Compact Edition of the Oxford English Dictionary*, s.v. "mother." For the historical introduction, see pp. viii–x.

3. Other, newer dictionaries add to the definition in ways that merit more discussion than is relevant here. The development of what the *American Heritage Dictionary* calls "vulgar slang," whereby *mother* refers to "something considered extraordinary, as in disagreeableness, size, or intensity" (e.g., the mother of all wars), is particularly worth further feminist exploration. Notably, the *American Heritage* and other dictionaries follow the *OED*'s lead in offering a second lexical entry, *mother 2*, to refer to "a stringy slime composed of yeast cells and bacteria that forms on the surface of fermenting liquids."

4. Sara Ruddick, *Maternal Thinking: Toward a Politics of Peace* (New York: Ballantine Books, 1990), pp. 17, 22. It would be tedious to cite all the definitions that stress this relational identity, but it is widespread, not particular in any way to Ruddick's work. To note just one more example, see Evelyn Nakano Glenn, quoting Alison M. Jaggar: "As a working definition, I propose looking at mothering as a historically and culturally variable relationship 'in which one individual nurtures and cares for another.'" Jaggar, *Feminist Politics and Human Nature* (Totowa, N.J.: Rowman and Allanheld, 1983), p. 256, quoted in Glenn, "Social Constructions of Mothering: A Thematic Overview," in *Mothering: Ideology, Experience, and Agency*, ed. Evelyn Nakano Glenn, Grace Chang, and Linda Rennie Forcey (New York: Routledge, 1994), p. 3.

5. For overviews that are helpful see Nancy Chodorow and Susan Contratto, "The Fantasy of the Perfect Mother," in *Rethinking the Family*, ed. Barrie Thorne and Marilyn Yalom (New York: Longman, 1982), pp. 54–73; Hester Eisenstein, *Contemporary Feminist Thought* (Boston: G. K. Hall, 1983), chaps. 7–9; Margaret A. Simons, "Motherhood, Feminism, and Identity," in *Hypatia Reborn: Essays in Feminism Philosophy*, ed. Azizah Y. Al-Hibri and

Simons (Bloomington: Indiana University Press, 1990), pp. 156–74. Simons, among others, argues that the gap between feminist repudiation and recuperation of motherhood is less "absolute" than it is sometimes said to be, and she discusses the possibility of a more "integrative feminist resolution" of this opposition.

6. Deborah Babcox and Madeline Belkin, comps. *Liberation Now! Writings from the Women's Liberation Movement* (New York: Dell, 1971), p. 106.

7. This point is made in Deborah Rosenfelt and Judith Stacey's review essay, "Second Thoughts on the Second Wave": "The reaction to the fifties' cloying cult of motherhood freed millions of women like us to consider motherhood a choice rather than an unavoidable obligation, but it may also have encouraged many to deny, or to defer dangerously long, our own desires for domesticity and maternity. One of the ironic effects of this history is the current obsession with maternity and children that seems to pervade aging feminist circles, a romanticization that occasionally rivals that of the fifties." *Feminist Studies* 13, no. 2 (summer 1987): 351.

8. Interesting critiques of various types of eighties recuperation are found in works such as Parveen Adams, "Mothering," in *The Woman in Question,* ed. Adams and Elizabeth Cowie (Cambridge, Mass.: MIT Press, 1990), pp. 315–27; Drucilla Cornell, *Beyond Accommodation: Ethical Feminism, Deconstruction, and the Law* (New York: Routledge, 1991), especially chapter 1, "The Maternal and the Feminine," pp. 21–78; Patrice DiQuinzio, "Exclusion and Essentialism in Feminist Theory: The Problem of Mothering," *Hypatia* 8, no. 3 (summer 1993): 1–20; Janice Doane and Devon Hedges, *From Klein to Kristeva: Psychoanalytic Feminism and the Search for the "Good Enough" Mother* (Ann Arbor: University of Michigan Press, 1992); Ann Ferguson, *Blood at the Root: Motherhood, Sexuality, and Male Dominance* (London: Pandora Press, 1989); Jane Gallop, "Reading the Mother Tongue: Psychoanalytic Feminist Criticism," *Critical Inquiry* 13 (winter 1987): 314–29; Sarah Hoagland, "Some Thoughts about 'Caring,'" in *Feminist Ethics,* ed. Claudia Card (Lawrence: University Press of Kansas, 1991), pp. 245–61; Nancy Scheper-Hughes, *Death without Weeping: The Violence of Everyday Life in Brazil* (Berkeley: University of California Press, 1992); Domna Stanton, "Difference on Trial: A Critique of the Maternal Metaphor in Cixous, Irigaray, and Kristeva," in *The Poetics of Gender,* ed. Nancy K. Miller (New York: Columbia University Press, 1986), pp. 157–82.

9. Several feminist critics have made this observation. In the words of Terri Apter, with reference to new feminist arguments in the eighties about why women should mother: "Where do they leave us? There is no going back, no prodigal's return to the kitchen, no fond farewell to the outside world. Yet how can we go forward in a working world created for man, but with a mother's responsibility?" Apter, *Why Women Don't Have Wives: Professional Success and Motherhood* (New York: Schocken Books, 1985), p. xi. Or as Susan Rubin Suleiman says in "On Maternal Splitting: A Propos of Mary Gordon's *Men and Angels*": "Can we choose or discard at will our most deep-seated fantasies and self-representations? Do we dare, in a time of increasing social conser-

vatism and/or disintegrating family life, to give up our sense of an absolutely privileged relationship with our children?" Suleiman, *Signs* 14, no. 1 (autumn 1988): 25–41. These are also the questions asked by all of the novels that I look at here.

10. Ann Snitow, "Feminism and Motherhood: An American Reading," *Feminist Review* 40 (spring 1992): 32–51. For a briefer version, see "Motherhood—Reclaiming the Demon Texts," *Ms*, May/June 1991, 34–7. See also Snitow's "A Gender Diary," in *Conflicts in Feminism*, eds. Marianne Hirsch and Evelyn Fox (New York: Routledge, 1990), pp. 9–43. The notion of "impasse" has been current in feminist thinking about motherhood since the late seventies; for example, Barbara Ehrenreich and Deirdre English argued that feminism had already reached a theoretical impasse in this regard as early as 1978, in *For Her Own Good: 150 Years of Experts' Advice to Women* (New York: Doubleday, 1978). But I speak here of the more recent articulation of this impasse, which responds specifically to the various modes of eighties recuperation of motherhood. I take Snitow as a particularly persuasive voice in this regard, but there are others making equally interesting cases for the failures of feminism to carry through on its original insights. Frequently these are also arguments that seek to justify childlessness as an ethical choice in the wake of eighties backlash. See, for example, Carolyn M. Morell, *Unwomanly Conduct: The Challenges of Intentional Childlessness* (New York: Routledge, 1994): "The strong public feminist voice of the early 1970s, arguing that women could have good lives without motherhood, is barely a whisper today. A maternal revivalism has occurred over the past two decades within feminism as well as in the dominant culture" (xvi).

11. Snitow, "Feminism and Motherhood," p. 34. In *Reproducing the Womb: Images of Childbirth in Science, Feminist Theory, and Literature* (Ithaca: Cornell University Press, 1994), Alice Adams implies agreement with Snitow when she argues that although the "essentialism" of early feminists may have been misguided, "the visions contained in the seventies-era utopias . . . still represent some of the most advanced thinking [about mothering] produced in second-wave feminism" (177).

12. "Preface," *Feminist Studies* 20, no. 1 (spring 1994): 3.

13. My focus here is only on the original prose contributions. The two poems included in this section, by Joan Cusack Handler and Susan Ticky, are easier to understand as belonging under the rubric of "maternal scenarios," and the same may be said of Cora Kaplan's "Fictions of Feminism: Figuring the Maternal," *Feminist Studies* 20, no. 1 (spring 1994): 153–67, a review essay. Kaplan takes on what she sees as "a dangerous overinvestment in idealized fictions of maternal and sororal relations" in two books published in 1989, but because of the five-year time lag, this well-thought-out critique doesn't seem particularly new and is not meant to explore alternative feminist ways of thinking about motherhood in any detail.

14. Judith Kegan Gardiner, "Empathic Ways of Reading: Narcissism, Cultural Politics, and Russ's *Female Man*," *Feminist Studies* 20, no. 1 (spring 1994): 91, 104.

15. Stacy Alaimo, "Cyborg and Ecofeminist Interventions: Challenges for an Environmental Feminism," *Feminist Studies* 20, no. 1 (spring 1994): 133.

16. Ibid., 149.

17. Molly Hite, "Mother Underground (Fiction)," *Feminist Studies* 20, no. 1 (spring 1994): 66.

18. Patrice DiQuinzio, "Exclusion and Essentialism," *Hypatia* 8, no. 3 (summer 1993): 12.

19. Jane Price Knowles, *Motherhood: A Feminist Perspective*, ed. Jane Price Knowles and Ellen Cole (New York: The Haworth Press, 1990), pp. 6–7.

20. Doane and Hodges, *From Klein to Kristeva*, p. 28.

21. Snitow makes a brief reference to Sue Miller's *The Good Mother*.

22. Biddy Martin, "Lesbian Practice and Changing Lesbian Identities," in *Destabilizing Theory: Contemporary Feminist Debates,* ed. Michele Barrett and Anne Phillips (Stanford: Stanford University Press, 1992), p. 103.

23. Judith Butler, *Gender Trouble: Feminism and the Suversion of Identity* (New York: Routledge, 1990), pp. 148–9.

24. In "Why Novels Make Bad Mothers," Jessamyn Jackson argues that whereas the novel in its earliest forms in English was associated with prominent female authors, the status of women writers and the redefinition of the novel as "a preserve of masculine authority" can be precisely located in the second decade of the nineteenth century. Jackson, *Novel* 27, no. 2 (winter 1994): 161–73.

25. See, for example, Deanna L. Davis, "Feminist Critics and Literary Mothers: Daughters Reading Elizabeth Gaskell," *Signs* 17, no. 3 (1992): 507–32.

26. Margaret Homans, *Bearing the Word: Language and Female Experience in Nineteenth-Century Women's Writing* (Chicago: University of Chicago Press, 1986). For an interesting critique of Homans, see Davis, "Feminist Critics," pp. 18–20.

27. Marianne Hirsch, *The Mother/Daughter Plot: Narrative, Psychoanalysis, Feminism* (Bloomington: Indiana University Press, 1989), p. 10. Hereafter, page numbers to this volume are cited parenthetically.

28. Deborah Kelly Kloepfer, *The Unspeakable Mother* (Ithaca: Cornell University Press, 1989).

29. Rachel DuPlessis, *Writing beyond the Ending: Narrative Strategies of Twentieth-Century Women Writers* (Bloomington: Indiana University Press, 1985), p. 61.

30. Susan Winnett, "Coming Unstrung: Women, Men, Narrative, and Principles of Pleasure," *PMLA* 105, no. 3 (May 1990): 505–18.

31. Ellen G. Friedman, "Where are the Missing Contents? (Post)Modernism, Gender, and the Canon," *PMLA* 108, no. 3 (1993): 240–52.

32. Claire Kahane, "Questioning the Maternal Voice," *Genders* 3 (1988): 82–91. For a brief discussion of how metaphor also serves to create a "transitional space" as an alternative to the play space that the mother fails to create in *Beloved* and *Sula,* see Laurie Vickroy, "The Force Outside/The Force Inside: Mother-Love and Regenerative Spaces in *Sula* and *Beloved,*" *Obsidian II* 8, no. 2 (fall-winter 1993): 28–45.

33. Susan Rubin Suleiman, *Subversive Intent: Gender, Politics, and the Avant-Garde* (Cambridge: Harvard University Press, 1990), p. 161.

34. Ibid., p. 165.

35. Magdalene Redekop, *Mothers and Other Clowns: The Stories of Alice Munro* (New York: Routledge, 1992), pp. 8–10.

36. Cited from Alice Munro, *The Progress of Love* (Toronto: McClelland and Stewart, 1986), emphasis added.

37. For a good exploration of the mother's inability to play games and tell jokes, see Tillie Olsen's story, "Tell Me a Riddle."

38. Sara Ruddick, "Thinking about Mothering—and Putting Maternal Thinking to Use," *Women's Studies Quarterly* 11, no. 4 (winter 1983): 5.

39. Since my goal was depth and specificity of analysis rather than coverage, I have not included all of the fictional subcultures (such as Asian American or Latina) where I think the figure of the mother without child is also being explored, and I have chosen only one author to represent the postwar encounter of pronatalism and feminism outside North America, in England.

40. See, for example, Angus McClaren, *Reproductive Rituals* (New York: Methuen, 1984) for discussion of the loss of women's control over reproduction from the sixteenth century on.

41. A few examples of the many books and essays debating this concern include Ruth Hubbard, *The Politics of Women's Biology* (New Brunswick: Rutgers University Press, 1990); Linda M. Whiteford and Marilyn L. Poland, eds., *New Approaches to Human Reproduction* (Boulder: Westview Press, 1989); Michelle Stanworth, ed., *Reproductive Technologies: Gender, Motherhood, and Medicine* (Minneapolis: University of Minnesota Press, 1987); *Science as Culture* 3, part 4, no. 17 (1993); Hilary Homans, ed., *The Sexual Politics of Reproduction* (Aldershot: Gower Publishing, 1985); Judith Rodin and Aila Collins, eds., *Women and New Reproductive Technologies: Medical, Psychosocial, Legal, and Ethical Dilemmas* (Hillsdale: Lawrence Erlbaum Associates, 1991).

42. Jean F. O'Barr, Deborah Pope, and Mary Wyer, eds., introduction to *Ties That Bind: Essays on Mothering and Patriarchy* (Chicago: University of Chicago Press, 199), p. 14.

43. As I noted earlier, some, like Rosenfelt and Stacey in "Second Thoughts on the Second Wave," have argued that "the current obsession" with motherhood is an effect of the earlier repudiation, which caused women to deny maternal instincts. If this is so, then certainly stories about lost children could be explained as a manifestation of that denial, a projection of the sense of loss. Rosenfelt makes this point explicitly in another essay when she speaks of the "sense of terrible loss" she finds in what she identifies as the "post-feminist" novel: "Though often they grieve explicitly for the loss of a child, I am convinced that the less tangible loss they mourn is the certainty of the feminist dream, the myth of progress toward liberation surely attainable within the immediate future." Deborah Rosenfelt, "Feminism, 'Postfeminism,' and Contemporary Women's Fiction," in *Traditions and the Talents of Women*, ed. Florence Howe (Urbana: University of Illinois Press, 1991), p. 287. Nancy Miller,

in an interesting footnote, speaks of the "double truth of liberation and deferral" that marks the experience of motherhood for many feminists, including herself. Miller, "Decades," in *Changing Subjects: The Making of Feminist Literary Criticism,* ed. Gayle Greene and Coppelia Kahn (London: Routledge, 1993), p. 46. Compare my argument in the epilogue that the figure of the mother without child represents a "double strategy," expressing the need both to resist pronatalism and to revalue maternal experience.

44. Davis, "Feminist Critics," p. 513.

45. Ruddick, "Thinking Mothers/Conceiving Birth," in Bassin, Honey, and Kaplan, *Representations of Motherhood,* p. 30. Here Ruddick also insists, again, that "maternal concepts can be reflective of mothers, and a help to them, only if they are anchored in thinking about children."

46. For examples of such criticism, see Lisa C. Bower, "'Mother' in Law: Conceptions of Mother and the Maternal in Feminism and Feminist Legal Theory," *differences* 3, no. 1 (1991): 20–38, and the introduction to Bassin, Honey, and Kaplan, *Representations of Motherhood,* pp. 1–25.

47. Elsa First, "Mothering, Hate, and Winnicott," in Bassin, Honey, and Kaplan, *Representations of Motherhood,* pp. 147–61.

48. Mary Jacobus, "Dora and the Pregnant Madonna," in *Reading Woman: Essays in Feminist Criticism,* ed. Mary Jacobus (New York: Columbia University Press, 1986), p. 147. See also Suleiman, "On Maternal Splitting," pp. 25–41. For yet another suggestive discussion of the unconscious and motherhood that takes a very different tack, see Mardy Ireland, *Reconceiving Woman: Separating Motherhood from Female Identity* (New York: Guilford Press, 1993). Ireland's argument is too complex to summarize here, but notably she contends, as I would, that the current uncertainty about what motherhood means serves to open up what she calls "a psychic 'space' wherein additional signifiers of female identity may emerge into culture" (135). Childless women in particular, Ireland proposes, are "an apt metaphor of our postmodern times" and "the decentered or divided nature of the self" (142); as "other women," holding "a third position" in the gender system and representing the paradox of absence, they also call needed attention to "the undervalued presence of the unconscious" (145–6).

49. Madelon Sprengnether, *The Spectral Mother: Freud, Feminism, and Psychoanalysis* (Ithaca: Cornell University Press, 1990), p. 234.

50. Knowles, introduction to *Motherhood: A Feminist Perspective,* pp. 6–7. This point has been made by many others. For one formulation, see Shirley Nelson Garner, Claire Kahane, and Madelon Sprengnether, eds., preface to *The (M)Other Tongue: Essays in Feminist Psychoanalytic Interpretation* (Ithaca: Cornell 1985): "Psychoanalysis, whether it posits in the beginning maternal presence or absence, has yet to develop a story of the mother as other than the object of the infant's desire" (25). See also Suleiman's essay "Writing and Motherhood," in *The (M)Other Tongue,* p. 356, and Jane Gallop's "Reading the Mother Tongue."

51. In a chapter that includes a brief discussion of 1 Kings 3:16–28, Danna N. Fewell and David M. Gunn discuss the use of the metaphor of "whoring"

for religious apostasy and point out an irony: "female prostitutes as a class constitute a serious challenge to the patriarchal control of women's bodies"; although prostitutes serve men's needs, they also represent "the possibility of a woman controlling her own sexuality, her own body." Fewell and Gunn, *Gender, Power, and Promise: The Subject of the Bible's First Story* (Nashville: Abington, 1993), p. 170. This is an issue that Fay Weldon addresses extensively in *Praxis,* a novel I consider in the final chapter of this volume. For another discussion of the Hebrew term *zona* ("prostitute") and the movement from a characteristic associated specifically with women, "whoring," to a metaphor for the bad behavior of Israel, see Phyllis Bird, "'To Play the Harlot': An Inquiry into an Old Testament Metaphor," in *Gender and Difference in Ancient Israel,* ed. Peggy L. Day (Minneapolis: Fortress Press, 1989), pp. 75–94. For this and other references to the Solomon story in religious studies, I am indebted to Anne McGuire. For recent contributions to the discussion among legal feminists about the topic of motherhood, see Martha Fineman and Isabel Karpin, eds., *Mother in Law: Feminist Theory and the Legal Regulation of Motherhood* (New York: Columbia University Press, 1995), and Martha Fineman, *The Neutered Mother, the Sexual Family, and Other Twentieth Century Tragedies* (New York: Routledge, 1995).

52. One of the most fully developed treatments of the patriarchal mother is in Nicole Brossard's *These Our Mothers* (Toronto: Coach House Press, 1984); see my discussion of this argument in the following chapter. For another brief discussion, see Suleiman, *Subversive Intent,* pp. 163 ff.

53. Not all feminist readings of the Solomon story would see it my way. This quotation is in fact taken from Phyllis Trible's pioneering feminist analysis of the Old Testament story, in which Trible more or less accepts the model of motherhood that I have critiqued here. Trible assumes that A was both the woman whose child was alive and the woman who brought the case to court and that the other woman, the bad mother B, is "the agent of both death and deceit" in this tale. The king is credited with exposing the fact that both women are locked in a power struggle as long as each claims possession of the fruits of her womb; only when compassion motivates the real mother to sacrifice justice for life does the possibility of "transcendent love which brings truth and life" appear. See Trible, *God and the Rhetoric of Sexuality* (Philadelphia: Fortress Press, 1978), pp. 31–3.

54. For a brief overview of *East Lynne* and other novels that punish the mother who abandons her children, see Rosie Jackson's *Mothers Who Leave* (London: Pandora, 1994), pp. 50–7. It is difficult to find instances of more subtle literary treatments of the mother who abandons her child, but one interesting text that merits further feminist discussion is Oscar Wilde's *Lady Windermere's Fan.*

55. As Ann Kaplan suggests, "liberatory discourses" about issues like single motherhood, female sexuality, and custody of children may exist "in complex relation" to something she calls "a renewed sentimentalizing of motherhood," and Sue Miller's *The Good Mother* (New York: Harper and Row, 1986) is a case in point of such sentimentality. As Kaplan also points out, "mothering is

presented as a woman's only satisfying activity. Anna is destroyed when she loses primary custody of her child." Kaplan, "Sex, Work, and Motherhood: Maternal Subjectivity in Recent Visual Culture," in Bassin, Honey, and Kaplan, *Representations of Motherhood*, p. 262. For a discussion of Hollywood treatments of mothers who give up their children, such as *Kramer versus Kramer*, see Jackson, *Mothers Who Leave*, pp. 65–76.

56. Thomas Laqueur, "The Facts of Fatherhood," in Hirsch and Fox, *Conflicts in Feminism*, 205–21. See also Ruddick's response to this essay in the same volume, pp. 222–33.

57. Butler, *Gender Trouble*, p. 93.

58. Suleiman, *Subversive Intent*, p. 166.

59. For a usefully comparable argument that lesbians should practice an "elemental resistance to being either included or excluded" in the category of the family, with particular referencence to legal practice and theory, see Ruthann Robson, "Resisting the Family: Repositioning Lesbians in Legal Theory," *Signs* 19, no. 4 (summer 1994): 975–96.

CHAPTER TWO

1. For a recent critique of current social reform from a lesbian separatist point of view, see Jackie Anderson, "Separatism, Feminism, and the Betrayal of Reform," *Signs* 19 (1994): 437–48.

2. B. Drummond Ayres Jr., writing about the Sharon Bottoms case in "Judge's Decision in Custody Case Raises Concerns," *The New York Times*, September 9, 1993, p. A16. It is interesting to note that the child's name in this custody suit is rarely mentioned, whereas the most publicized custody case of the year goes by the child's name: the Baby Jessica case. This might be because we name a story after its perceived victim. Or it might be because the only really newsworthy mother is the "bad" mother, and while it's clear that as a lesbian Sharon Bottoms is "bad," it's harder to say which is the bad mother—or which is the real mother—in the Baby Jessica case (as in the even more famous case of Baby M). Naming the case after the baby deflects attention away from the more problematic question of who the mother is.

3. This point is confirmed from two different directions in Ellen Lewin's 1993 study, *Lesbian Mothers: Accounts of Gender in American Culture* (Ithaca: Cornell University Press, 1993), and Harriet Edwards's 1989 study, *How Could You? Mothers without Custody of Their Children* (Freedom, Calif.: The Crossing Press, 1989). Lewin looks at custodial mothers who try to stay out of court by concealing their lesbianism; Edwards surveys lesbians without custody and observes that "*None* of the lesbian women tried to gain custody in the courts, and most of them said the major, if not sole, reason for that decision was their sexual preferences and their awareness that such a preference has almost always precluded success in a custody contest" (54).

4. Audre Lorde, "Turning the Beat Around: Lesbian Parenting 1986," in *Politics of the Heart: A Lesbian Parenting Anthology*, ed. Sandra Pollack and Jeanne Vaughn (Ithaca: Firebrand Books, 1987), p. 310.

5. Bonnie Zimmerman, "Lesbians Like This and That: Some Notes on Lesbian Criticism for the Nineties," in *New Lesbian Criticism,* ed. Sally Munt (New York: Columbia University Press, 1992), p. 3.

6. See Marilyn Frye, "Lesbian Community: Heterodox Congregation," in *Willful Virgin: Essays in Feminism, 1976–1992* (Freedom, Calif.: Crossing Press, 1992), pp. 120–3.

7. Anderson, "Separatism, Feminism, and Reform," p. 446.

8. Jeffner Allen, *Lesbian Philosophy: Explorations* (Palo Alto: Institute of Lesbian Studies, 1986), pp. 61–88.

9. Minnie Bruce Pratt, "Identity: Skin Blood Heart," in *Yours in Struggle: Three Feminist Perspectives on Anti-Semitism and Racism,* by Elly Bulkin, Minne Bruce Pratt, and Barbara Smith (Brooklyn, N.Y.: Long Haul Press, 1984), p. 27

10. Ibid., p. 39. For another example of a woman writing from the position of a lesbian who gives up custody of her children, seemingly less reluctantly than Pratt, see Lucia Valeska, "If All Else Fails, I'm Still a Mother," in *Mothering: Essays in Feminist Theory,* ed. Joyce Trebilcot (Totowa, N.J.: Rowman and Allanheld, 1984), pp. 70–8. Valeska describes herself as comparable to that contradiction in terms, the mother without child, that I explore in this study: "I am a mother and then again I am not" (70). She sees her position as both personal and political and argues that transferring custody is an option women should consider: "It is the surest, quickest, most personal survival. It is also a political statement" (75). She adds, however, that the "childfree" have a responsibility to take on child care.

11. Theresa de Lauretis, "Sexual Indifference and Lesbian Representation," in *Performing Feminisms: Feminist Critical Theory and Theatre,* ed. Sue-Ellen Case (Baltimore: Johns Hopkins University Press, 1990), pp. 17–39.

12. For a classic description of this view, see Frank S. Caprio, *Variations in Sexual Behavior* (New York: Citadel, 1955). I am indebted to Kate Adams's work in "Making the World Safe for the Missionary Position: Images of the Lesbian in Post-World War II America," in *Lesbian Texts and Contexts,* ed. Karla Jay and Joanne Glasgow (New York: New York University Press, 1990), pp. 255–74, for calling my attention to this and other works that contextualize Rule's 1964 novel.

13. Sheila Ortiz Taylor, *Faultline* (Tallahassee: The Naiad Press, 1982), p. 8.

14. Meg Turner, "Two-Part Inventions: Knowing What We Know," in *Women, Girls, and Psychotherapy: Reframing Resistance,* ed. Carol Gilligan, Annie G. Rogers, and Deborah L. Toman (New York: Haworth Press, 1991), p. 163.

15. Adrienne Rich, "Compulsory Heterosexuality and Lesbian Existence," *Signs* 5 (1980): 183.

16. See Ann Ferguson's critique of "compulsory heterosexuality" arguments of Rich, Charlotte Bunch, Julia Penelope, and others. She sees these as guilty of "false universalism" and points out that if a girl's original love for her mother is based on social fact (women do the mothering in most cultures), then neither lesbian nor heterosexual preference can be seen as "natural." Ferguson,

Blood at the Root: Motherhood, Sexuality, and Male Dominance (London: Pandora Press, 1989), pp. 189–93. Compare Mardy Ireland's more general critique of the emphasis on motherhood in the kind of feminist work associated with the Stone Center and an "ethics of care" model: "The feminist interpersonal-social learning perspective can appear to overemphasize and overidealize the mother-daughter bond to such a degree that it is unimaginable why or how a woman would ever chose not to become a mother herself, or how she could ever develop a positive sense of identity if childbearing is denied her for physical reasons." Ireland, *Reconceiving Women: Separating Motherhood from Female Identity* (New York: Guilford Press, 1993), p. 103. The bad mother is attended to in theoretical work like Melanie Klein's, assumed by a host of mother-blaming arguments, or critiqued as an effect of motherhood under patriarchy by feminists including Rich herself.

17. See Rosemary Curb, "Core of the Apple: Mother-Daughter Fusion/Separation in Three Recent Lesbian Plays," in Jay and Glasgow, *Lesbian Texts and Contexts,* pp. 355–76, for a discussion of three plays in which we see the common pattern—lesbian daughter, straight mother—and the further presumption that "coming out" is equivalent to separation from the mother, so that the lesbian daughter's fear is a type of every woman's fear. Curb concludes by emphasizing the importance and difficulty of separation in standard terms: "Mothers and daughters can never be entirely separated. The healthier the separation of mother and daughter, the more likely the lesbian daughter can form loving bonds with other women. Lovers can never replace the mother but always shadow her in some fashion. In healthy lesbian relationships both women mother the other out of the strength of their love rather than the weakness of mutually unfulfilled needs" (374).

18. In "Lesbians Choosing Children: The Personal is Political Revisited," in Pollack and Vaughn, *Politics of the Heart,* p. 50, Nancy Polikoff notes that lesbians who choose to mother rarely claim that lesbian childrearing is superior to traditional childrearing, or that raising children will enable the lesbian mother to put her politics into practice.

19. Martha Gimenez, "Feminism, Pronatalism, and Motherhood," in Trebilcot, *Mothering: Essays in Feminist Theory,* p. 293.

20. Barbara Love and Elizabeth Shanklin, "The Answer Is Matriarchy," in Trebilcot, *Mothering: Essays in Feminist Theory,* p. 277.

21. Nicole Brossard, *These Our Mothers, or: The Disintegrating Chapter* (Toronto: Coach House Press, 1984), p. 26.

22. The kind of symbolic mother Brossard imagines is also described in Penelope J. Engelbrecht's discussion of Susanne de Lotbiniere-Harwood's "Turning to Woman," in "'Lifting Belly Is a Language: The Postmodern Lesbian Subject," *Feminist Studies* 16, no. 1 (1990): 85–113. Speaking of a line from Lotbiniere-Harwood's poetry, "the womb is our first context," Engelbrecht says that "womb" isn't an "essential element," but rather "symbolizes an abstract, rather than a physical thing . . . 'the womb' is but de Lotbiniere-Harwood's sign for language, knowledge, context, . . . process. Not an end, but a means to an end"(107–8).

23. Alice Parker, "Nicole Brossard: A Differential Equation of Lesbian Love," in Jay and Glasgow, *Lesbian Texts and Contexts*, p. 314.

24. This phenomenon is also reported by Sarah Bruckner, writing as a lesbian mother of two adopted children: "Oddly, the friends who have had the hardest time accepting our family are childless gays and lesbians who do not comprehend our loss of freedom and the new way we have gone public with our commitment to each other. Married friends with children have had fewer problems understanding." Bruckner, "Two Moms, Two Kids, and a Dog," in *Mother Journeys: Feminists Write about Mothering*, ed. Maureen T. Reddy, Martha Roth, and Amy Sheldon (Minneapolis: Spinsters Ink, 1994), p. 41. Writing in 1989, Marilyn Frye said that lesbians still do not agree "on whether the practice of friendship . . . requires active support of lesbians who have male babies." I can only assume that Frye believes that support of lesbian mothers of girls, at least, brooks no disagreement (*Willful Virgin*, 121).

25. Ellen Lewin, *Lesbian Mothers*, pp. 186 and 192.

26. Ibid., p. 191.

27. In keeping with Brossard's theory, the lesbian who adopts would be the best example of a "symbolic" mother, but in Lewin's study, "fear that their sexual orientation might undermine the adoption" appeared in most cases to compromise the possibility of subversion (Lewin, *Lesbian Mothers*, pp. 71–2).

28. Harriet Edwards in *How Could You?* suggests that the answer to this question is yes. Edwards surveyed one hundred women who had "given up" custody of their children (in most cases, after several years of marriage) and notes that none of the lesbian mothers in her study even bothered to try to get court-ordered custody of their children; the advice they received and took was "don't try it." Edwards says these women went "outside the system altogether, and have met with a good measure of success"; their responses to living apart from their children were the only ones with "any real humor," and in her assessment lesbian mothers without custody seemed "the most joyful, the most settled, the most self-accepting, and the most thoughtful" (53). Lewin's worries about the complicity of custodial lesbian mothers are also noted by many contributors to Pollack and Vaughn's *Politics of the Heart,* including both women who have given up custody (such as Jeanne Vaughn) and women who haven't (such as Nancy Polikoff). But contrast in that same volume the view of Sue Overstreet in "No Apology Offered," pp. 38–9, who believes her strength to fight for and attain custody of her children came from both the anger and pride of her lesbianism, and the story of Rosalie Davies, in "Confronting the Courts," pp. 43–6, whose political action as founder of C.A.L.M. (Custody Action for Lesbian Mothers, founded in 1974) resulted from threatened loss of her children. See also Phyllis Burke, *Family Values: Two Moms and Their Son* (New York: Random House, 1993): *Women's Review of Books* says, "With neither a biological or a legal tie to Jesse, her [Burke's] issues were different from the start. Motherhood was transformative for Burke, as it was for the women Lewin interviewed; it did not move her toward the center, but in a radical, political direction" (*Women's Review of Books* 11, no. 2 [November 1993]: 25).

29. Zimmerman, "Lesbians Like This and That," p. 13. She also notes, "Most theorists today are anti-essentialist, suspicious of 'experience' and 'truth' as categories, and enamored of disruption and fragmentation; most lesbians in everyday life believe they always have been lesbians, rely on their experience and sense of what's real to make literary judgments, and seek the condition of wholeness and normality."

30. Bonnie Zimmerman, *The Safe Sea of Women: Lesbian Fiction, 1969–1989* (Boston: Beacon Press, 1990), p. 144.

31. Ibid. Zimmerman points out that mothers may be characterized differently in novels by lesbians of color and ethnic lesbians: They are often "sources of personal and collective identity" (191). Her discussion of utopian versus realistic fiction recalls Catherine Stimpson's earlier division of lesbian novels into two "modes": "lesbian romanticism," in which "ruthlessness rejects a stifling dominant culture and asserts the value of psychological autonomy, women, art, and a European cultivation of the sensuous, sensual, and voluptuous," and "lesbian realism," in which there is "tension between the role of mother, which the lesbian may desire, and the traditional family structure, in which women are subordinate" ("Zero Degree Deviancy: The Lesbian Novel in English," *Critical Inquiry* 8 (1981): 363–79). Stimpson does not mention Rule's fiction.

32. Judith Roof, "'This Is Not for You': The Sexuality of Mothering," in *Narrating Mothers: Theorizing Maternal Subjectivities* (Knoxville: University of Tennessee Press, 1991), p. 167.

33. Ibid., p. 171.

34. Ibid., p. 172.

35. The alternatives presented by these two terms speak also to the division between women who voluntarily and women who involuntarily find themselves without children, a division that nonprocreative motherhood—and Rule's fiction—hopes to avoid.

36. Simone de Beauvoir, *The Second Sex* (New York: Vintage Books, 1974), p. 462.

37. Ibid., pp. 464, 466.

38. I use the term "maternal representation" in the psychoanalytic sense to refer to the internal construct of the mother, in the child's mind; it is "a function of both objective events and subjective experiences," but not a persona and certainly not a person (see Adria E. Schwartz, "Thoughts on the Constructions of Maternal Representations," *Psychoanalytic Psychology* 10, no. 3, (1993): 331–44).

39. In de Beauvoir's *Second Sex*, for instance, we read: "It is only when her fingers trace the body of a woman whose fingers in turn trace her body that the miracle of the mirror is accomplished" (465). For arguments about lesbian writing as the space of sameness as opposed to difference, see Marilyn Farwell, "Toward a Definition of the Lesbian Literary Imagination," *Signs* 14, no. 1 (1988): 100–18.; see also Engelbrecht, "'Lifting Belly Is a Language.'"

40. Each character also suggests both essentialist and nonessentialist understandings of lesbianism. Ann, who is said to be bisexual, seems to view her

desire for women, like her decision not to marry and bear children, as a matter of choice, although at the same time the narrative of her family romance suggests that there is something predetermined, if not essentialist, about her sexual orientation toward the mother she never had, away from a domineering father. Evelyn seems more socially constructed, in the sense that she is given little family heritage and clearly espouses a belief in will and intention. But then again, she is the one who speaks of her feelings for Ann as a matter of for once following "nature" and giving into "desire."

41. Compare Kate Adams's argument in "Making the World Safe for the Missionary Position," in Jay and Glasgow, *Lesbian Texts and Contexts,* that the truly radical book of the postwar period is *The Price of Salt,* where lesbians appear without the psychoanalytic stereotypes—but as Adams also argues, they are therefore "invisible" to the mainstream as lesbians. She warns of the dangers of "defensive posturings," but I think *Desert of the Heart* avoids these not just by announcing her lesbians as such but by showing both how they are constructed by the psychoanalytic confusion and how they dismantle it. Note here Jane Rule's comment in *Lesbian Images* (Trumanburg, New York: The Crossing Press, 1975): "For anyone who would genuinely like to understand the nature of lesbian experience, the field of psychology should probably be off limits since just this brief, incomplete survey exposes the state of conflict and confusion which exists among the `experts.' But the myth that psychology has the answers about human experience is now deeply embedded in our culture, and people do turn there to increase their understanding or relieve their suffering" (45).

42. It might be worth exploring the idea of Ann as victim of abuse—not sexual abuse, but the emotional abuse of a father so controlling and despairing that he either instigates or actually helps Ann's suicide attempt. For a good description of the danger of fathers who "love" their children the way Mr. Childs seems to have loved Ann, see Sally Ruddick's piece on fathers in *Conflicts in Feminism,* ed. Marianne Hirsch and Evelyn Fox (New York: Routledge, 1990)..

43. The word "tenderness" is used repeatedly to describe what Ann and Evelyn feel for each other. A striking link that I cannot explore further at this point is the use of this word in *The Bell Jar,* published the year before *Desert of the Heart.* When Esther Greenwood, thinking about lesbians she has heard of in college and the mental asylum, asks the female psychiatrist who oversees her recovery what two women would see in each other, Dr. Nolan answers with one word: "tenderness."

44. Rule says she puts a piece of herself into every character, and this may be one of the authorial bits of Evelyn, for Rule herself really had an Aunt Ida. Ireland, in *Reconceiving Women,* says that about a third of the women without children whom she interviewed had an auntlike figure (a biological aunt or family friend), "a significant woman in her early life who did not have children and who left a positive mark on her development" (61).

45. Lucia Valeska, "If All Else Fails, I'm Still a Mother," in Trebilcot, *Mothering: Essays in Feminist Theory,* p. 72.

46. Although she does not mention this particular passage, this is Gillian Spraggs's reading of the problem of "nature" in *Desert of the Heart*. Spraggs sees the move in Evelyn's thinking—from "nature" as an explanation of her perversity, which can be "ransomed" only by will, to her decision that loving Ann is "natural"—as a step that evades moral responsibility, ignores the social construction of lesbianism, and fails to articulate a context within society for lesbianism, thereby leading to a "dead end" ("Hell and The Mirror: A Reading of *Desert of the Heart*," in Munt, *New Lesbian Criticism*, pp. 115–32). Spraggs's reading of the novel raises interesting questions, but I stress instead that Evelyn is finally able to stay with Ann, however temporarily, because she recognizes precisely the need to take responsibility.

47. Jane Rule, "The Question of Children," in *A Hot-Eyed Moderate* (Tallahassee: Naiad Press, 1985), p. 95. The parenthetical reference is to Sara Ruddick, *Maternal Thinking* (Boston: Beacon Press, 1989), discussed at greater length in the preceding chapter.

48. The work Evelyn does as mentor-pedagogue should be understood as a positive alternative to rather than a compensation or displacement of her maternal desires, anticipating Adrienne Rich's comment that "poetry was where I lived as no-one's mother, where I existed as myself." Rich, *Of Woman Born: Motherhood as Experience and Institution*, tenth anniversary edition (New York: W. W. Norton, 1986), p. 31.

49. See for example Marilyn Schuster's reading in "Strategies for Survival: The Subtle Subversion of Jane Rule," *Feminist Studies* 7, no. 3 (1981): 431–49. Spraggs also discusses intertextuality, and in several years of teaching this novel I have received a good number of student papers on the topic of various literary allusions and rewritings in *Desert of the Heart*.

50. To understand the subversiveness of Rule's pregnant women, it might be useful to compare the actual vulnerability of the unmarried pregnant woman as outlined in a study like Rickie Solinger's "Race and 'Value': Black and White Illegitimate Babies, 1945–1965," in *Mothering: Ideology, Experience, and Agency,* ed. Evelyn Nakano Glenn, Grace Chang, and Linda Rennie Forcey (New York: Routledge, 1994), pp. 287–310.

51. The toast is raised by Ann's ex-boyfriend Bill, who uses the occasion to announce that he is marrying Joyce. The scene might also be read in light of Rule's hearty critique of compulsory heterosexuality and the oppression of women who marry. Alluding to Silver's pregnancy, Bill, a sympathetically portrayed and even "tender" man, tells Ann: "'That's what I should have done to you . . . I've solved my problem. I've got a girl who's already got a baby and I'm going to marry her'" (*Desert of the Heart,* 191).

52. Jane Rule, *The Young in One Another's Arms* (Tallahassee, Fla.: The Naiad Press: 1977).

53. Jane Rule, *Memory Board* (Tallahassee, Fla.: The Naiad Press, 1989), pp. 20–1.

54. Jane Rule, *Against the Season* (New York: McCall Publishing Co., 1971), p. 60.

55. According to Rickie Solinger in her comparative study, "Race and 'Value': Black and White Illegitimate Babies, 1945–65," it was in fact quite rare

for a black woman to be able to give up her child for adoption, both because of official "white" policy and because of the attitudes of the black community toward maternal responsibility.

CHAPTER THREE

1. Cited as reprinted in Patricia Bell-Scott et al., eds., *Double Stitch: Black Women Write about Mothers and Daughters* (New York: Harper Collins, 1993), p. 203.

2. Joanne Braxton, "Ancestral Presence: The Outraged Mother Figure in Contemporary Afra-American Writing," in *Wild Women in the Whirlwind: Afra American Culture and the Contemporary Literary Renaissance*, ed. Joanne Braxton and Andree Nicola McLaughlin (New Brunswick: Rutgers University Press, 1990), p. 314.

3. Barbara Christian, "'Somebody Forgot to Tell Somebody Something': African-American Women's Historical Novels," in Braxton and McLaughlin, *Wild Women in the Whirlwind*, p. 335.

4. Suzanne Carother, "Catching Sense: Learning from Our Mothers to be Black and Female," in *Uncertain Terms: Negotiating Gender in American Culture*, ed. Faye Ginsburg and Anna Lowenhaupt Tsing (Boston: Beacon Press, 1990), pp. 232–47. Patricia Hill Collins also critiques the inapplicability of several "Eurocentric," white views of motherhood; Collins, "The Meaning of Motherhood in Black Culture and Black Mother-Daughter Relationships," in Bell-Scott et al., *Double Stitch*, pp. 41–60. Elsewhere, Collins points out that "work that separated women of color from their children also framed the mothering relationship"; Collins, "Shifting the Center: Race, Class, and Feminist Theorizing about Motherhood," in *Representations of Motherhood*, ed. Donna Bassin, Margaret Honey, Meryle Mahrer Kaplan (New Haven: Yale University Press, 1994), p. 63.

Several scholars have recently commended Morrison's *Beloved* for turning from white models and inscribing more Afrocentric perspectives. Karla Holloway compares *Beloved* to an African novel, Flora Nwapa's *Efaru,* in terms of their shared depiction of "contradictions between childbirth and wholeness" for women. Whereas for white women, Holloway observes, motherhood has been thought to block potential development as an artist, in both African and African American women's works, "childbirth is often framed as a threat to survival rather than the (comparatively) benign worry that pregnancy will 'sabotage' their creative drive"; Holloway, *Moorings and Metaphors* (New Brunswick: Rutgers University Press, 1992), p. 171. Barbara Hill Rigney addresses the connections between *Beloved* and an African rather than an American heritage: Sethe evokes the power of the African Great Mother, and the barely remembered language of Africa and Sethe's mother, carried too in the songs that Sethe and Paul D sing, is "subversive and unintelligible to white listeners"; Rigney "'A Story to Pass On': Ghosts and the Significance of History in Toni Morrison's *Beloved*," in *Haunting the House of Fiction: Feminist Perspectives on Ghost Stories by American Women*, ed. Lynette Carpenter and Wendy K. Kolmar (Knoxville: University of Tennessee

Press, 1991), p. 234. A third example of this approach to *Beloved* is Maggie Sale's argument that Morrison, in her expressed intention to write "Black Art," structures the novel on the principle of "call and response" drawn from oral African culture; Sale, "Call and Response as Critical Method: African-American Oral Traditions and *Beloved*," *African-American Review* 26, no. 1 (1992): 41–50.

5. See both Mae Henderson's "Response" (pp. 155–63) and Houston A. Baker Jr.'s "There Is No More Beautiful Way," in *Afro-American Literary Study in the 1990s,* ed. Houston A. Baker Jr. and Patricia Redmond (Chicago: University of Chicago Press, 1989).

6. Deborah McDowell, "Boundaries: Or Distant Relations and Close Kin," in Baker and Redmond, *Afro-American Literary Study in the 1990s,* p. 58.

7. Hortense Spillers, "Response" to Deborah E. McDowell, in Baker and Redmond, *Afro-American Literary Study in the 1990s,* pp. 71–3.

8. Hortense Spillers, "Mama's Baby, Papa's Maybe: An American Grammar Book," *Diacritics* 17 (summer 1987): 80.

9. Ibid. Other readings, however, view Sethe's destruction of Beloved as a type of universal or at least widespread maternal (mis)behavior, instancing "a mother's will to dominate" and the threat of the engulfing maternal bond to children's individuality. Laurie Vickroy, "The Force Outside/The Force Inside: Mother-Love and Regenerative Spaces in *Sula* and *Beloved*," *Obsidian II* 8, no. 2 (fall-winter 1993): 28.

10. White feminist scholars have been at least as interested in this book as black critics, in large part perhaps because it allows them to exorcise some of their own ghosts. In the 1980s, (white) feminist (literary) theory was charged with exclusivity and bias not only for its failure to include nonwhite, non-middle class, nonwestern women's writings, but also for its prejudice toward or presumption of the daughter's point of view. *Beloved* affords critics the opportunity to redeem many past lapses in one gesture, as the interests of "mother theory" (most often, in writing about this novel, a psychoanalytically informed discourse) converge with the interests of taking the experience of African American (female) subjects more seriously.

11. Alice Walker, *Meridian* (1976; reprint, New York: Pocket Books, 1986), pp. 90–1. Parenthetical references hereafter will be to the 1986 edition of the novel.

12. Rickie Solinger, "Race and 'Value': Black and White Illegitimate Babies, 1945–1965," in *Mothering: Ideology, Experience, and Agency,* ed. Evelyn Nakano Glenn, Grace Chang, and Linda Rennie Forcey (New York: Routledge, 1994), pp. 287–310.

13. Judith Modell, "'How Do You Introduce Yourself as a Childless Mother?' Birthparent Interpretations of Parenthood," in *Storied Lives: The Cultural Politics of Self-Understanding,* ed. George C. Rosewald and Richard L. Ochberg (New Haven: Yale University Press, 1992), pp. 76–94. The editors' introduction critiques Modell's interpretation of the birth parents' narratives by observing that these stories "invite skepticism" in their professions of unambivalent love; as the editors see it, this is because "women who hope, against

public policy, to reestablish connections with lost children cannot acknowledge that they were ever ambivalent" (10–1).

14. This, for instance, is Melissa Walker's formulation: "The core narrative is about a black man and the two women in his life—one black and one white"; M. Walker, *Down from the Mountaintop: Black Women's Novels in the Wake of the Civil Rights Movement, 1966–89* (New Haven: Yale University Press, 1991), pp. 173–4. Nancy Porter's brief summary of the plot also omits mention of the loss of Meridian's son; Porter, "Women's Interracial Friendships and Visions of Community in *Meridian, The Salt Eaters, Civil Wars,* and *Dessa Rose,*" in *Tradition and the Talents of Women,* ed. Florence Howe (Urbana: University of Illinois Press, 1991), pp. 251–7.

15. Alan Nadel, "Reading the Body: Alice Walker's *Meridian* and the Archeology of Self," *Modern Fiction Studies* 34, no. 1 (spring 1988): 55–68, says that "to become an activist," Meridian "has to *relinquish* her role as mother" (59, emphasis added); her body, which "reflects the conflict between her role as a mother and a self-fulfilling woman," must be overcome or renounced" (62), and she finally plays an "androgynous" role (66). Dianne F. Sadoff, "Black Matrilineage: Walker and Hurston," *Signs* 11, no. 1 (1985): 4–26, suggests that Alice Walker's "ambivalence" about the idealization of black motherhood emerges "even if dispersed, in the fictional texts" and that Meridian sacrifices her motherhood to pursue politics. Melissa Walker says the novel "dramatizes the power of public commitment to overwhelm the demands of private ties"; M. Walker, *Down from the Mountaintop,* p. 175. Lindsey Tucker, "Walking the Red Road: Mobility, Maternity, and Native American Myth in Alice Walker's *Meridian,*" *Women's Studies* 19 (1991): 1–17, sees Meridian struggling between maternity, which entails entrapment, and escape into the more spiritual, creative life associated with Native American symbols like the hoop, the sacred flowering tree, and Thought-Woman. Deborah McDowell argues that Meridian moves to an androgynous, fluid selfhood; McDowell, "The Self in Bloom: Alice Walker's *Meridian,*" *CLA Journal* 24, no. 3 (1981): 262–78. Karen Stein, "*Meridian:* Alice Walker's Critique of Revolution," *BALF* 20 (1986): 129–41, speaks of Meridian's female journey to "mature self-knowledge," wherein she can resist domination and gain authenticity.

16. However, as Margaret A. Simons points out, whereas early radical critiques like Shulamith Firestone's were better known, many feminists in fact tried from the beginning to offer more "integrative" solutions to the problem that motherhood can be both oppressive and empowering for women. See Simons, "Motherhood, Feminism, and Identity," in *Hypatia Reborn: Essays in Feminist Philosophy,* ed. Azizah Y. Al-Hibri and Margaret A. Simons (Bloomington: Indiana University Press, 1990), pp. 156–74.

17. Barbara Christian, "An Angle of Seeing: Motherhood in Buchi Emcheta's *Joys of Motherhood* and Alice Walker's *Meridian,*" in *Black Feminist Criticism* (New York: Pergamon, 1985), pp. 211–52. Christian discusses the destruction of the Sojourner Tree (by Saxon students) as evidence that "it is sometimes black women who deny our own maternal history (often unintentionally)" (230). This essay provides the fullest reading to date of *Meridian's*

complex treatment of motherhood and its contradictions for African American women.

18. Marjorie Agosin points out that a common way to "break" women activists in Latin American countries is to threaten their children, "making it clear to the woman that [by becoming an activist] she has lost the ability to protect them" (17). Agosin, introduction to *Surviving beyond Fear: Women, Children, and Human Rights in Latin America* (New York: White Pine Press, 1993). For further discussion of the Latin American motherist movements, see Jean Bethke Elshtain, "The Mothers of the Disappeared: Passion and Protest in Maternal Action," in Bassin, Honey, and Kaplan, *Representations of Motherhood*, pp. 75–91. See also Sara Ruddick's discussion of a maternal politics of peace, in *Maternal Thinking: Toward a Politics of Peace* (New York: Ballantine Books, 1990), and Amy Swerdlow's *Women Strike for Peace: Traditional Motherhood and Radical Politics in the 1960s* (Chicago: University of Chicago Press, 1993). For an interesting discussion of both the political advantages and disadvantages of motherist organizing in one American city, see Mary Pardo, "Mexican American Women Grassroots Community Activists: Mothers of East Los Angeles," *Frontiers* 11, no. 1 (1990): 1–7.

19. See Collins, "Shifting the Center," for a relevant discussion of "motherwork" as a key to rethinking motherhood: "Whether it is on behalf of one's own children, children of one's racial ethnic community, or children who are yet unborn . . . the space that this motherwork occupies promises to shift our thinking about motherhood itself" (59). Susan Willis, in *Specifying: Black Women Writing the American Experience* (Madison: University of Wisconsin Press, 1987), notes this point: Meridian's refusal to mother shows us that "mothering . . . is the single most insurmountable obstacle to a black woman's self-affirmation," yet Meridian also seeks to define a "new social function, which includes a form of mothering, but in the larger sense of an individual's caring for her community" (123). The fate of Meridian's friend Anne-Marion, a young revolutionary, ironically suggests how seductive the white rather than the Afrocentric definition is. Far more certain of herself as an activist than Meridian ever is, Anne is nevertheless easily co-opted by success and motherhood; near the end of the novel, a parenthetical note observes that "Anne-Marion . . . had become a well-known poet whose poems were about her two children, and the quality of the light that fell across a lake she owned" (201). It is interesting to note that this sentence serves as an epigraph to Adrienne Rich's recent discussion of the difficult necessity of combining writing and political activism. Rich argues that both seek "connection with unseen others" (1159), a particularly interesting formulation if we consider how motherhood too offers such connection; Rich, "The Hermit's Scream," *PMLA* 108, no. 5 (October 1993): 1157–64.

20. See Tucker, "Walking the Red Road."

21. Rita Felski, *Beyond Feminist Aesthetics: Feminist Literature and Social Change* (Cambridge: Harvard University Press, 1989); the quotations are found, respectively, on pp. 140, 131, 132, 141, 142, and 124. The argument is similar to one made by Homans and Hirsch about earlier novelists; it mer-

its fuller discussion with regard to claims by psychologists like Chodorow and Gilligan, made contemporaneously with the rise of the "feminist bildungsroman," that women have more fluid ego boundaries than men do.

22. So too her friend Anne-Marion calls her obsolete (124), and she is accused of "holding on" to the past (14).

23. Alice Walker, quoted in Claudia Tate, ed., *Black Women Writers at Work* (New York: Continuum, 1983), p. 176.

24. See M. Walker, *Down from the Mountaintop,* pp. 171–2, for an interesting discussion of the formal structure of *Meridian* that comes to rather different conclusions than I do about its meaning. For discussion of the fragmented and cyclical structure of the novel, see Christine Hall, "Art, Action, and the Ancestors: Alice Walker's *Meridian* in its Context," in *Black Women's Writing,* ed. Gina Wisker (New York: St. Martin's Press, 1993), pp. 96–110.

25. Dianne Sadoff suggests that "in celebrating her literary foremothers . . . the contemporary black woman writer covers over more profoundly than does the white writer her ambivalence about matrilineage, her own misreadings of precursors"; Sadoff, "Black Matrilineage: The Case of Alice Walker and Zora Neale Hurston," in *Black Women in America,* ed. Michelene R. Malson, Elisabeth Mudimbe-Boyi, Jean O'Barr, and Mary Wyer (Chicago: University of Chicago Press, 1988), p. 198. But my reading of *Meridian* suggests that here is the novel in which Walker uncovers and explores just this ambivalence.

26. Mary O'Brien, *The Politics of Reproduction* (London: Routledge and Kegan Paul, 1981); see especially chapter 1, "The Dialectics of Reproduction." It is particularly telling that both O'Brien and the narrator of *Meridian* identify a common historical turning point or dividing line in women's reproductive consciousness. O'Brien argues that the first significant historical change in the reproductive process was "the historical discovery of physiological paternity"; the second—far more recent, if anything more revolutionary, and still in the dialectal process of negotiation—is the technology that offers women the freedom to choose or not choose to be mothers (21–2). Speaking of Meridian's sense that she inherits an impossible legacy of endurance from her mother, the narrator observes: "It never occurred to her that her mother's and her grandmother's extreme purity of life was compelled by necessity. They had not lived in an age of choice" (124).

27. For one critical reading of O'Brien's alleged biologism and ahistoricism that is sympathetic, as I am, to her efforts to think about motherhood from a feminist perspective, see Reyes Lazaro, "Feminism and Motherhood: O'Brien vs Beauvoir," *Hypatia* 1, no. 2 (fall 1986): 87–102.

28. Susan Willis points out that Marilene is "the embodiment of the congealed labor that exemplifies the commodity form. In death, as was probably the case in her life, the white woman's labor power is the basis for her husband's livelihood"; Willis, "I Shop Therefore I Am: Is There a Place for Afro-American Culture in Commodity Culture?" in *Changing Our Own Words,* ed. Cheryl A. Wall (New Brunswick: Rutgers University Press, 1989), p. 180. In fact, however, Marilene didn't "labor," her husband insists, and what does it mean that as a commodity she is probably more valuable to her husband dead than alive?

29. For discussion of Othermothers ("women who assist blood mothers by sharing mothering responsibilities") as an Afrocentric concept, see Collins, "The Meaning of Motherhood in Black Culture," esp. pp. 46–50. See also Gloria Joseph in *Common Differences: Conflicts in Black and White Feminist Perspectives* (New York: Anchor Books, 1981), pp. 75–126, and Rosalie Riegle Troester, "Turbulence and Tenderness: Mothers, Daughters, and 'Othermothers' in Paule Marshall's *Brown Girl, Brownstones*," in Bell-Scott et al., *Double Stitch*, pp. 163–72.

30. Margaret Homans, "Her Very Own Howl," *Signs* 9, no. 2 (1983): 186–205, mentions *Meridian* together with *Sula* and *Surfacing* as novels that call into question the very possibility of representing women's voices in discourse; the Sojourner is a symbol of "both the persistence and the self-subversion of women's expression" (194–5).

31. I differ here from those who see the destruction of the Sojourner Tree as a tragic example of black-on-black violence, although I understand this reading. It seems to me, however, that the story of Louvinie is one of those ambiguous inheritances that does not serve its descendants altogether well, a story like Beloved's and Meridian's, as I argue in the conclusion of this chapter, "not to be passed on."

32. For one of many recent discussions of the psychological and material threats to black children, see Beverly Greene, "Sturdy Bridges: The Role of African-American Mothers in the Socialization of American Children," in *Motherhood: A Feminist Perspective,* ed. Jane Price Knowles and Ellen Cole (New York: The Haworth Press, 1990), pp. 205–25. Greene mentions, among other things, this grim list of statistics: "Black children are six times as likely as their white counterparts to show excess exposure to lead; six times as likely to contract tuberculosis; ten times as likely to die before the age of one year from nutritional deficiencies. . . . Black children are found in correctional facilities at 400 times the rate of their white counterparts and are placed in psychiatric, foster care and health care facilities at a rate 75 percent higher than that of their white counterparts" (214).

33. Although I do not develop this argument here, it is clear that Meridian's role as Othermother can be understood as a version of the argument that maternal functions, normally thought of as private, need to take the lead in reforming public policy. Here the analogy between Meridian and Latin American motherist movements is also clear: given the emphasis on mothering as a private responsibility, it is when mothers lose their children that they can or must enter into the public space. (In chapter 5, we see a similar pattern in the figure of Connie Ramos in *Woman on the Edge of Time.*) Several recent books also explore this notion that women need to become mothers of society as well as individual mothers: in addition to Ruddick's discussion of the basis of peace politics in maternal thinking, see for example Perdita Huston, *Motherhood by Choice: Pioneers in Women's Health and Family Planning* (New York: Feminist Press, 1992); Arnlaug Leira, *Welfare States and Working Mothers: The Scandinavian Experience* (New York: Guilford Press, 1992); and Theda

Skocpol, *Protecting Soldiers and Mothers: The Political Origins of Social Policy in the United States* (Cambridge: Harvard University Press, 1992).

34. See for instance Gloria Joseph, "Black Mothers and Daughters: Their Roles and Functions in American Society," in *Common Differences,* for the suggestion that the "rituals" of respect and reverence celebrated on Mother's Day "can be traced to Africa and the slave quarters" (90).

35. The passage cited in the epigraph to this section is taken from the first flashback in the novel, in which Meridian faces what is often taken to be the philosophical core of the novel: the question of whether killing for the revolution is justified. What strikes me as interesting is that the initial presentation of this problem focuses attention less on the issue than on Meridian's experience of her hesitation as an involuntary disconnection between the parts of her body necessary for normal speech: she feels that her tongue refuses to move and hears instead an internal voice. Even when Meridian is finally able to move her tongue, at the end of this flashback, it is only to utter this characteristic language of self-doubt, marking the distance between the certainty she desires and the involuntary reluctance she feels. Nancy Walker, *Feminist Alternatives: Irony and Fantasy in the Contemporary Novel by Women* (Jackson: University of Mississippi, 1990), has described Meridian as suffering from "periodic spells of disassociation" (126–7). Walker sees this as a "sickness" that Meridian must recover from, whereas I want to read it a little differently; but Walker too begins to link Meridian's out-of-the-body experiences and her subsequent connectedness, an issue I explore in the following discussion.

36. L. J. West, cited in Frank W. Putnam, *Diagnosis and Treatment of Multiple Personality Disorders* (New York: The Guilford Press, 1989). The following overview of dissociation is taken mainly from chapter 1 of Putnam's book and from his chapter on "Dissociative Phenomena" in *American Psychiatric Press Review of Psychiatry,* vol. 10 (Washington, D.C.: American Psychiatric Press, 1991), pp. 145–60.

37. As Ellen Rose pointed out to me, Meridian here can be compared to another fictional mother who gives up a child, Doris Lessing's Martha Quest, who has a similar moment of ecstatic dissociation on the veld.

38. This is compatible with feminist revisions of Freud. See Madelon Sprengnether, *The Spectral Mother: Freud, Feminism, and Psychoanalysis* (Ithaca: Cornell University Press, 1990), who argues that we can "avoid some of the problems in Freud's portrayal of the preoedipal mother," including the denial of the mother's desires, by seeing separation as primary, and "subjectivity . . . as an elegiac construct, the product of an internalized loss" of the mother's body (9). I suggest that "subjectivity" also take into account the loss of the child to the mother.

39. For a reading of *Sula* that suggests how Sula too disconnects herself in order to examine herself, see Vickroy, "The Force Outside/The Force Inside."

40. For a contrasting reading of this episode, see Elizabeth Schultz, "Out of the Woods and into the World: A Study of Interracial Friendships between Women in American Novels," in *Conjuring,* ed. Marjorie Pryse and Hortense

J. Spillers (Bloomington: Indiana University Press, 1985), pp. 67–85. The relationship is also discussed by Susan Danielson, "Alice Walker's *Meridian,* Feminism, and the 'Movement,'" *Women's Studies* 16 (1989): 317–30; Suzanne W. Jones, "Dismantling Stereotypes: Interracial Friendships in *Meridian* and *A Mother and Two Daughters,*" in *The Female Tradition in Southern Literature,* ed. Carol S. Manning (Urbana: University of Illinois Press, 1993), pp. 140–57; and Nancy Porter, "Women's Interracial Friendships." Martha J. McGowan, "Atonement and Release in Alice Walker's *Meridian, Critique* 23, no. 1 (1981): 25–36, also discusses their friendship, although her emphasis is less on the interracial question than on Meridian's ability to sympathize with Lynne as a turning point in Meridian's life that leads away from her destructive feelings of guilt, because she is not able to blame herself for Camara's death.

41. Critics who see Meridian transformed by her moment of realization in the Black Church include Danielson, Hall, and Stein. Susan Danielson, "Alice Walker's *Meridian,* Feminism, and the 'Movement,'" *Women's Studies* 16 (1989): 317–30; Christine Hall, "Art, Action, and the Ancestors: Alice Walker's *Meridian* in Its Context," in *Black Women's Writing,* ed. Gina Wisker (New York: St. Martin's Press, 1993); Karen F. Stein, "*Meridian:* Alice Walker's Critique of Revolution," *Black American Literature Forum* 20, no. 1–2 (spring-summer 1986): 129–41.

42. Spoken aloud, the two words might not seem quite so nearly identical, since the stress probably is meant to fall on the second syllable in the proper name as opposed to the first syllable in the common noun. However, as McDowell observes in "The Self in Bloom," the nearness of the two spellings may suggest an analogy between Meridian and a camera, "an image suggesting distance and detachment" (273).

43. Lorraine Liscio, "*Beloved*'s Narrative: Writing Mother's Milk," *Tulsa Studies in Women's Literature* 11, no. 1 (spring 1992): 44.

44. Jean Wyatt, "Giving Body to the Word: The Maternal Symbolic in Toni Morrison's *Beloved,*" *PMLA* 108, no. 3 (May 1993): 484.

45. The first quotation is from the American Psychiatric Association's *Diagnostic and Statistical Manual of Mental Disorders,* 3d edition, 1987, as cited in David Spiegel, "Dissociation and Trauma," chapter 12 of *American Psychiatric Press Review of Psychiatry,* p. 264; the second quotation is Spiegel, p. 261.

46. Judith L. Herman, *Trauma and Recovery* (New York: Basic Books, 1992), p. 9.

47. Ibid., p. 33.

48. Cathy Caruth, "Introduction," *American Imago* 48, no. 4 (1991): 417.

49. Herman, *Trauma and Recovery,* p. 38.

50. Spiegel, "Dissociation and Trauma," p. 261.

51. Caruth, "Introduction," p. 417.

52. Ibid., p. 420, emphasis added.

53. B. A. van der Kolk and Onno van der Hart, "The Intrusive Past: The Flexibility of Memory and the Engraving of Trauma," *American Imago* 48, no. 4 (1991): 450.

54. Caruth, "Introduction," pp. 422–3.

55. Compare Marianne Hirsch's claim that infanticide in *Beloved* "takes the text . . . to the point of antinarrative," in "Maternity and Rememory: Toni Morrison's *Beloved*," in Bassin, Honey, and Kaplan, *Representations of Motherhood,* p. 104.

56. Herman, *Trauma and Recovery,* p. 40.

CHAPTER FOUR

1. Rayna Green, "Native American Women," *Signs* 6, no. 2 (1980): 257 and 250, respectively. Green adds that the early colonizers "misunderstood Eastern tribes so profoundly that they sabotaged their own treaties in making them with men who did not have the right to make such decisions" (250).

2. Paula Gunn Allen, *The Sacred Hoop: Recovering the Feminine in American Indian Traditions* (Boston: Beacon Press, 1986), pp. 28, 251.

3. Brooke Medicine Eagle, *In Childlessness Transformed: Stories of Alternative Parenting,* ed. Jane English (Mount Shasta: Earth Heart Books, 1989), p. 25.

4. Kate Stanley, "Thoughts on Indian Feminism," in *A Gathering of Spirit,* ed. Beth Brant (Ithaca, New York: Firebrand Books, 1988), p. 214.

5. Brant, *A Gathering of Spirit,* p. 11. See also Bea Medicine, who says "Indian women do not need liberation . . . they have always been liberated within their tribal structures," in Gretchen M. Bataille and Kathleen Mullen Sands, *American Indian Women: Telling Their Lives* (Lincoln: University of Nebraska Press, 1984), p. vii.

6. Furthermore, although I have stressed arguments like Allen's here about the matrifocal nature of many Native American cultures, it is important to remember that tribal and regional differences militate against sweeping generalizations about the power of "the" mother. Assumptions about "aboriginal matriarchy" were also mistakenly made by early western observers, as Cara E. Richards argues in "Matriarchy or Mistake: The Role of Iroquois Women Through Time," in *Iroquois Women: An Anthology,* ed. W. G. Spittal (Iroqrafts Indian Reprint Series), pp. 149–59.

7. Louis Owens, *Other Destinies: Understanding the American Indian Novel* (Norman: University of Oklahoma Press, 1992), p. 5.

8. Patricia Hill Collins, "Shifting the Center," in *Representations of Motherhood,* ed. Donna Bassin, Margaret Honey, Meryle Mahrer Kaplan (New Haven: Yale University Press, 1994), p. 65.

9. I pass over here the question of what "counts" as Native American literature, which, like questions of Indian identity and authenticity, is an ongoing problem. Recent examples of the voluminous discussion of this question include Michael Castro, *Interpreting the Indian: Twentieth-Century Poets and the Native American* (Norman: University of Oklahoma Press, 1983); Vine Deloria Jr., *Custer Died for Your Sins* (Norman: University of Oklahoma Press, 1988); Michael Dorris, "Native American Literature in an Ethno-Historical Context," *College English* 41, no. 2 (1979): 147–62; Susan Hegeman, "Native

American 'Texts' and the Problem of Authenticity," *American Quarterly* 41, no. 2 (June 1989): 265–83; Arnold Krupat, *The Voice in the Margin: Native American Literature and the Canon* (Berkeley: University of California Press, 1987); Simon Ortiz, "Towards a National Indian Literature: Cultural Authenticity in Nationalism," *MELUS* 8, no. 2 (summer 1981): 7–12; Rodney Simard, "American Indian Literatures, Authenticity, and the Canon," *World Literature Today* (spring 1992): 243–8.

10. Judith Antell, "Momaday, Welch, and Silko: Expressing the Feminine Principle through Male Alienation," *American Indian Quarterly* (summer 1988): 213–4.

11. Quoting from James Welch, *The Death of Jim Loney* (New York: Harper and Row, 1979), p. 34.

12. For a correspondent discussion of the figure of the absent mother in Leslie Marmon Silko's *Storyteller,* see Patricia Jones, "The Web of Meaning: Naming the Absent Mother in *Storyteller,*" in Silko, *"Yellow Woman,"* ed. Melody Graulich (New Brunswick: Rutgers University Press, 1993), pp. 213–32. Arguing for the importance of reading significance into the gaps in the characteristically fragmentary Native American text, Jones points out that "the most notable gaps and silences in *Storyteller* revolve around the absence of Silko's mother" (215); hence the mother is, as in Antell's view, both "absent" and "through her palpable absence, the very center of the text" (217). Jones relates the absent mother in Silko, especially in the Yellow Woman stories, to common myths of the mother who in one way or another fails an individual child, but with "good results" for the community and with an emphasis on the "ultimately creative act" of female sexuality.

13. I speak of Erdrich and Dorris as a team here because of their own frequent insistence that they work together. See Hertha D. Wong, "An Interview with Louise Erdrich and Michael Dorris," *North Dakota Quarterly* 55, no. 1 (winter 1987): 201. For ease of reading in discussions of particular texts, I subsequently use just the one author's name under which a novel has been published.

14. Robert Silberman, "Opening the Text: Love Medicine and the Return of the Native American Woman," in *Narrative Chance: Postmodern Discourse on Native American Literatures,* ed. Gerald Vizenor (Albuquerque: University of New Mexico Press, 1989), pp. 101–20.

15. Hertha D. Wong, "Adoptive Mothers and Thrown-Away Children in the Novels of Louise Erdrich," in *Narrating Mothers: Theorizing Maternal Subjectivities,* ed. Brenda O. Daly and Maureen T. Reddy (Knoxville: University of Tennessee Press, 1991), pp. 174–92. This point is also stressed in Owens, *Other Destinies,* in the chapter on Erdrich and Dorris.

16. Wong, "Adoptive Mothers," p. 186.

17. Karl Kroeber, editor of the first special issue of *Studies in American Indian Literatures* devoted to Erdrich's work, is one of the first to point out that *Love Medicine* "poses a question about novelistic unity," and he argues for Erdrich's "sensitivity to the peculiarly poly-ethnic character of Americanness" as reflected in the novel's multiply voiced structure; Kroeber, *Studies in American*

Indian Literatures 9, no. 1 (1985), pp. 2–3. In her contribution to the same volume, Kathleen Sands describes the novel's narrative technique as "compellingly tribal in character," although she believes it moves toward the traditional end of presenting "a complete story in stable form." See also Sands' insightful discussion of the way in which the novel works as and through "the secular anecdotal narrative process of community gossip"; Sands, *Studies in American Indian Literatures* 9, no. 1 (1985): 12–24.

18. Louise Erdrich, *The Bingo Palace* (New York: HarperCollins Publishers, 1994), p. 5.

19. It is much simpler to make this claim for *Yellow Raft on Blue Water* than for *Love Medicine,* because it is clear who the central protagonists of the former are. Different readers have tended to see different persons in the collectively told *Love Medicine* as central. Robert Silberman and Thomas Matchie underscore June's importance; Matchie compares June to Moby Dick: "her presence pervades the entire story and gives it depth. She is not there and yet there" (483). Matchie, "*Love Medicine:* A Female *Moby Dick,*" *Midwest Quarterly* 30, no. 4 (1989): 478–491. Deborah Rosenfelt says that the "warp and woof" of the fabric of *Love Medicine* are the "entwined" narratives of Nector (and his "attempt to reconcile his divided love for Marie Lazarre . . . and Lulu Lamartine") and Lipsha's quest for his parentage (wherein he needs to know who his mother is, indeed), but "this plot remains essentially a quest for identity and manhood—a quest predicated on the importance of knowing one's paternity" (281–2). Rosenfelt, "Feminism, 'Postfeminism,' and Contemporary Women's Fiction," in *Tradition and the Talents of Women,* ed. Florence Howe (Urbana: University of Illinois Press, 1991), pp. 268–91.

20. A genogram is "a diagram that portrays the family tree of the individual for two or three generations"; for discussion, see Karen G. Howe, "Daughters Discover Their Mothers through Biographies and Genograms: Educational and Clinical Parallels," in *Motherhood: A Feminist Perspective,* ed. Jane Rice Knowles and Ellen Cole (New York: Haworth Press, 1990), pp. 31–40.

21. Quotations are taken from Michael Dorris, *Yellow Raft on Blue Water* (New York: Warner Books, 1987).

22. Sara Ruddick, "Thinking Mothers/Conceiving Birth," in Bassin, Honey, and Kaplan, *Representations of Motherhood,* p. 38. As Patricia Hill Collins also points out, "For many women of color, choosing to become a mother challenges institutional policies that encourage white middle-class women to reproduce and discourages low-income racial ethnic women from doing so, even penalizing them" ("Shifting the Center," p. 65). See also Virginia Held, *Feminist Morality: Transforming Culture, Society, and Politics* (Chicago: University of Chicago Press, 1993), who repeatedly addresses the question of the voluntary or involuntary nature of human motherhood.

23. As Louis Owens implies in *Other Destinies,* the optimism may be problematic to some readers: "Resolution and closure come with a somewhat unpersuasive rapidity and ease in this novel" (223). *Yellow Raft* ought to be compared to *The Crown of Columbus,* which I omit from this study, because there the biracial daughter, Violet, is also a positive, hopeful mix of at least two

cultures. For a reading of the novel that addresses this issue, see Ann Rayson, "Shifting Identity in the Work of Louise Erdrich and Michael Dorris," *Studies in American Indian Literatures* 3, no. 4 (1991): 27–36.

24. This idea is echoed in several recent stories, poems, and autobiographical pieces by Native American women writers. For instance, see Beth Brant's introductory statement in *A Gathering of Spirit:* "As I unravel, I also weave. I am the storyteller and the story" (8).

25. Owens, *Other Destinies,* p. 223. For a comparable reading of the way in which "the mothers' reclaiming of storytelling is an act of self-creation, one by which they enact, with a full complement of ambivalence and doubt, their passage from loss and dispossession to hope and affirmation" (608) in another subculture, see Marina Hueng, "Daughter-Text/Mother-Text: Matrilineage in Amy Tan's *Joy Luck Club,*" *Feminist Studies* 19, no. 3 (fall 1993): 597–616.

26. The dilemma is a familiar one: James Flavin points to a similar problem in *Tracks* when Nanapush says that since his name loses power every time it is written (speaking particularly of its inscription in "a government file"), he has only given it out once (32). This is "an awkward moment," as Flavin sees: "The character/narrator won't give it out, yet the novelist must use the name again and again throughout her story." See Flavin, "The Novel as Performance: Communication in Louise Erdrich's *Tracks,*" *Studies in American Indian Literatures* 3, no. 4 (1991): 1. In a somewhat contrasting argument about using "the languages of the colonialists" for indigenous purposes of resistance, Simon Ortiz points out that "it is entirely possible for a people to retain and maintain their lives through the use of any language" ("Towards a National Indian Literature," 10). The novel may run some risk in asking us to accept on faith that Ida's story is told "in my own language," although we read it in English; is nothing lost in translation?

27. Wong, "An Interview with Louise Erdrich and Michael Dorris," pp. 201–2.

28. Braiding is the final image of the novel, as Ida sits in the dark on the roof of her house with Father Hulbert. He asks her what she is doing, and in the last sentence of the novel she observes: "As a man with cut hair, he did not identify the rhythm of three strands, the whispers of coming and going, of twisting and tying and blending, of catching and letting go, of braiding" (*Yellow Raft,* 372).

29. In *Other Destinies,* Owens says June is the "mythic catalyst" of the novel (196). Sands also uses the word "catalyst" in her commentary (*Studies in American Indian Literatures* 9, no. 1, p. 16). Claire Crabtree identifies the death of June and the revelation that she was Lipsha's mother as "a thread running through the novel," in "Salvific Oneness and the Fragmented Self in Louise Erdrich's *Love Medicine,*" in *Contemporary Native American Cultural Issues,* ed. Thomas E. Schirer (Sault Ste. Marie: Lake Superior State University Press, 1988), p. 50.

30. For a discussion of Lulu as Erdrich's "vision of a wholly transpersonal state of being," see Jeanne Smith, "Transpersonal Selfhood: The Boundaries of

Identity in Louise Erdrich's *Love Medicine*," *Studies in American Indian Literatures* 3, no. 4 (1991): 13–26, esp. 18–9.

31. Deborah Rosenfelt calls this an image of "female reparenting," in "Feminism, 'Postfeminism,' and Contemporary Women's Fiction," p. 283.

32. Several recent discussions of "Native American" identity have made a similar point. See for example Gerald Vizenor, *The People Named Chippewa* (Minneapolis: University of Minnesota Press, 1984), p. 107.

33. Erdrich and Dorris's fiction thus participates in the effort to revise the myth of the mother's "ultimate responsibility," an effort that feminist critics like Susan Suleiman have called for. Suleiman, "On Maternal Splitting: A Propos of Mary Gordon's *Men and Angels*," *Signs* 14, no. 1 (autumn 1988): 25–41.

34. It has been pointed out, however, that Mary Adare, Adelaide's daughter, has "stringy black hair," which might indicate Indian blood and suggest a motive for Adelaide's flight. Leslie Marmon Silko, cited by Susan Perez Castillo, "Postmodernism, Native American Literature, and the Real: The Silko-Erdrich Controversy," *Massachusetts Review* 32, no. 2 (1991): 287.

35. Quotations are taken from Louise Erdrich, *The Beet Queen* (New York: Bantam Books, 1986).

36. Quoting from Louise Erdrich, *Tracks* (New York: Harper and Row, 1988).

37. Note that closure again comes with parental reunion and a child's possible forgiveness. Some indication of how difficult it was for parents to retrieve their children from Indian boarding schools is given in Brenda Child's discussion, with several examples of correspondence, in "Homesickness, Illness, and Death: Native American Girls in Government Boarding Schools," in *Wings of Gauze: Women of Color and the Experience of Health and Illness*, ed. Barbara Bair and Susan E. Cayleff (Detroit: Wayne State University Press, 1993), pp. 169–79.

38. For discussion of the trickster figure in the first three Erdrich novels, see Catherine M. Catt, "Ancient Myth in Modern American: The Trickster in the Fiction of Louise Erdrich," *Platte Valley Review* 19, no. 1 (1991): 71–81. One of the few discussions of the female trickster is Jay Cox, "Dangerous Definitions: Female Tricksters in Contemporary Native American Literature," *Wicazo Sa Review* 5, no. 2 (1989): 17–21.

39. Flavin discusses Nanapush's use of words to bring Lulu back to her native culture in "The Novel as Performance."

40. For just one of several discussions that make this assumption, see Annette Van Dyke, "Questions of the Spirit: Bloodlines in Louise Erdrich's Chippewa Landscape," *Studies in American Indian Literatures* 4, no. 1 (spring 1992): 15–27.

41. The quotations are taken, in order, from: Victoria Walker, "A Note on Narrative Perspective in *Tracks*," *Studies in American Indian Literatures* 3, no. 4 (1991): 40; Jennifer Sergi, "Storytelling: Tradition and Preservation in Louise Erdrich's *Tracks*," *World Literature Today* (spring 1992): 279; Van Dyke, "Questions of the Spirit," p. 22.

42. Nancy J. Peterson, "History, Postmodernism, and Louise Erdrich's *Tracks*," *PMLA* 109 (October 1994): 989. Peterson's reading stresses the way in which Erdrich seeks to represent the problems of historical narratives about the precontact past; I stress the way in which this is figured in the search for the (preoedipal) maternal subject. As Peterson observes in a footnote, presumably written before the publication of *The Bingo Palace*, Fleur can be compared to both June and Adelaide, and these novels also "revolve around the disappearance of a key mother figure" (992).

43. Daniel Cornell, "Woman Looking: Revis(ion)ing Pauline's Subject Position in Louise Erdrich's *Tracks*," *Studies in American Indian Literatures* 4, no. 1 (1992): 52. In "A Note on the Narrative Perspective," Walker also sees that Nanapush is slightly suspect, "a self-confessed, charming 'talker'" (40).

44. Compare Magdelene Redekop's identification of the "mock mother" in Alice Munro's stories, also discussed in chapter 1: "The mock mother is constructed as a result of the impossibility of picturing the 'real' mother. Often she performs as *a kind of trickster* who challenges our old ways of looking at the relation between the work of art and the human body" (4). Redekop, *Mothers and Other Clowns* (London: Routledge, 1992).

45. For a discussion that situates *Tracks* in women writers' tradition of using the ghost story to reflect an alternative epistemology, see Wendy K. Kolmar, "'Dialectics of Connectedness': Supernatural Elements in Novels by Bambara, Cisneros, Grahn, and Erdrich," in *Haunting the House of Fiction*, ed. Lynette Carpenter and Wendy K. Kolmar (Knoxville: University of Tennessee Press, 1991), pp. 236–49. Written before the publication of *The Bingo Palace*, Kolmar's discussion notes that Erdrich's novels, like others she examines, are not classic ghost stories in that there is no encounter between the protagonist and a literal ghost; rather, "in each novel, the supernatural elements exist undifferentiated from the 'present,' 'the real,' 'the natural.' Characters and readers do not confront them as *other*, they are simply part of the experience of life and of the text" (238). In Erdrich's fourth novel, however, we see both the central "encounter" with a ghost *and* this blurring of natural and supernatural in the experience of text and characters.

46. See Sands in *Studies in American Indian Literatures* 9, no. 1 (1985): 12–24.

47. In "June's Luck," Erdrich touches on the problem of domestic violence in Native American communities (as she does in the scene with King Jr. and Lynn near the beginning of *Love Medicine*). For one interesting biographical/autobiographical essay about an Alutiiq woman and healer who escaped a violent marriage that suggests a more optimistic possibility than June's life, see Joanne B. Mulcahy with Mary Petersen, "Mary Petersen: A Life of Healing and Renewal," in Bair and Cayleff, *Wings of Gauze*, pp. 148–68. Retrospectively, June's alienation from her own body at the beginning of *Love Medicine* takes on added significance. For discussion of this and other moments when characters are split off or dissociated from their bodies, see Jeanne Smith, "Transpersonal Selfhood," p. 13–26.

48. Scott Sanders, *Studies in American Indian Literatures* 9, no. 1 (1985): 9.

49. Fleur's presence as Othermother is worth noting: We also learn in *Tracks* that before her own children are born, Fleur is a kind of surrogate mother to young Russell, and in a brief scene in *Love Medicine* she still seems to be taking care of him, after he is a wounded war veteran confined to his wheelchair. In *The Beet Queen*, where she seems to be living as an itinerant, she rescues and heals the broken bones of Karl Adare.

50. For a discussion of how this works in *Tracks*, see Peterson, "History, Postmodernism, and Louise Erdrich's *Tracks*." This scene is evocative of Tayo's entry in Silko's *Ceremony* into the home of Betonie, the medicine man who lives with his combination of old and new ritual objects.

51. Compare Donna Haraway's frequently cited claim: "The Coyote or Trickster, as embodied in Southwestern Native American accounts, suggests the situation we are in when we give up mastery but keep searching for fidelity, knowing all the while that we will be hoodwinked. . . . I like to see feminist theory as a reinvented coyote discourse obligated to its sources in many heterogeneous accounts of the world." Haraway, "Situated Knowledge," *Feminist Studies* 14 (1988): 592, 593–4.

52. Both stories are anthologized in *The Woman That I Am: The Literature and Culture of Contemporary Women of Color*, ed. D. Soyini Madison (New York: St. Martin's Press, 1994), pp. 200–6 and 256–63, respectively.

CHAPTER FIVE

1. Quotations are taken from the Fawcett Crest edition of Marge Piercy, *Woman on the Edge of Time* (New York: Ballantine Books, 1983).

2. Although in general it might be argued, as I suggest later, that Piercy valorizes the imaginative power of the mother's position in a way comparable to that of the French feminists, in this regard I take Piercy's view as antithetical to Julia Kristeva's position that the maternal is a site of constitutive splitting and radical otherness. For this view, see especially "Herethique de la'amour," *Tel Quel* 74 (winter 1977): 30–49; reprinted in *Histoires d'amour* (Paris: Denoel, 1983).

3. The fact that Connie is Chicana is interesting in light of my findings in chapters 2 and 3 about other racial and ethnic minority women, but I think the representation of the Chicana is not Piercy's main concern, so I do not discuss it extensively here.

4. Note that this is an act Connie has just imagined doing—when Geraldo breaks in, her hatred "gave her a flush in the nerves like speed coming on," and she imagines destroying his elegance in creative ways that foreshadow her visionary capacity: "She dreamed of peeling off a slickly polished antiqued lizard high-heeled boot and pounding it down his lying throat" (13).

5. Later, in utopian Mattapoisett at the end-of-mothering ritual, we learn tellingly that "aunts" (chosen, not biological) play an important role after naming, when the adolescent no longer goes to her mothers for advice, but to the aunts she selects as advisers for the next few years (116). Contrast Margaret Atwood's characterization of "the Aunts" in *The Handmaid's Tale*, an elite

female gestapo who brutally train and police other women and serve the interests of the antifeminist state.

6. Not only does Dolly have the abortion, at Geraldo's insistence, but in the few brief visits Connie has with her niece we learn that Dolly, working harder than ever as a prostitute, is growing further and further estranged from her own daughter Nita, who is cared for by her grandmother.

7. Alice Adams, "Out of the Womb: The Future of the Uterine Metaphor," *Feminist Studies* 19, no. 2 (summer 1993): 275. See also Adams's discussion of *Woman on the Edge of Time* in *Reproducing the Womb: Images of Childbirth in Science, Feminist Theory, and Literature* (Ithaca: Cornell University Press, 1994).

8. Piercy's vision in the novel is often taken to idealize androgyny, and she has sometimes been criticized for letting men into her utopia. See for example Peter Fitting, "For Men Only: A Guide to Reading Single-Sex Worlds," *Women's Studies* 14 (1987): 101–18.

9. Evelyn Nakano Glenn, "Social Constructions of Mothering: A Thematic Overview," in *Mothering: Ideology, Experience, and Agency,* ed. Evelyn Nakano Glenn, Grace Chang, and Linda Rennie Forcey (New York: Routledge, 1994), p. 7. For elaboration, see Sau-ling C. Wong, "Diverted Mothering: Representations of Caregivers of Color in the Age of 'Multiculturalism'" in Glenn, Chang, and Forcey, *Mothering: Ideology, Experience, and Agency,* pp. 67–91. See also Evelyn Nakano Glenn, "From Servitude to Service Work: Historical Continuities in the Racial Division of Women's Work," *Signs* 18, no. 1 (fall 1992): 1–43.

10. Quotations are from the Fawcett Crest edition of Margaret Atwood, *The Handmaid's Tale* (New York: Ballantine Books, 1987).

11. For discussion of this interpretation, see Amin Malak, "Margaret Atwood's *The Handmaid's Tale* and the Dystopian Tradition," *Canadian Literature* 112 (spring 1987): 9–16.

12. Helen Yglesias, "Odd Woman Out," calls this the "the Atwood woman," in *The Women's Review of Books* 6, no. 10–11 (July 1989): 3.

13. To cite just one more example: when she finally understands what has been obvious to the reader for some time, that there is an underground resistance and that her walking partner is a member, she is given a chance to join their efforts. Her partner urges her to use her nightly secret meetings to find out something about the Commander; "'Find out what?' I say" (289).

14. In this passage she criticizes her lack of sympathy for another Handmaid, who has gone mad: "I look after her. Easy out, is what I think. I don't even feel sorry for her, although I should. I feel angry. I'm not proud of myself for this, or for any of it. But then, that's the point" (361). This leaves her readers to ask: The point of what? *What's* the point?

15. For a discussion of Atwood's relation to "postfeminism" in the novel preceding *The Handmaid's Tale* that has implications I cannot explore here, see my earlier essay, "(Post)Feminism in Atwood's *Bodily Harm,*" *Novel* 19 (1985): 5–21.

16. Aunt Lydia expresses just this reasoning when she explains why the promiscuity of the past was a mistake: "A thing is valued, she says, only if it is rare and hard to get. We want you to be valued, girls." The Handmaid's reflection, as the passage continues, highlights the tyranny and corruption of this ideology: "We sitting in our rows, eyes down, we make her salivate morally. We are hers to define, we must suffer her adjectives" (145).

17. It could even be argued that the Handmaid retrospectively highlights Connie's perhaps equally unsettling inability to give up the myth of individual and utter responsibility. Whereas the women of Mattapoisett have apparently relinquished the myth and share the work of mothering with a whole community (and do so only until the child reaches adolescence), Connie still embodies in her fairly standard brand of individual heroism another very ancient, long-lived, and romantic myth about good mothers: their willing and utter and lonely self-sacrifice.

18. Susan Rubin Suleiman, "On Maternal Splitting: A Propos of Mary Gordon's *Men and Angels*," *Signs* 14, no. 1 (autumn 1988): 25–41.

19. Adrienne Rich, *Of Woman Born: Motherhood as Experience and Institution*, tenth anniversary edition *(New York: W. W. Norton, 1986)*, p. 240.

20. In "Balancing Acts," an interview of Kathi Aguero and Marea Gordett conducted by Ruth Perry, *Women's Review of Books* 5, no. 10–11 (July 1988), one contemporary mother and writer has publicly said that her fiction is useful in exorcising her fears about her children. Gordett observes, "Well, when I was pregnant I was somewhat obsessed with the fear of having a child who had some handicap, and I wrote a story about it and it helped me tremendously" (29).

21. Perry, "Balancing Acts," p. 30.

22. Domna C. Stanton, "Difference on Trial: A Critique of the Maternal Metaphor in Cixous, Irigaray, and Kristeva," in *The Poetics of Gender*, ed. Nancy K. Miller (New York: Columbia University Press, 1986), pp. 156–82, quotation on p. 174.

23. bell hooks, *Talking Back: Thinking Feminist, Thinking Black* (Boston: South End Press, 1989), p. 37.

24. Tillie Olsen's "As I Stand Here Ironing" was first published in 1956; quotations are taken from Olsen, *Tell Me a Riddle* (New York: Dell, 1976).

CHAPTER SIX

1. Although most critics have approached Weldon as a feminist writer, some have disputed this designation; see, for example, Alan Wilde, "Bold, But Not Too Bold: Fay Weldon and the Limits of Poststructuralist Criticism," *Contemporary Literature* 39 (1988). For discussion of the subversive technique and effect of Weldon's satire, see Ann Marie Herbert, "Rewriting the Feminine Script: Fay Weldon's Wicked Laughter," *Critical Matrix* 7, no. 1 (1993): 21–40.

2. Denise Riley, *War in the Nursery: Theories of the Child and Mother* (London: Virago, 1983), p. 96.

3. See Jessica Benjamin, "The First Bond," in *The Bonds of Love: Psychoanalysis, Feminism, and the Problem of Domination* (New York: Pantheon, 1988), pp. 11–50.

4. Juliet Mitchell, *Psychoanalysis and Feminism* (New York: Vintage Books, 1975), pp. 228–9.

5. Ann Dally, *Inventing Motherhood: The Consequences of an Ideal* (New York: Schocken Books, 1982), p. 90.

6. Mary O'Brien, *The Politics of Reproduction* (London: Routledge and Kegan Paul, 1981); see especially chapter 1, "The Dialectics of Reproduction."

7. Fay Weldon, *Female Friends* (New York: St. Martin's Press, 1974), p. 116. Hereafter page references to Weldon's novels will appear in parentheses.

8. The phrase closes the first chapter and opens the last chapter. It also opens four of the first eight chapters of the novel (the first three of these chapters, 4, 6, and 7, focus respectively on brief comments about each friend in turn), and at less frequent, irregular intervals, it opens six subsequent chapters (24, 32, 36, 44, 52, 58). The refrain appears only once in the third person: "Marjorie, Grace, and Chloe" (the first words of chapter 24).

9. For the suggestion that Joanna May in *The Cloning of Joanna May* is also both first-person and third-person narrator, in a revision of the role of Eliot's Tiresias, see Betsy Ford, "Belladonna Speaks: Fay Weldon's Wasteland," *West Virginia University Philological Papers* 38 (1992): 322–33.

10. In Drabble's recent trilogy, *The Radiant Way, A Natural Curiosity,* and *The Gates of Ivory,* friends Liz, Alix, and Esther take turns as the center of the narratives; the plots may focus on their individual experiences, but their friendship is of ongoing importance. Margaret Atwood's latest novel narrates the relations between three friends, Toni, Charis, and Roz, to a fourth character, Zenia, who has deceived and injured each of them. Rachel DuPlessis discusses a related phenomenon, what she calls the "group" protagonist or the "collective" or "communal" protagonist, in both the late novels of Virginia Woolf and in the more recent speculative fiction of Joanna Russ, Marge Piercy, and Doris Lessing, in *Writing beyond the Ending: Narrative Strategies of Twentieth-Century Women Writers* (Bloomington: Indiana University Press, 1985), especially in chapter 11, pp. 178–97.

11. For a somewhat different reading that stresses the irony of the title, see Nancy Walker, *Feminist Alternatives: Irony and Fantasy in Contemporary Novels of Women* (Jackson: University of Mississippi Press, 1990), esp. pp. 104–7.

12. In Weldon's *Hearts and Lives of Men,* it is difficult to know whether the story is about Helen or Nell, the mother or the daughter. The narrator alternately tells what happens to each of them during a fifteen-year period when Nell is lost and insists that the novel is about Nell. But readers know a lot more about Helen's feelings; Nell may be too lucky, indeed, to be penetrated by representation.

13. Fay Weldon, *The Cloning of Joanna May* (William Collins Sons, 1989; reprint, New York: Penguin Books, 1991), p.108. References are to the reprint edition.

14. The phrase is Donna Haraway's in "Situated Knowledges: The Science Question in Feminism and the Privilege of Partial Perspective," *Feminist Stud-*

ies 14 (1988): 575–99, an essay that speaks directly to many of the concerns raised in *The Cloning of Joanna May.*

15. Judith V. Jordan, "Empathy and Self Boundaries," in *Women's Growth in Connection: Writings from the Stone Center,* ed. Jordan et al. (New York: Guilford Press, 1991), p. 79.

16. Praxis's self-division is particularly interesting in light of the fact that she is also the author of the novel and hence a figure of the woman writer. In "Me and My Shadows," Weldon approaches the task of writing an autobiographical essay by splitting herself into two parts, the Interviewer and the Answerer, and further discusses the multiple personalities she experiences in daily life. "The writing of fiction," Weldon claims, "for me, is the splitting of the self into myriad parts" (162); Weldon, "Me and My Shadows," in *On Gender and Writing,* ed. Michelene Wandor (London: Pandora Press, 1983).

17. Fay Weldon, *Praxis* (Hodder and Stoughton, 1978; reprint, New York: Penguin Books, 1990). References are to the reprint edition.

18. Other minor characters in Weldon's fiction who go mad in part at least because they know too much (about others or about sides of themselves that they fear) include Miss Martin in *Puffball* and Marion in *Words of Advice.* Such women protect the "self" that has been abused and disbelieved by retreating like Lucy into madness.

19. *Atlantic,* August 1980, p. 84. A version of the following discussion of *Puffball* appeared in the *Alumni Magazine of Haverford College,* Spring 1994 (pp. 24–31).

20. Anita Brookner, "The Return of the Earth Mother," *Times Literary Supplement,* February 22, 1980, p. 202.

21. Pauline Palmer, *Contemporary Women's Fiction: Narrative Practice and Feminist Theory* (Jackson: University of Mississippi Press, 1989), p. 102.

22. Susan Bordo, "Are Mothers Persons? Reproductive Rights and the Politics of Subjectivity," in *Unbearable Weight: Feminism, Western Culture, and the Body* (Berkeley: University of California Press, 1990), p. 94.

23. Gayatri Spivak, "French Feminism in an International Frame," *Yale French Studies* 62 (1981): 183.

24. Iris Marion Young, "Pregnant Embodiment: Subjectivity and Alienation," in *Throwing Like a Girl and Other Essays in Feminist Philosophy and Social Theory* (Bloomington: Indiana University Press, 1990), p. 160.

25. The novel also addresses a question posed by Barbara Johnson in "Apostrophe, Animation, and Abortion," the final chapter of *A World of Difference* (Baltimore: Johns Hopkins University Press, 1987), p. 190: "How might the plot of human subjectivity be reconceived (so to speak) if pregnancy rather than autonomy is what raises the question of deliberateness?"

26. The position is exemplified in statements such as: "Childbirth establishes the offspring's independent existence and simultaneously transforms the woman into a particular kind of social being, a mother"; Paula Treichler, "Feminism, Medicine, and the Meaning of Childbirth," in *Body/Politics: Women and the Discourses of Science,* ed. Mary Jacobus, Evelyn Fox Keller, and Sally Shuttleworth (New York: Routledge, 1990), p. 117. The fact that

Liffey has a C-section adds another complication to the problem of including birthing labor in definitions of what makes a mother.

27. In *Women Writing Childbirth: Modern Discourses of Motherhood* (Manchester and New York: Manchester University Press, 1994), Tess Cosslett points out that the wording in these passages is very close to that of a popular manual, Gordon Breach's *Pregnancy*. Cosslett suggests that either Weldon used Breach or they had a common source (70).

28. Fay Weldon, *Puffball* (Hodder and Stoughton, 1980; reprint, New York: Penguin Books, 1990). References are to the reprint edition.

29. As Emily Martin puts it, "In this view [postmodern anthropology] scientific discourse is not more privileged in its relation to reality than any other form of description." Martin, "Science and Women's Bodies: Forms of Anthropological Knowledge," in Jacobus, Keller, and Shuttleworth, *Body/Politics*, p. 71.

30. This perspective corrects the bias that Young points to in "Pregnant Embodiment":

> The dominant model of health assumes that the normal, healthy body is unchanging. Health is associated with stability, equilibrium, a steady state. Only a minority of persons, however, namely adult men who are not yet old, experience their health as a state in which there is no regular or noticeable change in body condition. . . . Regular, noticeable, sometimes extreme change in body condition, on the other hand, is an aspect of the normal bodily functioning of adult women. Change is also a central aspect of the bodily existence of healthy children and healthy old people, as well as some of the so-called disabled. Yet medical conceptualization implicitly uses this unchanging adult male body as the standard of all health. (169)

31. In *Reproducing the Womb: Images of Childbirth in Science, Feminist Theory, and Literature* (Ithaca: Cornell University Press, 1994), which appeared after my discussion of *Puffball* was originally published, Alice Adams makes a similar point: "I think that the project of 'getting in touch with'—or 'writing through'—the body is more likely to confirm the inseparability of culture and biology than it is to help us rediscover an essential and constant woman's body" (7).

32. Hélène Cixous, "The Laugh of the Medusa," in *New French Feminisms: An Anthology,* ed. Elaine Marks and Isabelle de Courtivron (Amherst: University of Massachusetts Press, 1980), p. 261.

33. Tess Cosslett also stresses the "ambiguous" meaning, for a feminist critique, of the natural childbirth movement that Weldon so clearly articulates. See the introduction to *Women Writing Childbirth,* pp. 1–8.

34. See for example Janelle Sue Taylor, "The Public Foetus and the Family Car: From Abortion Politics to a Volvo Advertisement," in *Science as Culture* 3, part 4 (#17) (London: Free Association Books, 1993), pp. 601–18.

35. The literature critiquing visualization is too extensive to cite in full, but a few examples have particular relevance: Barbara Duden, "Visualizing Life," in *Science as Culture,* pp. 562–600, and *The Woman beneath the Skin: A Doctor's Patients in Eighteenth-Century Germany* (Cambridge: Harvard University Press, 1991); Jane Gallop, *Thinking through the Body* (New York:

Columbia University Press, 1989); Ann Kaplan, "Look Who's Talking, Indeed: Fetal Images in Recent North American Visual Culture," in *Mothering: Ideology, Experience, and Agency,* ed. Evelyn Nakano Glenn, Grace Chang, and Linda Rennie Forcey (New York: and London: Routledge, 1994), pp. 121–37; Bruno Latour, "Visualization and Cognition," *Knowledge and Society* 6 (1986): 1–40; Rosalind Petcheskey, "Fetal Images: The Power of Visual Culture in the Politics of Reproduction," *Feminist Studies* 13, no. 2 (1987): 263–92; Susan Squier, "Conceiving Difference: Reproductive Technology and the Construction of Identity in Two Contemporary Fictions," in *A Question of Identity: Women, Science, and Literature,* ed. Marina Benjamin (New Brunswick: Rutgers University Press, 1993), pp. 97–115; Barbara Maria Stafford, *Body Criticism: Imagining the Unseen in Enlightenment Art and Medicine* (Cambridge, Mass.: MIT Press, 1991). For an interesting historical discussion of the link between eighteenth-century embryology and the fetal rights movement of the twentieth century, see Julia Epstein, *Altered Conditions: Disease, Medicine, and Storytelling* (New York: Routledge, 1995), pp. 123–56.

36. The absence of any first-person narrator in *Puffball* may also reinforce the sense that we are trying to understand and discuss here experiences and feelings that are not readily available to verbal consciousness and linguistic representation. It recalls Daniel N. Stern's observation that "experience in the domains of emergent, core- and intersubjective relatedness, which continue irrespective of language, can be embraced only very partially in the domain of verbal relatedness"; Stern, "The Sense of a Verbal Self," in *The Woman and Language Debate,* ed. Camille Roman, Suzanne Juhasz, and Christanne Miller (New Brunswick: Rutgers University Press, 1994), p. 199. Another effect of this technique is that readers remain somewhat distanced from all the characters, including Liffey and Mabs, and questions of sympathy and judgment are complicated. Perhaps this is why some readers find that the novel "valorizes" precisely where I find that it strongly critiques.

37. For one strong statement of this argument, see Maureen McNeil, "New Reproductive Technologies: Dreams and Broken Promises," in *Science as Culture,* pp. 483–506.

38. Liffey's meditation on her own new auditory perceptiveness also suggests that it is now difficult to sort out her self and her capacities and needs from those of the fetus:

> Liffey wondered if she had always heard the other voice, the tone that lies behind the words and betrays them; and if she had heard, why had she not listened? Perhaps she listened now with the baby's budding ears? And certainly this disagreeable acuity of hearing diminished within a week or two: perhaps because Liffey could not for long endure her new sensitivity to the ifs and buts in Richard's voice when he assured her he loved her: perhaps because the matter of hearing was, once properly established, less in the air so far as the baby was concerned. (147)

39. In fact, she has borne her husband only one child; her second baby was fathered by another man, demonstrating that what she viewed for years as her own maternal incapacity was in fact an effect of "the male factor."

40. See for example Nancy Scheper-Hughes's discussion of the effect of culture and scarcity on "maternal thinking" in a Brazilian shantytown in *Death without Weeping: The Violence of Everyday Life in Brazil* (Berkeley: University of California Press, 1992).

41. She commits this theft by treating other women's children with more indulgence than "any natural mother" could, adds the sententious narrator in this third-person section: "The natural mother is ambivalent towards the child. The unnatural one behaves much better" (*Female Friends*, 273).

42. It is useful to compare another badly behaved woman in Weldon's fiction, Madeleine in *Remember Me,* who finds the will or energy to come back from the dead because she is worried about who will care for her adolescent daughter, Hilary.

43. In prison, moreover, the meager diet brings back memories of the past that are also almost tangible, and mind and body come closer to sharing a sense of coherence: "Her body as much as her mind she felt—was allowed for once to feel, in the boring tranquillity of prison routine—was the sum of its experience" (*Praxis,* 244).

44. At one point, one of the voices of reason and insight in the story, a teacher named Mrs. Pelotti, reassures the distraught Isabel that her son isn't lost, as she has assumed when she comes to collect him from school and finds the classroom empty. The boy has been taken home by a neighbor, as in fact Isabel informed the school he would be. As Mrs. Pelotti comforts Isabel with a glass of medicinal sherry, she observes: "I'm quite sorry for mothers these days. They have lost their children to the nation's education system. I quite often find them roaming the school, looking for children they fancy they've lost who are perfectly safe somewhere else"; Weldon, *The President's Child* (Hodder and Stoughton, 1982; reprint, New York: Penguin Books, 1992), p. 171. No doubt Mrs. Pelotti bespeaks a genuine problem, the psychological effect of social change in the way children are raised and educated and the way it gives a particular force to the Worm Anxiety. But just because women fancy their children are lost doesn't mean they aren't. The next time Isabel comes to school, Jason is indeed gone—kidnapped by Homer. Isabel thus represents the actual experience that so many female characters in Weldon's novels (not to mention the real world) imagine and fear, a woman's worst nightmare come true.

45. Useful representatives of the vast literature on this subject include the volume of *Science as Culture* noted earlier; Rita Arditti, Renate Duelli Klein, and Shelley Minden, eds., *Test-Tube Women: What Future for Motherhood?* (London: Pandora Press, 1984); Ruth Hubbard, *The Politics of Women's Biology* (New Brunswick: Rutgers University Press, 1990); *Man-Made Women: How New Reproductive Technologies Affect Women,* ed. Gena Corea et al. (Bloomington: Indiana University Press, 1987); Linda M. Whitford and Marilyn L. Poland, eds., *New Approaches to Human Reproduction: Social and Ethical Dimensions* (Boulder: Westview Press, 1989); Michelle Stanworth, ed., *Reproductive Technologies: Gender, Motherhood, and Medicine* (Minneapolis: University of Minnesota Press, 1987); Hilary Homans, ed., *The Sexual Politics of Reproduction* (Aldershot, England: Gower, 1985); Judith Rodin and Aila

Collins, eds., *Women and New Reproductive Technologies: Medical, Psychosocial, Legal, and Ethical Dilemmas* (Hillsdale, N.J.: Lawrence Erlbaum Associates, 1991).

46. Given the actors in this plot, Ann Ferguson's concept of "husband patriarchy" seems particularly apt; see Ferguson, *Blood at the Root: Motherhood, Sexuality, and Male Dominance* (London: Pandora Press, 1989), pp. 102 ff.

EPILOGUE

1. In the third-person narrative, some connectedness can be glimpsed, and as the narrative unfolds, debilitating divisions between Praxis and several women are at least partially closed. Praxis expresses some insight into her own similarity to her mother; her sister Hypatia/Hilda is to an extent understood, forgiven and embraced; Irma, before her death, becomes a better friend and supporter; and Mary tells lies to save Praxis from a longer jail sentence. Praxis has at least temporary friendships with women to whom she is connected in more irregular, even socially disapproved ways, including Mary's mother, Miss Leonard, the schoolteacher who briefly becomes something of a surrogate mother to Praxis; and Elaine, the local chum with whom Praxis engages in a career of midday prostitution. The suggestion here as usual is that women who are sexually active outside the law, like Miss Leonard and Elaine (or like the lesbian character of the same name, Elaine, and her companion Olive in *Female Friends*) have better relationships with other women. Mothers, daughters, sisters, and wives are divided in large part by their possessive, competitive relationships, especially to husbands or lovers, as Chloe with some accuracy understood.

2. Praxis comments on how women turn to motherhood as an easy form of connection, but suggests it is at best a "quick fix": "Women of child-bearing age have it easy: if all else fails they can always give birth to another human being, who will love them, at least for a time" (100). She addresses her "sisters" with an argument against "Nature," a force for procreation that "does not know best, or if it does, is on the man's side" (133), and commends them to struggle against the "natural": "When anyone says to you, this, that or other is natural, then fight" (133). She repudiates other conventional feelings and beliefs that constrain women, like possessiveness and jealousy. She replaces the notion that her prostitution was "shameful and disgraceful" with the understanding that it was "a way out, not a path down," and she wonders, "Why was I so easily made to feel it was distasteful, when my own experience indicated that it was not?" (148). In the same meditation, she decides that Hilda's madness needs to be revalued: it "at least enabled her . . . to function as a man might do. . . . If it was madness, it served her very well, as obsessional interests—company, religion, country, politics—serve men very well, to relieve them of the more exacting chores of family and domestic relationships" (148).

3. This makes sense too of Isabel's perceived connection with President Sukarno's mistress, who also bore her famous lover a son and eventually had to be gotten rid of. See pp. 160–1 for Isabel's recognition that "when male

power and prestige is at stake the lives and happiness of women and children are immaterial."

4. Ann Ferguson, *Blood at the Root: Motherhood, Sexuality, and Male Dominance* (London: Pandora Press, 1989); Miriam Johnson, *Strong Mothers, Weak Wives: The Search for Gender Equality* (Berkeley: University of California Press, 1988).

5. Terri Apter, *Why Women Don't Have Wives: Professional Success and Motherhood* (New York: Schocken Books, 1985), p. 26.

6. Paul Smith, *Discerning the Subject* (Minneapolis: University of Minnesota Press, 1988), p. 149. Compare the notion that the mother without child serves as a "double strategy" to Alice E. Adams's discussion of "subjective flexibility"—the possibility of occupying the position of the "essential" self of individualism when it is useful, while taking advantage of a more contradictory sense of "self-in-process" at other points; Adams, *Reproducing the Womb: Images of Childbirth in Science, Feminist Theory, and Literature* (Ithaca: Cornell University Press, 1994), p. 68.

Index

abandonment themes, 22; in Erdrich's novels, 119–20, 126, 130, 134–41, 144–45, 146, 148, 149, 151–52; in Rule's novels, 41–42, 44
abortions, 10, 18
absent mothers, 119–20, 126, 130, 134–40, 157
Adams, Alice E., 241n.11, 268n.7, 276n.6
Adams, Kate, 251n.41
adoption, 67, 118
adoptive mothers, 4, 31, 121, 126, 249nn.24, 27
African American mothers, 63–114 passim
After the Fire (Rule), 54, 59–60
Against the Season (Rule), 54, 59
Agosin, Marjorie, 256n.18
Aguero, Kathi, 179, 269n.20
Alaimo, Stacy, 8
Allen, Jeffner, 30, 31
Allen, Paula Gunn, 116–17, 120, 123
Althea, 25
ancestral mothers: among African Americans, 63, 79–82, 83, 115; among Native Americans, 123, 130, 148–52
Anderson, Jackie, 30
androgyny, 166
Antell, Judith, 119–20, 157
Apter, Terri, 235, 240–41n.9
Arnold, June, 37
artificial insemination, 31
"As I Stand Here Ironing" (Olsen), 182–83
Atwood, Margaret, 12, 175, 189; mother without child narratives of, 16, 158, 167–76
—works: *The Edible Woman,* 170; *The Handmaid's Tale,* 158, 159, 167–83, 223, 228, 229, 231, 267–68n.5; *The Robber Bride,* 270n.10
Austen, Jane, 12

Baby Jessica case, 246n.2
Baby M case, 23, 168, 246n.2
bad mothering, 10, 23, 66–72
Baker, Houston, 64
Bambara, Toni Cade: "My Man Bovanne," 69
Bearing the Word (Homans), 11
Beauvoir, Simone de, 5
Beet Queen, The (Erdrich), 121, 136–40, 146
Bell Jar, The (Plath), 251n.43
Beloved (Morrison), 12, 65–66, 68, 71, 88, 89, 93, 109–12, 114, 152, 242n.32, 253–54n.4
Benjamin, Jessica, 186
Bingo Palace, The (Erdrich), 115, 121, 122, 127, 130, 147–54, 157
birth mothers, 2
birth parents, of adopted children, 67
black mothers. *See* African American mothers
Bordo, Susan, 199–200, 201, 224
Bottoms, Sharon, 28, 36
Bowlby, John, 185–87, 210, 215
Bradley, Henry, 2
braiding metaphor, 129, 264n.28
Brant, Beth, 117, 120; *A Gathering of Spirit,* 264n.24
Braxton, Joanne, 63
Brontë, Anne, 12
Brontë, Charlotte, 12
Brontë, Emily, 12
Brookner, Anita, 200
Brossard, Nicole, 48, 60–61; *Mauve Desert,* 34; *These Our Mothers,* 33–34, 36, 245n.52
Brown, Rita Mae: *Rubyfruit Jungle,* 38
Bruckner, Sarah, 249n.23
Butler, Judith, 10, 26

C.A.L.M. (Custody Action for Lesbian Mothers), 249n.28

language: Lacanian theory of, 11; of
motherhood, 1–5, 49; in *Tracks*
(Erdrich), 145
Laqueur, Thomas, 25
Latin American motherist movements,
69, 161, 258–59n.33
"Laugh of the Medusa, The"
(Cixous), 199
Lesbian Images (Rule), 53, 251n.41
lesbian mothers, 10, 15–16, 28–62 pas-
sim, 246n.59
Lessing, Doris, 259n.37, 270n.10
Lewin, Ellen, 49, 60–61; *Lesbian Moth-
ers,* 34–36, 37
Life Force (Weldon), 185, 192, 214,
218–19
Liscio, Lorraine, 109
Lives and Loves of a She Devil, The
(Weldon), 184, 192, 195, 214
Lorde, Audre, 29
Lotbiniere-Harwood, Susanne de,
248n.22
Love, Barbara, 32–33
Love Medicine (Erdrich), 120–21, 123,
130–36, 141, 143, 146, 148, 149,
151–52, 153

Madame Bovary (Flaubert), 25
male eroticism, 13
Martin, Biddy, 10
Martin, Emily, 272n.29
Mary (mother of God), 146
masculine voice, in writing, 11
maternal consciousness, 7, 20
maternal deprivation, 186, 210–15
maternal sacrifice, 125, 173
maternal surrender. *See* surrender
Maternal Thinking (Ruddick), 252n.47
maternity. *See* motherhood
matriarchy, 116
matrifocality, 116, 261n.6
matrilineality, 116
Mauve Desert (Brossard), 34
McDowell, Deborah, 64, 105, 255n.15
Medea, 25
Medicine, Bea, 261n.5
Medicine Eagle, Brooke, 117
Memory Board (Rule), 56–57
Meridian (Walker): ancestral mothers in,
79–82, 83, 115; bad mothering in,
66–72; dissociation in, 89–108;
mother without child narrative in, 62,
66–108 passim; reproductive consciousness depicted in, 56, 72–74, 78,
79, 82, 84, 88, 90; self-discovery narratives in, 70–71, 83, 85, 107; struc-

ture of, 73–74, 96, 100, 103, 123;
trauma and recovery narratives in,
110, 112–14, 233
metaphorical motherhood, 4, 9
metaphors. *See* braiding metaphor; crazy
quilt metaphor; time travel metaphor
Miller, Sue: *The Good Mother,* 25,
242n.21, 245–46n.55
Millett, Kate, 5
mind-body dichotomy, 202
miscarriages, 10, 212
Mitchell, Juliet, 5, 186
mock mothers, 14, 266n.44
Modell, Judith, 67
Mohanty, Chandra Talpade, 116
Moll Flanders (Defoe), 25
Momaday, N. Scott, 128
Morell, Carolyn M., 241n.10
Morrison, Toni, 12, 16; trauma and recovery narratives of, 174, 237
—works: *Beloved,* 12, 65–66, 68, 71, 88,
89, 93, 109–12, 114, 152, 242n.32,
253–54n.4; *Sula,* 64, 242n.32,
259n.39
mother-daughter relationships, 8–9, 138,
160, 176
motherhood, 2–4, 11–14, 25, 127, 179;
among African Americans, 63–114
passim; changing definition of, 1–5,
19–20, 25–26, 238; critique of recuperation of, 6–11, 184; feminist critique of, 5–11, 19, 24, 235; as gender-
constructing experience, 3, 13;
inherent dichotomy in, 160, 167,
172–73, 235–36; lesbian perspective
on, 28–62 passim; marginalized,
63–115 passim; metaphorical, 4, 9;
mockery of, 14, 266n.44; among Native Americans, 115–57 passim; new
narratives of, 14–27; nonprocreative,
38–62 passim, 116, 188, 224–27, 237;
patriarchal, 33, 36; procreative, 54,
55–56; recuperation (reclamation) of,
5–6, 11, 184, 201, 235; reevaluation
of, 26, 235; relational aspect of, 4, 5,
17, 26–27, 235; repudiation of, 5, 6,
11, 68, 184, 200–201; as subversive,
13, 14, 26, 139, 162; types of, 1, 10,
14; Victorian, 12
mothering. *See* motherhood
mothers, 1, 2; absent, 119–20, 126, 130,
134–40, 157; adoptive, 4, 31, 121,
126, 249nn.24, 27; bad, 10, 23,
66–72; biological, 4, 17–18, 30, 31,
72, 165, 167–68, 171–72; lesbian, 10,
15–16, 28–62 passim, 246n.59; mock,

Compositor:	BookMasters, Inc.
Text:	10/13 Sabon
Display:	Sabon
Printer and Binder:	Maple-Vail Book Manufacturing Group